ALEC GUINNESS
The Unknown

Le Théâtre en Grande-Bretagne

French Theatre Today

Different Circumstances *(play)*

Dialogue Between Friends *(play)*

The Pursuit of Perfection: A Life of Maggie Teyte

Ralph Richardson: An Actor's Life

Darlings of the Gods: One Year in the Lives of
Lawrence Olivier and Vivien Leigh

Olivier: In Celebration *(editor)*

Sean O'Casey: A Life

The Mahabharata

Darlings of the Gods *(novel)*

William Shakespeare: A Life

Campion's Ghost: The Sacred and Profane Memories of
John Donne, Poet *(novel)*

Alec Guinness: Master of Disguise

The Secret Woman: A Life of Peggy Ashcroft

William Shakespeare: A Popular Life

Paul Scofield: The Biography

GARRY O'CONNOR

ALEC GUINNESS
The Unknown
A Life

SIDGWICK & JACKSON

First published 2002 by Sidgwick & Jackson
an imprint of Pan Macmillan Ltd
Pan Macmillan, 20 New Wharf Road, London NI 9RR
Basingstoke and Oxford
Associated companies throughout the world
www.panmacmillan.com

ISBN 0 283 07340 3

Typeset by SetSystems Ltd, Saffron Walden, Essex
Printed and bound in Great Britain by
Mackays of Chatham plc, Chatham, Kent

To Emilie,

and to the memory of

Angela Fox

'The readiness is all'

Hamlet

Contents

PART TWO: ILLUMINATION

List of Illustrations

In Text

Plate Sections

Acknowledgements

Every effort has been made to contact copyright holders of material
reproduced in this book. If any have been inadvertently overlooked, the
author and publishers will be pleased to make restitution at the earliest
opportunity.

[1] Clive Francis   [2] Author's own collection   [3] Robert Barrett   [4] Annie
Salaman   [5] *Illustrated London News*   [6] *Guardian*   [7] *Punch*   [8] *Daily
Mail*   [9] Associated Press   [10] H. C. G. Stevens   [11] Zoë Dominic
[12] Michael Noakes   [13] Snowdon   [14] Mander and Mitchenson   [15] Howard
Coster and National Portrait Gallery   [16] BBC Hulton   [17] John Vickers
Archive   [18] Alistair Muir and *Daily Telegraph*   [19] British Film Institute
[20] Harmsworth Photo Library   [21] National Film Archive

Acknowledgements

For more than a decade and a half I have fluctuated in and out of this biography with its large and ever-changing cast of contributors and sources, consulting and talking to some only once, others as much as four times, as successive layers of comment, anecdote and information have been scraped off or painted over, and the whole composition of the portrait completely rethought from the beginning. What started – and then had a life of sorts – as one book, has largely disappeared and emerged as something different entirely, while discarded material has found its way back, sometimes, into unexpected prominence. My view or point of view on the subject himself has changed considerably from its awkward and prejudiced beginnings, and I am grateful to all those who have broadened, or tried to broaden my understanding. Like God, to whom Angela Fox compared Alec without any hint or suggestion of blasphemy, we know about Alec only what he wanted or wants us to know, and I suspect it will always be like this. I am reluctant at last to let go with some questions unanswered, but happy to acknowledge that my time with Alec is now ended. Especially I must register the vivid and enriching hours spent with all those who gave me their time and memories, who sent or gave me sight of letters written to or from Alec or Merula Guinness or other material that I would not have thought of myself or dreamed of finding. Many of those I list below are sadly no longer with us, but their witness to the extraordinary presence and life of Alec reflects often their own vivid individuality and uniqueness as much as that of the force that has brought them together.

*

Mark Amory, Peggy Ashcroft, Clare Astor, Eileen Atkins, Jill Balcon, Frith Banbury, Robert Barrett, Michael Billington, John Bird, Roger Bolton, Melvyn Bragg, Gyles Brandreth, Coral Browne, Kevin Brownlow, Elaine Burrows, Simon Callow, Father Philip Caraman, Humphrey Carpenter, Don Chapman, Michael Codron, Peter Copley, Michael Coveney, Betty Coxon, Charles Crichton, Anthony Daniels, Alexander Davion, Frank Delaney, John Dexter, David Drummond, Elaine Dundy, Christine Edzard, Charlotte Elson, Martin Esslin, Barbara Everett, Ronald Eyre, Richard Findlater, John Fortune, Angela Fox, Edward Fox, James Fox, Robert Fox, Clive Francis, Stuart Freeborn, Patrick Garland, Andrew Geddes, Lord Geddes, John Gielgud, René Girard, Christopher Good, David Gothard, Simon Gough, Simon Gray, Graham Greene, Kate Griffin, Peter Hall, Margaret Harris, John Harrison, Ronald Harwood, Frank Hauser, Janis Hayward, Nick Hern, Michael Holroyd, Nigel Horne, Nicholas Hunter, Miles Hutchinson, Emrys Jones, James Cellan Jones, Dominic Lawson, David Lean, Roger Lewis, Geoffrey Levy, George Lucas, Leueen MacGrath, Alexander Mackendrick, Kenneth MacReddie, Patrick Maloney, Richard Mangan, E. Mattison, Michael Meyer, David Miller, John Mills, Sheridan Morley, John Mortimer, Michael Noakes, Margaret Philipsborn, Michael Pickwoad, J. B. Priestley, Anthony Quayle, Corin Redgrave, Michael Redington, Michael Relph, Simon Relph, George Rylands, Annie Salaman, Nick Salaman, Rosemary Say, Ned Sherrin, Andrew Sinclair, Donald Sinden, Douglas Slocombe, Lord Snowdon, Oliver Stockman, Alix Stone, Anthony Storr, Monsignor Roderick Strange, Tom Sutcliffe, Ion Trewin, J. C. Trewin, Wendy Trewin, John Tydeman, Kathleen Tynan (to whom I am grateful for permission to quote from *Tynan's Letters*), Leslee Udwin, Gore Vidal, Alexander Walker, John Walsh, Simon Ward, Irving Wardle, Eric Warne, Francis Warner, John Warner, Michael Warr, Sue Westwood, Clifford Williams, Audrey Williamson, Peter Wood, Irene Worth, Franco Zeffirelli.

*

I am grateful, also, to the following institutions who have been helpful in my searches: the Court Service, Liverpool Record Office, Banbury Public Library, the Bodleian Library, the British Library, the Garrick Club, the Savile Club, the Players Club (New York), the British Film Institute, the New York Library for the Performing Arts at Lincoln Center, the British Theatre Museum, the Old Vic Archives, the BBC Written and Sound archives.

Last but not least I thank all those involved in the publication of this book: Samantha Hill, for her typing, at Macmillan, Gordon Wise, Ingrid Connell, for their many suggestions; also Philippa McEwan, Jon Mitchell – and not to forget the editing of Talya Baker and her amazing tolerance for last-minute changes; likewise at Applause, New York, Glenn Young for his structural ideas, Kaye Radke and Matthew Callan.

Prologue: Truth Is Not Privileged
to Be Used All the Time

In the first lines of his autobiography, *Blessings in Disguise*, published in 1985, Alec Guinness describes his own birth as an actor as that of a raw and youthful Ego, entering, pursued by fiends, the public stage from the wings. When Guinness discussed with Graham Greene the writing of this book, 'I'll give you one tip,' Greene told him. 'Sit down to write in the morning. It doesn't matter how long you write and when you stop. But before you stop you must have the next sentence in mind.' Alec had to sigh: the advice came too late, the book was written. 'If only he'd said that eighteen months ago.'

Alec claimed that, being an amateur, he worked swiftly for three or four days on *Blessings in Disguise*, then became stuck and abandoned it. This was a little motif he whistled aloud many times and could orchestrate into, 'brief suave chapters ... finding a sentence, oh heavens, there's a paragraph, and then I would stop for three months ... I was terribly nervous, etc. ...'

Or, 'I found it a pretty frightening experience because I didn't realize what extraordinary recall I had ... I'd set off on a chapter about something thinking I'd known the basic things I wanted to say and suddenly yards of dialogue which I know is pretty well authentic or little incidents came whizzing back from the past, from thirty, forty, fifty years ago and that I found alarming.' He had his diaries upon which he could draw. There were articles he had written, interviews he had given, reviews and letters he had kept. He could fictionalize delicately, or uproariously, within the realm, or limits, of the known.

The genesis of the book was characteristic. He had had plenty of experience as a writer: he had adapted Dickens and Dostoevsky for the stage; his script for *The Horse's Mouth* had been nominated for an Oscar. *Yahoo* had been his own acerbic and lurid assemblage of Jonathan Swift's life. He had written up his wartime landing on Sicily in 1943 several times; likewise his first theatrical encounters with John Gielgud in the 1930s, even his failure as Hamlet in 1951, had long before, in the many forms listed at the back of this book, found their way into the public domain. The daily practice of writing to his friends and correspondents had aided him to become a competent prose stylist. He would, as his confessor Father Caraman noted to me, receive and answer up to thirty letters a day.

He had over the years resisted the advances of publishers, taking cover under the shelter of his friend Hamish Hamilton, by asking him, 'Could I say I've promised a book to you?' This after some time, turned into Hamilton saying to him, 'Look, we've protected you from others, so where's the book?' A brown-paper parcel, containing the bulk of the manuscript, was handed over some years later to Hamilton's successor Christopher Sinclair-Stevenson.

Anyone looking at Alec's record of writing, even setting aside the public heroes and geniuses he played, would at once remark that here was a born biographer. Given his desire for mystery and anonymity, the problem would be how to make his gift for observation, as extended to others, become more than anecdotal biography. But actual autobiography? He must often have pondered this as he looked through his scrapbooks and his diaries.

He had taken pride in having once started an autobiography and then abandoned it, using a quotation from W. Watson, the post-Tennysonian derivative poet, as authority: 'I have not paid the world the evil and the insolent courtesy of offering it my baseness as a gift.' ('Gift' and 'blessings' – the word of Alec's title – are synonyms.) The interviewer (Bel Mooney) on the occasion he discussed writing his book, sensibly pointed out that 'to abandon your autobiography is the final proof of privacy, that the actor's "real" self is nobody's business but his own'. Alec did not give that final proof of privacy. He never abandoned his autobiography. Quite the reverse.

His solution was judicious and in keeping with his character. He wouldn't write up his own career and, if he mentioned it at all, this would be by way of passing, the impressionist backcloth, so to speak. Against this backcloth he would parade his friends. They would be given their entrances and exits, the number of words allowed to each would convey the pecking order. And then they would be carefully and compositionally placed as in a Franz Hals multiple portrait: each in turn would do his or her act. Due attention would be given to their star status and gifts. Their 'act' would be Alec filling them with life, impersonating them with a life of his own.

We come back to Graham Greene. Your bank balance as a writer, Greene once said, was your childhood. You go on drawing carefully on it all your life. Or you spend it all at once. Alec dipped into his just enough to intrigue us with it. The glorious events in Alec's childhood were his visits to the variety and music-hall stages. He would build up his book like a wonderful, suave and magical variety show and mystery tour, with incursions into the world of pantomime, which he didn't like (his pantomime family, that is), with himself as Master of Ceremonies. Here was the perfect disguise in autobiography.

The first turn would be Alec's. He would come on to the stage, a few pages of childhood, a few juggling acts, a little tap dance (a 'Totentanz'?) of early misery, and then the master magician would withdraw. Inscrutably present, he would still remain in full view of the audience. He would sit down onstage in a comfortable ducal chair – or the eighteenth-century 'gout' chair he kept in his London flat – and introduce the rest of the acts with comments in his own special brand of humour, 'a curious mixture of the fey, the sly and the marginally macabre', always clear that he was more after 'the secret grin than an open laugh'.

Mother, Agnes de Cuffe, would occasionally erupt onto the scene, the evil godmother or wicked fairy of his life, while there would be no end of eccentrics and curiosities, of good fairies and influences, beginning with Nellie Wallace and her parrot-like movements of the head; exotic Argentinian-born Martita Hunt, the Miss Havisham of his story; Sybil Thorndike, and on and on.

This was an ideal method for Alec: he was the perfect imper-sonator – you only had to hear him mimic Gielgud or Laurence Olivier to know that he could not only catch perfectly their accents and intonations, he also understood exactly the right words to put into their mouths, the words that they would actually say; it would be as if he knew them better than they knew themselves. Although Alec called it memory, it would be much more. His mimetic desire and genius was such that he could become *them*.

His method of presenting his turns, as well as those who had influenced him, as items on a variety bill, also carried respectability. It had a snobbish or fashionable appeal, just as the royal family in the old days mixed with the stars of variety, and T. S. Eliot wrote of the virtues of old music-hall performers such as Marie Lloyd. Like stories of the royals, it would appeal to every class of reader. Above all, the method was authentic and truly autobiographical because it enacted what had moved and involved him as a child, providing his escape and the route to his future. With a nugget of realistic narrative at the centre of the book – the vivid account of his life at sea during the war – he could thereafter return to his biographical sketches of friends and peers, bringing them alive through their 'own' words and actions.

Then a final, sudden, few dark pages on the mystery of his birth: after the merriment of the stars letting down their hair, with glimpses into their secret selves, with a little gentle pricking of their foibles and other quiet but firm debunking – all of them brilliantly impersonated by Alec – the air grows chill.

'I am sorry, madam, for the news I bring.'

The finish is perfect. Here am I, at heart a lonely illegitimate child, with no father that can be traced, or if a father then one who just on one single occasion confessed the sin of my birth to his legitimate daughter. But what I am most proud of is that I never lost a friend. And so the entertainment would be perfectly rounded off, as Shakespeare rounded off *Love's Labour's Lost*:

> The words of Mercury are harsh after the songs of Apollo.
>   You that way, we this way.

We all leave the theatre.

But where did this leave the actor Alec Guinness? One thing *Blessings in Disguise* did not demonstrate is Rosaline's statement from that same early and mischievous comedy, which was perhaps more autobiographical than some of his other plays:

> A jest's prosperity lies in the ear
> Of him that hears it, never in the tongue
> Of him that makes it.

*

Comedians (and by extension character actors) are more often than not dark and unsatisfied people. *Blessings in Disguise* and its sequels, *My Name Escapes Me* (1996) and *A Positively Last Appearance* (1999) were a treat for their readers: polished, accomplished, sly, amusing, witty, but did they, could they, really satisfy as a frank and honest confession of what, or who, Guinness was? Yes and no. They revealed that he was always revealing himself, a little bit at a time and as a tease, otherwise he would never have been what he was. 'There are lots of things I don't wish to admit, but come through willy-nilly . . .' and, 'In my views of most things I'm swayed like a very busy weather-cock.' And so on. So, in fact, his flaws and vanities are purged in the main portraits he paints of others, but again they are disguised. As Stanley Cavell the Harvard philosopher writes in *Disowning Knowledge*,

> A first-person account is, after all, a confession; and the one
> who has something to confess has something to conceal. And
> the one who has the word 'I' at his or her disposal has the
> quickest device for concealing himself.

As in his acting, Guinness revealed himself indirectly in his writing. What was significant was how the texture of his writing became imbued with his acting talent and skill. The first book (but not the later two quite to the same extent) had the quality of what Irene Worth pointed out about his acting, quoting Edith Wharton, that of working like the Gobelin weavers, 'on the wrong side of the tapestry'.

> If now and then he comes round to the right side and catches
> what seems a happy glow of colour or a firm sweep of design,
> he must instantly retreat again.

One good example of indirect explicitness is the way Alec writes up Ernest Milton, whom he had invited round to give a piece of his Lear in front of the young Richard Burton in 1946 when Milton was appearing in Alec's adaptation of *The Brothers*

Karamazov. 'He could scarcely take his eyes from the beauty of Burton's head,' he says. Milton performed miserably, telephoning Alec the next day to say he was sorry: 'I was *distracted* by such beauty. Ah, the breasts (pronounced "braasts") and the eyes of the young men are *damning*.' Alec continued, suavely, covering Milton's – and indirectly, I suspect, his own – infatuation with Burton's beauty. 'Not long after this his wife, Naomi Royde Smith, died . . .'

He next celebrates Milton's great love for his wife Naomi in affectionate prose. Yet Milton confides to Alec that the only woman who ever roused him sexually was Lilian Baylis (yet she was, as most people described her, an 'old battleaxe'). It's all quicksilver, a touch of homosexual titillation, a slanting reference to arousal, a sudden, dark contrast of the death of a spouse. So Alec writes on of his mother, his search for his father, the birds-and-the-bees talks in his early school dormitories, at all times swiftly moving on to the next subject, not lingering over anything, the most skilled of raconteurs.

In this book and the sequels – and in his acting – Alec Guinness, the great magician, entertained vastly while he concealed. It is the very essence of the actor's art. But in his writing the sleight of hand becomes more plainly evident as he simultaneously beclouds and illuminates his world. Readers such as myself who have enjoyed his three autobiographies and the dozens, nay hundreds, of articles written about him, can be counted in millions. He had, deservedly become a British institution; as one obituarist wrote after his death in 2000, 'the best known and loved English actor of the 20th century'. But the books go little way to explaining what made Guinness tick, and what made him great. In them we see only the disguises he wanted us to see, the one or many he miraculously maintained, virtually from boyhood. They show nothing of how this great actor, this great illusionist, developed these magical skills to hide himself from his own history, from his very inner life, and that a by-product of his Herculean effort of self-deception was one of the theatre's and the cinema's most entertaining artists.

Even his name was a sham. His parents a mystery . . .

PART ONE: INCUBATION

Conversation enriches the understanding, but solitude is the school of genius; and the uniformity of a work denotes the hand of a single artist.   **Edward Gibbon**

As a boy, even as a child, I was thrown much upon myself. I have explained, when speaking of my school days, how it came to pass that other boys would not play with me. I was therefore alone, and had to form my plays within myself. Play of some kind was necessary to me then, as it has always been. Study was not my bent, and I could not please myself by being all idle. Thus it came to pass I was always going about with some castle in the air firmly built within my mind.

Anthony Trollope

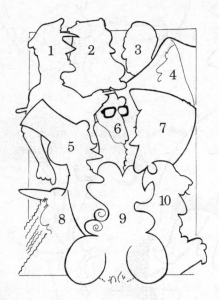

1. Colonel Nicholson, *The Bridge on the River Kwai*, 1957
2. Prince Feisal, *Lawrence of Arabia*, 1962
3. Adolf Hitler, *Hitler: The Last Ten Days*, 1973
4. Obi-Wan Kenobi, *Star Wars*, 1977
5. Herbert Pocket, *Great Expectations*, 1946
6. George Smiley, *Tinker, Tailor, Soldier, Spy*, 1979
7. Lady Agatha D'Ascoyne, *Kind Hearts and Coronets*, 1949
8. Fagin, *Oliver Twist*, 1948
9. Charles I, *Cromwell*, 1970
10. Professor Marcus, *The Ladykillers*, 1955

Some of Guinness's many faces in a drawing by Clive Francis

1. The Ambush of Younger Days and Some Preliminary Confessions

> A book is really talk, glorified talk, and you must read it
> with the knowledge that the writer is talking to you.
>
> E. M. Forster

I first met Alec Guinness in the spring of 1989. We were at the publisher's party given for the tribute edited by playwright Ronald Harwood for the actor's seventy-fifth birthday.

The book was a handsome volume, produced in an age before the dumbing down of culture, so continually disparaged by Alec, when publishers took pride not only in their surroundings, in this case Hodder and Stoughton's twin eighteenth-century houses in Bedford Square, but also in the quality as well as the marketability of their books. I had much valued my visits to Bedford Square, mainly because the writer still had a freedom to pop his head unexpectedly round the door of most of those connected with the production of his book, he could circulate his ideas horizontally, he could explore the archives and even be offered coffee by editorial staff who had nothing to do with his own book. For ten years I had enjoyed the buildings, the elegant staircases and grand candelabra, and I am sure their books gained something from the proportions of their surroundings, as did the workers where, separated from one another, they could gather together their best thoughts in the quiet, secluded offices of a publishing house. I liked the two front doors, one locked so that if you were visiting someone at the top of the second staircase you had to mount the first, descend by another staircase, then mount again. Many encounters could happen on the way.

Alec, surprisingly, attended this party given for his book in these handsome buildings – while having grumbled at and opposed some stages of its production, sometimes with good, sometimes with ill-concealed bad, humour.

We chatted briefly when we were introduced. I must have made some kind of impression on him, apart from the essay I contributed on his films to the symposium, because when about a year later I wrote and asked him for an interview he readily agreed. I must hasten to add that this was no longer in connection with writing his biography or a book about his acting, which I had begun to contemplate in the previous year.

This false start had led me to drive four and a half hours through rain and flying wet mud on 18 January 1988 to Dulverton, a North Devon village, in order to meet Alec Guinness's confessor, who introduced him into the Roman Catholic Church. Father Philip Caraman's house was a tiny cottage on the main road in front of the Catholic Church. It had by way of identification a pencilled sign – 'Bridge House'.

The Jesuit priest was a thin spare man with glasses and wiry white hair who wore a fisherman's jersey. He reminded me of Samuel Beckett with whom I had spent time years before in Paris. But while Beckett was gentle, affable, here there was something distant, even defensive, with no expression of sympathy or concern. He grumbled, 'Shouldn't have taken you so long to get here . . .'

I found myself tongue-tied. Confessor to Graham Greene, Evelyn Waugh and other high-octane Roman Catholics, many of them converts, Caraman had attended the Stonyhurst Jesuit college, aptly named perhaps and – although a public school – the Sandhurst or West Point of orthodox Catholic teaching. A contemporary was Peter Glenville, Alec's lifelong friend and one of a list of likely lovers who while openly having a male partner or partners sponsored Alec as godfather for his conversion into the Catholic faith. When Glenville died from a heart attack in 1991, Alec contacted Caraman (in *My Name Escapes Me* he mistakenly said that Caraman lived in Dorset not Devon), to say a memorial mass at the Brompton Oratory.

Guinness called Caraman 'a loving friend of mine'. He was seventy-eight years old, though looked barely older than sixty-five. I shuddered in his unfriendly presence, consoling myself that Peter Hebblethwaite, biographer of popes, had once described him to me as 'completely mad'.

My intention had been to enlist Father Caraman's help. Over the next hour or so I tried my hardest to engage him in providing some spiritual background to writing a life of Guinness. Over a frugal meal of barely defrosted cold chicken and eight tiny boiled potatoes liberally covered in chives, I asked him about the life of St Ignatius Loyola, the founder of the Jesuits, which he was writing. When questioned about Graham Greene – a figure in my mind close to Alec – he said, 'Greene reveals all his spiritual life in every book, but he is the electric hare – always ahead of everyone else.'

Among the pieces of chicken stood out a stubbily shaped, smoked German salami sausage which, when its thick skin was pierced tasted delicious – the one indulgence of the meal, perhaps. The hospitality, for which I was grateful, was otherwise minimal: a thimbleful of sherry before lunch, a small quantity of lager from a shared can during it.

But the going got pretty sticky. Caraman mentioned there was a Father Bartlett in Oxford who knew Guinness; that he thought the most significant play in Guinness's life (and indicator of his spiritual torment and subsequent conversion) was Bridget Boland's *The Prisoner*. As for my request for an introduction to Guinness he was unhelpful. 'I can't help you in what you ask for. I'm very sorry you have come such a long way for nothing. But there it is.'

When I returned during coffee to this topic he again said he would grant no introduction, and that it would not serve my purpose. I should write a letter and introduce myself, he said, and enclose a stamped addressed envelope. He said he thought Guinness would see me. Throughout my visit I kept asking myself, 'How is it that Waugh, Greene, Alec Guinness had made him their father confessor, or asked him for spiritual services?' Could it be because he was as wily and as uncompromisingly tough as they were themselves? Or was it his literary credentials (he spoke fluent Latin and had translated Father John Gerard's autobiography, the account of the Jesuit's escape from persecution)? Did he, because of his European aura, appeal to their sense of alienation and exile? By a little stretch one could imagine him as a priest in charge of the Inquisition.

He told me Guinness received thirty letters a day. All of which, promptly rising at dawn, he answered personally. But he was wrong about the response. Guinness replied by return that he wouldn't see me – even the stamped addressed envelope did not help.

Father Caraman wasn't a man I warmed to. 'Is there any other matter I can help you with?' the priest asked me before I hurriedly left, perhaps with an ominous reference to my confused state of mind. This had mainly been caused by his poor reception of me. I did wonder about his ability to reconcile the dogmatic demands of the Church with the uncontrollable urges of the flesh in his elite circle of sinners. But I never asked.

I had then given up the Guinness idea, because Hodders, on the strength of two synopses I had shown them, one for a life of Shakespeare, the other for a novel about John Donne, had commissioned both works, which would take up the next three years. My first and as I thought novel and original approach to writing a life of the shadowy and elusive Shakespeare, about whom little is known and even less can be verified, was to interview those whose lives had been intimately connected with him through their work. High if not first on my list was Guinness, whose own intellectual grasp as well as literary originality had been displayed four years earlier in *Blessings in Disguise*. I expected him to have plenty to say about Shakespeare that would be both challenging and memorable. I had written to him reminding him we had met at the Hodder party, and gently asked for an interview on this subject.

After the ritual self-demolition, saying he knew little about Shakespeare and had acted even less in his plays (a claim I was able to discount immediately to my own satisfaction, although I did not point it out to him), he said he would meet me. He invited me to lunch at his favourite restaurant, the Greek White Tower in Soho.

True to what I had hoped or expected, Alec talked extremely well about Shakespeare, so that I was able to use the interview or parts of it in a preamble to my biography. Whether or not he had prepared what he was going to say I do not know, although I suspected he must have done, but looking back on the interview I realize that while he talked about Shakespeare it was, in a way similar to most of those I talked to, also as if he was looking at himself in a mirror, and revealing much about himself in an unguarded, even vulnerable way.

The first revelation he made to me about Shakespeare was that he had seen or found a new portrait, which after some detective work I tracked down to being in the possession of Michael Holroyd's literary agent, Hilary Rubinstein. I remain convinced, as was Alec, that this is an authentic portrait of Shakespeare in old age – although by no means a flattering image of the exhausted pen-pusher, actor and theatre manager, whether it was a true likeness copied from life could not subsequently be proved one way or the other. The Chandos portrait, which is Number 1 in the National Portrait Gallery collection, has no stronger claim to be authentic or a true likeness. The cases for and against this new portrait are outlined fully in my life of Shakespeare.

But Guinness, who as a collector of paintings and drawings showed all his life an unusual sensitivity to painting and art history, was convinced that he had seen the real, the true Shakespeare in this painting. It was, he told me, 'a lived-in face, a genial face – a tired, sweet face, not at all like that austere thing in Leicester Square.' I could not be other than impressed by the force of his insight and the reasons he gave.

I don't remember how the talk then progressed, but we moved on to Daphne du Maurier's account of Francis Bacon's brother Anthony in *Golden Boys*, who was a homosexual arrested and almost executed for what was then considered a capital offence: 'accused of buggery with a pageboy,' said Alec. It is only now that I can relate the description of Shakespeare's face, a reductive grey-haired old man's image, to the seventy-five-year-old actor chain-smoking Silk Cuts before me – and to the bisexuality which, as our lunch went on, seemed to figure more and more in his conversation.

For after the discussion of Anthony Bacon, Alec told me that because of no radio and television, 'Everyone took in each other, and probably Shakespeare told tales of others like the way Terry Rattigan used to tell tales of Somerset Maugham.' Later in the lunch Alec said, that while Shakespeare 'kept a very clever balance, for professional and political reasons – about his religious beliefs for instance – I wonder whether he was not a Somerset Maugham

– time-serving'. I knew little about Maugham's personal life except what I learned from the extended fictional autobiography of Kenneth Toomey, the homosexual narrator of Anthony Burgess's *Earthly Powers*, closely based on Maugham, who had been married and was bisexual.

The most unusual part of our talk about Shakespeare, apart from detailed thoughts Alec had about Hamlet (which belong later where I discuss the two Hamlets he acted), was his description to me of how the nineteenth-century writer Samuel Butler was obsessed with the Sonnets. Butler, according to Alec, had each one pasted on a separate piece of paper, then laid out on a large or billiard table, because he was never satisfied with the order in which they were printed in the first Folio edition.

'He shuffled them,' Alec told me, and this went on for years until he had a notation – and final notation. 'He found he had exactly the same sequence as was in the first edition, except for four.' Alec added that he found a copy of Butler's re-ordered sonnets in a bookshop signed by Butler himself and he gave it to Joan Plowright – 'I don't think she was very interested in Shakespeare,' he said to me in a kind of mock aside.

I did not ask myself at the time what all that was about, but thought later that I should have done. Here again I could see, looking back, there could have been a hidden or disguised homosexual agenda in what Alec was telling me. Most likely he was unconscious of it himself. Towards the end of his life he did say, I read later, that he had a lifelong fondness and admiration for Samuel Butler – beginning when he was aged twenty – for who could not love and respect a man who wrote, 'The Three Most Important Things a man has are briefly, his private parts, his money, and his religious opinions'? The times he'd quoted it suggested it had become his motto as well. The question I found myself asking, was 'Yes, but in what directions did these important things point?'

Butler, I found out later, felt the Sonnets lifted the veil that cloaked Shakespeare the dramatist, and in them 'we look upon him face to face.'

In other words, Shakespeare's sonnets were love letters that tell a very squalid tale of youthful indiscretion, when the playwright fell for a navy steward called Willie Hughes or Hewes and was lured into a rendezvous with the sailor lad, whereupon both indulged their mutual homosexual inclinations. Willie Hughes later hurtfully reflected, 'The love of the English poet for the Mr W. H. was, though only for a short time, more Greek than English.' Shakespeare himself was caught in the act, beaten and lamed. 'Speak of my lameness and I straight will halt.' (Sonnet 34) He was forced to flee leaving his cloak behind: 'And make me travel forth without my cloak.'

To speak of Shakespeare's single transgression is at once to be put in mind of the now well-aired incident, first reported in Sheridan Morley's authorized life of John Gielgud, of Alec Guinness's arrest for homosexual soliciting just after the war, and preserving his anonymity by giving the name of the offender as Herbert Pocket. Was it a single transgression, a one-off lapse, or was it an indicator of something deeper or a longer-lasting trend?

Butler forgave Shakespeare, although his own life, uncannily similar in many ways to that of Guinness, showed in his specu-lation about Shakespeare's 'pederastic interlude' a projection of his own failure when it came to resisting his handsome male friend, Charles Pauli, who sponged off him and at whose funeral, Butler discovered, had fleeced him of £600 or £800 pounds, a consider-able fortune. Butler reflected with chastened hindsight, 'Very handsome, well-dressed men are seldom very good men.'

Although in the first decades of the twentieth century Butler was discovered by the mainly homosexual Bloomsbury literati, in particular Lytton Strachey and E. M. Forster, who praised his 'independent mind', he remained an elusive and paradoxical figure. Denounced on the one hand by Malcolm Muggeridge as a timid homosexual and money-obsessed snob, he was exalted by others in a similar way to Oscar Wilde as an arch-mocker, who campaigned against and overcame 'earnestness' – according to Butler, 'the last enemy that shall be subdued'.

But with Shakespeare, or through Shakespeare – so often through Shakespeare we look at ourselves – Butler looks at himself and forgives his own homosexuality. Onto the Sonnets, it could be claimed, Butler projected himself as the victimized poet; and in forgiving Shakespeare he came to terms with his own guilt about his sexuality. Similarly Guinness, close to Shakespeare, in 1951 played a very personal Hamlet, as naked and unadorned on stage as he was ever likely to be.

It is fascinating to note that while Guinness in later life publicly and in print skirted round homosexual acts and practices with euphemistic delicacy, Butler's own libidinal preoccupations never once led to his use of the words sex or sexuality – as impassioned counsel for the defence he spoke of Shakespeare's 'lapse':

> Considering, then, Shakespeare's extreme youth . . . his ardent poetic temperament, and Alas! it is just the poetic temperament which by reason of its very catholicity is least likely to pass scatheless through what he so touchingly describes as 'the ambush of young days'; considering also the license of the times, Shakespeare's bitter punishment, and still more bitter remorse – is it likely that there was ever afterwards a day in his life in which the remembrance of that 'night of woe' did not at some time or another rise up before him and stab him? nay, is it not quite likely that this great shock may in the end have brought him prematurely to the grave? . . . I believe that those whose judgment we should respect will refuse to take Shakespeare's grave indiscretion more to heart than they do the story of Noah's drunkenness; they will neither blink it nor yet look at it more closely than is necessary in order to prevent men's rank thoughts from taking it to have been more grievous than it was.
>
> *Shakespeare's Sonnets Reconsidered, and in Part Rearranged* (1899)

Not only with Butler, but with others, in their treatment of their own bisexuality and their tendency to guilt and confusion over their sexual identity, but above all in their roundabout way of reference to it, Alec would come to show well-defined parallels.

But there were also two main differences, as well as many minor ones. Where Butler was extremely faithful to the truth about his own family and background, and especially his childhood, in his autobiographical novel *The Way of All Flesh* – 'I am telling the truth, the whole truth and nothing but the truth' he told a friend – he, Alec, instinctively shied away from the truth, confessing – he was always to show how personal and individually revealing his taste was – that his exception to his admiration for

Butler was *The Way of All Flesh*, 'which I could never get on with'.

Second, Butler seemed to have adhered more to a rigid moral and sexual code than Guinness. He distrusted and feared women. He paid for sex with prostitutes, but would never allow intimacy with them, he never married or had children – he channelled his 'unusually strong' sexual impulse 'in that prosaic way which some men adopt who dread emotional disturbance in their lives'. While Alec led an ostensibly companioned and loving relationship with his wife Merula, he would seem, at least in his later years, for most of the time to have suppressed or ignored as much as he could the demands of his sexuality.

Perhaps I would come to see this as the key to his greatness, his altruism and his lifelong identification with – to take a phrase describing Machin, whom he played in *The Card* – 'the good cause of cheering us all up'. Lunch with Alec, for which he generously footed the bill, was to launch me on a very challenging exercise in discretion and taste.

2. The Sins of the Father

'I had to steal my own birthright, stole it, and was bitterly punished,' wrote Samuel Butler. 'My most implacable enemy from childhood onward has certainly been my father.' Cowed and subjugated by a father who never liked him and gave him no scope to be loved by him, Butler as a child received an intense hurt which he locked away. His mother did not help, continually submitting him to a domestic confidence trick by wheedling him and stroking him on the sofa into making confidences, then betraying these by telling his father. In the often repeated sofa episodes he wrote, in *The Way of All Flesh*, of 'the mangled bones of too many murdered confessions which were lying whitening round the skirts of his mother's dress'.

While he never doubted his father's good intentions, Butler deduced a general principle from his own family:

> The Ancients attached such special horror to the murder of near relations because the temptation was felt on all hands to be so great that nothing short of this could stop people from laying violent hands upon them.

Early on in life Alec Guinness himself had such a sense of his own damaged nature it is hardly surprising he should gravitate towards those who had a similar sense of themselves as victims. Maybe the sexual delving is beside the point. Like Butler, Alec's main desire was to 'conceal how severely I had been wounded and to get beyond the reach of those arrows that from time to time still reached me'. Like Butler also, he learned to fashion for himself an alternative life. Almost from the outset this duality became a game as well as a reality, a form of artistry of not being who you

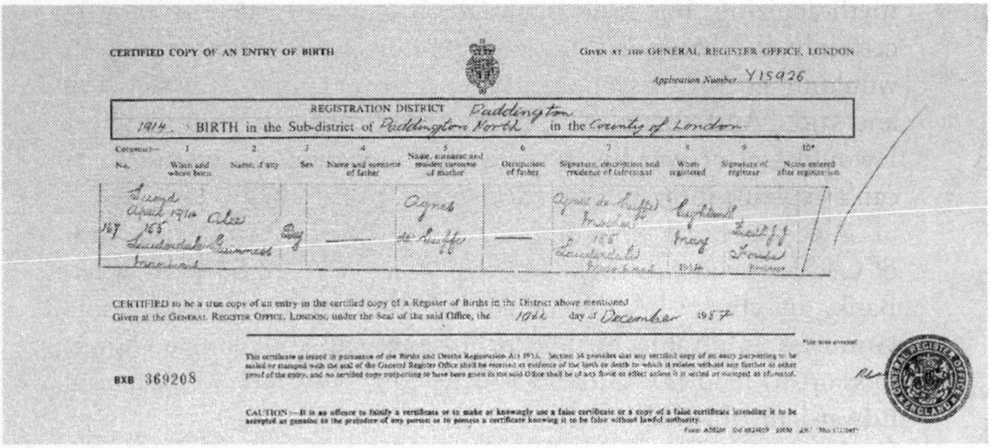

CERTIFIED COPY OF AN ENTRY OF BIRTH

GIVEN AT THE GENERAL REGISTER OFFICE, LONDON

Application Number Y15926

REGISTRATION DISTRICT Paddington

1914. BIRTH in the Sub-district of Paddington North in the County of London

Columns:—	1	2	3	4	5	6	7	8	9	10*
No.	When and where born	Name, if any	Sex	Name and surname of father	Name, surname and maiden surname of mother	Occupation of father	Signature, description and residence of informant	When registered	Signature of registrar	Name entered after registration
167	Second April 1914 155 Lauderdale Mansions	Alec Guinness	Boy	—	Agnes de Cuffe	—	Agnes de Cuffe Mother 155 Lauderdale Mansions	Eighteenth May 1914	[illegible] Registrar	

CERTIFIED to be a true copy of an entry in the certified copy of a Register of Births in the District above mentioned.
Given at the GENERAL REGISTER OFFICE, LONDON, under the Seal of the said Office, the 10th day of December 1957

*See note overleaf

BXB 369208

This certificate is issued in pursuance of the Births and Deaths Registration Act 1953. Section 34 provides that any certified copy of an entry purporting to be sealed or stamped with the seal of the General Register Office shall be received as evidence of the birth or death to which it relates without any further or other proof of the entry, and no certified copy purporting to have been given in the said Office shall be of any force or effect unless it is sealed or stamped as aforesaid.

CAUTION:—It is an offence to falsify a certificate or to make or knowingly use a false certificate or a copy of a false certificate intending it to be accepted as genuine to the prejudice of any person or to possess a certificate knowing it to be false without lawful authority.

GENERAL REGISTER OFFICE ENGLAND

The missing birth certificate

are. The tangled roots out of which he grew kept and sustained at their knotted centre a terrible anger.

Today we probably know more about the identity and history of the man we suppose was Alec's father than ever he did during his lifetime. Although on his birth certificate the box for father's name was left blank, his father, with little shadow of doubt, was Andrew Geddes, a Scottish banker and friend of the titled banking and brewing Guinness family. Alec, however, preferred to live all his life guarded by the shades of uncertainty. He played a game with what he knew or heard, it became part of his self-mythologizing, but really, you felt, he did not want to know too certainly the truth. As he confessed in an interview in 1985, 'I wouldn't go to a psychoanalyst in case he unravelled something and said, "And that is the springboard of such talents as you have." I would feel, it was just that, was it? – instead of something you can't explain, something tucked inside.'

Alec was born in London on 2 April 1914, the illegitimate son of Geddes, who was then a roving director of the South American Bank, in charge of the bank's London operations. The name Guinness is on his birth certificate because Geddes asked permission to lend the Guinness name to an unwanted child. It was Edwardian practice for a best friend, or at least a friend, to give (or in this case probably have taken by the child's mother), his name to a love child. This was Alec's version of his naming, as revealed at the very end of his first autobiographical memoir, *Blessings in Disguise*. One of these blessings was, by ironic or humorous implication, Alec himself.

Agnes de Cuffe, Alec's mother (and the bearer of an equally mysterious name) would not – or could not – clear up the mystery for him. But he did see Andrew Geddes several times during his childhood. He also found himself the possessor of a small allowance, which suggests some provision made for him by a wealthy father.

Alec also revealed in *Blessings in Disguise* that the last time he saw his supposed father Geddes he was eight years old. Guinness came one day on a visit to him. The cynical smile Geddes wore when he handed him half a crown may well have reflected the link of guilt and financial support. Alec himself commented, identifying with the strong possibility he felt that Geddes *was* the father, that the cynical smile was the Geddes personality he remembered and which he had, through the years, seen in himself: 'Something very similar when I have felt hurt or taken advantage of.' He added swiftly, coveringly, 'He died when I was sixteen.'

If we add to this a more conclusive statement Alec made earlier in a newspaper article about his father – 'My father generated me in his 64th year. He was a bank director. Quite wealthy. His name was Andrew' – we have a father who should have been eighty years old when he died. In fact he was sixty-eight and died in 1928, so he generated Alec in his fifty-third year.

Everything Alec has said points to the likelihood that his father, if called Geddes, was a well-connected Geddes, in other words 'a Geddes'. The most famous member of this family, Sir Eric Geddes, was a businessman and politician who served in Lloyd George's coalition cabinet of 1919 as minister of transport and later wielded the famous 'Geddes Axe' of post-First World War economic planning. Another Geddes, Sir Auckland, also reached cabinet rank and was made a baron in 1942.

Later Alec was to become subject to the misunderstanding of being assumed to be a member of the more famous Guinness family. Possibly his mother liked the name because it conferred on her son a bit of class, and might help to give him a start in life. Her social ambitions and the curious form they took might well have set him on the path to becoming, as he did, a one-man institution outweighing by far his confused family 'lettres de crédit'.

But the Geddes connection well outweighed the Guinness connection. One day in November 1986 – he told me when I interviewed him in 1990 – at King's Cross Station book stall, the present Lord Geddes picked up a copy of *Blessings in Disguise*, then number one on the paperback lists, and read it with amusement and interest until page 308 when suddenly the name 'Andrew Geddes' – a regular name in his family – sprang out at him.

Beginning on that page Alec spends six pages talking about his ancestry during which he says that since earliest childhood and from the time he first recognized he was illegitimate he believed, although 'without any good reason', that his father was Andrew Geddes, 'a Managing Director of the Anglo-South American Bank, who had been born, I discovered later, in 1860'.

Lord Geddes became intrigued. The Geddes clan was a large one and, as he wrote to a close relation, it would be quite fun to 'find a beknighted illegitimate relation'. Taking his cue from Alec's assertion that the search for his father had been a 'constant, though fairly minor speculation for fifty years', he wrote to Alec that he had grown intrigued by his supposition that his father might have been an Andrew Geddes born in 1860. He then went on to say that he himself had long had an interest in Geddes genealogy and for that reason was occasionally referred to by members of his family as 'Head of the Family'.

There was no Andrew Geddes in their direct descent, although a son of one of the four brothers of his great grandfather Acland Geddes (1831–1908) might have been an Andrew Geddes. However, Lord Geddes told me, so curious had he become that he wondered whether Alec might care to join him for a drink or lunch. Alec promptly replied that he would. He now realized that the date he had given for the birth of his father, 1860, was more likely to have been 1850 (in fact it was 1861), but this too did not fit in with any possible connection with the Geddes family. Alec had also, he wrote, found out that there was a Catholic bishop called Geddes who lived in New Zealand in the last half of the nineteenth century, but that he himself most likely could not be laid at his door. He had heard when small that the Geddes who may have been his father came from Dumfriesshire, or Ayrshire. He was sure that there was no Andrew Geddes. All this had been in Alec's letter to Lord Geddes, of which I have a copy.

Geddes replied that the different dates did not help establish any connections with his family, and while there was a strong branch of the family who were in shipping and trading, based in Rachan, Peeblesshire, none of these fitted what Alec knew. Although they then arranged to meet for a drink, this fell through so that not for the first or last time, the chance that Alec might find out more about his father than he already knew, came to nothing. Frankly, it seemed, Alec did not want to know.

Were there any other, non-factual connections between Guinness and the Geddes family that might be worthy of note? Hardly, although it must be said that Alexander Geddes, father of a present-day Andrew Geddes (born 1943), a distinguished barrister and judge, had a distinct resemblance to Alec in certain features of

the face, that physically the Geddeses were quite small, stocky men
with big heads (Guinness is similar here), and that the existence of
a famous cabinet minister and a tradition of public speaking
suggested certain talents that might have been shared. That is as
far as they go.

But the most significant aspect of the contact between Lord
Geddes and Alec was that, for all the protestations of interest on
Alec's part and the warm tactful interest on Geddes's part, the
elaborate courtesies that surrounded these, the prestigious suggestions of places where they should meet – the Connaught Hotel,
'my too expensive hideaway', the guest bar of the House of Lords
– the meeting between them did not in the end actually material-
ize. It was as if, without either of them noticing quite how or why,
Alec slipped away again and was seen no more. What might have
been remained – in the words of T. S. Eliot, the favourite poet of
the actor – a possibility only in a world of speculation. After
seventy-odd years of not knowing the exact identity of his father,
did Alec really want to know? The answer is probably not.

Alec did not know either the circumstances in which Andrew
Geddes came to accept his paternity. The cynical smile which he
gave Alec could be interpreted in a different way. It may even have
been a reflection of complicity in a deception. He was not to
know how much, or how little, Alec believed himself to be his
true son.

In spite of Guinness's assertion to the contrary, Andrew
Geddes *was* born in 1861. Alec may have changed the date to 1850
to put Lord Geddes off the scent. But if Geddes was not directly
related to the titled family, the Cuffs believe that he was a Scot
and a self-made man, the son of a blacksmith in Dumfriesshire.
Confident and with a good head for figures, he had left for South
America when there was a mining boom in Chile. Geddes had
not, despite what Alec told *Time* magazine in 1958, generated him
in his sixty-fourth year, but in his fifty-third. There's a big
difference here. Alec wrote in *Blessings in Disguise* that he died
'when I was sixteen [he died when Alec was fourteen]. *The Times*
printed a fairly long, dull obituary, representing him, if I remember correctly, as an industrious and conscientious man.' In fact,
there was no obituary in *The Times*, so no mention of his qualities.
This shows a typical Guinness ability to finesse. There was a brief

report of his will and his age at death in *The Times* of 26 June 1928. This is what Guinness saw:

Andrew Geddes (68) of Meadside, Northumberland-road New Barnet, late of the Anglo-Saxon American Bank [*sic*], Limited, and lately also a director of the Allanza Company, Limited, and of the Pan de Azucar Nitrate Company, Limited (net personality £51,468)–£53,460.

A photograph taken of Geddes in his sixties showed a face strongly resembling Alec's, especially if compared with that of him in the role of Freud (at a similar age).

Geddes left a considerable fortune. According to the certificate issued in Barnet, Geddes died at home on 18 March 1928 from pneumonia and mental degeneration. In his will – which I have consulted and which describes him as 'formerly known as Gaddes' – Geddes had directed that his money and estate should for the most part be left to his four daughters and put in trust for his only son, Andrew, who was in permanent care as a mental invalid. There was no mention of his wife or of Guinness. 'Catherine Weldon', who many years later introduced herself to Guinness after a performance in Brighton as the youngest daughter of Geddes, was left £3,300. She told Alec nothing about her father or herself. But Geddes's granddaughter Margaret Aubrey, aged eighty-three, said he lived 'a rich man's life'. There was a very large detached house in Barnet, a maid called Louie, Humphrey the chauffeur and a gardener. She never knew him as a ladies' man since she was only eleven when he died. Mrs Aubrey also recalled Geddes towards the end: 'I just remember a tall, white-haired and rather distinguished man mostly sitting in a wheelchair. I don't remember even anyone mentioning Alec Guinness, but they wouldn't, would they?'

But what if a Guinness from the banking and brewery family had been his father? From what we know of Andrew Geddes (or Gaddes), it would seem unlikely that he was a Guinness family friend and therefore on the family yacht anchored in the Solent during Cowes week in 1913, at the place and time when the subject of this book was conceived. The family of Alec's mother, the Cuffs, did understand that one of their guests was Andrew Geddes, then aged fifty-three and married with six children. Alec was born in the following April, eight months later. 'Quite how they met we don't know, but it's part of our family history that Andrew Geddes is his father,' said Mrs Janis Hayward, whose grandmother Elizabeth was Agnes's elder sister. 'There has never been any doubt about it.'

On the other hand, some members of the Guinness family with whom I talked still strongly believed that the Hon. Anthony Ernest Guinness, or 'Uncle' Ernest (1876–1959), was Guinness's father. Ernest, who became vice-chairman of the brewery firm, had married into the English aristocracy in 1903 and had three daughters. They believe he met Alec's mother Agnes when the family yacht was moored in Cowes, and she was working as a waitress or chambermaid in a hotel. Alec distanced himself from any connection with the family, although when he met Honor Guinness, Lord Iveagh's daughter, on the *Queen Mary* in 1959, she told him he was definitely a Guinness. Perhaps the date was significant because it was the year of Ernest's death, and therefore he was not around to deny it. Several Guinnesses of his generation also looked uncannily like Alec. But then Alec uncannily looked like a lot of other people, one of the secrets of his art. When he was taken to meet Lord Iveagh he remained reluctant to be claimed as a one of the family. He liked the name and was by no means blind to its uses. He became quite comfortable, even blasé, with his surname, commenting later on a Phiz illustration in *The Pickwick Papers*, 'On the wall above the fireplace are lightly sketched in a few sporting prints: propped up on the mantelpiece are a couple of framed advertisements. One reads CIDER and the other GUINES'S DUBLIN STOUT. Being so familiar with the misspelling of my surname I immediately felt at home' (*A Positively Final Appearance*). Reports in the press of a DNA test to establish Alec as a Guinness before he died were simply not true. 'We'd love to have him as a member of the family – who wouldn't?' said Lord Moyne, head of another branch of the family. But there was no evidence.

The wound of illegitimacy was one thing; what must have hurt as much if not more was that Alec had no father who acknowledged him as his son and fulfilled the role of a father. It seems likely that at some point when very young, Agnes told him his father was Geddes; but Alec's diffidence to acknowledge this may well have come from his deeply wounded pride; he felt unwanted by his father. He would keep it to himself.

Thus, early on, the power and atmosphere of a hidden secret as opposed to an open secret came to permeate Alec's life. But while being his secret, it was also a secret hidden from him or so he liked to keep it. The quality of unsolved mystery and its seductive, Janus-faced nature – shame and guilt, yet desire for success – were to become important components of his personality.

Secrecy lies at the core of power. Secrecy and terror are a double act. Someone with something to hide arranges his or her secrets to guard each other. The secret confirmed and hid, as hiding became second nature, two other secrets: that of his sexuality and that of his anger. There is a saying in the Arabic *Book of the Crown*: 'It is the privilege of kings to keep their secrets from father, mother, brothers, wives and friends.' Did Alec assume this kingly privilege for himself?

3. The Bewitching of Naughtiness Doth Obscure Things

There was no doubt in my own mind, although I could have been mistaken, that when I began first to approach Guinness, then write about him, that it was his fear of being, to use that word, 'outed' as a homosexual or bisexual that constituted the main reason for his strong objection. But now I am not so sure. As part of one letter I wrote, I said to him – rather naively with hindsight:

> I believe in respecting and preserving mystery where some of it still fortunately exists. There must be an enormous and greatly suppressed desire for something *good* to be said.
>
> I do understand your reluctance to cooperate, and to be written about, but having hovered and dithered over the idea [which I have wanted] for over four years [to do], I hope you can understand that I would like to make the attempt. If you can see any way – without conceding the principle – that you might assist in, even slightly, I believe that you would not be unhappy at the outcome.
>
> With best wishes
> Garry O'Connor

However, as he wrote back to me (together with the rather spurious reason that there had been too many books written about him already), he had further ambitions of his own which he was to realize. He had already published *Blessings in Disguise* in 1985, and had then two further volumes to write: *My Name Escapes Me* (1996) and *A Positively Final Appearance* (1999), to which may be added *A Commonplace Book*, posthumously published in 2001.

As it was, I was caught in a difficult if not impossible situation. Discouraged, I did not really want to go ahead and write the book, finally published as *Alec Guinness: Master of Disguise*. The publishers, however, would not agree to my delaying the book until after Alec's death. I decided therefore to make some references, not too overt, to the duality of Alec's sexual nature, integrating these with his performances and his confusion over his identity, summarized in his relationship to playing Hamlet, also a seeker after his own unfinished identity. All along, however, I did hope – and even half expect – that he would change his mind upon reading, as I intended to show him, the final typescript of my book. But when I approached him about this his response was, to say the least, curt:

> A. E. Housman wrote, in 1936, to a would-be-biographer – 'Do not send me your manuscript. Worse than the practice of writing books about living men is the conduct of living men supervising such books'. Would you please accept that as being my own sentiment and possibly make it clear to your publisher.
>
> Yours sincerely
> Alec Guinness

Clearly Housman and I would not have got on.

I could not help noticing that he quoted Housman, who like Butler, like E. M. Forster, was another of those shadowy and undeclared (during their own lifetime, that is) figures in English literature, reticent to acknowledge their sexuality (and not necessarily through their own fault, but because of society's attitude and fear of the criminal law). *A Shropshire Lad*, a favourite poem of Alec's, had a 'hidden agenda'. Forster wrote incidentally, of Housman, 'He was an unhappy fellow and not a very amiable one.'

As it was I was surprised and confess that Alec's response provoked not only dismay but for some time antagonism and anger – I had not plumbed the depth, the virulence, the anger in that proprietorial sense he had of himself. I never recall Gielgud, who wrote some four or five volumes of autobiography, being in the slightest bit put out by the number of books written about him. Yet Guinness had forbidden his friends on pain of cutting off communication with them from cooperating with me. (As a Catholic this was his own form of excommunication.) He subsequently did not speak to various of those who had disobeyed for three or so years after my book came out. Yet many who read the book, including Sister Felicitas Corrigan of Stanbrook Abbey where Alec used to stay for retreats, pointed out to him that his reaction was exaggerated and unjustified.

In late spring 2001, just before the publication of Morley's life of Gielgud there was a flurry of articles in the press on Guinness's sexuality. The reason was that Morley, drawing a parallel with his subject Gielgud, who had cooperated with Morley, revealed this piece of gossip well-known in theatrical circles: that Alec had been arrested and fined for a homosexual offence in a public lavatory in Liverpool in 1948. 'Alec was clever enough to come up with a false name,' Morley told me. Maintaining his anonymity in a quick-witted way, something the more open Gielgud was incapable of doing, Alec gave his name as Herbert Pocket, the character in *Great Expectations* which he had acted before the war in a production devised by himself and had just, to general acclaim, been playing in David Lean's film of the classic. 'Pocket's name is still solemnly inscribed in the [Liverpool police] list of offenders,' wrote Morley. 'This never came out in Guinness's lifetime.' Questioned about this, Piers Paul Read who had been asked to write an authorized biography by Merula Guinness, Alec's widow, just before she died, in October 2000, replied that he was 'not at all surprised' at Guinness's bisexuality. 'I would not be surprised, too, if he was tempted.'

The broader subject of Guinness's sexuality had never been dealt with before in print, and like most aspects of this secretive, many-sided and rich personality the truth was far more complex and hard to unravel than might be revealed in the reportage. This, in our age's reckoning, could be discounted as little more than the peccadillo of a young man (although Guinness was thirty-two and had served long years in the navy as a landing-craft captain and had by then become a much-hardened figure).

There is an anguished cri de cœur in the closing pages of *A Positively Final Appearance* which goes some way if not quite to the heart of the matter: 'If,' Alec writes with his usual indirect, evasive, escape clause, 'I have one regret (leaving aside a thousand failings as a person, husband, father, grandfather, great-grandfather and friend – and my lazy, slapdash, selfish attitude as an actor) it would be that I didn't take the decision to become a Catholic in my early twenties. That would have sorted out a lot of my life and sweetened it.'

But then, it is most unlikely we would have had the Alec Guinness we know today; and probably even more unlikely that I would be writing this book. For the great performances that made his name and established his reputation came directly out of this confusion.

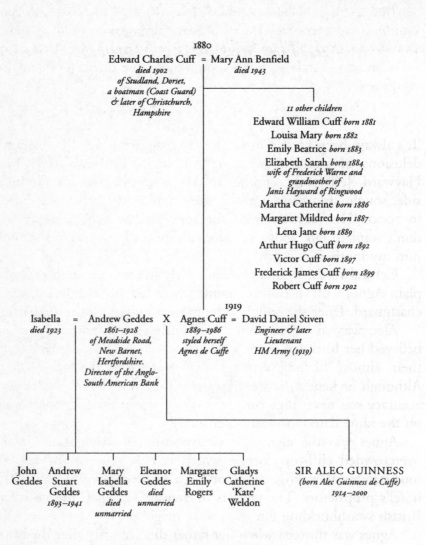

1880

Edward Charles Cuff = Mary Ann Benfield
died 1902   *died 1943*
of Studland, Dorset,
a boatman (Coast Guard)
& later of Christchurch,
Hampshire

11 other children

Edward William Cuff *born 1881*

Louisa Mary *born 1882*

Emily Beatrice *born 1883*

Elizabeth Sarah *born 1884*
wife of Frederick Warne and
grandmother of
Janis Hayward of Ringwood

Martha Catherine *born 1886*

Margaret Mildred *born 1887*

Lena Jane *born 1889*

Arthur Hugo Cuff *born 1892*

Victor Cuff *born 1897*

Frederick James Cuff *born 1899*

Robert Cuff *born 1902*

1919

Isabella = Andrew Geddes X Agnes Cuff = David Daniel Stiven
died 1923   *1861–1928*   *1889–1986*   *Engineer & later*
of Meadside Road,   *styled herself*   *Lieutenant*
New Barnet,   *Agnes de Cuffe*   *HM Army (1919)*
Hertfordshire.
Director of the Anglo-
South American Bank

John   Andrew   Mary   Eleanor   Margaret   Gladys   SIR ALEC GUINNESS
Geddes   Stuart   Isabella   Geddes   Emily   Catherine   *(born Alec Guinness de Cuffe)*
          Geddes   Geddes   *died*   Rogers   'Kate'   *1914–2000*
          1893–1941 *died*   *unmarried*   Weldon
                     unmarried

The Cuff–Guinness family tree

4. The Sins of the Mother

'It's always been known in the family that Agnes was the one with delusions of grandeur who wanted to be different,' says Mrs Hayward. Jeff Cuffe, another of Alec's relations on his mother's side, sought information about their family just before Alec died in 2000. 'His reaction from the start was politely go away – I don't want to talk about it.' Alec told him, 'I am too old to look into my mother's history.'

Central to the drama of Alec's early life was his mother, born plain Agnes Cuff in Bournemouth where her father Edward was a coastguard. Later she adopted the more grandiose form, de Cuffe.

Alec was so vague about his mother's background that he believed her birthday – not a celebration he acknowledged due to their almost lifelong estrangement – was 6 December 1885. Although he kept a diary for the last thirty years of his life, factual accuracy was never high on Alec's list of priorities. Agnes was born on the same date four years later in 1889.

Agnes was the eighth of twelve children brought up in an overcrowded cliff-top cottage which is now part of the resort's four-star Swallow Highcliff Hotel – a fact unknown, even to the hotel's proprietors. The parents of Stewart Granger, the post-war British swashbuckling film star, were neighbours.

Agnes was thirteen when her father died, shortly after the birth of his last child, by which time he had left the coastguard to work as a caretaker for a shopping arcade in the Westbourne area of Bournemouth. What work Agnes was doing at this stage of her life, the Cuff family are uncertain. Alec believed she was in service before becoming a barmaid. His friend David Cornwell, the author John le Carré, understood her to be a prostitute (*Daily Mail*, 2000) who fell pregnant with Alec while entertaining members of

the aristocracy. Alec's son Matthew, highly offended at the suggestion, disputes this. And according to Agnes's great-niece Janis
Hayward, she was a showy young woman who yearned for the
theatre and went to London to become a bit-part actress but never
found either the success or fame that her son was to enjoy.

Agnes's mother, Mary Ann Benfield, outlived Edward her
husband by forty-one years and Alec, very late in life, did record
she had a whitewashed cottage overlooking the bay (at Christchurch, possibly). She resembled, he said, a vast black widow
spider and when aged about five he visited her she 'scared the
pants off me. Her great crimson face was surrounded by black
hair, fiercely parted in the middle; she was a bundle of shiny
black clothes and glittering jet jewellery.'

This gypsy-like woman, treating him with something between
indifference and dislike gave him a tiny polar bear on skis, which
he came to treasure: he became Alec's friend to whom he whispered secrets. Later he found she was a heavy drinker.

Agnes was auburn-haired and freckled. Alec mentions his birth
certificate on the first page of *Blessings in Disguise*. But in his three
books he either gets the place of his birth wrong or distorts it in
order to cloak or hide it. He says that he was born in Marylebone,
which is not true. The certificate gives Lauderdale Mansions as her
address: this strictly is in Lauderdale Road, Maida Vale, near
Warwick Avenue and Elgin Avenue, two streets away from the
Paddington recreation ground. If his mother moved within six
weeks of his birth she must have gone down in the world. As
A. A. Gill, the columnist, wrote in 2001, 'Maida Vale is the suicide
capital of London: a strange shrouded and muttering place'. At
this earlier time it was an area associated with the demi-monde
and prostitution.

Alec was born in the first year of the First World War, declared
in August 1914, a few months after his birth. His mother was
twenty-five when he was born, his father, assuming this was
Geddes, twenty-eight years older than she was. They never lived
together. There is no doubt that at the time of Alec's conception
Agnes was in the Isle of Wight on an extended visit to her close
sister Elizabeth, who had fallen in love with a young man from
the island, Frederick Warne, whom she later married. To be born
just before the war meant that, personal conditions of chaos and

unhappiness apart, the whole of his infant and early life was steeped in an atmosphere of optimism and formal discipline. Whatever his mother may have been doing, the country before and during her pregnancy was gearing itself up for war, and there was always a sense of life larger than oneself.

Not only was this feeling of nationhood an integral part of his early life, but it must have been reinforced, although not entirely in a salutary way, by his mother's immediate post-war marriage to a demobbed 'captain', David Stiven, who had apparently served in Ireland during the war (or just after), and who kept a loaded revolver beside his bed in case members of Sinn Fein came after him.

Several millions of men were away from home, many mothers lived with their children alone during these years, so Agnes de Cuffe's situation was hardly remarkable. But illegitimacy in those days was much less common than it is today, and knowing this fact from an early age inevitably set Alec apart. It is hard to know the exact date Alec first discovered he was illegitimate, but he presumably knew before his mother married in 1919 and if he didn't, the brute who became his stepfather probably told him in no uncertain terms. He guarded the knowledge as a secret, taking special pains to make himself respectable and build up for the outside world an image of himself so he could feel accepted. You might keep quiet about yourself, but you would always be suspicious that someone else knew. Alec's exact sense of what was right, his punctiliousness and self-discipline, came from a need and a determination to show he was better than the facts of his birth. The guard was never lowered.

Alec's birth, on 2 April 1914, had not been registered at once. It was delayed for the legal limit of six weeks before his mother, reluctantly one imagines, went along from Flat 155, Lauderdale Mansions to the nearest register office which was Paddington North. The certificate is enigmatic for it contains his name ('if any' in the words of the form) 'Alec Guinness'; his mother's name, Agnes de Cuffe; the date of his registration, one calendar month and sixteen days after his birth. The name of the father and his occupation have both been left blank. Long delay over the registering of the birth was quite a common occurrence with an unwanted or illegitimate child. Alec later told someone that whenever he talked over with his mother the question of his father, she went into a catatonic state.

As for the Cuffs, apart from Agnes herself and Alec, there are no other known actors in the Cuff family. Years later, when Guinness was famous, a young cousin wrote to him saying she wanted to go on the stage and he sent her a kindly and encouraging reply. But she never did.

The twelve children of Edward Cuff and his wife Mary took a variety of paths through life. The family had fallen on hard times after Edward's death and, desperate for her children not to go hungry, Mary Cuff managed to have two of the boys – Alec's late uncles Victor and Fred – admitted by Dr Barnardo's as 'orphans'.

They were shipped to Canada while still children, where they were given work as farm labourourers and treated as virtual slaves – according to the Cuffs – who bore the scars of whip marks until their deaths in Canada in the 1980s. Alec nominated as the most inane remark he had ever heard: 'Worthwhile Canadian initiative which is not boring as a whole but boring word by word' (from the *New Statesman*).

*

Dr Johnson believed complete submission of the young must be beaten into them, but Montaigne, from whose *Essays* Alec became fond of quoting, wrote, 'I have never seen caning achieve anything except making souls more cowardly or maliciously stubborn.' Alec's early deprivation and suffering was of a different kind. 'An unhappy childhood and adolescence?' he inquired of himself. 'Yes, it could be judged as such, except that I think the young accept their own lives as the norm.' He depicted his early isolated upbringing at preparatory private schools as a mixture of privilege and deprivation. He was sent off to private boarding schools, but when his mother arrived she would borrow ten pounds off a master. (Our factual biographer could claim he exaggerated. Ten pounds would have been at least three hundred pounds at 2002 values.) Alec hardly spoke publicly of her more than five times, and what he said was less than warm: she was unhelpful; even less helpful was the solicitor who channelled the money into his schooling and abruptly turned off the dribble of funds when he ceased being a drama student.

The first blow in his early life was his mother's marriage on 9 August 1919, at the St Giles Register Office, London, to David Daniel Stiven – the 'captain' Alec called him. Agnes grandly claimed on the certificate that her father, coastguard Edward, also was a 'Captain RN'. He was no such thing. Alec's memories of his short-term stepfather of inflated rank were not happy. Stiven, recently demobbed from the service, had not become properly detached from the habits of military life. He may not even have been demobbed at all, but still a serving officer, for he gave his address to the marriage registrar as the Ordnance Depot, Didcot. The 'captain', like Geddes a Scot, became at once to Alec a threatening and exploitative figure. 'Why are Scots so attracted to the secret world?' wonders Smiley in *Smiley's People*, the le Carré character Alec was later to play on television. 'Ship engineers, colonial administrators, spies. Their heretical Scottish history drew them to distant churches.'

In fact, Stiven had never been a captain but a Royal Army Service Corps lieutenant, a master gas engineer, like his father before him. He was twenty-eight years old and had divorced, or been divorced by, his first wife Winifred. Stiven not only kept a loaded service revolver, he could be violent. He once menaced Alec with the revolver, holding it to his head, saying he would kill both him and Agnes to get whatever he wanted out of Alec's mother. On another occasion, or so Alec reported, he dangled his young charge upside down from a bridge, threatening to drop him into the river below.

Much later, Alec felt, or so again he reports, he may have provoked the 'captain' to behave in the way he did. Reluctant as he was to speak ill of his mother after she died, there was an undercurrent of resentment at the way he was treated by her which coloured his relationship with certain of the opposite sex and may have made him contained, even shy, towards feminine sexual attraction.

The marriage to Stiven lasted four years, during which time Alec said they lived in a depressing three-roomed top-floor flat in St John's Wood, not far from the Victorian block in Lauderdale Road where he had started life. But Agnes gave her address when she and Stiven married as 31 Upper Bedford Place, Bloomsbury, quite a distance away. The personal family complexity or muddle

19¹⁴	Marriage solemnized at *the Register Office*				in the County of *London*			
No.	When Married.	Name and Surname.	Age.	Condition.	Rank or Profession.	Residence at the time of Marriage.	Father's Name and Surname.	Rank or Profession of Father.
36	Ninth August 19¹⁴	David Daniel Steven	38 years	*Widowed [last pub. of Dorothy Whitefield Steven formerly Margt Spinks]*	*Lieutenant R.A.S.C. Gas Engineer Student]*	Ordnance Depot Didcot Berks	David Steven (deceased)	Gas Engineer
		Agnes Cuff	32 years	Spinster	—	31, Upper Bedford Place, Bloomsbury	Edward Charles Cuff (deceased)	Captain R.N.

Married in the	*Register Office*	according to the Rites and Ceremonies of the		by *Licence* before	*by me.*
This Marriage was solemnized between us, {	D. D. Steven Agnes Cuff	In the Presence of us. {	Anne Blanch Steven B. Pearce Lucas	P. H. Townsend, *Registrar* Sydney Ashley, Superintendent Registrar	

1887
32

Agnes Cuff's marriage certificate

must have given Alec a further early drive towards becoming an actor, for he played other people in his fantasies of escape, and while the schools he subsequently attended did not provide much by way of stimulus or academic achievement, they did provoke that most important element in anyone's education, namely curiosity.

When later on Alec recalled these early days of misery, he found the experiences which returned alarming: the effect was powerful and Proustian, as a smell or some other memory would suddenly smack him in the face. He had much hidden recall. 'I only had to say I went to a pre-prep school at Bexhill at six, and suddenly a vision of a master picking off the tree a diseased crab apple, crawling with maggots, haunted my days. Something with a shiny outside that hid the corruption.'

The first of his schools, Normandale boarding school in Collington Avenue, Bexhill, had a headmaster named Mr Salmon. Bexhill was a flourishing area for preparatory schools because it was quiet and respectable, the air was healthy, while it possessed two railway lines to London. His second school, Pembroke Lodge, Southbourne-on-Sea, which he attended from the ages of seven to thirteen, had the same qualities: a 'School for Young Gentlemen', preparatory for Public School and the Royal Navy, it was a stone's throw from the Dorset beach. His third, Roborough School in Bournemouth, saw him through to the age of eighteen, establishing a lasting basis of discipline in him, mostly by means of a series of prohibitions which, if broken, threatened dire punishments.

Remarking on ugly physical characteristics became to Alec a distinctive trait early on. He was never to lose it, stemming from a vanity only too aware of physical shortcomings: at Pembroke Lodge the masters in their thirties already 'had knobbly knees, revealed by their long, floppy football shorts, and at forty they often had ghastly Adam's apples which not only bobbed up and down in a jokey way but sometimes sprouted single tough hairs. None of these physical attributes of age were desirable, and as for tufts of hair in ears and nostrils, they were not to be mentioned except with horror and youthful contempt.'

Joking is a familiar means for brazening out shame, calling enlarged attention to the thing you do not want naturally noticed. Both in mental and physical forms Alec sported disfigurement for its comic effect. Shame is discomfort produced by the sense of being looked at; guilt is a different matter, producing a reflex that discovery must at all costs be avoided. Alec's memories by the age of eighty-four had mellowed when he recalled setting off two by two, in loose crocodile form on obligatory walks, scuffing through the fallen leaves in residential roads which wound through South-bourne or Bournemouth, or out to sniff the steel-cold sea at Hengistbury Head. What on earth did we chatter to each other about, he wondered? He felt that they were too young and ignorant to whisper about sex.

On winter evenings, inside, they would get on with their hobbies, in Alec's case the construction of a collapsible card-board model theatre, for which he had designed a variety of baronial halls, dungeons, drawing rooms and 'a glade in a forest'. He used pocket torches to achieve highly dramatic effects in the smaller, darkened schoolrooms. There were little cut-out paper or cardboard figures, which he attached to pieces of wire and eased on and off stage from the wings or sometimes dangled them from above. 'Needless to say I did all the voices for the quite incredible dialogue. Usually I managed to collect an audi-ence of about three or four, suitably spellbound. Even if there was no audience I still carried on, but perhaps in low heart.' (*My Name Escapes Me*)

'In low heart', with low expectations, were the operative feelings. He wrote the short pieces himself, sophisticated they were, about titled people. Remove the shell of these nostalgic sketches and there remained the kernel of anger, of resentment. He was not, at Pembroke Lodge, put down for an admired school such as Marlborough or Fettes, which he would have liked, but the near anonymous solicitor guardian who intermediated to pay the fees provided by Geddes sent him to the mediocre Roborough School. Before he left his prep school he asked the headmaster if he could be in the end-of-term play, farces which were often funny. The request was dismissed. 'You'll never make an actor,' the headmaster told him. 'It dumbfounded me at the time . . . in retrospect I believe I turned it to a useful warning, because it put in my soul a little grain of iron determination.'

Out of school Alec had little in the way of family stability or structure. According to the Cuffs there had been more to Alec's relationship with his father Andrew Geddes – and to his mother's, too – than he ever wanted or felt inclined to record.

Alec had been five when his mother married Stiven, a step-father whom he says in his memoirs was a brute whom he 'hated and dreaded'. By the time they divorced, Geddes's wife Isabella had died, and from this moment Alec was to spend most of his summer holidays with his aunt Elizabeth Warne and her husband, who had by now settled in Westbourne, Bournemouth in a house later knocked down to make way for a local branch of the supermarket chain Waitrose.

Why wasn't Alec holidaying with his mother? The answer, say the Cuffs, is that Agnes and Geddes had reopened their affair and were again seeing each other.

'Agnes used to join Geddes in the South of France,' Eric Warne, one of Elizabeth's grandchildren, told me in 2002. 'She was different from the rest of the family by then, you know, lots of airs and graces.

'Alec used to play with my uncles John and Victor who were about the same age. By all accounts he really loved coming here because it was a real family atmosphere which he didn't have at home and Elizabeth was so like his mother. But my uncles found him rather toffee-nosed, though this might have been simply because they went to the local school and he was being privately educated.'

What about the character of Agnes? I repeat that I do not believe she made Alec feel from a very early age well disposed, or naturally attracted, to women. Reluctant though he was to speak ill of Agnes, he did mention the sound of unknown male footsteps up and down the stairs outside his bedroom door, suggesting a succession of client lovers. His resentment and anger towards Agnes may well have been the reason he felt contained, even very shy towards feminine sexual attraction, especially if it was in any way predatory. This became evident later on in his acting: the last thing he could convey was passionate attraction towards women, although this of course is not to say he did not feel it. I don't think in any of his seventy-seven films he was shown in bed with a woman, although most were made before this became obligatory. His refusal, when rehearsing, to kiss when it was called for is well known; he would save this for the performance.

Yet there were benefits as well as downsides to having Agnes as a mother. Alec's retrospective resentment is not wholly to be trusted. Memories of negative experiences, of unhappy life periods, are more accessible in a negative mood than in a happy mood. Agnes must, I suspect, have been quite rich in character, many-sided and, with a love of drink, quite feisty. With her phobias and assumed airs, a role, surely, for Maggie Smith.

His doubt about who he really was, and the loneliness of his position, developed his imagination more than that of other children. 'If I look back now I can see traces from being very, very small and escaping into something of a fantasy world,' he said in a 1975 radio interview. His early capacity to be alone became also crucially linked with self-discovery and self-realization. As well as a false self there was some inner scheme or system developing which sought to make sense of his distress. He must also have been reasonable, for as Goya the painter wrote, 'Phantasy abandoned by reason produces impossible monsters; united with her, she is the mother of the arts and the origin of their marvels'.

The recall of autobiographical memories is influenced by the current mood of the individual. As Alec's anecdotal eye developed, the observing side of his personality also became important to him. He found, perhaps as a reaction to the pain that had been inflicted on him, that he could easily merge 'with the background when he wants to', as Michael Noakes, who painted Alec's portrait over a two-year period in 1970–71, noted. 'When I was young,' said Alec himself, 'I used to follow people for miles sometimes, women as well as men, just studying them. It was a kind of obsession.' But he developed a hatred, a phobia of being followed himself, of being looked at too earnestly, of being questioned directly, of being analysed. Sometimes he made light of this. Once, he said, an anxious-looking lady followed him relentlessly only to tell him, 'Mr Guinness, your buttons [fly-buttons] are undone.'

In 1928 Alec was told, presumably by his mother, that his real name was Guinness, which it was not, although this was the name on his birth certificate, and that de Cuffe and Stiven no longer applied. Yet by this time he and his mother had moved thirty times (so Guinness said, although much of the time he was away at school which gave an institutional framework to his life). In the hotels and lodgings where they lived they left behind them, as in a paper chase, a wake of unpaid bills. Again we must allow for autobiographical licence on Alec's part. While there is no proof of a shady profession, one does suspect the means by which his mother came by her money. You do not ever get a sense that Alec trusted her or that she ever made him the centre of her attention. This generated feelings of aloofness, detachment, sometimes despair. But her own fantasy life, her aspiration to become an actress, unfulfilled as it was, must have become rooted in him. Later, when he became an actor, he did not see her for long periods, or so he reported, although this may not have been true.

Frith Banbury, who acted with Alec in 1934 in the Gielgud company and saw him every day for six months, told me in 2001 that every Friday, on pay day, 'Mum appeared at the stage door' and that out of the six pounds a week, 'One pound had to go to keep Mum in booze.' In view of this, Gielgud was 'very generous, but a frightfully hard master'. Banbury commented how terribly awkward Alec was about his mother – 'very buttoned up about a drunken mother while he was very sensitive all his life, with a very short fuse. He easily got upset. My impression was that he didn't like himself.'

What Agnes did do was to stimulate his aspiration to have a family, to escape from his past (if that was possible), to 'belong' in a wider sense, for which he developed an extraordinary capacity – an appetite which he fulfilled meticulously and conscientiously. Without a father he had to be the father he never had. Yet the more formless threat of Agnes continued all the time to threaten him, as if she might suddenly appear to embarrass him, pitch him into a confused and shamed state of mind. He became precise in his attachment to form, sought an exaggerated correctness in details such as dress, manners, articulation and even handwriting.

Agnes instilled phobias in her young son. She dragged him past London pillar boxes for fear Irish revolutionaries had posted bombs in them. She created a terror in his youthful psyche of black-hatted Trotskyites lurking round corners waiting to kill. Rag-and-bone men were poised to kidnap him and spirit him away under a heap of old clothes. This superstitious, premonitory element persisted in Alec throughout his life; he had a sense of auras, of foretelling disasters, of ultimate nightmares of his imagination – lasting right to the end. Tidal waves that engulfed him (usually in the company of approved celebrities such as Lady Diana Cooper) seemed a particular recurrent phobia, but this sense of mystery had its delicate, appealing side, connected with wildlife, birds for example: 'So often I feel that birds are around to keep us informed in some mysterious way, or at least to suggest to our imaginations a larger, unknown world. This is possibly some throwback in my genes to a pagan past, the shade perhaps of a Roman augur in the blood.'

*

At an early age Alec began theatre-going. This provided fairyland vistas of happiness, or at least comic relief. His first visit to a London theatre was when he was four. This was to *Chu Chin Chow* at the Coliseum. It made a 'huge impression' on him. Two years later he was taken to one or two shows, 'which I hated, a pantomime which I was scared by. I think the kind of dressing-up and pretending to be someone else probably happens to all children. And I think as my particular background wasn't a very happy one I probably did console myself with make-believe a lot.' (Radio interview 1975)

In his childhood and youth Alec always had to keep quiet, gaining respectability and good report by the calm quality of his behaviour. But inwardly this little boy seethed with a guilt and resentment often near to boiling point. As le Carré said to Frank Delaney in 1982 of an upbringing in some ways similar, 'I was scrupulously well behaved, appallingly polite, a little butler, not able to do anything naughty.' It was a dangerous condition to be in, akin to that 'of a liar or a spy'. As le Carré said of Alec in 1996, 'The deprivals and humiliations of three-quarters of a century ago are unresolved.'

'I must have been struck in the holiday time by something I'd seen.' Escaping into a fantasy world had developed at about the age of eight, and Alec used to tell stories in his dormitory, rather overdramatizing them. 'I acted my head off . . . Other boys were fast asleep when I was still droning on.' There were the school plays, at least at the pre-prep stage, before the later rejection. He scored a 'great hit' in *Macbeth* because, as the Act Five Messenger, he ran round the soccer field for six minutes before he made his entrance to deliver his news in a state of exhaustion. At another

time, when he was nine, a conjuror came to school and he joined
in his act, sitting on a chair and then getting up. Alec felt a need
to underplay: 'He wanted me to scream and shout. I knew it was
phoney.'

During his schooldays and after, Alec expressed or described
little or no awakening of sexual feeling or attraction to girls or
young women. Given what had happened to him this was not
surprising. Not until he was fourteen, he said, had he been told
his 'real' name was Guinness. Rejected by the men in his life, his
true father, his short-lived stepfather, he formed more trust with
the female side of his personality than the male. The extreme,
bizarre antics of middle-aged female music-hall stars engaged his
attention more, as did some odd notions about the sexual organs,
discussed in the dormitory after lights out, where the headmaster
made an occasional visit to 'tickle' the captain of the First XI.
About sperm ('male seed') one school friend assured Alec, one had
to be very careful, as it was a black pip which popped out of the
penis unexpectedly and had to be caught when you micturated, or
you would never be a father. One suspects Alec knew more about
this subject than he was prepared to say. And his awareness of the
hypocrisy of grown-ups was acute.

In the school holidays when he visited London, he mainly
stayed in hotels with his mother, one in particular in the Cromwell
Road, where he had fun working the hydraulic lifts and he became
friends with chambermaids who brought up hot water. Again one
senses something impermanent and seedy about this background,
but not without its own kind of mystery and glamour. It was a
world whose atmosphere T. S. Eliot caught forcefully in his poems
of 1909–25, which are contemporary with Alec's early years: the
evocation of the half-deserted post-war city streets, the one-night
cheap hotels, the yellow smoke outside the window panes, the
smells of cheap eau de cologne and cocktails in bars, the rattling
breakfast plates in basement kitchens – all breeding an oblique,
hidden and yet insidious undercurrent of sexuality.

The emotional outlet Alec so desperately needed was provided
by the variety stage and, in later childhood, the 'legitimate'
stage. 'I used to be always asking for bits of pocket money to get
into the gallery or pit somewhere.' He described with joy in
The Observer in 1984 Nellie Wallace bending over the stage to the

accompaniment of farting sounds from the orchestra: 'She was an extraordinary comic, in loud tweeds and boots with a long feather in her hat. She was hideous as a parrot.' He found himself leaving the Coliseum in a daze, trying to talk like her, and repeat her act of assisting a surgeon in a baroque, surreal operation. She made him want to be a clown. He caught imaginary corpses in the air, glared with wildly shocked eyes at innocent passers-by, and generally misbehaved himself.

He could never remember not wanting to be an actor, while the delight of escaping from himself came at the age of fourteen. 'Somehow I had got hold of a long, straight-haired wig. One night before going to bed I put it on, then teased some wool out of my blanket and stuck on a moustache and a little beard. I looked in the mirror and thought, "I look like Charles I". And I began to *feel* like Charles I. It was much better than feeling like me.'

In Eastbourne's Devonshire Park Theatre Alec found nourishment for his passion for the theatre, savouring 'frothy comedies, or thrillers, and now and then what were considered torrid sex dramas!' These pre- or post-London productions familiarized him with such stars as Godfrey Tearle, Sir Frank Benson, Irene Vanbrugh and Phyllis Neilson-Terry. He realized early the sad ephemeral nature of the actor's art, and how the 'Positively Final Performance' gimmick was just an effort to sell a few more seats. This ability to feel the character in almost instant acts of self-transformation became a hallmark of Alec's genius.

On Eastbourne's pier he claims he saw a very lazy production by the Ben Greet Players of *Julius Caesar* when he was sixteen. Because the men had spent the day on the beach they were scarlet except for white areas showing in spite of togas or Roman armour 'where their one-piece bathing costumes with shoulder straps had protected them. Ben Greet himself shuffled around as Caesar and you caught glimpses of his rolled-up trousers under his costume.'

He experienced at the Pier Theatre the moment which indicated his future career. He was 'seized' by Henry Baynton as Shylock, a 'bit of an old ham', whom he saw with his Shakespearean company of 'mostly undergraduates he picked up on the cheap'. Baynton, said Alec, modelled his Shylock on Henry Irving's. He made some 'curious and obviously phoney gestures but they were very arresting, and a sort of strange Eastern waving of the hand . . . I remember spending the rest of that term, it was the summer term, in the cricket pavilion. I couldn't be less interested in the sports side of things, but [was] making this strange Eastern signal to my school fellows.'

By the age of eighteen Alec had severed all close living connection with his mother, although she stayed as this constant threat and sometimes unwelcome presence. The headmaster of Roborough School helped him to get a job as a copywriter in Ark's advertising agency in Lincoln's Inn Fields. In a later account, not long before he died, Alec revised this to confess it was not the headmaster but his daughter Beryl Daniels, with whom 'like several other boys in their late teens' he had fallen in love, in spite of her being seven years older. She seemed distantly safe and unattainable, like one of the virtuous ladies pursued by Samuel Butler in between assuaging his sexual needs with prostitutes. She found him his advertising job and he would write to her weekly 'sixteen page outpourings'. Once a fortnight she would reply in 'short, reassuring and wise' letters. She expressed confidence in his future, and she began for Alec a lifelong habit of prolific correspondence.

At the agency Alec was paid a pound a week. Later this was increased to thirty shillings. He wrote about razor blades, Rose's Lime Juice and radio valves. 'I learnt a lot. I learnt to trim my English quite a bit.' They wanted to try him out in all sides of the business. One day he took into the printers a four-foot square block instead of a four-inch square block. 'They didn't sack me, of course.'

He wanted to go to the Royal Academy of Dramatic Art, and they sent him a form. He got in touch with John Gielgud whom he admired 'dottily . . . I think I must have had some secret hope he'd say come round to the theatre and I'll put you through it . . . which could have been terrible.' It would probably have been to his father, who was away in South America, he told a BBC interviewer in 1975, 'a great shock to hear his son had gone into the theatre'. But Andrew Geddes was not then away in South America; he had died four years earlier in Barnet.

Towards the end of her life Agnes lived in a cottage Alec had built in the grounds of Kettlebrook Meadows. One Sunday morning after breakfast, Alan Bennett told John Bird, when Bennett was staying for the weekend, Alec said, 'I'd better go and see Mother.' Bennett accompanied him as they walked down the path and when they reached the cottage he saw Agnes lying flat out on the floor. He was horrified, fearing she had collapsed from illness or died. But Alec gently pulled him away, saying, 'Oh, it's just . . .' and made a drinking gesture with hand and elbow.

And so they left her. It seemed the heartlessness she engendered in him had persisted through life. The last we hear of Agnes de Cuffe in public utterances, is when Alec made an entry for 17 February 1996 in his diary manufactured for publication entitled, with a typically self-effacing flourish, *My Name Escapes Me*. He reports sadly that ten years before, in 1986, in a Sue Ryder home just a few miles from where he lived in Petersfield his mother died. 'My poor, very old, rather unhappy mother'. She would then have been ninety-seven. Sitting with her in her room at Bordean House, 'listening to the rasp of her stertoreous breathing,' a tall nurse appeared and cheerfully asked if he would like a cup of tea. He accepted whereupon the nurse plied him with questions such as 'Were you a lonely little boy?' which made Alec cross, who then demanded to be left with his dying mother. But he returned home for a breather; and while he was away they telephoned him to say she had died.

The passage reveals mixed feelings, concealed in jokes about the upward formal half of an undertaker kept on late: 'in offering his condolences he only half-rose from the desk, hoping I wouldn't spot his nether-garment (blue-jeans and white sneakers)', and drinking rather a lot of whisky with their perfect house guest, Peggy Ashcroft – 'absolutely the right person to have around'. The shame and loneliness of the little boy was still here, one feels, perhaps even more so, at her death. At another time he evoked from that South Coast childhood he loved the little electric railway which ran from near the Palace Pier to Black Rock and which had a section of its line running out over the sea. 'When the sea was a bit rough this was a thrill; when it was really rough the cissy little train didn't function. I must have spent many happy, if lonely, hours to'ing and fro'ing. Not absolutely lonely. I have always found the sea, in whatever mood it was in, good and sufficient company.'

This is echoed in a Victor Hugo anecdote Alec included in his *Commonplace Book*. Hugo's son asks his father what he would do in his Guernsey exile. 'I will gaze at the ocean. What will you do?' The son answers, 'I shall translate Shakespeare.' Hugo: 'The two activities are one and the same.'

There must have been also considerable anger and shame about Agnes vulnerably confessed – although conveniently disguised – in Bridget Boland's *The Prisoner*, which Father Caraman had observed to me was 'the most significant play' in Alec's life, performed in 1954. The powerful impact of *The Prisoner* on those who saw it, or later saw the film of the play, was that Alec seemed to be 'confessing' – at one level removed and in emotionally safe circumstances – the shameful background of his own life (and if not the actual truth, then the feelings he had about it).

> *Interrogator:* What were you hiding? Why were you
>   ashamed?
> *Prisoner:* Unclean flesh.
> *Interrogator:* Yes. Yes?
> *Prisoner:* My body of her flesh and blood.
> *Interrogator:* Your mother.
> *Prisoner:* Filth of her filth, me at the root of it, her lust.
> *Interrogator:* Behind the Fish Market. A prostitute?
> *Prisoner:* Not even for money. A whore. Not even for
>   money, for lust . . . Remembering the smell of the
>   women who bent over you to try and kiss you good
>   night. Where, before I was born or after it, would I find
>   a heart?

Later the Prisoner is even more explicit when he says what should go into his confession: 'That I am the son of my mother, and my whole life is a fantasy to hide me . . . I prayed for forgiveness, but I knew I had no heart.'

Most actors and incidentally writers act or write with their surface personalities. They never let down, in the phrase of E. M. Forster, 'buckets into their underworld'. Alec managed continually this rare feat – disguising from the world that he was doing it.

There was yet another side of Agnes Cuffe that Alec carried with him throughout his life. In him remained the component which had made his mother what she was: not only the potential, as in everyone, but the actual ability to sell herself cheap. Early on in his life his outlet for this was to become attached to those tawdry music-hall figures who sported themselves, tarted their talents on the stage; he developed a 'wicked' side to himself, a sense of subversive fun, a lavatorial humour – that kind of 'don't-leave-your-fan-on-the-seat' smart remarks that were the catchphrases of his adolescence. These were to become even a deliberately outrageous side of his personality in later life, and not always and necessarily a pleasant side – a way of living out an exhibitionist streak in his nature. Outwardly, except for a few odd references to her, he successfully hid Agnes de Cuffe from the world.

5. *The Dancing Star*

On 2 April 1934, Alec's twentieth birthday, he appeared in his first West End role, ironically that of a non-speaking Junior Counsel in *Libel!*. Edward Wooll's famous play opened at the King's Theatre, Hammersmith and then transferred for a run at the Playhouse. Alec gained upon the transfer a couple of lines to speak. He later said he was a non-speaking juror, but the biographies list his part as Junior Counsel.

About that time Samuel Butler's *Erewhon* and *Notebooks* first came his way. Alec carried disillusionment in his heart; now were added a sense of failure and guilt as if they were his birthright. He dipped much into W. N. O. Barbellion's *Journal of a Disappointed Man*, published some fifteen years earlier, soaking himself in the despondent observations about life and nature. One of these struck Alec in particular, when Barbellion quoted Nietzsche as saying, 'You must carry a chaos inside you to give birth to a dancing star.' Barbellion added, 'Internal chaos I have, but no dancing star'.

Alec identified with this negative self-assessment. Worse, his weekly allowance of twenty-five shillings, now he was of a mature age, was stopped by the solicitor who administered the legacy or trust put aside by Geddes for his education. He dreamed of being a star one day, but he knew he would never be one. A friend, a girl, with whom he sat one day by the lake in Regent's Park, made a suggestion. She and he were fellow students at the Fay Compton Studio of Dramatic Art in Baker Street, and during a break in rehearsals sat watching the elderly gentlemen feathering on the lake's boats. Guinness had not been very long at the Studio, a former dingy drill hall with a stage at one end, where he attended classes in voice production, fencing, dancing and movement, musical comedy and the classics. Before coming he had applied for a scholarship audition at the Royal Academy of Dramatic Art but he could not afford to pay, and the scholarship was suspended. The extravagant character actress Martita Hunt, who lived the life of a rich eccentric ('Martita always put druggets over her carpeting except when she was expecting important guests, fearing what lesser mortals might tread into her flat'), thought he was a rich Guinness and gave him ten private but costly lessons. On their first meeting she tried to drag him across the room by his upper lip: 'Flab!' she commented, 'No muscle. If you want to be an actor you must have muscle in your upper lip.' Later she told him, 'Take care you don't fall in with the wrong set.'

Now the Geddes subsidy and the two-year scholarship he had won at the Fay Compton Studio (free tuition only) had come to an end possibly well ahead of time, and he had to leave and find work. His companion by the lake in Regent's Park stubbed out her cigarette with the sophistication of the inexperienced smoker, so Alec noted, and told him very forcefully he ought to go along and see John Gielgud.

Alec had encountered Gielgud once, on the prize-giving rostrum at the Fay Compton school, when Gielgud, as judge of the acting, together with Jessie Matthews and Ronald Adam, had awarded the prize to him. When his friend suggested he see Gielgud he thought Gielgud may have voted against him; he also spurned her suggestion to lend him a pound to take a taxi, and set off to walk to Wyndham's Theatre alone, to catch Gielgud there, before he went on.

The Maitlands, Gielgud's new play, opened in July 1934. Gielgud played a schoolmaster engaged in attempting to cure a mentally ill young man, a role at odds with his gilded matinee idol appeal, and he was dressed shabbily and sported a moustache. He claimed in one of his autobiographies that he remembered Alec, 'being struck by the evident talent of a skinny boy with a sad Pierrot face and big ears', to whom they all agreed the prize should be given:

> The plot of the short play in which he appeared was about the owner of the Punch and Judy show who, in despair at losing his customers as they drifted away to some other attraction went home, and, like Mr Punch, battered his wife

to death. It seems to me that there was no dialogue, and that the boy's compulsive miming impressed us all very much.

Early Stages

When Alec arrived at the theatre he later expressed astonishment to be shown straight to the star's dressing room.

He had remembered my name though he looked somewhat surprised when he saw what I looked like. I was in rather dirty grey flannel trousers, a check shirt (to keep down the laundry bill) and skimpy sports jacket. Also I was very thin, large-eared and strange.

He sat making up for the evening performance of *The Maitlands*, and I told him of the absolute necessity for my finding work. This was the first time I had seen a real live star actor applying his make-up; I believe I was even more fascinated by that than by being in the presence of a man I had hero-worshipped so long.

He was friendly and kind, but under the unpowdered grease-paint, which gives actors the look of china dolls, I couldn't tell whether he was really interested in my predicament and talents or not. He painted his eyebrows for a moment or two in silence and then became immensely practical.

Sunday Times

One must allow for romantic, or more often than not self-deflationary, retouching in these accounts of Alec's, for example it was nonsense for him to say 'the first time I had seen a real live star actor applying his make-up', when he had already acted in a West End play. John le Mesurier says that at the Fay Compton school there were two males (himself and Alec), and twenty-two girls: 'It was obvious from the start that Alec Guinness would be a great character actor, that he had the ability to inhabit the skin of whoever he portrayed.' There was no doubt Alec had a sense of inferiority, a chip on his shoulder, thin-skinned and aware as he was of his own limitations. Perhaps this was exaggerated for a young man of twenty, but retrospectively, he, with ironic detachment, saw his younger self as a victim, telling us of the continuing presence of his shortcomings and resentment. He had small expectations: 'I was very lightweight, a thin, cadaverous creature . . . I was never a glamorous juvenile.'

He never detailed how many times he had been turned down at this time, but Douglas Fairbanks Jr recounted an incident typical of the life of the twenty-year-old Guinness. Fairbanks was playing the lead in *Moonlight is Silver*, which was based on *Othello*'s jealousy theme:

> Binkie (Beaumont) interviewed a keen and serious young actor for the job of my understudy. His name was Alec Guinness. Binkie and Winifred heard him read a scene or two and politely told him he had not yet had enough experience and let him go. Alas.   *The Salad Days*

Alec had played three tiny parts in Noël Langley's *Queer Cargo*, at the Piccadilly Theatre. As well as his three small parts, he understudied the six leading men. *Queer Cargo* was a tale of piracy on the China Seas, in which Franklyn Dyall played a magnificent pirate. Alec shaved his hair for one of the parts, the Chinese Coolie, and claimed that thereafter his hair never grew back on. His memory for lines was, and remained, extraordinary. In 1939 he was to learn the whole of Macbeth's part in four days. He also memorized Dubedat in *The Doctor's Dilemma* in a few days in 1938, using cold compresses on his head while Merula Salaman, an actress (later to become his wife), heard him in the train to Richmond.

Was Gielgud, on Alec's unannounced arrival in his dressing room, that interested in Alec's predicament? Alec thought that he might just have been impressed by the aristocratic name and said nothing to disenchant him. Anyway, to begin with, Gielgud's efforts on his behalf yielded no result. Alec did a brief audition of Mercutio's 'Queen Mab' speech for the director Henry Cass, not getting further, he said, than 'little atomies' when Cass stopped him, told him he had no business in the theatre and 'wouldn't take me as a gift'. ('Howls of derision from the director in the darkened stalls ... "You're no actor!" he shouted. "Get off the fucking stage,"' ran the later Guinness version.)

In an earlier version of this episode Alec went back to Gielgud after the failed audition and Gielgud was at the end of his resourcefulness but by no means at the end of his generosity. Alec recalled:

All I had left was the proverbial half-crown. On the side of his make-up table was a neat pile of one-pound notes. 'The next time I do a play I'll give you a part,' he promised, 'but you are far too thin. Here's twenty pounds – for God's sake go and eat properly.' He frantically painted his eyebrows with embarrassment. I stared at the money. I had a vision of eating, buying clothes (particularly shoes), of spending four-pence a day on park chairs for twelve hundred days. Then I saw myself being thrown into gaol for debt. 'I am all right for money, thank you,' I said, so foolishly that it makes me blush even twenty-two years later, and walked out of his room.

Sunday Times, 1956

Much later Gielgud went over the same incident in his own words. 'He was extremely shy and diffident and refused to accept the few pounds I offered him.' Gielgud had probably forgotten the whole episode but accepted what Guinness wrote. All the later accounts, which read like return volleys in tennis, hinge on Guinness's refusal of the loan, but in one earlier account (in *Early Stages*; later in *Dear Alec*) Gielgud had simply lent him ten pounds and Alec pocketed the money gratefully, returning it as soon as he could. Only weeks later Gielgud signed him up for his New Theatre Company with which he remained until July 1936.

Alec tended in retrospect to heighten his sense of isolation and that of being a victim. Anxious people tend to overestimate the chances that unfortunate events will happen to them. He was far far younger (by ten years) than the person he put straight away on a pedestal, and yet ahead of him at a similar age (if only by a year) in being in the theatrical swim.

Alec avidly soaked up other plays, too, at this time, forging more links with that small, intensely talented coterie which, forming around 1934, and with an injection of continental genius (through the directors Theodore Komisarjevsky and Michel Saint-Denis), came with its offshoots and tributaries to dominate the English theatre for most of the rest of the twentieth century.

He went in November 1933 to see *Fräulein Elsa*, adapted by Komisarjevsky from a story by Arthur Schnitzler, a censored play performed in a club performance. Peggy Ashcroft acted Elsa, a young woman who in an attempt to save her father from bankruptcy approaches a supposed philanthropist who offers her money if she will meet him in a wood and take off her clothes. Instead of complying she swallows laudanum and, stripping completely, covers her nakedness with a cloak to face the dirty old man in the hotel lounge where he is waiting. She removes her cloak, then falls to the ground dead.

This scene, for which the Lord Chamberlain banned the play, triggered in the audience, Alec told the critic Michael Billington, at the sight of Peggy's naked back, a sudden intake of breath (she was 'suitably covered in front for the near-onlookers'). It caused a touch of 'Mrs Whitehouse outrage'. Only a little later Alec appeared familiar and as a friend sitting in the front row at the first night of Terence Rattigan's *French Without Tears*, a landmark triumph in English light comedy. ('I barely knew Terry but I suppose I must have met him at a party and that he extended an invitation.')

At once Alec had an introduction to and moved in theatre's elite and 'unashamedly homosexual circles' – the two were roughly synonymous, as Sheridan Morley points out in his biography of Gielgud. Although theatre was more tolerant towards homosexuality than the rest of society, it was 'still necessary for its workers to form a kind of secret network, behaving rather like spies'. The theatre, it would seem, was in microcosm an indicator of the future profession of treachery, a quintessentially British art.

Alec's deep attraction to secrecy would now seem to have deepened and broadened in time. 'In a famous phrase of the period you could either joint the Comintern or the Homintern, and like Guy Burgess sometimes even both.' Alec had no appetite for the former, while on the brink of the latter he hovered uncertainly, unsure which way to go – either to take the plunge or to seek a winding, mainly undetectable path. He was, from all accounts, afraid and unsure of himself. As well as the Nietzschean chaos he carried inside him, he picked up on what he identified, in the words of Alphonse Daudet, as this 'horrible duality . . . this terrible second me . . . that I have never been able to intoxicate, to make shed tears, or put to sleep'. The chaos, the overriding desire and need for secrecy about it were always there.

While Alec went on carrying around inside him a chaos,

Gielgud was for these early years the dancing star Guinness aspired to give birth to. While they had, and must have recognized in each other, similarities, they also had great differences. The greatest difference, apart from the gap of ten years in their ages – so that Gielgud was far more experienced and exerted the kind of influence Guinness felt he needed – was in their relationship with their mothers.

We see Gielgud developing quite late a freedom from his inhibitions over his inherent homosexuality. One person above all, until her death at the age of eighty-nine in 1958, held his heart in unwavering loyalty, and this was John's mother Kate Terry, sister of the legendary Ellen Terry. Reading through the hundreds of thousands of words he wrote to his mother, beginning aged eight in 1912, and ceasing, according to the collection acquired by the British Library on Gielgud's death, in the years only just before her death, I discovered in these largely overlooked letters Gielgud was the most loving and meticulous correspondent as well as dutiful son. In tiny, well-formed and close-packed handwriting similar to Alec's, he covered page after page of letter-headed, expensive hotel, or embassy notepaper.

Gielgud shared a private preparatory and public boarding school education with Alec, and while Alec regretted not being put down for Fettes, Gielgud fell short of expectations by not getting into Winchester or Eton. When he was in his teens, living in a school house only a few miles from home, he wrote passionate anguished letters to Kate asking to be a day boy. 'Vile and rotten – woke up this morning with a deadly fear of waking up . . . I don't know what I really want, but I think it is something: otherwise the feeling is utterly impossible.' So ran his passionate appeals when aged fourteen: 'everlasting worry and horrors . . . I feel inclined to either cry or shriek . . . the whole world might be plotting against me alone, and you and father be out for assassination . . .' And in another letter: 'Please mother, have me home – I am quite willing to make my bed and clean my boots.'

Practically the first thing he thought of when in 1953 he was arrested for homosexual soliciting in Chelsea was his school days at Westminster. 'I was thoroughly ashamed, not of what I had done but of being caught, and I couldn't bear to hear the anger or disappointment in Binkie's [Beaumont's] voice. Then again, I had some vague Westminster schoolboy idea that when you were in trouble you had to stand on your own two feet and "take it like a man".'

Gielgud's attractive personality, endearing him to men and women alike, was that he was not a jealous man and he had an artless innocence, not to say naivety about his lack of guile, his openness. Alec later asserted in a rather misanthropic way that we all deny being jealous and to prove it Peter Brook once said, when directing Gielgud as Laertes, 'John, I don't get any feeling of jealousy from you.' Gielgud replied, 'I don't know what it means. I've never been jealous in my life.' After a pause, he added, 'But I admit I did burst into tears when Larry Olivier got such good notices for his Hamlet!' This example surely indicates the opposite of the point Alec wanted to make, because it is more often than not concealed jealousy that gives others the feeling of jealousy, not that which is so naively open.

Gielgud's early letters to his mother show well how he developed a complete confidence in what he did, allied with a kind of social insouciance that often led him into trouble. You feel from his letters that although he had high standards and was well connected with the elite, and the grand traditions of English society, he was never really a snob and he saw people as they were, often with embarrassingly clear honesty. He mocked the hypocrisy of theatre managers who condescendingly worded their offers to him. He saw through Noël Coward, whom he understudied in an early bid to stardom: 'His early brilliance,' he told his mother, 'cannot find a stronger phase as he gets older and I fear his friends, too, do not criticize him with any discrimination and he is very obstinate.'

Gielgud might at times, as his biographers show, assuage his insecure appetite in cottaging, in advancing artistic minions who granted him sexual favours, as in some Renaissance court, but mother – aside from all this – held steady his heart's sway with unwavering devotion. There must again inevitably have been an element of deception because Kate, when she heard of his arrest and conviction for soliciting, didn't believe it. She wrote to Dodie Smith, the novelist and playwright, who had expressed her sympathy over the 'misfortune' that his magnificent achievements would never fade and no one in the theatre was more loved and admired – 'John has done nothing to his discredit, save one drink too many at a Chelsea party.'

As for Gielgud's long-lasting liaisons, it seemed that like many respectable mothers of gay people Kate Terry took the view that his liking for and continual attention to her confirmed the fact that deep down, he really did prefer members of the opposite sex but had never quite found the right one to marry. He was able to move out of home, set up with his first love, John Perry the Irish-born actor, in the West End and he would frankly write of Perry's illness and their holidays together as if they were two schoolboy chums.

Possibly the relationship with Perry was more about power than lasting love and so when Perry was detached from Gielgud by Binkie Beaumont it took Gielgud many years to realize that his domestic needs would better be served by someone who existed completely under his thumb. (Martin Hensler became his partner and domestic dependent.)

In the intervening years, before he reached this point, he was much at sea and, like Marcel Proust's mother Jeanne Weil, or Kenneth Williams' mother Louie, Kate Terry, judging from the frequency and intensity of his letters to her, occupied the important role of being the lightship and emotional rock of Gielgud's life. 'To the world's best mother from a sometimes, very selfish son' he wrote when twenty-six.

> You are an incorrigible woman, and one is inclined to say you seem to have so much pleasure in doing things for other people that one cannot sufficiently express one's appreciation of the pleasure you give them in return. But I am sure you know how very much we all rely on you and if you have spoilt us rather, and we do not always express properly the gratitude and devotion we feel, it is only because you have shamelessly led us on to expect you to be incredibly devoted and generous, and you always living up to it, and a bit over.
> **British Library letters**

I have gone into Gielgud's overlooked relationship with his mother at some length because for Alec it was the opposite. The spectre and reality of Agnes de Cuffe inside him, her constant and unexpected demands on him for money – Frith Banbury told me how he kept the grief to himself, 'He never said how having a drunken mother was a pain in the arse' – made him guarded, on the defensive. It may, when Alec went to stay with Gielgud alone at weekends at the retreat he and John Perry shared in Harpsden, in the hills above Henley-on-Thames, have made him suspicious of any sexual advance, or even frisson. We do see, almost from an early age, how Alec's mood swung between a great anger, which could erupt in a cold haughtiness, even arrogance, and this exaggerated humility. This was an anger people often would feel in him but never saw expressed. It exploded in family private circumstances, later with his wife or son, but rarely with friends or in public. He concealed his true feelings from others to spare them, he claimed, the sting of his sharp tongue. 'Would it be fair to say of John Gielgud, "He is a great actor and his most appreciative audience?"' recorded Alec in later years. 'Alan Bennett says Gielgud has running through him an iron streak – of tinsel.'

At bottom there was still the chaos, the unsorted emotional darkness. It gave rise in Alec to what one psychiatrist and author has called 'disintegration anxiety'; to quote Anthony Storr:

> The individuals whom [Alex Kohnt] considers liable to this are those who, because of the immaturity of their parents' responses to them in childhood, or because of the absence of empathic parental understanding, have not built up a strong coherent personality . . . one might compare Kohnt's conception with looking in a mirror. A clear, clean, polished mirror will repeatedly reflect the developing personality as he actually is, and thus give him a firm and true sense of his own identity. A cracked, dirty, smeared mirror will reflect an incomplete, obscured image which provides the child with an inaccurate and distorted picture of himself.
>
> *Solitude: a Return to the Self*

In spite of his doubts Alec strove to have a better image of himself. It was a continual struggle and struggle as he might, having the sense of being an unwanted child was already very difficult to get over.

The redoubtable Angela Fox – friend and later neighbour, wife of Robin Fox, theatrical agent, and the mother of actors Edward and James and producer Robert, grandmother of Emilia Fox –

also knew only too well that sense of not belonging anywhere. She was the illegitimate daughter of Frederick Lonsdale, the playwright, who had another, legitimate family on the go. She came to terms with her deprivation but found it difficult. 'You think they had you by mistake,' she told me when talking about Alec. 'You feel rejection, by life, by people, and by God. My mother never looked at me as if I was an ordinary child. You were a problem. And don't forget they tried so hard to get rid of us. The mother loathes the illegitimate child for he or she makes *her* feel a mess.' Yet Angela became, in the words of John le Carré about one of his characters, 'fearless, formidable, eccentric, upper-class and athletic. She had a ten-acre voice!'

Only too well Alec knew his own mother and now he was beginning to make a reputation for himself she would call round at the theatre or even raid his bedsit and cart off any spare cash, realizable assets or pawn tickets. It sounds sometimes as if she was trying to get her own back on him for having been born. Desperate feelings she caused sought desperate remedies. 'You do something stupid for relief or get blind, bloody drunk,' said Fox.

Alec's appearance told very much against him. Angela Fox, whose friendship with him went back to the 1940s, described him to me as 'colossally unattractive, like a shrimp . . . My God, he would want to be liked.' Alec throughout his life assessed adversely his physical appearance, in itself a form of negative narcissism. His ears, he said, made him look 'like a bat straight out of hell' – (yet he hoped they might wing him to heaven in the end).

He reported how Martita Hunt told him scornfully, 'You're not exactly an athlete.' As with Gielgud, although in a very different way, there was something he could not quite acknowledge about himself from the very start. That he was to others very likeable, endearing, witty, excellent company, while at first, as indeed much later, people wanted to mother him and could become fiercely protective of him, was ignored by him.

Christopher Fry said later of Gielgud, when he directed and acted the lead role in *The Lady's Not for Burning*, 'Ideas came not as single spies but in battalions . . . I was constantly struck by John's never-diminishing eagerness to learn his craft, as though he were always at the beginning of his career, and still seeing the fun of it all.'

Translated into direction of his newest acolyte and protégé, the machine-gun frequency of Gielgud's comments might seem sometimes cruel, for according to Frith Banbury, also a minor member at this time (as an actor) of Gielgud's company, every one of them was made at some time or other to feel terribly inadequate: 'We all got bullied and told we had to go away and learn to act: John had no patience or understanding of other people's talent. Once, when Lueen McGrath giggled John told her to go away and write out one hundred times, "I must not giggle on stage".' Loner as he was, it is important to note that Alec experienced this as happening *only* to him.

Alec was, said Banbury of these months when Alec played Osric in *Hamlet*, 'very awkward with his body'. Alec's own recall of John's method suggested that he saw himself as being singled out for bouts of unpredictability. In awe of Gielgud, even overwhelmed, he had been told after a week's rehearsal in October 1934, 'What's happened to you? I thought you were rather good. You're terrible. Oh, go away! I don't want to see you again!'

Alec loved imitating Gielgud the director: exact tone of voice, exact mannerisms:

> Come from the left. No! No! The other left – oh, someone make him understand! Why are you so stiff? Why don't you make me laugh? Motleys! [the designers Sophie Harris, Margaret Harris and Elizabeth Montgomery] Would it be pretty to paint the whole thing gold? Perhaps not. Don't fidget, Guinness; now you are gabbling. Now turn upstage. No, not you. You! Turn the other way. Oh, why can't you all act? Get someone to teach you how to act! Why is your voice so harsh? It really is quite ugly. Do just do something about it.
>
> **Sheridan Morley,** *John Gielgud*

Ostensibly given the sack Alec, who had already learned at least a little about the volatility of John's moods, knew enough to hang about until the end of that day's rehearsal. 'Excuse me, Mr Gielgud, but am I really fired?'

'No! Yes! No, of course not. But do go away. Come back in a week. Get someone to teach you how to act. Try Martita Hunt – she'll be glad of the money.'

In the event, Alec decided not to go anywhere near Martita, to whom Gielgud had already sent him and whose teaching was to say the least a little eccentric, but instead to walk around London's parks for a week and then report back to Gielgud at the New. 'He seemed delighted to have me back, heaped praise on my Osric and laughed at everything I said. I couldn't swear that I was doing anything I had not done a week earlier. But suddenly and briefly I had become teacher's pet, and John told the Motleys that I should have a hat with a lot of feathers, just like the Duchess of Devonshire.'

Hats played a major part in the early mythology of these two rapidly balding young actors. When Alec earned his first weekly salary as an actor the first thing he did was to buy himself a cheap replica of the kind of hat Gielgud wore. It gave him as he thought, 'a sort of elegance in the second class'. Later, when Gielgud had given him more than his first job, he reflected that no quality could be 'put on the head in the shape of someone's hat'.

It seemed that even offstage Gielgud and Guinness might also a little be playing Hamlet and Osric, for, so far from being the Prince himself, Osric had a symbiotic presence in Hamlet's psyche. Alec took John Gielgud seriously as the judge of his talent: as, moreover, a strict disciplinarian, intolerant of any slovenliness of speech, a living monument of impatience. While Ralph Richardson perceived John as a spluttering Catherine wheel sparking off in all directions which 'happily have never been resolved – tongue and mind work so closely together that it is sufficient for him to think of something for it to be said' – Alec noted his emperor-like head held 'higher than high', his patrician Polish breeding – both grandparents on Gielgud's father's side were Polish – and that he lacked nothing 'as far as I could see, except tact'. Yet, oddly enough, tact would seem to be exactly the quality later valued above all others by Alec. Tact, reticence, silence, studiedness: none of these did Gielgud possess.

Gielgud's Hamlet was a technical tour-de-force, beautifully scored, exalted in spirit, a prince, in no way a rogue and peasant slave; he was also, however, 'swayed by a thousand subtle influences, physiological and pathological . . . sensitive and disillusioned'. By all accounts it was the definitive performance of the 1930s, perhaps in the appeasing, 'sensitive' spirit of the times. The duty of revenge terrified poor Gielgud. The performance mesmerized every young actor: according to Donald Sinden, who was also in the cast, John spoke Shakespeare's lines, 'as if he had written them himself'. Sinden pointed to the effect that Gielgud had when Hamlet has just seen and talked with his father's ghost. He has just pronounced that, 'The time is out of joint', and he turns to Horatio and Marcellus and says, 'Nay, come, let's go together'. Gielgud conveyed in that simple line, 'Please go with me'; 'I don't want to let you out of my sight'; 'It would be better if we arrived together'; 'Let us leave this awesome place'; and 'Don't leave me'. This taught Sinden the many possibilities open to an actor in just one line.

Likewise with Alec, who confessed himself also spellbound by John's Hamlet because it showed so much of what he himself would have liked to have shown in Hamlet. But there was a great danger of being sucked into imitation. Night after night he watched it from the wings, for ten whole months: overall he saw the performance 155 times and knew every inflection of every line: it was 'the lovable, distressed and romantic prince of all time'.

Hamlet, the portrait of a genius, could also have been seizing control over Alec at a level deeper than the play. The mark of a certain kind of genius is that he is all of one piece: everything he does changes the order and balance of the rest. Alec might not have known it at the time but this first encounter with *Hamlet* had begun to feed a deeper quest, one that would emerge increasingly as the actor grew older. He had begun to strive for unity, for integration in the way that Hamlet did: he wanted everything he did to be part of some greater wholeness.

Gielgud had an inkling of this deeper, stranger integrity inherent in Alec when for Christmas 1934 he presented, 'To Alec, who grows apace' an edition of his aunt Ellen Terry's letters, quoting Act Five's motto, 'The readiness is all'. In the context of learning to become an actor, this sentence could have meant any of a dozen different things: it could even be seen as an uncomplimentary comment on his talent – or lack of it. 'Only wait and one day it may arrive, you poor idiot!' It could be construed as an acknowledgement of Alec's independence of spirit. The refusal of Gielgud's twenty pounds may tell us from Alec's point of view that there could have been something excessive about the offer and sensibly suspicious inferred about the refusal.

In the following spring, according to Frith Banbury, Frank Vosper, who played Claudius and was quite a well-known playwright – 'dear chap, very nice' but on stage, together with Laura Cowie as Gertrude came over as two sleek evil cats – came down at the end of one performance and finding Alec asked him, 'How old are you?' to which he received the reply, 'I'll be twenty-one in a few weeks' time, on 2nd April.'

'Oh, I'll give you a party,' declared Vosper.

Before moving to Acacia Road in St John's Wood, Vosper had lived in Upper St Martin's Lane in a flat which Gielgud then took over, finding sexual independence for the first time with his lover John Perry. It had no proper kitchen, while the bathroom halfway downstairs featured an erratic geyser. 'Vosper had covered the sitting-room walls with brown hessian, and there was a Braque-like ceiling in one of the bedrooms, with a lot of large nudes sprawling about,' recalled Gielgud. It was here, away from home, John had begun discreetly to lead his own independent life.

Vosper's new house had similar eccentricities. When Alec had given him a list of names of invitees and Vosper had looked at the four names remarking, 'That all? I was expecting a lot more,' he added he would like to invite John, while Vosper's sister, Margery, who acted his hostess would think up some others. Then, after a lapse of some time, Alec had heard no more.

Seeking to jog his memory he went one night to the tent-like carrel Vosper had in the wings where he withdrew to repair his make-up and take a rest – without the fatigue of climbing the stairs to his dressing room. He could see him hunched over his dressing-table, a glass of whisky in his right hand, staring at himself in the mirror . . . 'sad and rather sinister with his puffy white face, pencil-thin arched eyebrows and shiny red wig'. He spotted Alec's reflection in a mirror and terrified, jumped up with a screech.

Alec was to become attached, in writing his memoirs, to such vignettes of lonely gay bachelor actors (Douglas Byng and Ernest Milton were further examples), suggesting he partly identified as a very young man with what could in time become the narcissistic lower depths of ageing loneliness. At the same time he seemed darkly attracted by them, at least they drew him in imagination, like Baudelaire's *Les Fleurs du mal*.

The party in Acacia Road went with a great swing. When Banbury many years later told Alec he had been at his twenty-first birthday party, the pair, he said, had a rather heated argument as to who was actually there: Alec did not remember accurately, Banbury claimed. Alec did record himself overwhelmed by the occasion, staggering back to his tiny bedsit in Hasker Street, for which he paid one pound a week, and loaded with gifts of books, gramophone records, neckties and scarves. Later Vosper asked him to read a play entitled *Monkey on a Stick*, which he said he had written for Alec (one presumed the 'monkey' was Alec), but he never saw it. Vosper was soon to drown mysteriously at sea, on a transatlantic liner, either drunkenly pushing himself through a porthole (could you open portholes? – I thought they were firmly bolted) believing he would land on a lower deck, or, it was rumoured, shoved overboard by someone.

Alec expressed gratitude to Gielgud:

> I could write you a very long letter thanking you not only for giving me a part, but also for your countless little kindnesses, which have made working with you so delightful, but I will spare you all that. It was very courageous of you to give an inexperienced person a part like Osric, and knowing how bad I was even at the end of the run, and how much you said I had improved, I shudder to think what I must have been like at the beginning. I suppose one never forgets one's first part – I certainly shall never forget how happy I have been during these last six months. I am not a very gay or happy person by nature, but I find the confidence you have in me a great source of happiness. I want to write this because it's one of those things which mean a lot to me, but I find very hard to speak.
>   *John Gielgud*

Was Gielgud's Hamlet for all its success, as great as it was cracked up to be? Certainly it was a key revival, but comments such as, 'Hamlet attends the funeral of Ophelia in a sort of white fur coat, which as usual suits Gielgud, but not the scene,' made by Raymond Mortimer, rather suggest it would not impress us unduly today. I myself was rather surprised and dismayed, on recently examining the Gielgud archive, at the hundreds of flattering letters Gielgud himself had kept which praised his performances.

Perhaps I shall be proved wrong, but Alec certainly seemed not one to attach himself to mementos singing his praises. He was, or could be described as, narcissistic in his own very defined way: negatively more than positively. He was again cast as Osric in the Old Vic's 1936–7 season, this time with Olivier as Hamlet, and Tyrone Guthrie directing.

The Salaman family with their cats.
A Christmas card drawn by Michael Salaman

6. A Gift from God

'The way he swept on the stage with his plumed hat he bewitched me,' commented Kay Walsh on that first entrance. Alec's Osric was by all accounts one of the most memorable minor performances of the time, cleverly placing the water-fly in the treachery of the duel, winning laughter 'easily without losing the hint of the courtier's craft beneath the mask'. He played him as a prodigally endowed invertebrate who none the less had the function of, according to the critic Eric Auerbach in his *Mimesis*, 'a significant reflex of Hamlet's temperament and state of mind'.

The two years spent under John Gielgud's pernickety and impatient direction had unnerved him; the pages of his script were 'filthy grey' with the rubbing out of conflicting directives written in 'soft lead pencil and sometimes smudged with tears'. He had gone on viewing himself as greatly limited: 'I was never a handsome chap. I didn't think I had anything personal to offer.' But he had made the important discovery that he could transform his persona. 'All I could offer is through my imagination.' Tyrone Guthrie, the director of the 1936–7 *Hamlet* advocated a more creative and imaginative process than Gielgud, and rebuked him for pencilling notes in his script: 'If I've given you a good move you'll remember it, if bad you'll forget it.' His method of work contrasted sharply with Gielgud's. Guthrie shied away from, even despised, the star-actor system as personified by Gielgud.

So Alec was on the way, if only beginning, to formulate a complex grammar of indirect discourse to master the invisible gesture and the unspoken word. These might seem to be the reverse of the heroic or romantic acting qualities practised by his slightly older contemporaries – his models John Gielgud and Laurence Olivier – but they were not. He was to find, with time, the ability to internalize all Gielgud's gesture and showiness, scale them down, make them show in the face's hidden yet discernible musculature, hint at them, shadow them into inferences of mind. Emphatically the influence of Gielgud was to remain the strongest of all, but with the difference that he could turn Gielgud, in time, into Guinness. This realized the first stage of his mimetic desire, his desire to become like others.

At a personal level there remained in Alec some kind of stroppiness, resistance or refusal towards John. John in a handwritten tribute published on Alec's seventy-fifth birthday, regretted not working with him more – they appeared in later life together only once, in a television dialogue by Friedrich Dürrenmatt called *Conversation at Night* (1970) – and John added, perhaps with a touch of tartness, 'I know I should have learned much by studying at first hand some of the fascinating mysterious secrets which have enabled him to create so many different types of characters with so much subtlety and skill.'

'In spite of my fondness for him,' he summed up, 'Alec is not an easy man to know. He has never confided to me his ambitions, his hopes and his despairs.' But did he confide them to anyone at this young age?

*

'I am evasive,' Alec said in an interview on *The South Bank Show* in 1993. 'I do know I'm evasive, because I wish to be. My private life is my private life, and I have very much taken the attitude that I share it with my wife, who is inclined to be rather a shy person. She didn't know when we married that I would make a name for myself.'

Alec first met the actress Sylvia Merula, as she was known at the time, 'otherwise Merula Sylvia' Salaman, during rehearsals of Saint-Denis's production of André Obey's *Noah*. This was, after the break for spring touring, the next Gielgud star vehicle. Red-headed Merula was only months younger than Alec. Her name was the ancient Italian word for the blackbird that flew into her mother's room at the birth. Of *Noah*, Alec recalled in a Saint-Denis memorial broadcast:

I only played a tiny part. I think Gielgud tried to get me a very nice part as Shem. That was the first time I ever met Saint-Denis. He obviously thought I was too inexperienced: quite rightly ... And I was offered the part of the Wolf who doesn't say anything at all, just trots across the stage. I understudied someone and incidentally met my wife who was playing the Tiger.

Subsequently Merula played, in the same company as Alec, small parts or attendants in *Richard II, The School for Scandal, The Three Sisters,* and *The Merchant of Venice.*

Merula, on her mother's side, was not 'a Guinness' or 'a Geddes' but 'a Wake' (after Hereward the Wake). On her father's side she was descended from the Saloman, a Sephardic Jew, who had brought Haydn to London in the 1790s. So perhaps Alec was not right in claiming Merula did not know he would make a name for himself: the family, as well as being talented, had an eye for spotting talent in others. The Saloman patron of Haydn was an entrepreneur as well as an impresario. He had emigrated to England from Livorno in 1740. One of his descendants joined the British navy, fighting at Trafalgar, changing his name to Salaman to make it appear more English.

Thus Alec joined a well-established and highly cultured family, something he had never had.

The Salamans had great charm, great wealth and fine taste. Physically the men were small and presented no threat, but they had a puckish quality. Chattie, Merula's mother, first became engaged to Michel Salaman when they were fellow students at the Slade School of Art. She, like Merula, had chestnut red wavy hair and hazel eyes. Like her, Michel was small and slight with an almost identical shade of curly auburn hair, so that they were often mistaken for brother and sister. The Salamans were a large clan: Michel's father, Merula's grandfather, made a fortune in straw hats, while at one time the family owned most of the ostrich farms in South Africa. He had fourteen children, and Michel was the youngest but one. Family money was diminishing fast and they invested in property and had an office, S. M. N. Salaman Estates, in Southampton Place in London. They were a rich, leisured set, with a lot of friends, and they entertained generously. Chattie was beautiful when young, but she was determined not to be a housewife so she occupied herself with painting and gardening. She was a better painter than Michel, though neither of them painted after leaving the Slade. Chattie kept a goat, as did Merula later on.

They had five children, two sons and three daughters. The eldest, Susie, was a choreographer with the Ballet Rambert, and worked at the Mercury Theatre. She was the first to fall under the spell of Michel Saint-Denis's touring Compagnie des Quinze and she joined it as an assistant stage manager. Aged thirty she suffered a hernia of the brain, resulting in encephalitis. She partly recovered, but her brain was seriously impaired and she was partially paralysed. She lived on into her eighties, cared for by her parents and a succession of live-in nurses. Jill, a potter, was two years younger. The elder son Eustin, or Eustie, took a degree in architecture at The Queen's College, Oxford. Michael, or 'Mike' as he was known, was two years younger than him – he became a distinguished Parisian left-bank artist considered after his death in 1987 as overlooked and under-nurtured. Some years after Michael, in 1914, the same year as Alec, Merula, the youngest, was born. Like her mother, Merula was keen on ponies and riding, she left school to attend the Randell Phillips riding school and was scornful at first of the arty crowd. Michel had wanted her to train as a dancer and when she was sacked from her riding school for reading a book she too trained at the Ballet Rambert School, receiving personal tuition from Madame Rambert.

The Salamans lived at Ruckmans, a large rambling house with fifteen bedrooms and a music room designed by Lutyens, set in a large and beautiful garden in Ockley, ten miles south of Dorking in Surrey. They kept open house, inviting down many well-known people from the worlds of art and theatre. They used to sit down to a large party at every meal. Michel, a retired major of the Royal North Devon Hussars (a Territorial Regiment), and who 'graduated from an art student into a fox-hunting squire', was the dominant figure. Several of Merula's aunts, who often stayed at the house, also had red hair. Two of them had studied at the Slade, and Michel used to joke in a good-natured way that they spent all day sleeping in armchairs.

Peggy Ashcroft came to Ruckmans; so did Ninette de Valois,

the dancer, and Theodore Komisarjevsky. Michel, a member of the Athenaeum Club, was fond of Michel Saint-Denis. When Merula took part in Komisarjevsky's famous production of *The Seagull*, Michel gave a party for it. Elsie Fogarty, Olivier's acting teacher, he also knew well.

The Salaman family had many other artistic connections. Michel's younger brother Clement married Dora Tullock, the Scottish actress who had been an infant prodigy and acted with Sir Herbert Beerbohm Tree. Clement had once taken up with Ira Nettleship, but she jilted him and went off with Augustus John, the painter, who had been a close friend of Michel's at the Slade. Both Augustus and his sister Gwen wrote to Michel frequently. Michel lent John money, part of which he repaid by painting Michel's mother. The family owned a lot of John's paintings.

The impression Michel and Chattie gave Alec was that of a marvellously happy and amusing pair. Michel was a bit of a flirt and he had a wry sense of humour, to the point of telling jokes against himself, as his son-in-law would learn to do. But he would not suffer fools gladly: he liked charm *and* danger.

At first Alec found the house alarmingly hearty. Martin Esslin, later head of BBC radio drama and a well-known writer on the theatre, was taken up by the Salamans when he arrived in April 1939, aged twenty-one, from Vienna as a refugee, and stayed with them until the outbreak of war. To some degree, he believed, they hoped he might be company for Susie. After his harrowing experiences he found it difficult to adapt to the wealth and Bloomsbury informality, the interacting strength of family emotions. There was a great deal of talk of Alec's marriage to Merula. One night Esslin was eating dinner with them and felt upset, asked to be excused and so retired to his room. He shut himself in, broke down and just howled with grief. There was a knock on the door. Esslin pulled himself together. It was Alec Guinness.

'May I come in?' He came in and they sat down on the bed. 'I understand just how you feel,' said Alec. '. . . No, you will never be part of this . . . I . . . I have managed to become part of this and it has been difficult for me too.' Put more bluntly by an old friend, Alec was at first 'completely overawed, terrified by the Salamans'.

Merula Salaman has been described as a woman with a restful air, and a charming, enigmatic smile. Her appearance was statuesque: 'Titian hair melting perfectly with her freckled skin and brilliant eyes'. She was to become a strong, harmonizing influence in Alec's life and in some way, like Michel and Chattie – they too having married very young – she and Alec were like brother and sister. They were both natural loners, attracted to the similar aspirations they found in each other. They became engaged during a late-night rehearsal of *The Merchant of Venice* at the Queen's Theatre, which Gielgud was directing and in which Alec was playing Lorenzo. On 20 June 1938 they were married quietly at Reigate Register Office, in the presence of Juliet O'Rourke and Michael Salaman as witnesses. To avoid embarrassment, it would seem, Agnes had not been invited.

It was a very 'agnostic' wedding, Alec said afterwards, while Chattie interrupted proceedings with a repeated need to go to the loo, and he himself, from nerves, dropped his trilby half a dozen times. They flew from Croydon to Dublin, spending their nuptial night at the Gresham Hotel. No description of sexual bliss: Alec recalled the dozen or so priests at the bar sipping their 'usquebaugh and dragging on crumpled cigarettes' – they felt lost in an atmosphere thick with smoke, raucous laughter and betting talk.

The newly married couple visited Tyrone and Judy Guthrie, spending a week at the Guthries' ramshackle family home in County Monaghan, but here Alec spent most of the time discussing the Hamlet he was about to play in Guthrie's next production. Merula passed the hours with Guthrie's eccentric wife Judy. When you allow for Alec's careful study of John Dover Wilson's *What Happens in Hamlet* and Ernest Jones's Freudian interpretation of why the prince's power to act is paralysed by his Oedipus complex, it does not sound as if they had much time for one another.

Next they hiked to Donegal, with rucksacks on their backs. While on their last days in Donegal they tried to find a bed in a derelict lodging. In their bedroom Merula pulled back the top sheet of the bed, which made a crackly, retching sound as the sheets were stuck together with 'old sweat and grease'. Alec's foot connected under the bed with a full chamber pot and 'floating on top a pink swansdown powder-puff'. This was his recall of it, anyway.

I do not know what Merula could have made of this romantic beginning to their marriage when she read it later in life (and if she read it), but it fitted in well with Alec's fairly fixed attitude of small expectations. Before she died less than two months after Alec, Merula told a friend she was contemplating some kind of memoir herself. I paraphrase what has come to me, so these are not her exact words.

She began by saying she needed to jot down things that biographers and obituary writers wouldn't know: things that had nothing to do with films or theatre or Alec's social life, in other words the humdrum homely domestic bits and pieces of everyday life. She went on that Alec's strength came out of his weakness, and that perhaps it was 'the humdrum that finds out one's weaknesses'. His lack of self-confidence, his fear of the future, his need to be loved and his rejection of love, his need to give and rejection of gifts – all these made it so difficult for him to be thanked.

Peter Glenville once told Merula, 'He's the most complicated person I have ever known,' – she added, 'and Peter must have known plenty of complicated people.' She confirmed Alec's anxiety over joining the Salaman family. 'When we were first married I was alarmed, having come from a big noisy family where one could hurl abuse at one's brothers and sisters without offence, that the tiniest pinprick could cause such pain for days. He was like someone without an outer skin. He bled. I felt I had to approach him on tiptoe with gloves on.'

She felt they were opposite in all things, even incompatible: that he was a 'towny, I a country girl'. He went round shutting windows, she opened them. 'He was physically lazy, I mentally lazy; he was a shopping addict whilst I hated shopping. We were Mr and Mrs Jack Sprat.'

The negativity, his depressed predictions and pessimism could get her down. If their daily lady forgot to say 'good morning' he would be convinced that she was about to give notice – she spoke in a whisper anyway. When their two-year-old granddaughter threw a tantrum he feared she would have an uncontrollable temper for the rest of her life. If one of the dogs made a mess in the kitchen then it was going to go on doing that forever, and so on.

Finally she confessed, 'My crassness and stupidities were agony to him, until "grounds for divorce" became a household joke.'

This moving avowal explains why he liked her so much. It seemed she had the capacity to put up with his basic grumpiness. But could she, or did she, really trust him? Perhaps she was a married partner who, in the Bloomsbury tradition of the 1930s, could, without jealousy or a sense of betrayal, separate sexual practice from married life and friendship? The accounts of their early marriage suggest they knew little of romantic love or sexual passion and with only a limited desire to have children they went ahead to achieve a contented and sanctioned equilibrium through tolerance and good sense. Perhaps she simply never knew, or had an attitude of out of sight, out of mind which was common in that era, that 'boys will be boys' and do their own thing. Of her own faithfulness there would never be a shred of doubt.

'All shall be well, and all manner of things shall be well' was a motto Alec tried with difficulty to adopt after he came across the quote from St Julian of Norwich, pointed out Merula. But the true motto of his life was 'The readiness is all' even to the point of dealing with his correspondence before breakfast. This meant he could not be late. Being a split second late for anything was not tolerated: the hours of wasted time they spent cruising round London before a party or first night, or sitting on railway stations were uncountable. Even Alec found it laughable, but it never altered, he couldn't help it.

'Help for those who were up a gum tree was always immediate and practical, but sympathy for one's stupid mistakes was in short supply. His criticism could be devastating, but a drop of praise or encouragement one could wallow in for days.

'He didn't suffer fools gladly, nor the garrulous nor the verbose nor gushers. With all the contradictions of his make-up there was always the rod of truth up the middle which was what I recognized when we first fell in love. I knew I could always trust him.'

Alec told Simon Callow years later, confessing to his early involvement with men as sexual partners, that when he married Merula he 'gave up all that kind of thing'. 'My guess would be,'

Alec's journalist friend Tom Sutcliffe told me, 'that if Alec ever had done something or gone in for much in the way of homosexual or bisexual activity, it would have been when he was quite a lot younger – and by the time I was being entertained by him I should not have thought it was something that was still going on. He was then in his early sixties.' Certainly in those early years, as a member of Gielgud's company there was a continuum of quietly discreet homosexual activity, sometimes rather random and impulsive, and probably not with acting colleagues or peers, but more with social inferiors – 'rough and ready boys' in the Oscar Wilde phrase – rented for the occasion or picked up at parties. There is no reason to believe Alec did not behave like the others. This other self was to surface briefly, with some notoriety, after the war.

Publicly it never became known, which is amazing when you think how much was known or rumoured privately in the profession. Alec created for himself, out of his sexuality and his homosexuality, a secret identity akin to that of a spy. He needed it, he drew unconsciously on it, and it succoured him. But also terrified him because of its nature and his fear of being found out.

As John le Carré wrote in 1980 describing the 1930s Oxbridge models for his spy characters, they were 'not only a self-selecting élite, but a self-loving one as well. One forgets nowadays the extent to which homosexuality at that period, was itself a commitment to a secret world.' (*Observer*) The remark to Callow, 'I gave up all that kind of thing', is often echoed by those fearful of discovery. Alec Guinness was a complicated person, as was his lifelong friend, the director who had been to Stonyhurst, who was unashamedly homosexual. Was Peter Glenville – charming, witty, handsome – a sexual partner of Alec's? Certainly a number of colleagues and friends thought so. But this is not hard evidence. Do we need it? Does it matter? Glenville remained Alec's closest personal friend until his death in 1996.

Merula became his family, his security, the mother he never had, the woman he could trust – in contrast to his own mother, Agnes de Cuffe. What perhaps Merula was saying, when she said 'I knew I could always trust him', was a sign of that dependence on one another that often happens in married life, when one of the pair transfers to the other their own feelings. What in effect she was saying was that, in her own sense of strong self-esteem and family well-being, she could trust herself, while his own psychological need of her, as a background friend and spouse he could trust – and trust not to rival or impose herself before his own selfish needs and the demands of his career – remained deep, solid and lifelong. She became a remarkable woman and wife. Alec, apart from his wayward moods towards her and his reprehensible tendency to put her down, even in company, was appreciative and grateful.

Alec was also grateful to have what he had never had: a family. For the next five or six years that was to prove enough, especially with the intervention of the war; for those years apart from Merula Alec was able to regulate his secret, double life – seemingly it was not so important that he would risk the threat of death or humiliation. After the war, with the return to peace and the quickening of Alec's career and all the pressure, as well as fame and money, this brought, it seemed to gather momentum towards a mounting sense of crisis.

There was more than one Alec: to emphasize what Glenville said, 'He's the most complicated person I have ever known.' Many others echoed his remarks; one could fill a notebook with such comments about Alec. I like the notion that, in the phrase Ralph Richardson used of himself, Alec was 'a whole pack of cards'.

Without them being close confidants the affection between Michel, the Salamans and their newly acquired member remained close. Alec described Salaman in old age with warmth as 'my very wise old father-in-law who died at the age of ninety-five or ninety-six, saying don't kid yourself' (about the decrease of desire):

> He said – he was a well-read man – that he used to think he would sit down and read everything he had never read, and that everything would be under control. 'Not a bit of it,' he said, 'you revert in a strange way to your younger ways of thinking. You're not past it. And the younger and prettier the girls that go by the more you think, oh it would be lovely, you know.'
> *Guardian*, 7 October 1985

We are back, are we not, to the first of Samuel Butler's 'Three Most Important Things'?

7. The Prince of Denmark Passes
Unnoticed through London

For the next few years, Alec's career rose in a straight trajectory to the most important role he played in his youthful, pre-Second World War days, possibly the best stage performance he ever gave in his career. His Hamlet, in Tyrone Guthrie's Old Vic production, opened in October 1938 and took Alec, with Merula at his side, on a historic tour of Europe and the Near East. From the time of *Noah*, when he met Merula, and in the next four years of intense formative acting that laid the groundwork for his future great career, the devils in his system did not play him up unduly. Or not for a while, anyway. He would seem to have found in the religion of being an artist a foretaste, or a premonition, of the relief and deeper mixed torment and satisfaction he was later to find in organized religious faith. As he confessed, in this short period of early fulfilment a door in his heart had been opened for him, and it dawned on him that acting could have an affinity with the greater arts.

This was due to an uncompromising, rather gruff, sometimes belligerent Frenchman whom this present author knew rather well, for he worked for a time as his directorial assistant. In the pre-war and post-war English theatre until his death in 1971 the influence of Michel Saint-Denis was considerable. Again, it was Gielgud's entrepreneurial flair – and perhaps his continental blood, for he was part Polish – that brought Saint-Denis into the mainstream of classical company work. Characteristically unselfish in his exploration but upset by the consequences, Gielgud had asked Saint-Denis to direct *Noah*, in which Alec and Merula played two of the masked animals. As the biblical principal, in velveteen trousers and fur cap, Gielgud felt uneasy. Saint-Denis, the perfectionist from his Compagnie des Quinze training, was the nephew of Jacques

SEASON 1938—39

THE OLD VIC

Founded by EMMA CONS 1880 Managed by LILIAN BAYLIS from 1912.

RUN IN CONNECTION WITH

SADLER'S WELLS

Re-opened by LILIAN BAYLIS 1931

Lessee and Manager : BRUCE D. WORSLEY.

25th CONSECUTIVE SEASON of DRAMA at the OLD VIC

TUESDAY, OCTOBER 11th at 7.15

HAMLET

(IN ITS ENTIRETY)

MODERN DRESS

Nightly at 7.15

Theatre Closed on Mondays

Matinees, Thursdays and Saturdays, at 1.45

LAST PERFORMANCE, SATURDAY, NOVEMBER 19th, at 7.15

Programme—PRICE THREEPENCE

A programme cover for Alec's first Hamlet

Copeau, the Catholic presiding genius of French theatre of that era, a progenitor of much of the spectacular post-Second World War flowering of French theatre. He unnerved Gielgud from the start of rehearsals, making him feel lazy, ignorant, and self-satisfied. Even the minor players, such as Alec, must have sniffed this significant wind of change, and felt a certain pleasure in their taskmaster's discomfort. At the New Theatre (now the Albery) Michel changed his whole attitude to acting. But there was opposition to this new basic approach. Alec heard a robust elderly actor called Frederick Lloyd asking Tony Guthrie what it would be like working with Saint-Denis. ' "*Very* interesting," Tony said, "very pleasant – so long as you don't object to rehearsing for three months in a chicken-run in preparation for the *Ghost Train*." ' Alec might have sided in sympathy with the actresses being admonished to abandon high-heeled shoes and cartwheel hats when they came to rehearsal. But Saint-Denis's powerful vision took hold of him and he joined the London School: a school for aspiring actors which formed round Peggy Ashcroft, George Devine and Glen Byam Shaw. In Peggy Ashcroft's case 'commitment to art' became so bound up with her personal development and need for love and sexual passion, that while she was married to Komisarjevsky she had affairs with both George Devine, and more seriously with Saint-Denis, whom at one stage she intended to marry.

Michel, as Guinness pointed out, smoked a rather chunky curved pipe, while George and Glen (like Alec, 'very much a cigarette man') dropped their fags to follow suit: 'I maintained that for a time they all spoke with French accents.' Alec, as part of the group, paid one pound a week and they met at 14 Beak Street in Soho five mornings and sometimes an afternoon or two. Alec kept his distance but learned a lot from what he called a great theatrical guru. This was, he said, his early road to Damascus, though the conversion was blurred by his own selfish ego. Yet, notwithstanding, 'The trouble with Michel was his secret conviction that he could break down young personalities, as if a psychiatrist . . . He didn't attempt it with older actors, set in their ways, and he failed singularly with Peter Ustinov, James Donald and myself, all of us choosing to go on our merry, separate ways. If the truth be known, I suspect we each resented the onslaught on our integrity – a sort of rape of unformed talent – while admiring the man.' (*A Positively Final Appearance*) Peter Brook emulated this practice of Saint-Denis as he reached maturity as a director in the 1960s, but Alec from the start was waiting for a greater, deeper or at least different faith to which to convert.

Noah was followed by another Gielgud production, something of an anti-climax for Alec: he played the Apothecary and Samson in a *Romeo and Juliet* in which Gielgud and Laurence Olivier alternated as Romeo and Mercutio every other night; in 1999 Alec claimed he could still hear the clicking of foils from this production in the New – not from the stage but from the topmost corridor where those with little to do practised fencing (he took lessons in épée from the excitable Capitaine Félix Gravé). He didn't seem much enamoured of Olivier's Mercutio which he called 'macho, vulgar, rumbustious'. Edith Evans acted the Nurse, and when he was offstage Alec would hold open doors for her and not 'get even a nod, let alone a thank you'. Later she was to tell him, hearing of his marriage – 'No-ah! You're an artist! You shouldn't marry.' In the next production, *The Seagull*, in which Ashcroft played Nina, Komisarjevsky was impressed by Alec – Saint-Denis was leaving his mark. When Guinness, in the small role of Yakov the workman, had mimed pulling a rope, Peggy told him: 'I've had a quarrel with Komis about you.' She maintained there was no rope there; but Komis had said, 'Yes there was: I saw it when he was pulling.'

But Alec was to finish stalking the mighty ones and begin to come into his own. In the summer of 1936, after *The Seagull* closed, he joined the Old Vic Company. Now he was working for seven pounds a week. He was still almost beneath the notice of Lilian Baylis, manager of the Old Vic Company. She spoke to him only twice. On the first occasion, at his audition, she said, 'Let's have a look at your legs, dear,' and, having looked, she said, 'You'll do'. On the second occasion he dropped three pennies in a corridor, just as she came round the corner. She eyed the coins, remarked, 'Father, Son and Holy Ghost', and swept on.

Alec played, wrote Audrey Williamson, Boyet in *Love's Labour's Lost* as 'a perfect and stylish cameo of the middle-aged courtier'. Alec himself considered he was wretched and humourless, but

Michael Redgrave, who felt he had been passed over for Berowne in favour of Alec Clunes and who therefore played Ferdinand instead, commented that Alec 'had a rather tiresome part, and succeeded against the odds in bringing it to life. He had, and still has, the most valuable asset for comedy: the appearance of possessing an impenetrable secret.'

Alec later cleverly doubled Le Beau and the rustic William in *As You Like It*, in which Edith Evans, as Rosalind, set a standard for the times and Michael Redgrave played Orlando as a handsome, well-spoken 'stripling'. This production was directed by Esme Church, the woman director of the Old Vic School.

If Gielgud provoked something which, for so reticent an actor as Alec, approached loquacity, Olivier continued to stimulate disapproval. When on 5 January 1937 Olivier opened as Hamlet in Guthrie's 'uncut' production, Alec who understudied Olivier, professed himself 'outraged at the gymnastic leaps and falls required by his example. I never liked the performance or Guthrie's production, but it was huge box office . . . It would have been fatal if I had had to go on. I would have fainted rather than throw myself off a twelve-foot rostrum.' Later he conceded that it had been 'necessary for Olivier to do what he did – and it laid the foundations for his becoming a truly great actor'.

Olivier admitted that his first consideration in playing the part was to seduce Vivien Leigh (who came to nearly half the performances) with what the critic Kenneth Tynan later called his 'physical virility and acrobatic flash'. James Agate wrote, 'Mr Olivier's Hamlet is the best performance of Hotspur that the present generation has seen.' John Gielgud did not mince his words, according to legend, going backstage after the opening night, and saying, 'Larry, it's one of the finest performances I have ever seen, but it's still my part.'

Alec had perfected the impact he made as Osric, which had now become the essence of Osric; his Reynaldo also made a strong comic impact. In *Twelfth Night*, the next Guthrie production at the Old Vic, Alec's career took a major step forward. In this downbeat, melancholy production, in which with bustling ebullience Olivier played Toby Belch, Alec took the risk of underacting as Belch's foil, Sir Andrew Aguecheek, in a way which emphasized the production's haunting sense of fatality:

A wistful flaxen gull with the sad ingenuous eyes of a Dan
Leno, and the same upstanding quiff of hair on the forehead.
The character had a harmless, amiable silliness that was
likeable as well as funny.   **Audrey Williamson**

Agate commented that he was too youthful in his capers.
Guthrie himself hated the production, calling it 'baddish' and
'immature', while Alec himself was not too keen on it. For some
'quirky reason of my own I played him as if he were Stan Laurel,'
Alec remembered. 'It was a very undisciplined affair, not good at
all, but I was thrilled to be acting my first important part . . . Like
every Aguecheek that has ever been I got a laugh on the line, "I
was adored once, too". One midweek matinee, with a sparse
audience, no laugh came although I undoubtedly sought it. Larry
hissed in my ear, "Fool, you should know a matinee audience
would never laugh at that." '
    Olivier perceived that Alec was never to become a great stage
actor in relation to audiences. He became a great stage actor, yes,
but as a presenter of perfectly shaped and organized roles. He
gained by experience the skill to play off audiences and mesmerize
them (by always keeping something back). He never took command: he simply had not this gift, rather he put audiences
immediately at their ease. But he did have the gift of creating
mystery.
    In the Guthrie production of *Henry V* which followed with
Olivier as king, Alec's Exeter passed without comment. The play
was chosen to chime in with George VI's coronation. Immediately
after this he came back to *Hamlet* for the much-celebrated
performance at Elsinore. This was billed as an outdoor gala
performance by the first British company to play in the turreted
and flagged courtyard of Kronborg Castle since the late sixteenth
century. A cloudburst saturated the stage and the courtyard
benches which should have held 2,500 people. They had to move
to the ballroom of the Marienlyst Hotel where the company was
staying.
    'Be polite to Kings and Queens if they get in your way. Alec,
make your entrance through the French windows,' barked Guthrie.
Alec shivered on the bench, soaked to the skin, although well-
fuelled with Danish liquor:

Outside, waves were riding high in the narrow water between Denmark and Sweden, and it was plain that the storm had set in for the night, with a noise like the ride of the Valkyries. All the costumes and property had been brought over from Kronborg; hotel bedrooms became dressing-rooms; and not so long after eight o'clock the ballroom, with Danish royalty [Prince Knud and Princess Caroline Mathilde] in the front row, was filled for what, in effect, would be an improvisation. It had been left to the players, directed by Laurence Olivier whom Guthrie had put wisely in command, to get the night together with only the sketchiest idea of ways and means . . .

Guthrie came forward to apologise briefly for 'the strangest performance of *Hamlet* on any stage,' and presently Francisco and Barnardo were 'on the platform before the castle,' Horatio and Marcellus were on their way up through the audience, and somewhere, within a few moments, the bell was beating one.   J. C. Trewin, *Five & Eighty Hamlets*

'Never was there such a performance,' commented Lady Diana Cooper, who was in the audience.

Alec's own small contribution was, he said, heavily affected by the schnapps with which his Danish dresser supplied him prior to his 'blowing in' through the French windows. He smiled rather too much. He rested his sword on the King of Sweden's lap, and blocked the view of at least two crowned heads.

This was the third of Alec's appearances in *Hamlet* and he added the Player Queen to his repertoire. Offstage, the furtive affair between Laurence Olivier and Vivien Leigh was at its height. Jill Esmond, Olivier's wife, accompanied Olivier everywhere on the tour. In a gloating tone in *Confessions of an Actor* Olivier said he found himself making love to Vivien 'almost within Jill's vision. This welding closeness tripped the obvious decision and two marriages were severed.'

Alec recalled more indirectly and enigmatically that 'many bedroom doors were locked, or slammed or opened that night'. Drawing a discreet veil over his own activities, Alec could be loquacious in revealing the biography of others. He informed one of Vivien Leigh's biographers that he was delegated to take Jill out on afternoon trips to give the lovers time to be together. Had Jill not gone to Elsinore with Olivier, said Alec, 'It might just have been an exciting new affair.' But the participants ensured it was always more than that, while even at Elsinore Vivien fell into extreme fluctuations of mood, screaming at Olivier one moment, then 'becoming suppressed and silent and staring blankly into space'.

In the meantime Gielgud had become manager of the Queen's Theatre and on his return Alec again joined Gielgud's 'family', as he had at the New Theatre in 1935–6. In this second season he appeared in all four productions: *Richard II*, Sheridan's *The School for Scandal*, Chekhov's *The Three Sisters* and *The Merchant of Venice*. In John's own production of *Richard*, Alec played Aumerle and the Groom. In *School* Guinness played Snake. (Herbert Farjeon wrote in the *Bystander*, 'From the tip of his nose to the acid in each syllable he utters Alec Guinness's Snake is as arresting as Hogarth'.) Gielgud's Joseph Surface was acclaimed as a dazzling masterpiece but the production, by Guthrie, was poor, for Gielgud and he did not see eye to eye. In *The Three Sisters* Alec played the humble Fedotik; and in *The Merchant* he was the pallid lover Lorenzo to Gielgud's 'challenging and unusual' Shylock. These were hardly stimulating roles but Alec made them so; on the one hand one can imagine Gielgud dishing them out in an offhand way to this new arrival of no fixed talent and easily pliable substance. On the other hand Gielgud had an acute and generous sense of the talent of others and would surround himself only with the best. And Alec made each role distinctive: Peggy Ashcroft recalled Lorenzo's 'grave Italian look', Snake's 'sly mischief' and Fedotik's 'ingenious youth'. As Lorenzo he was fitted by Motley's with a suit of white calico: he went back to the theatre saying the costume was a disaster and he looked dreadful, not realizing they had still to cut and spray the calico and trim it with black velvet.

He still attended the classes of Michel Saint-Denis, who directed *The Three Sisters*, deepening his Stanislavskian sense of realism and continuing to open up his imagination. He recalled, at various times, the later, ill-fated production of *The Cherry Orchard* which failed to open because of the war:

I wish I could describe something which I remember taking place when Michel Saint-Denis was rehearsing *The Cherry Orchard* . . . It involved another actor who was playing

Epihodov, whose boots squeak. Saint-Denis was so insistent on the way the actor *listened* to his boots squeaking ... Witnessing that altered my whole attitude to acting which I thought had been would-be romantic, admiring flourishes of various sorts – although I couldn't do them. And here was something very basic.

Alec expanded this earlier account, given to Irving Wardle, to a fuller 'memory', which showed his elaborative skills: it was, he said, the middle of an afternoon rehearsal. Marius Goring played Epihodov, the clumsy, wrong-footed clerk on the Ranyevsky estate, who has to complain about the squeaking of his boots. After waiting a short while Michel said, 'Marius, I don't hear the squeak in your boots.' Marius replied, 'Of course not. I'm wearing gym shoes with rubber soles.' Michel persisted, 'But I should hear the squeak.'

He got up to demonstrate what he meant. (His own shoes, of course, were squeak free.) With great concentration and concern, his head on one side, he listened to a shoe as he bent his instep up and down. I could swear we all heard a squeak, though naturally it was only in our imagination. From then on I was in love with the idea of trying to exercise a touch of magic on an audience, of persuading people to see and hear what wasn't there.   *A Positively Final Appearance*

Peter Daubeny, the impresario, aged sixteen at this time, met Guinness. He was, he said, nervous, and he could sense Guinness's own shyness.

There was something curiously unemotional, inaccessible, beyond his gentleness. Even then he had the kind of intellectual humility which was described by Matthew Arnold: 'You must get yourself out of the way to see things clearly.' But he listened kindly and with understanding, as if in a confessional – and, indeed, the sort of help our meeting gave me was similar to that which I might have obtained by pouring myself out to a priest in some shadowy cathedral stall. I came away feeling relieved of a psychological wound.

My World of Theatre

Alec told him to study with Saint-Denis at the London Theatre School. 'You can't get away from Stanislavsky,' he declared buoyantly. 'You'll like him.'

As Richard II, Gielgud was the commanding 'presence'. On the morning of the first night Alec finally got to rehearse with Gielgud, who told him that he wasn't as good in the role of the Groom as Leslie French when Gielgud did the play before. 'Try coming on from the right tonight instead of the left and see if it makes a difference.'

When Alec asked, as he said, cheekily, 'Which right?', Gielgud replied, in a fatigued manner, 'Oh, have it your own way. Do it as you've always done it. I can't be bothered.'

Gielgud was not like this only with Alec (Alec, like a news reporter, even in these early days makes every story he told sound like an exclusive), but with everyone. Margaret Harris said he was 'a strange mixture of thoughtfulness and thoughtlessness'. Alec undervalued his own impact. He 'always made an impression', Margaret Harris told me. 'I don't think he was ever better. His sense of character was amazing.' Everyone saw his potential, but especially Tyrone Guthrie.

The production of greatest value was *The Three Sisters*, which Peggy Ashcroft called 'the particular triumph of the season'. Alec played the humble Fedotik, the 'ingenuous youth', commended by Ashcroft but criticized by Michael Redgrave for overstepping his inventiveness. Saint-Denis had demanded seven weeks' rehearsal, which in those days was unheard of: 'I think the company, under his influence, reached its climax as a wonderfully welded ensemble.' Alec added, 'Lots of people flowered in *Three Sisters*: it was like going to some delightful and sad party: we couldn't wait to get back to the place every night.'

*

Guthrie and Gielgud represented opposing theatrical traditions. It was now into Guthrie's camp that Alec was drawn. If it took more than ten years for Alec to throw off the influence of Gielgud (what Redgrave called 'the dazzling virtuosity of phrasing and breathing') – if throw it off he ever did – it was now Guthrie who perceived the twenty-two-year-old actor's acute intellect and essential ordinariness. He tried to champion them long before they found their full integration into his acting. He was never much of an admirer of West End stars and did not like or get on well with Gielgud. Ralph Richardson thought Guthrie the most stimulating and extraordinary man of the theatre since Harley Granville-Barker; but, Richardson also commented, it was as if he were trying to take the scene away from the leading actor and give it to the man who carried the spear.

Or, in Alec's case, the Groom; for now Guthrie, almost, it seemed, in an act of defiance to Gielgud, summoned Alec back to the Old Vic and asked him if he would care 'to give us your Hamlet . . . Think we should do it in modern dress. You could wear that nice grey suit you've got on.'

Alec nearly fainted. By no stretch of the imagination, he thought, was he ready for Hamlet, so he would be taking an absurd risk. But he had long studied the role. The first Hamlet he had ever seen had been that of Godfrey Tearle, at the Haymarket Theatre in 1931, when he was seventeen. This had not been the Hamlet he was going to love for the rest of his life, while Tearle's voice brought to his mind a 'very dark Christmas pudding with a dollop of brandy butter'. He probably saw other Hamlets, but the revelation came when he was nineteen. He witnessed a Hamlet in the playing of which the actor confronted his own vulnerability and helplessness. He was not the first, he knew, to claim they experienced their first 'overwhelming theatrical experience' watching Ernest Milton, the American actor of Jewish descent who had settled in England and become one of the greatest interpreters of Hamlet. Yet he was by no means universally applauded. Forty-two years of age when Alec saw him, he was often called a classical actor who would not stick to the rules of the game: 'an emotional force sometimes almost demonic', wrote one critic: 'speech after speech he double-charged'. 'Hamlet, I knew the man – you will remember that,' Milton later told that same critic.

Alec confessed himself shattered by the impact of this performance. He found that Milton and Shakespeare seemed to be of one mind, 'presenting the Renaissance Prince *par excellence*, a man familiar with the ways of mankind – not unlike Montaigne – who could always see the two sides of a coin, tortured by conscience and burdened by duty, a man of sharp wit but exquisite manners . . . I returned to my bed-sitter in Bayswater, incapable of speaking for about twenty-four hours, knowing I had witnessed something I can only call both transcendental and very human.'

These early impressions had been overlaid by the constant viewing of Gielgud in the role and more recently the rigorous understudy of Olivier (he never got to play the role and one suspects Olivier would never willingly have given his understudy the chance). So perhaps, on reflection, no young actor of twenty-four could have had a better grounding in the role.

Yet Alec, being Alec, still heard the scathing words of John about his *Richard II* Groom ringing in his ears, 'You're not nearly as good in the part as Leslie French was,' while in 1938 just before rehearsals began, he met John in Piccadilly:

'I can't think why you want to play big parts. Why don't you stick to those funny little men you do so well instead of trying to be important' (Alec reported this in a letter to Enid Bagnold in December 1964: this was found in a Wiltshire bookshop in May 1991).

No doubt Alec's first, negative instinct was to agree. His humility, or negative narcissism – sometimes one is not quite sure which it was – aligned him more to Alfred Prufrock:

> No! I am not Prince Hamlet, nor was meant to be.
> Am an attendant Lord, one that will do
> To swell a progress, start a scene or two.

He was not Prince Hamlet. Politic, cautious, and meticulous, he had the mentality of a small-part player. Is this what Guthrie found so attractive? Here, in embryo, was the personality of the anti-star, the anti-celebrity. The young actor was malleable and Guthrie, nearing his fortieth year, was in full rivalry for power with the active stars of the theatre. He was impelled to succeed with Alec where he had failed with Olivier, in a production of *Hamlet* without a star player in which, at every point, the quality of the thinking in the production and the integrity of his own vision of the play could be realized. Significantly, yet again he had chosen to do the text in its 'entirety'.

'I could never emulate the pyrotechnics of Olivier, or the classic formality of Gielgud.' With Guthrie's approach Alec would never need to, because the daring and radical idea was to play the tragedy in modern dress. Up to then Shakespeare had rarely been acted in contemporary fashions. In 1925 there had been a 'Hamlet in plus fours', with Colin Keith-Johnson mouthing in a soft colloquial manner, Ophelia skipping about in short skirts and 'light' (transparent?) stockings and Claudius with whisky and a soda siphon in his prayer cabinet. Guthrie eschewed such gimmickry, saying in 1933 that he did not much care for modern dress. He set out to achieve, instead, six years later in Roger Furse's permanent design of classical pillars and changing backcloths, a timeless atmosphere and a 'racy tumult' of visual effects; overall he described the new approach he had in mind as a 'cadenza on the familiar theme of the Painted Smile and the Breaking Heart'.

The laid-back atmosphere suited Alec, allowing him his own pace of assimilation. He found Guthrie superior even to Michel Saint-Denis, who had driven him mad with meticulous little moves. Guthrie shared a quality with Gielgud, Olivier and Peter Brook that Saint-Denis the purist lacked: the faculty by sheer physical presence of galvanizing a company into good work. Under his tutelage Alec learnt, gradually, and with much backtracking and mistakes, to make his own decisions about how his own talent should develop. No doubt he would have loved to escape from this agonizing process – who wouldn't? – but Guthrie saw more deeply and more wisely the need not to interfere and impose. He practised a kind of inspired indifference which strikes one as truly remarkable in what is now such a power-hungry profession, and it did not seem to bother him much if his actors made fools of themselves. This unconventionality appealed to Alec, who yet, forever grappling with uncertainty, hankered after certainty. Later he would complain that Guthrie had failed to wean him away from his 'pale, ersatz Gielgudry'. In truth, Guthrie was sensible, just letting him grow in his own time. Before *Hamlet* opened, Alec paid the penance for such an opportunity by acting the unrewarding role of Arthur Gower, the ineffectual hero of Pinero's *Trelawny of the Wells*, which they put on to commemorate the Old Vic's first quarter-century of cooperation with its sister theatre.

The predominant note of the reviews of *Hamlet*, which opened on 11 October 1938, was a surprised interest. The settings and costumes struck the audiences as timeless and Ruritanian rather than modern: as Hamlet Alec wore sombre black and plum-coloured dress jackets, Horatio unassuming civilian tweeds, the women long and sweeping evening dresses. Everyone carried open umbrellas at Ophelia's graveside – possibly an effect touched off in Guthrie's mind by the downpour at Elsinore. Alec entered the graveyard in sailor's jersey and thigh boots. The production was much praised for its atmosphere. 'For the first time,' wrote Audrey Williamson in *Old Vic Drama*, 'one realised how a modern-dress production may give new life and reality to Shakespeare's characters without losing intellectual excitement or beauty.'

Alec's Hamlet fitted admirably into the production: 'essentially sane', Williamson called it, or as Alec might translate it: 'lacking in emotional turmoil'. Even worse, she picked up the similarity to Gielgud's early Hamlet:

> a sensitive young intellectual temperamentally incapable of meeting violence with violence – an interpretation aided by Guinness's youth and fragile appearance, as well as by the curiously impotent expression with which he regarded his sword at the words, 'Oh cursèd spite!'

This response mortified Alec when he read it in his press books and he was to call attention to it later (as well as claiming he never read reviews).

James Agate attacked the performance for lacking power, pointing out that, as Alec had chubby, practical hands, he attempted few rhetorical gestures. This Hamlet, according to the magisterial Agate, failed because it deliberately refused to succeed. He seemed to be adding another complex to Dr Ernest Jones's Freudian theories of the Oedipus Complex. 'This young actor attempts neither play of feature nor gesture. He reflects mordancy ... Yet this non-acting comes, in the end, to have a value of its own.' In an astonishing volte-face Agate still found it, in spite of the performance by Alec and the modern costumes, 'the most moving performance of *Hamlet* in my experience'.

Robert Speaight, the actor, went further along this road. In his memoir *The Property Basket*, he describes the performance as 'sensitive and *intimiste*, spurning spectacular effects'. J. C. Trewin, who saw well over a hundred different Hamlets in his lifetime, dubbed it the youngest and quietest of them all, above all 'a thinking man'. Trewin noted that Guinness was the first Hamlet sitting alone by the Players' property basket before the conscience of the king speech who found himself tapping out the rhythm upon the upturned drum: 'As he would so often, he seemed to be creating a character as he moved, without previous calculation.'

Alec may, by his own high standards, have failed as Hamlet but in his work and his life he was to embody more and more of its central message: 'The readiness is all'. Tyrone Guthrie's way was ultimately the liberating path for Alec's own unique and individual talent, while Guthrie's own choice of supporting actors, especially that of Anthony Quayle for Laertes and Andrew Cruick-shank for Claudius, brought very definite qualities into influential play over Alec that were entirely different from those of Gielgud.

Quayle was an excellent but cool, prosaic actor who brought to Laertes a stricken stillness in his grief over his sister's death and a self-harrowing guilt in the duel. Cruickshank, more crucially, was a Claudius who had lost the love of Gertrude and who knew it: 'But that I know love is begun by time,' yields, in Harley Granville-Baker's suggestion, this interpretation. Cruickshank's performance became an exposition of the Stanislavsky theory that an actor playing an evil man should look for the good in him. Looking for the good in his characters was to become the creed of Guinness.

Alec himself did claim originality for his wild outburst of misogyny after the 'To be or not to be' soliloquy, saying he interpreted that, from Ophelia's attitude and false orisons, she was a decoy; also for the drumming, which he said came about almost by accident. Otherwise, for being over-familiar with Gielgud's manner of timing, he quoted Dr Johnson to the effect that, 'almost all absurdity of conduct arises from the imitations of those we cannot resemble.'

Here he was being too hard on himself, for he did not resemble Gielgud unduly in style or manner. Yet he felt and confessed to me in 1989 that he had hardly penetrated below the surface of the part. There was no grasp of the complexity. 'Why, it was ridiculous,' he said. 'It was like water off a duck's back.' He marvelled that they had performed the play in its 'entirety' text, nearly 'five' hours of it.

This may have been no bad thing. He had followed Gielgud in obeying his own instinctive feeling and Guthrie thought that Alec's youth, combined with rare intelligence, humour and pathos realized a great deal of the part. 'He had not yet quite the authority to support, as Hamlet must, a whole evening, or to give the tragedy its full stature. The performance demanded that the public reach out and take what was offered. To this demand the public is rarely equal.'

Gielgud wrote to Guthrie that he was stirred and provoked. 'I was deeply touched by Alec's performance,' commented John, 'which I thought grew in distinction and quality all the time as it went on . . . I thought that the Recorder scene was fussed by the busyness of the production, and you haven't got any further than anyone else in solving the problem of the ghost. I also hated the new punctuation, but perhaps that is only my Terry blood crying out . . . I was terrifically moved by the closet scene, almost the best I have ever seen . . .'

The public's response was depressing, at first anyway. Guthrie admitted the production wasn't doing very well, even though he declared proudly, 'Alec is much *much* better in the part than Larry, but Larry with his beautiful head and athletic sexy movements and bursts of fireworks are what the public wants . . . [The production] represents my very utmost effort. It's easily the best work I've done so far and may well be the best I shall do – in this job, as in all semi-creative work, experience tends to kill invention and it is a blow to have it fall very flat.' Guthrie summarized his overall response in *A Life in the Theatre*:

> It's been far more difficult for Alec to weather. The actor's position to success or failure is so terribly personal. The work of art is inseparable from himself. It's *him* 'they' like or fail to like. And it's a very personal ordeal to have to tussle through that enormous physical effort to empty houses. Still, he's got great spirit and sense of proportion and the houses though empty are immensely enthusiastic and nearly all the people whose opinion we value have been sincerely and wholeheartedly praising him.

Among those people still to be valued is Stuart Burge the director who, at the very beginning of his career, played minor parts in this Old Vic season, including the Player Queen in *Hamlet*. He recalled in 2001 the 'wonderful, dry self-analytic quality' in Alec's performance, and how, 'as a classical actor he thought out every aspect of a character in a self-effacing way'. Burge also told me it was the best Hamlet he'd ever seen.

In view of Alec's future conversion to Catholicism it was prophetic of Kenneth Tynan to write in his monograph on Alec, published in 1953, that:

> Apart from Claudius, a short-lived penitent in the prayer scene, Hamlet is the only person in the play who cares about God. He doubts the provenance of the ghost – is it from hell or heaven? He will not kill the King until his heels may 'kick at heaven'; having seen the ghost, he'll 'go pray'; he would dispatch Ophelia to a nunnery; he swears 'by the rood' and reflects that man is 'in apprehension, how like a god!'; he talks of the abuse of 'god-like reason' and envisages himself as heaven's 'scourge and minister'; he enjoins Gertrude to confess herself to heaven; and it is not just by formal chance that Horatio invokes flights of angels to sing him to his rest. And when Laertes returns, sword in hand, to avenge his own father's murder, the contrast between the two men is violent and immediate. 'I dare damnation', shouts Laertes; and we are at once reminded that Hamlet's tragedy is that he cannot dare damnation, cannot bring himself to perform an act unsanctioned by heaven. I suspect that Guinness, an actor who specialises in men with obsessions, might be able to emphasise this religious melancholy more tellingly than anyone else.

He might have added that Alec, when he later turned to Catholicism, increasingly could not bring himself to perform acts unsanctioned by heaven.

Guinness's Hamlet went on tour and won more plaudits abroad than ever it did at home. The British Council tour included Portugal, Italy, Greece and Egypt. No still barely peace-time period could be so politically sensitive as was early 1939: Hitler was threatening western Europe, while the Anschluss of Austria had merged the German-speaking powers, and Italy had invaded Abyssinia. This tour of mainly right-wing or fascist countries provoked an outcry: 'shaking the blood-stained hand of Mussolini', some papers said. Scotland Yard warned of a demonstration outside the theatre, but nothing much happened.

The company travelled with eight productions, including *The Rivals*, *Trelawny of the Wells*, *Hamlet* and *Henry V*. The enterprise was huge and incredible – a company of forty-two and nearly twelve tons of scenery. The irony of it was that while they had taken all these productions with them, most audiences wanted to see only one – that of *Hamlet* with Guinness.

They first played Lisbon, where their scenery was lowered into the Tagus by mistake and where the victory of Franco over the Republican-led Barcelona was celebrated with delirium; they played Milan, where Alec and Merula had a day off visiting Como. Next it was Florence and on the Sunday night of their arrival Alec went along to see what the theatre looked like, and here he found an Italian company of eight just leaving. Scenery of waxed paper, costumes and props were strapped to bicycles: Alec reflected on the arduous life of the itinerant performer – but he was now paid a princely twenty pounds per week, still not a great salary, while Merula also received company pay. Merula and he experienced the tour as a second honeymoon, but he took no pictures – he lost his costly wedding present from Merula of a Leica camera by dropping it into Lake Como.

They played Rome, where Mussolini invited Alec to take tea with him in his box, then cancelled the arrangement because of the sudden death of the Pope – he had to attend the funeral. In Rome and Naples the audiences wore black in mourning for Pius XI, appropriate for *Hamlet*, which became popular in Italy and helped promote the lost cause of Anglo-Italian relations. Lewis Casson, who was now playing Polonius, tried to encourage Alec to show more confidence. Later he would defend Alec's interpretation as the ordinary man's Hamlet.

They sailed from Naples to Cairo. Sir Sydney Cockerell, the art historian, was in the audience in Cairo. Cockerell was the first literary figure of importance that Alec, in his new-found eminence, collected and diligently cultivated. The 'ordinary man's Hamlet' paradoxically had as strong an impulse to woo and correspond with the influential as more blatantly self-promoting publicists. Yet Alec would do this in his own discreet, self-effacing, even anonymous manner, by attracting the influential figure's curiosity without flattery. Cockerell was extraordinary, as his biographer Wilfrid Blunt noted, on account of 'the empire he exerted over his innumerable friends'. Some questioned if it was toadyism or genuine hero-worship. Alec became at once a new object of his admiration. 'A charming young man of twenty-four, very serious about Shakespeare and about his profession. His wife is on the stage, and is also a lover of literature . . . I hope to see them again,' wrote Cockerell rather patronizingly in his diary.

In Cairo they stayed three weeks; King Faroukh's sister was marrying the Shah of Persia and there were many parties. Merula, diving from the diving board of the Gezirah Club pool, hit the side and had to be rushed to hospital. Fortunately she escaped serious injury, but she and Alec missed the celebrations.

John Bird tells how, in 1973, during the run of *Habeas Corpus*, after three or four dinners at Alec's expense, Bird managed to repay his hospitality by taking him out to Tratoo. Alec was very concerned that the table should be in the corner of the restaurant. During the course of the meal Alec told Bird and the others that when he had just got married they were in Cairo, and the only place they could afford to visit was the zoo. He was taken, Alec told them, by this secretary bird or crane. Alec then stood in his chair and adopted a frozen bird-like position. 'It was amazing,' says Bird, 'he was this bird.'

After Cairo they played in Alexandria where Alec saw Katina Paxinou – whom Sir Lewis Casson called 'the old and fish-wifey' grande dame of the Greek National Theatre – in her most famous role of Electra. She was barely forty and went on acting for another thirty years. Sailing past Rhodes and Naxos they docked in Athens. Alec and Merula loved Athens, for they strolled almost alone round the Parthenon and had the beach temple at Sunion to themselves. Returning by taxi to their hotel they narrowly avoided a head-on collision with a luxury convertible whose uniformed passengers Alec recognized as Goebbels and Goering. King George of the Hellenes visited almost every performance because he was smitten with Cathleen Nesbitt (Gertrude) and one evening shared his Royal Box with a tall and fair-haired youth of about seventeen. The poor chap, said Alec, was desperately bored, and Alec missed his name. He asked Alec shyly, 'Got a yacht?' 'I said I hadn't. That was the end of our conversation. He was Prince Philip.'

Then on to Malta. The social activity here was intense, but even more evident were the battle preparations of the English fleet in Valetta harbour. One performance of *Henry V*, in which Alec acted the Chorus, emptied halfway through as men were called back to their ships as the fleet had been 'scrambled' – an Italian midget submarine had entered the harbour. The fleet was, as the pacifist Casson put it, 'so horribly ready'.

Back in England in May 1939 Alec played his first Macbeth with the Sheffield Repertory Company, learning the role with lightning speed. In fact, although he denied it in later years, he was quite courageous about seizing opportunities that tested his range. His next role, that of Michael Ransom in Auden and Isherwood's *The Ascent of F6*, was based on the tortured hero Lawrence of Arabia. It began Alec's fascination with Lawrence, who was an icon for homosexual writers such as Auden and Isherwood, and later Rattigan, in whose *Ross* Alec was to star in 1960. He felt at once that Lawrence was an enigma, although unaware that this might have been as much for his ambivalent, undeclared sexuality as for his complexity, or confusion over his double identity. Alan Bennett in his play *Forty Years On* put his finger on a quality Alec was to come to share with Lawrence:

> Shyness has always been a disease with him, and it was shyness and a longing for anonymity that made him disguise himself. Clad in the magnificent white robes of an Arab prince with in his belt the short curved, gold sword of the Ashraf descendants of the Prophet he hoped to pass unnoticed through London.

As Ransom, Alec was able to impersonate Lawrence easily, as if he was already second nature to him, 'chucking a towel over my head and twisting a towel into a sort of burnous'.

In *Blessings in Disguise* Alec made a bizarre reference to another actor in the cast to whom he felt attracted, yet wanted to tease the reader and kept the identity to himself. He had first seen this actor in Ibsen's *Ghosts*, when he had gone to worship Sybil Thorndike and Lewis Casson. He was fourteen, or so he said, and found himself in Sybil Thorndike's presence, tongue-tied at her larger-than-life presence, and that of her husband Lewis Casson. Describing this production he made this strange veiled reference: 'I rather warmed to the feckless, handsome Oswald. (Ten years later, at the Old Vic, the Oswald played, quite excellently, the enigmatic, priggish Tibetan Abbot in Auden/Isherwood's *Ascent of F6*, in which I acted the even more priggish hero, Ransom).' Leaving the Thorndikes, he left the theatre to find: 'Only Oswald, who emerged from the stage-door in a camel-hair coat and full make-up-Leichner sticks numbers 5 and 9, a red dot in the corner of each eye and a lot of mascara. In my puritanical way I was rather shocked; also perhaps a little alarmed. There was something ambivalent about him which I couldn't grasp, but which also *glamorised me*' (my italics).

He had not been fourteen, the date had been 1930, and he had been sixteen and a half. Fourteen suggests innocence, sixteen something very different as far as sexual development, 'something ambivalent', goes. Had the shadowy Oswald/Tibetan monk made a pass at him? Was there suggestion of a sexual encounter? It seems possible or even likely. In his coded and veiled way Alec calls attention to the actor in retrospect without mentioning his name, as if somewhere he wanted it to be known and yet have the satisfaction of keeping it secret. (The actor's name, I later discovered, was Hubert Langley.)

Alec loved Merula, put her before anyone else and remained unwaveringly loyal and true to her. However, he had the not uncommon predicament which another gifted man described better than Alec was (as far as we know) ever able to. This was André Gide, French Nobel prize winner for literature, who confronted without flinching this truth about himself. A month before Alec was born in 1914 the playwright and poet Paul Claudel had written to his friend Gide after reading *Les Caves du Vatican*, that he had been 'brought to a stop on page 478' by a pederastic passage which had shocked him profoundly and threw 'a sinister light' on some of Gide's earlier works. Claudel wanted to know if 'you yourself are a participant in these hideous practices?' and went on to ask, 'If you are not a pederast, why do you have so strange a predilection for this sort of subject?'

As soon as he received Claudel's letter Gide answered, begging not to be misjudged, 'that I love my wife more than life itself, and I could not forgive any word or action on your part which might endanger her happiness'. He went on to confess to Claudel, whose 'binding duty is to keep my secret before God . . . [that] I have never felt any desire in the presence of a woman: and the great sadness of my life is that the most constant, the most enduring, and the keenest of my loves has never been accompanied by any of the things which normally precede love. It seemed, on the contrary, that in my case love prevented me from desiring.'

One wonders if, and to what degree, Alec felt this about Merula. The strong love between them grew and matured on the basis of a non-sexual attraction, and one can be fairly sure that Alec, while appreciating and loving women, indeed praising their attractiveness, felt not so much desire for the opposite sex but rather an affinity and even rivalry with it. The way he writes about women, the identification and sympathy he feels, suggests often that he is, in imitative desire at least, one himself. Yet this does not mean he did not experience heterosexual desire. And what could Merula have felt about all this? When Claudel wrote to Madame Gide in great consternation that the tortured Gide was leaving for equatorial Africa with the idea that perhaps he would never return, and suggesting they might meet and speak together, Madame Gide replied that she was anxious, yes, but they could best meet each other by praying for him. 'All those who love André Gide, as that very noble spirit deserves to be loved, must pray for him.' There was possibly something of a Madame Gide in Merula, and when he heard of her response to Claudel Gide was touched. 'Why aren't all Catholics like you?' he asked. 'You will tell me that the best are silent.'

The bisexual side of Alec's nature was there from the start. It had a strong, if not commanding influence on his art. The influence of personal sexuality or sexual preference may not be an important fact in the art of other actors or artists. One can name many in whom it was not, their sexuality being unimportant. But in Guinness's case it did figure highly. Because he had throughout his life to the end a highly ambiguous sexual nature which was often at the forefront of his roles and evident in his social behaviour, he would seem to have had, especially in these early years, a severe identity problem, or series of identity problems, which he struggled to solve, or at least survive or come through in a lifelong search for self-fulfilment and integration. But, as we shall see, his problems were closely related to the parts he was playing. How much or how little they were lived out or explored in sexual involvements outside his marriage and with other men is difficult to assess. He by no means became a great classical actor, but the outstanding precision – interior truth 'when he feels like a man he finds himself playing him' (Alan Brien) – and mocking self-doubt he brought to a great range of characters, was uniquely his. The uncanny ability to transpose himself totally onto the part was strongly related to these two lasting elements which never became properly resolved; and which at the same time he probably never wanted to resolve. These were the shame and darkness over his illegitimacy, together with the mixture of privilege and deprivation in his upbringing by his mother; and his ambivalent sexuality. Ambiguity and betrayal go together. Truth, said John Donne, is almost error's twin.

8. Plenty of Material to Embroider On

Apart from the shame and guilt he felt over his illegitimacy and his mother, unlike Gide, Alec kept to himself his longing for men, while at the same time he did like or feel attracted by the occasional woman: he always retained the need for a friendly and virtuous woman (but not a sexy one). The love for men became a love that literally dared not speak its name; it became a deep secret, hidden, with its own power – the secret, he was to discover, was an asset. Michael Redgrave had already pointed this out during his early season at the Old Vic. 'He has the most valuable asset for comedy; the appearance of possessing an impenetrable secret.' As his greatest asset, Alec made sure it was kept.

In *Dr Ibsen's Secret*, a play for radio broadcast in late 2000, the playwright, about to receive a high honour from the king of Norway, is posed the following dilemma: should he atone for the shame of a disgraceful action committed earlier in life – the fathering of an illegitimate child upon a poor working class girl – by fully acknowledging it, or should he keep the secret? His biographer Henrik Jaeger is in attendance, only too eager to pick up such a sensational detail, although the power of its revelation would have been taken from him by the subject himself. Ibsen's wife is also keen Ibsen should prove his greater social worth and humanity by owning up. She has, anyway, just met the former mistress of her husband, who is destitute and deserving. The bastard son, too, is around, a drunken no-good, confused by his paternity.

But no, having changed his mind from acquiescence to his humanity back to the earlier, self-protective self, Ibsen seals his lips, repudiates his promise to his wife to spill the beans at the public ceremony, and sends his biographer packing with comfortable hagiography.

The point Ibsen makes to his wife when explaining his action is that the 'artist' needs his secret. This is the source of his power, and if he gives it up he will lose his 'daemon', or his inspiration, that which drives him to create. In addition, Alec, with no father, no role model, was like, as Merula said, 'someone without an outer skin. He bled.' 'Anyone who is externally defenceless,' Elias Canetti, British Nobel Prize-winner of 1981, wrote, 'can retreat and arm himself inwardly. The inner armour against questions is possession of a secret, a secret being like a second body encased within the first, and better defended . . . Whatever its contents a secret is always dangerous.'

The libel lawyer's report on my submission of my earlier book's first draft tells its own story.

RE: 'ALEC GUINNESS'

SCHEDULE

A. HOMOSEXUALITY

Page	Comment
20–21	Camp, outrageous, queeny.
25	Cold to female attractions.
28	No awakening of sexual feeling to girls – 'claims' innocence in relation to boys, but describes homosexual attraction of Milton to Burton, of himself to Thatcher as drag queen.
156	Doesn't like to act with sexy or provocative women. AG and Robert Shaw – this is the clearest allegation of plainly homosexual feeling . . .

And so on. Listed were some sixteen references or instances of Guinness's alleged homosexuality. He was intimate with shadowy (i.e. gay) men; he kept silent about what he did in private; one performance (Dorrit) was 'shamelessly feminine . . . mutedly camp'. The references to the shifting sands of his sexuality – all going to form 'another link in a chain when read in context with the foregoing': finally, 'the unequivocal relationship with the feminine side'. Patrick Maloney, the lawyer who listed these, at the end simply asked, 'Is the author not simply praising AG for staying in the closet?'

In his covering letter Maloney pointed out that the great majority of the adverse comments in my book fell fairly and squarely within the defence of fair comment, and specifically the right of artistic criticism on plays, productions, acting perform- ances and literary works. The right extended, in the case of Guinness whose 'extraordinary personality (or lack of one) per- vades all his most celebrated work, to the kind of "psychoanalysis" which forms a large part of the book'.

He went on that the one aspect that stepped over the line from fair comment into allegation of fact and gave him serious concern, was the persistent undercurrent of insinuations that Guinness was in some sense homosexual, either deeply repressed who seldom if ever practised, or otherwise an active homosexual who had long led a secret life – the list he attached were examples pointing in this direction. Maloney further observed that the law which is based on interpreting what allegations the reasonable man could regard as injurious to reputation can change with time. It was highly like that 'homosexuality now being legal, it has ceased to be a defamatory allegation per se (unlike, say, dishonesty)'. However, he cited the recent Jason Donovan case (in 1994) which showed it was still highly defamatory to accuse a public person who puts himself forward as heterosexual of being gay, because it implied deceit and hypocrisy towards the public. An even more recent case would be that of Tom Cruise, who in 2001 was reported to have begun suing a writer for seventeen million dollars over a similar allegation.

The solicitor put forward three further considerations: the first that because Guinness had been married for almost all of his adult life any homosexual practice would be a form of adultery; the second that for most of Alec's adult life, pre-1967, homosexual practice was a criminal offence, so allegations now of such conduct at that time were certainly defamatory; finally that Guinness was well known to be an ardent Roman Catholic, which added a further element of religious hypocrisy. He advised me that every- thing tending in the direction he had pointed out, i.e. the 'secret life', should be removed although psychoanalytical criticism of Guinness's femininity as a source of his artistic strength could remain.

12 May 2000. I am in the British Library manuscripts room studying the Olivier papers which have just been sold by Olivier's family to the Library for 1.4 million pounds. Alec had a deep suspicion, not to say dislike of Olivier, and, as shown by this collection, the world of Olivier was crammed with enough syco-phants to fill the 160-odd boxes. No king or queen of England could have received more obeisance. If gratitude, according to La Rochefoucauld, 'is merely the secret hope of further favours', here is a monumental roll-call of such secret hopes. One wonders if and when the Guinness archive is opened to the public, what revelations about his character will be forthcoming.

Royalty never had as much power or patronage to dispose of as Olivier had before, during and after running the National Theatre from 1963–73 – 'This bloody thing I am attempting'. As if in acknowledgement of this fact royalty itself, and even Mrs Thatcher, bowed and scraped to him – as well as most of the up-and-coming stage and screen hopefuls; I saw letters from Kenneth Branagh, letters supporting Anthony Andrews's membership of the Garrick, John Mills's aspiration to knighthood, Michael Caine wanting residency status in the United Kingdom – 'I can vouch for him,' proclaims Olivier; there is Peter Shaffer needing a reference to say he would pay his rent. Why should Olivier have wanted to keep all this trivia? Marlene Dietrich, Gregory Peck, Noël Coward ('I love you' he tells Larry over and over again), Larry Adler, Bogie and those two would-be – posthumously and absurdly claimed – male lovers of Olivier, Richard Burton and Danny Kaye. The whole assembly bowed and scraped – why? Maybe as Swift wrote, 'climbing is but horizontal crawling'. Olivier had little sense of truth, of being able to distinguish between what was real and what was false: he responded to gesture.

What a feast is here (Hamlet might have said) of the great celebrity world: flatter that you may be flattered – a gram of hypocrisy is worth a kilo of ambition. The ambitious Olivier naturally excelled more than everyone else at collecting and keeping this display of refulgent voices to propel him into everlast-ing orbit (and to some extent compensate him for the insubstantial nature of the actor's fame). When George Cukor is honoured in Hollywood, Olivier who cannot be at the ceremony, writes, 'After so many years of so much love my heart is with you bouncing as from a mighty trampoline. I only wish my arms were around you on your glorious occasion.' Nothing succeeds like excess and Olivier in hyperbole outstripped everyone: so this must surely be the biggest collection of wind ever assembled in large cardboard boxes and then handsomely sold: 'Do I call you Lord Larry, or Sir Laurence, or Larry old boy, or dear old Larry darling . . .'

Not surprisingly one looks to Alec Guinness to be in some form the antidote to this general sycophancy. One is not disappointed. Alec played the humble part of Osric when Olivier played Hamlet at Elsinore, with Vivien Leigh as Ophelia. Osric stole the three-minute scene with Olivier: 'audacious, witty, wicked,' said Kay Walsh. Leigh and Olivier's clandestine affair under the nose of Jill Esmond, Olivier's first wife, was at its height. 'Everyone knew that Viv was a sexual dervish especially with Larry, and she probably put all the rest of us to shame in the bedroom,' said Margaret Leighton. But she was racked with insecurity: she was torn, a friend wrote to Olivier, 'with the anxiety of whether you were fucking someone else or not . . . when a girl has fucked a bit she finds it difficult to understand constancy.' When Vivien gave Olivier her everlasting and absolute love, quoting to him in a letter when their marriage was not going too well –

A woman's last word.
> Let's be content no more, love;
> Be a God and hold me with charm,
> Be a man and fold me with thine arm.
> Teach me my only heart: I must a little weep, for foolish me

– signing herself 'Baaa', Olivier promptly betrayed her with another.

These insecurities were formative in that, where Alec was concerned, in the third-person way he referred to himself, 'one' desired not to imitate them. And Alec, like Ralph Richardson, was a little different to the rest in his relationship to Olivier. Richardson teased and indirectly expressed his feelings to Olivier through his mask of allowed eccentricity. Like Richardson, Alec never really trusted Olivier and never allowed himself to be patronized or employed by Olivier at the National Theatre, or in Olivier's

other enterprises. Alec told me, when I met him, that his relationship with Olivier, since he played the Fool to his King Lear and
won the better notices, had been a distant one.

It would seem, from my reading through the Olivier papers,
that Alec used his self-deprecation as a form of self-defence:
continually run yourself down – what more successful antidote
could there be to exaggerated displays of false emotion? It was a
habit Alec used much to defuse envy, yet gain his own kind of
power and respect. Make yourself a small target and most will
miss you. To substantiate this I found in the British Library an
undated letter from Alec to Larry (probably written in the 1950s
when Alec's film career at its height far surpassed Olivier's): 'I
suspect I am the laziest actor in the world and always ill-
prepared . . .' while at another time, at the end of the 1960s, just
after a big West End success he wrote, 'I'm just going thru' a
weary, jaded phase knowing I'm not very good at the acting and
not greatly caring.'

Olivier, who was noted to be – and on his own admission too
– the great magpie and stealer of – well, just about everything –
was in awe or attracted by Alec's conversion to Roman Catholicism
in the 1950s. At a later period, just after the publication of his
Confessions of an Actor in 1982, and when he was quarrelling with
Joan Plowright, his third wife (so that they had recourse to their
separate lawyers), he felt he might assume the mantle of Alec's
Catholic conversion. He therefore wrote to Alec telling him that
he was seriously considering conversion to Roman Catholicism
as an answer to his tormenting problems, especially those of his
identity and his marriage to Joan Plowright. Alec mentioned this
request Olivier made to him in December 1983 as to how he
should go about converting to Roman Catholicism: 'I have had
Mass said for you at Farm Street . . . [the Jesuit church opposite
the Connaught Hotel where Alec always stayed in London – the
needs of the sybarite and acolyte sides of Alec's personality made
the propinquity of the Connaught and Farm Street fortunate] and
spent a fortune in candles.'

If Olivier wanted to see a 'Roman priest', Alec told him, he
would recommend someone at the Brompton Oratory, naming
Rev. Sir Hugh Barrett-Lennard, whom he described as probably a
saint; 'deeply eccentric, forgets to shave half his face, wears filthy

clothes, goes everywhere on a broken cycle and has alarming penetrating black eyes and very elaborate manner'.

In the upshot Olivier declined this confrontation and denied his soul its Roman salvation: he went elsewhere for spiritual fulfilment during the last years of his life, quaffing greater and greater draughts of fame. Elsewhere in this correspondence Alec confessed to him, just to make him feel good and put him at ease, 'I'm a pretty lousy Catholic, though I love the Church (in spite of some of its ghastly supermarket modern ways).' This was a common theme in letters and conversation: he told the novelist Piers Paul Read, who interviewed him, that the Church in America distressed him, in particular in Boston and New York, where he was shocked by offensive behaviour: he later reported 'I could clearly see, through the grille [in a New York Franciscan church] that the young priest was masturbating. Not stimulated by anything I said, I am sure.'

Six years later, after Olivier's death, it was natural that the acting profession should turn, when the memorial service was held in Westminster Abbey, to Alec to deliver the address. This was in spite of the fact that Alec did not seem to entertain that high a regard for Joan Plowright. Being called upon to deliver an oration for Olivier was an honour he felt he could not refuse. 'I am terrified of making the address about Larry,' he confided to me in 1989 when we talked – it happened to be just before the event – 'with two ex-wives in the audience' (as well as Joan Plowright, Jill Esmond would also be there). 'I have been to the Abbey to test the acoustics. They are so bad you have to speak very slowly.'

The address had to last eight minutes. 'I've written my piece. I am not going to make a single reference to any contemporary.' As he spoke to me about Olivier, Alec allowed his eyes, from between their now rather yellow eyelids, to circle the room and then swivel round on me, while he swept back with a hand from where it fell the ash of his Players Cut No. 1 cigarette.

> You know . . . Larry, I liked him and he was very nice to me
> but I knew how to survive him . . . He completely destroyed
> Redgrave. He tried to destroy Scofield, not deliberately but
> by animal cunning, instinctively. Also he could be very

pretentious, do things quite unnecessarily, silly things to show off.

When it came to the moment of the memorial service on 11 July 1989 the British nation seemed to go right over the top. The pomp was up there on the scale of a coronation. Olivier, a mere performer, an 'actor-laddy', was turned into something on the enormous and portentous American scale of treatment for its nation's fantasy life. Two thousand people attended. Some thought, after the grotesque ten years he had spent playing in expensive but bad films, the ceremony was ludicrously overdone. His Order of Merit was carried in procession by Douglas Fairbanks Jr, a film award by Michael Caine, and the sword once owned by Edmund Kean by Frank Finlay. It seemed more like idolatry than ceremony. John Gielgud recited in his perfect voice, described by Alec as a 'silver trumpet muffled in silk' (this sounds a good idea, but has anyone ever tried it?), Donne's 'Death be not proud' over yet another of his great contemporaries.

To many who were there Alec seemed to be the one person who was not unduly overawed. After giving a generous, non-sycophantic appreciation of Olivier as an actor and as a person, with a precisely tactful sense of weight, he gently deflated Olivier, telling how, when he played Malvolio interrupting the midnight riot of Sir Toby and his companions, he changed the line:

My masters are you mad, or what are you?

into

My masters are you mad, or what? *pause* Are you?

He delivered this so perfectly it brought to the Abbey a great, relaxing sigh of laughter. He went on to say that if you were on stage with Olivier and there was something you were doing of which he did not quite approve (the suggestion being that you were perhaps doing something a little too well) he 'could go very still and give you a steely look . . .' Thus Alec indicated, very slightly, that the worm could turn, and not in a sympathetic way at all. This brought, his old friend Peter Copley remarked, a sense that this god was a fallible creature. The occasion became real.

But there was a deeper reason for Alec's caution. All this

elaborate footwork and deception, for professional and social reasons, over the years, concealed a truth in the Olivier–Guinness relationship, which explained why, Guinness told a colleague and friend, he 'never really liked' Olivier (to put it mildly and politely, as was his way).

This went back to the early days, when in 1936–7 Alec played Osric and understudied Olivier's Hamlet in the production by Gielgud's company. Alec had already played Osric to Gielgud's Hamlet in 1935, and there must have been speculation (because in spite of often disparaging him Gielgud had clearly taken a shine to the actor ten years his junior) that because of Gielgud's well-known promiscuity at this time they were having a sexual liaison.

One night he was staying at Gielgud's cottage in Harpsden, the weekend country retreat John shared with his lover John Perry. Also dining with Gielgud, who was single that evening, were Olivier and Vivien Leigh. At the end of the evening they asked Alec if he would like a lift with them back to London, and Alec said no, innocently adding that he would come back the next day with John.

Upon this, Alec, in recounting this episode to Simon Callow, said he saw Olivier and Vivien exchange looks (as if to say, 'Well, well, we know what that means.'). Alec went to bed – 'he didn't so much as lay a finger on me' he said of John – and next day arrived at the Old Vic and dressed for the performance. When he stood in the wings waiting for his entrance, Larry came up to him – big louche manner, winking at him in a horrible way:

'Well, well,' he said. 'Did he put it in you, or did you put it in him?' Alec told Callow he was so angry, from that moment on he never liked Olivier. Tom Sutcliffe confirmed this incident, telling me that on one of the seven or eight occasions he was taken to lunch and dinner by Alec, he 'spent some time telling me how he didn't like being assumed to be an intimate little friend of John Gielgud's by Larry Olivier and his first wife.'

So, had insisted Alec, contrary to the rumours, Gielgud never made a pass at him. But if Alec didn't sleep with Gielgud he didn't escape him either. 'He was very impatient with the young, impatient of people's stiffness, of slovenly speaking. In York he heard me ask for a vanilla ice. Down the table came the spitting sound, 'There is no 'r' in *vanilla*'. You never escaped him. Everything in my generation stems back to Gielgud.'

*

It was Samuel Butler's words about man's 'Three Most Important Things' – his private parts, his money and his religious opinions (fondly quoted by Alec) which galvanized me therefore on a definite trail into the hidden and unknown, the mists and mysteries that composed Alec Guinness. The shrines found along the way were the characters he impersonated – intimately connected, most of them, to those 'Three Most Important Things.'

Much of my attempted tracking from now on reminds one of that aged courtier Polonius in *Hamlet*, who was based in real life on Elizabeth I's wily courtier and mentor, Lord Burghley. He advises his son, 'By indirections find directions out'. The original master of spying, Burghley hides behind the arras: 'I will find where truth is hid,' he says. Mainly by indirections, then, could I track (or chart) the strange progress of Alec's life during his lifetime. Now, some time after his death, the signposts stand out more clear – at least some of them – although they may point to deceive or lead you away, off the path or down the incline you came. But are they more than signposts and does one, in writing about Alec, ever arrive at destinations? The process of writing about him has somewhere been described (appropriately in a reference I have lost) as trying to find a fingerhold on a smooth and gently shining piece of plastic.

Attempting to trace the certainties – or uncertainties – of Alec's homosexual life is an intriguing as well as integral part of the whole mystery of his personal hinterland. I have absolutely no doubt that for some time in his life, and possibly even all of it, Alec had love affairs with men. Often these were romantic infatuations from which Alec would withdraw, hurt and unfulfilled, after trying in vain to express his yearnings or chase his quarry. Sometimes, but not always, he would seem to have profited from the role of the rejected lover in which he found himself. He never looked to analysis for a cure for the pain suffered, and would have agreed with Edward Thomas, the poet, who wrote, 'But seriously, I wonder whether for a person like myself whose most intense moments were those of depression, a cure that destroys that depression may not destroy the intensity – a desperate remedy.'

In the matter of sex, I speculate, Alec would recoil from, or feel guilt over, the acts of love themselves, probably mindful of the words of the sonnet:

> The expense of spirit in a waste of shame
> Is lust in action.

This did not mean he was deterred from being tempted again and again to seek union with men to whom he was attracted and most likely he gave in to temptation when the chances of discovery were minimal and the other person willing.

Most members of the older theatrical scene (for example, Angela Fox, Simon Callow, Ned Sherrin, Sheridan Morley and his father Robert, Peter Copley, Corin Redgrave, Robert Hardy, Eileen Atkins, Michael Codron, Ronald Harwood) knew by reputation that Alex was bisexual, while many believed that he participated early on in casual sex with young male prostitutes. No one seems to know exactly when or where – Liverpool or Rome? Malta? Shaftesbury Avenue? That it was rather more in the spirit of Abel Drugger than of Oscar Wilde, I have little doubt, while the prospect of being caught frightened him. As has been pointed out, English society, even going back as far as Elizabethan times, tolerated homosexuality only as long as one was not caught at it. To this extent, it could, during past times of legal proscription, be compared to Roman Catholicism.

While no evidence can be found that the Liverpool incident is true either it, or something very similar, happened at the time he was pursuing at least intermittently an active homosexual life. To have been caught must have scared Alec deeply. For better or worse, naked sexual detail today is the lingua franca of biography, so his preferences might be, as far as his friends have talked about them to me, noted. Richard Ellmann does not, in his biography of Oscar Wilde, diminish Wilde's stature or appeal, nor weaken our sympathy and understanding of him by describing, in his account of his sexual affair with Robert Ross, son of Canada's Attorney-General, that Wilde 'was not attracted to anal coition, so Ross presumably introduced him to the oral and intercrural intercourse he practises later'. We have already recorded Alec's disgust at Olivier's crude suggestions of anal penetration when Alec and John Gielgud spent the night under the same roof.

Many of Alec's closest friends, however, could not be so specific. One of them may yet come forward and say more. Eileen Atkins told me, 'I cannot fathom his sexuality.' She would like, probably in a way similar to most of his loving friends, to rest her case in, 'People will make up things. Alec had longings and became a Roman Catholic.' She also reports that she told Piers Paul Read, in the course of a long interview, that on the basis of Alec's enthusiasm over Robert Nye's fictional account (in his novel *Mrs Shakespeare*) of Shakespeare practising anal intercourse with his wife, 'that I thought Alec just liked buggery – but it was all always with the second-best bed' (a reference to another sexual partner, presumably). Eileen discussed this subsequently with Jean Marsh and Mark Kingston, other close friends of Alec, who told her emphatically that 'Alec could not bear the thought of buggery – it made him ill.' Eileen regretted what she had said, and telephoned Read to withdraw her previous statement.

Like most of Alec's friends, they knew of the bisexual side of Alec, but were short on details. Alec would no doubt have wished it so. Did he record them for himself in his diaries? Most unlikely. Atkins, who told me Kay Walsh, David Lean's wife, once accused her of having an affair with Alec, had assumed, when seen in public with him, that most theatre people thought she was a 'beard' – a female escort who at events such as Oscar ceremonies made him appear 'straight'. Once again, one feels, she was to some extent played with, manipulated by Alec, the master game-player. She had her reservations about him too: she said to me, rather cryptically, 'I thought something else about him and I still loved him.'

To Alec, it seems, it was part of the game, the constructive deceits that from the First World War, earlier even, made up and continue to form a fascinating strand of European cultural and political history. Roger Casement, Alfred Rendl (the Austrian spy hero of Osborne's *A Patriot for Me*), Burgess and Maclean, Anthony Blunt – and so on, the list indicates a whole stratum of the espionage game which became a British obsession. The connections between literature and the secret service were to provide Alec in the future with roles based on Kim Philby, the master technician of betrayal, and Maurice Oldfield, the head spycatcher. As well as being terrified of disclosure, Alec relished and enjoyed this side of his life, probably with his customary ironic detachment. 'The extreme artistry of not being who you are,' Peter Wood described it to me, recounting the anecdote of Emlyn Williams arriving one winter's night in his Rolls-Royce at a remote Welsh inn. (Emlyn and Alec were also 'very close', someone else tells me.) When asked about it the landlady replied, 'Oh it was a terrible night, the snow was deep, the wind howled, it froze everywhere – and he's a saint, you know, that man Emlyn Williams, he insisted on the chauffeur sharing his bed!'

'With Vita [Sackville-West] and Virginia [Woolf] leading the dance, who could not follow?' was Wood's assessment of the period between the wars. It was this passionate and sexually well-orchestrated affair (in Nigel Nicolson's account) which, like the fabled Helen of Troy, launched a thousand lesbian and homosexual printed revelations. Alec eminently and mysteriously qualifies for honorary Bloomsbury status. For the duality was part of the game, the Great Game which does not only 'belong to Kim' – in Wood's words, 'you finesse as best you may'. This was an area in which Alec showed consummate mastery.

In his acting, too –

> Le Carré met his match in Alec playing Smiley ... [in *Smiley's People*]. I thought one of the marvellous things about him was the way he could marshal the various things like the legion of betrayals, because he understood himself what it was to be unfaithful – to break faith with yourself (that was a hefty thing!) and whoever it is ... and what it demands of oneself.

As Wood pointed out to me, it was all reversible; in other words Alec could play Smiley 'beyond belief', because he knew what it was like not to live up to his own principles.

There were strong traits of unstraightforwardness in Alec. His close friends sometimes felt these keenly. Eileen Atkins and he had some bad rows. She hated him (in her most feminist period, she says) when she was performing in a one-woman show (as Virginia Woolf) because of the self-righteous tone of his rigid Catholic views about contraception. When, rather condescendingly, he talked about these to her it put her in a terrible rage. A more serious rift developed when, aged forty, she was asked by Patrick Garland, then directing the Chichester Festival, what part she would like to come and play in Shakespeare and she said Portia. 'It's such a tricky play to make work with an audience,' said Garland and asked who she thought should be cast as Shylock. Alec, she answered straight away. She did not hear anything further until one day Garland phoned and said Alec was going to play Shylock, but that 'Alec wanted to do it all with boys.' She was dropped. So, finally, was the all-male idea, but when she challenged Garland about herself and Portia she was told, 'Alec said I was too old.' What angered and offended her was that Alec did not have the openness to tell her himself but left it to Garland. She felt he behaved not only unethically, but also disgracefully towards her as a friend. Alec, at pains to make amends, sent her a 'bland' letter to try and placate her. One cannot but feel that Atkins was the right age to play Portia, but that Alec feared her, feared that her power and subtlety, her maturity, would show up his masterful but miniature character performance. He wanted a Portia who would not be able to attain Atkins's controlled passion. She would have run rings round him. Eileen and Alec effected a rather formal and elaborate reconciliation over lunch with Jean Marsh as umpire. Eileen also claims Alan Bennett, for all their dinners together, 'didn't like him particularly . . . Alec was cross because he preferred Merula.' It does seem, from these accounts, we are back in Bloomsbury. John Bird said much the same: 'Alan didn't approve of Alec very much. He thought him selfish.'

One has to remain cautious. Personal sexuality is never mentioned or evaluated by Alec in his writings, nor does one expect it to be. 'One simply refuses to put on a performance of one's private personality,' he said at different times in many forms.

9. A Warbler on a Cherry Tree

Leaving the tortured introverted genius of Lawrence/Ransom, to whose whole portrayal, wrote W. A. Darlington in the *Daily Telegraph*, Alec brought 'a sense of the concentration and integrity that belong to genius,' he next chose, in July 1939, to demonstrate his prowess as Romeo, the role of the full-blooded lover. In a bizarre touch Alec wore Olivier's 1935 Romeo costume for what apparently became comedy burlesque more than tragedy. It is hard to understand how it fitted, for Alec was considerably shorter, but it did. The wardrobe mistress had seen fit to adorn its dark red velvet with glittering spangles, so Alec, reacting to this with fury, made a tiny plasticine statuette of the mistress, sticking a needle in her left foot (Merula prevailed upon him not to impale her more vital parts). The poor lady then dropped a red-hot iron on her foot.

The first night was another bit of self-Schadenfreude, for to top the sequins Alec wore a red wig and a droopy moustache (presumably red). Was this because he thought it appropriate for the Perth Scottish Theatre Festival? Why did he so often want to disguise himself, even as Romeo? On the first night the garden wall he leapt over fell down and as he spouted the most famous (and most mocked) Shakespearean lines of all, the balcony toppled over revealing his Juliet, a prim ex-Queen Victoria, in her nightie. In the tomb with his 'Thus with a kiss I die' he transferred his upper lips' reddish growth to his dead consort's lips.

Romeo was above and beyond him somewhere; he chose to forget it and fortunately the disaster had happened in faraway Perth. It was with relief he journeyed south to the Waterloo Road to begin rehearsals for another Michel Saint-Denis production of Chekhov, this time of *The Cherry Orchard*, some of which he had rehearsed before at the London Theatre Studio. Edith Evans was cast as Madame Ranevsky, Peggy Ashcroft as Anya.

Edith Evans was not much over fifty, much admired by the younger, gentler sort of actors such as Alec and, in particular, by Michael Redgrave, whose infatuation for her bordered on obsession. She had witnessed the formative shame of Alec's dismissal from William Wycherley's *The Country Wife*, in the Old Vic 1936–7 season: he had started rehearsing in the role of Sparkish, and Ruth Gordon, the American star who was playing Mrs Pinchwife, had told Guthrie, 'Please! I can't act with this young man', so he had been dismissed. Edith Evans consoled him by saying that he was not right for the part.

In *The Cherry Orchard* Alec was cast as the student Trofimov, with the salary of twenty-eight pounds a week. Cyril Cusack, fresh from Ireland and intimidated at working with the exacting Saint-Denis, sidled over to address the actor with the lofty 'Irish patronymic . . . one that ranks among the Lords of the North' as he put it. The Guinness name, he mused, originally 'Mac Aonghusa, son of Aongus, God of the Birds'. He had not been disappointed, or so he reported, for 'Mr Guinness admitted diffidently there might have been an ancestral shade or two hovering, however mistily, amidst the hills of Donegal'. Alec was not above using the effect his name produced on others.

On the morning of 3 September, a Sunday, the by-now demoralized company of *The Cherry Orchard* assembled in the Queen's Theatre to hear the worst. Binkie Beaumont, the producer, told them, 'Theatres will be closed, productions will be cancelled. The future is just too gloomy and uncertain. I'm very afraid that we will have to call a halt.' While the body of the cast sat on stage Binkie, Bronson Albery, Gielgud, John Perry and Saint-Denis sat in the front stalls. At eleven o'clock, from a portable wireless they heard Neville Chamberlain declare war on Germany, followed by the testing of West End air-raid sirens sounding a false, wailing scream. Edith Evans started to panic and Binkie had to calm her. 'Fated never to reach the gods but condemned to limbo at the first off-stage roar of Mars,' concluded Cusack, who as an Irish citizen was not liable for military service.

'Alec, take me for a walk,' Edith Evans commanded. They

walked arm-in-arm slowly along Piccadilly to Hyde Park. Edith
Evans delivered a tirade at the slender young actor: 'I can't act
with bombs falling: what am I going to do?' . . . and so on and so
on. The future dead, the future dying, the young men lost, the
devastation: no concern for any of this, only her own career. Alec
felt chilled.

But Alec and Merula had other thoughts on their minds, for
Merula about this time or a little later in the month conceived
their first and only child; at such a time this was an expression of
optimism and hope for the future, as well as recognition, perhaps,
that Alec would have to go away and fight and possibly never
come back.

Beaumont gave a farewell lunch for Saint-Denis who forthwith
returned to France to join the infantry (he was shortly to return
with De Gaulle). Gielgud, after a cordial farewell, left the lunch
early. All theatres, by government order, were closed and the West
End became deserted.

This was not for long. By the following spring the theatres had
reopened. In the meantime, still in the autumn and winter of 1939,
Alec formed a little company with George Penne, Vera Lindsay
(later Poliakov, later Lady Russell), Martita Hunt and Marius
Goring, which they called the Actors' Company to put on 'intelligent' work. Alec, whose English at school had been good, had
literary as well as acting ambitions. He adapted *Great Expectations*,
and this was their first choice for production. They hired the
Rudolf Steiner Hall in Baker Street and planned to follow the
Dickens with *King John* and a Molière play: money was raised
from Marius Goring (£200), the department store John Lewis
(£10), and unexpectedly Edith Evans insisted on contributing
£700, the price of the most recent fur coat she had bought. 'I
can't let actors be out of work when I spend £700 on a fur coat,'
she told them.

Great Expectations, which was George Devine's first professional production, was, according to Alec, very good and also
very popular. Alec, who had earlier worked with George Devine
in Michel Saint-Denis's productions, played Herbert Pocket,
Marius Goring Pip, and Martita Hunt Miss Havisham. Merula
did the narration for the adaptation; she was becoming notice-
ably pregnant and when she told her mother, Chattie Salaman,

mother of six, she railed at her, 'How dare you bring a child into this filthy world?'

Alec's personal triumph was the role he himself chose to play. Herbert Pocket was 'The quintessential best friend, always on the sidelines, it would have been a surprising choice for any actor-playwright except Guinness,' wrote Guinness's first biographer, John Russell Taylor:

> and even with Guinness it was odd, because Pocket is such an open, sociable, communicative creature, the absolute opposite of Guinness's usual tortured solitary or droll misfit. It was a performance which so charmed people that they remembered. And among those who remembered, so it would seem, was a certain young film editor called David Lean.

Great Expectations ran for six weeks during the blackout, but they were thwarted in their hopes of transfer to the Shaftesbury Theatre and made a loss. During the run Alec met for the first time Edith Sitwell, who came backstage with her brother Osbert; she had sent Alec a book, and subsequently invited him to lunches at her Sesame Club where he met literary celebrities.

Alec may not have been suited to Romeo, but his next Shakespearean role was as Ferdinand in *The Tempest*. First though came *Cousin Muriel*, an unsuccessful Clemence Dane comedy at the Globe Theatre in which he played the juvenile lead and was paid thirty pounds a week. Peggy Ashcroft played the young feminine lead. Peggy, between affairs and with her failed marriage to Komisarjevsky not very far behind her, lived a nervous up-and-down private life. In an anecdote Alec often repeated to friends Edith Evans, restored to the stage as the play's middle-aged *éminence*, who was actually a kleptomaniac, gave way to hysteria during one rehearsal because she thought Alec, cast as her advertising-agent son Richard, in defending the way he played a line to 'Mummy' about stealing and financial fiddles, which she disliked and objected to, did not love her.

'Alec doesn't love me any more! ... He *hates* me!' screamed Evans, and threw herself down on stage, drumming with her feet, seizing (allow for hyperbole) and tearing the corner of the Persian rug between her teeth. Alec, recounting this episode in *Blessings in*

Disguise, failed to add how Peggy caught Edith's contagious hysteria and became so distressed she also threw herself down on stage wailing and screaming. Nor did Alec dare to report Peggy's sudden spates of bad language. When at one point she trod on her dress and tore it, she yelled, 'Shit!' Gielgud, also in the play, told me, 'So striking the way she did it. So striking!'

In *The Tempest* Gielgud's 'family' at the Old Vic was gathering for the last time before they were dispersed in battle. Gielgud was Prospero, Lewis Casson Gonzalo, while Jessica Tandy began as Miranda, to be replaced not long after by Peggy Ashcroft. Jack Hawkins played an excellent Caliban, and Marius Goring Ariel, in a production again directed by George Devine. Later, much later, Jessica Tandy commented in an article on leading actors that Alec was 'the most vulnerable actor I'd ever seen, terribly good, but if you said "boo" he'd die'. The vulnerability stayed with him, the difference being that in time he learned the secret of how to hide it.

Sybil Thorndike and Lewis Casson's son John had joined the Fleet Air Arm. He was in charge of a dive-bomber squadron on HMS *Ark Royal* when he was shot down over Norway by a Messerschmidt. Sybil went along to tell Lewis before one matinee of *The Tempest* that the Admiralty had telephoned that John was 'missing, believed killed'. As they played, every line about the drowned Ferdinand appeared to refer to his loss. Casson insisted on going on, but when Ferdinand and Miranda are discovered playing chess in the grotto, and father and son are reunited, Casson broke down and wept on stage. But John was not dead, and later he was reported captured by the Germans.

During *The Tempest*, in June 1940, Merula gave birth to Matthew Guinness at the Denmark Hill Hospital. 'Merula had a rather beastly time,' Alec noted. He saw his son between a matinee and evening performance. While the wartime trips to Denmark Hill were 'time-consuming and fretful', he grudgingly concedes, 'We had a son in whom we rejoiced.' He seemed to be more aware, at the time, of himself in his dazzling white costume designed by Oliver Messel with a great ruff of pipe-cleaners which bent or fell off, than the new little infant. Yet the birth of his son meant a great deal to him: with Merula and Matthew he now had his own family.

It marked the beginning of a new phase. By now Alec had enlisted in the Royal Navy, and was waiting for call-up. Twenty-six years of age, he had a wife, a son, and in the past six years had played thirty-four parts in twenty-three plays by Shakespeare, Sheridan, Pinero, Chekhov, Shaw and others. To a small loyal public he was something of a star. From an early life of dark contrasts, some of it rarefied and genteel yet some of it ugly and threatening, he was poised to enter a much larger universe.

*

It was a daunting if backward-looking social network that the Guinnesses were making for themselves since their marriage and in the early years of war, yet one that was to stand them in good stead during the immediate post-war years. The Bloomsbury circle was very choosy, but through Augustus and Gwen John they met Duncan Grant and Alec later befriended Keith Grant, with whom he would discuss painting at the Garrick Club. Peggy Ashcroft, through her friendship with George Rylands and Gielgud, and on the eve of war through her hasty marriage to Jeremy Hutchinson (whose mother Mary had a very public affair with Clive Bell), familiarized Alec and Merula with others in this circle. When they were in London the couple stayed with Peggy at 92 Camden Hill Road.

They moved out when Matthew was born and went to stay in a bungalow in Ockley, Surrey, on the edge of a wood near the Salaman family home, rented for seven shillings a week. The young Guinnesses continued to see much of Edith Sitwell. Her arrival in Alec's life gave rise to one of the best character vignettes in his first book: 'Immensely tall, although slightly stooped and in her early fifties . . . the long, oval face was chalk-white, the mouth small, thin and straight.' Their meeting, which I call historic because Alec was to follow Sitwell later into the Catholic Church, took place in the 'front parlour of the Sesame and Imperial Pioneer Ladies' Club in Grosvenor Street'. At the subsequent lunches, teas and one supper, Alec met her glamorous guests, among them the art historian Kenneth Clark and his wife, Stephen and Natasha Spender, Arthur Waley, Dylan and Caitlin Thomas, William Plomer and Somerset Maugham. Sitwell hosted these parties with 'grave courtesy, like a Plantagenet queen' and here for

Alec was a new grand pantomime dame, in her loony majesty, to rival those of his childhood and purge the evil fairy of Agnes de Cuffe. Was she real? Could she ever be real? She would denounce the Bloomsburyans. 'Virginia Woolf's writing is no more than glamorous knitting; I believe she must have a knitting pattern-book.'

Edith and her two brothers lived entirely in their own world. The friendship with Alec flourished, enhanced by Merula's supposed ancestor Hereward the Wake ('treated by Edith as a sort of cousin, at a vast number of removes'). The Sitwells went way back too, for early members of the family defended Charles I in the Civil War then became the principal world manufacturers of iron nails. Like the Salamans, in time the family became fox-hunting Tory squires and dilettantes, bankrupts and again became nouveau riche when in the late nineteenth century they found coal seams under their Derbyshire loam.

During that summer of the phoney war Edith did in fact sit well (as portrayed later in a Peter Cook sketch) – and knit. 'The unceasing misery, wretchedness, and, in minor ways, the boredom! . . . It is so dreadful seeing all these poor young men on the brink of this ghastly catastrophe,' she wrote to Anthony Powell, the novelist. She knitted for Alec, calling Merula 'a most sweet young creature', she knitted for Matthew, while she and her brother Osbert, aged forty-seven, settled down to spend the war years together. Many denounced the brother and sister, together with their brother Sacheverell, as literary curiosities of the 1920s. They reflected a society, wrote one critic, 'where dilettante art-worship is synonymous with culture'; best leave, wrote Geoffrey Grigson, these 'bower-birds, shining oddments of culture . . . mimicking, like starlings, the product of more harmonious throats . . . Best leave these minimal creatures, these contemptible elvers, wriggling away in their dull habitat.'

Alec enjoyed their attention. When Edith invited him to Weston Hall in Northamptonshire she introduced him to 'Sachie', who invited him to try some of George IV's snuff. 'I sniffed up a grain which lodged near my adenoids for several hours.' Alec noticed the curious, fastidious and disapproving glint in his eyes. A little later, when Alec was on a three-month tour with Robert Ardrey's *Thunder Rock*, in which he took over the lead of

Charleston from Michael Redgrave, who had played at the Globe Theatre, Edith persuaded Osbert to invite the Guinnesses to the Derbyshire family seat.

'Sachie liked talking about sex. Osbert very shy,' wrote Evelyn Waugh in his diary after a visit to the dark and forbidding Renishaw Hall. About the Hall's brooding presence, wrote Sacheverell, 'There was something of the extinct monster.' Victoria Glendinning, one of Edith's biographers, called the gardens, soon to be turned over to wartime's self-supporting vegetables, 'the best metaphor for Edith's submerged sexuality'. Sacheverell wrote of her:

> I have known no being so imprisoned in poetry
> As if besieged, embattled there . . .

Another visitor, another time, had this to say of them and their circle:

> The night before they had all dressed up as nuns, that morning they had all dressed up as shepherds and shepherdesses. In the evening they were all going to dress up as – God knows what – but they begged and implored me to return with them to share their rapture.

Lytton Strachey castigated the dreadful dullness of the Sitwells thus: 'Strange creatures, with just a few feathers where brains should be.' As the raw material of mimetic desire, they appealed to Alec's imagination and we are almost in the post-war world of *Kind Hearts and Coronets*. It was Alec's great gift to connect his fantasy world, the bizarre, the strange, with reason, with sound ordinary-seeming presentation. One recalls the bathos of the lines about the balloon death in *Kind Hearts*:

> I shot an arrow in the air
> She fell to earth in Berkeley Square,

or his shocked aside in *The Lavender Hill Mob* to Stanley Holloway when he opens the door to become aware of the police, 'Oh, helmets in the hall!'

Sturdy as Osbert Sitwell was, substantially built, there was about him a sexual elusiveness which, to his sister's chagrin, had recently flowered into a homosexual liaison. A sense of social

propriety even now his true sexual bent was established made him
unable to acknowledge this. His 'key emotion was fear', said a
friend. He was cautious and irresolute in his first approaches to
men, easily scared off: 'too sensitive and well mannered to press
his suit where he did not find it quickly successful'. He made
passes at William Walton the composer, who told him 'that sort
of thing was not his cup of tea', and he never asked again. 'That
sort of thing' was a favoured phrase of Alec's for homosexual
philandering. Constant Lambert, another composer of the era,
who became an alcoholic and wrote an engaging memoir called
Music Ho!, also came in for his pursuit in 'dormitory games –
scuffling on the sofa'. Lambert rebuffed it easily.

But he had David Horner as his lover; 'lost without you,'
Osbert told him, 'only half a rather depressed vacuum of a man
when you're not with me'.

Horner was a guest at Renishaw Hall when Merula and Alec
arrived, carrying Matthew in the carrycot. They were told Osbert
must not be informed of the baby's presence as babies made him
feel ill. So they smuggled Matthew in like a basket of dirty linen,
and during the day hid him in the walled garden.

In the evening, however, the 'house seemed vast and very dark
and there was much talk of a ghost who appeared periodically on
the staircase disguised as a piece of black lace'. This made Merula
and Alec jittery and when the butler entered to inform them,
'Young Master Guinness is in distress: he is screaming,' Edith
made Merula panic by saying, 'Nothing to worry about, my dear.
I expect the baboon has been looking at him.'

Merula threw down her napkin and sped from the table to
collect Matthew from the 'baboon', who turned out to be an old
housemaid. When she reappeared with the child, Osbert took
Matthew's presence with commendable calm. 'I assure you I do
not mind in the least,' he said, 'as long as you will excuse me
looking at him.'

Edith resented Osbert's intoxication with Horner and Horner's
power to awaken sexual passion in her brother: he was tall,
'slender, with golden curly hair, wide-set eyes, an indecently
smooth and cream complexion and a deep, languorous voice'. It
had been partly the need to contain and control the turmoil of her
feelings about Horner that drove Edith in the mid-1950s to take

the same step he had taken ten years before, for in 1944 Horner had himself converted to Roman Catholicism. Edith wrote to him on 2 April: 'I am certain this is going to bring you great happiness, and that you were absolutely right and absolutely wise to take the step. – I have never understood why people are afraid of constructive rules. Very few people are capable of coming to any great decision, but you have been.' She emphasized how it 'gives one an immense feeling of calm and of peace and security, and a great framework on which to build one's day'. After her own conversion, she remarked of Horner to some of her friends, 'If I had not been a Catholic, I would have murdered him.'

Many years later, the last occasion Alec saw Horner, Osbert and Edith together was at Osbert's castle not far from Florence. The lunch was sticky in spite of the picturesque surroundings. Parkinson's disease had begun to take hold of Osbert. When coffee was served and Osbert lit a cigarette it fell from his trembling hands onto the lace tablecloth but another guest quickly retrieved it and gave it back. Under his breath he asked, 'Did Edith see that?' 'I think not,' Marriot (the friend) replied and Osbert relaxed.

As they were leaving Edith hissed in Alec's ear, 'David Horner is a serpent. I can't tell you of his wickedness.' Alec then remarked that 'She cast her eyes heavenwards as if she was about to be assumed. Presumably it was in order to shake Horner's hand as we said goodbye but I felt uncomfortable doing so.'

On this occasion Alec refers to Horner as Osbert's 'intimate friend over many years', with the implication plain as to what he was. When Alec came to write his own three volumes of autobiography there was a distinct, strong similarity between the discreet tone of his writing and Osbert's, who in his famous volume, according to one biographer, 'was not the sort of man to expose the sexual peccadilloes of others to the world, still less to dwell upon his own'. He gave away virtually nothing about his emotional life; said not a word to indicate that he was homosexual; mentioned David Horner only three times and fleetingly, though referring to him once as 'a very dear friend of mine'. This was the practice Alec followed with Peter Glenville and later with Peter Bull and others who may or may not have been lovers.

Osbert, in his discursiveness, his apparent self-indulgence, owed as much to Lawrence Sterne as he did to Proust. Yet there is another way in which Osbert differed from, perhaps fell below the level of, Proust. His novel *Albertine Disparue – The Sweet Cheat Gone* – agonizingly conveys the horrors of jealousy and frustrated love. Osbert does not deal with passion; the pains of loneliness, of misunderstanding, of rejection, are often evoked with brilliant sympathy, but love is kept at arm's length.

10. Commander Cuffe and the Chintz-Covered Bunk

Alec entered a world of strange contrasts. In writing his life the image I have is of a journey round an old-fashioned seaside pier, perhaps Brighton's Palace Pier; at one point one finds an arcade of glittering, noisy, flashily illuminated wooden cabinets – ball-spinning, coin-spitting (Alec's films to come); in another a hall of distorting mirrors; in yet another a strange costume parade. Strangely haunting, sexually ambivalent characters hang around, either in drag or seedily dressed, smoking cigarettes, or as sequin-suited toffs. Around the pier's perimeter is the mystery train, chugging in and out of sight, emerging for a bit, then disappearing. Then there's a chamber of horrors: Alec's past, the terrors, the angsts.

But now one is down at the pier's base, among the sea-swept pylons, the smelly seaweeds, and the floating, bobbing detritus of man's pleasure and aggression with the tide lapping in and out. And death. Sea-bloated corpses aplenty.

The British navy. The sea. 'You know,' Alec told John Mortimer the playwright when in later life he played the role of Mortimer's father in *A Voyage round my Father*, 'the most difficult part I ever had to play was to be an officer and a gentleman for three years in the navy'. What he left out of this description and never once mentioned in any account of his wartime service, any of his books – nor did any of his friends call attention to it during his lifetime (not even Alan Bennett) – was that he did not play this part, did not join the navy under his own name, Guinness.

In 2001 I found this out when I was given by an old friend of Alec's a typewritten page from an unpublished diary; a curious document. It is worth seeing the whole page:

Extract from Augur East's diaries   Copy to Jake Thom

TUNISIA, Enfidaville   11th May 1943

After dark I went down to the plain with Jake Thom to meet
and lead up to our respective Company positions the battalion
of the French Foreign Legion who were taking over from us.

Walking back in the torrential rain I asked the company
commander if his troops were as cosmopolitan as one was led
to believe. 'Oh, yes' he replied, 'from every country'. 'Except
Germany, I imagine,' I said. 'On the contrary' said he, 'all
my N.C.Os are German. Germans make the best N.C.Os in
the world.'

They were the toughest looking troops I had ever seen.
They carried enormous loads but climbed the mountainside
like goats.

ALGERIA, The Med.   26th June 1943

Embarked at DJIDJELLI in a lean L.C.I. – most unusual –
and sailed at 1700 hours for a thirty-nine hour voyage to
SOUSSE.

Very decent skipper called Cuffe – Lt. Commander,
R.N.V.R., – who offered us the run of his cabin, alcohol and
food. The cabin was immaculate with chintz-covered bunk
and porthole curtains to match, and a tiny bookcase filled
with Shakespeare and the classics.

He spent most of his time on the bridge but I had several
meals with him in the course of which he told me he was an
actor by profession, that his ship had been built in New York
and that while he was there supervising its construction he
had been lucky enough to get the lead in 'Flarepath' on
Broadway. When I said I reckoned I ought to but didn't
recognise his name he said 'No. I use a stage name, I call
myself Guinness – Alec Guinness.'

SICILY, Sferre   19th July 1943

If one was lucky one learned from other people's mistakes as
well as from one's own.

Here we have mysterious proof (who was Augur East? Who
was Jake Thom?) of an extraordinary descent into a kind of
anonymity on Alec's part from the position of one who was now

quite a well-known actor, a distinguished player on the path to knighthood (leading a British Council tour seemed a good qualification), to the deliberate assumption of ordinariness, which was also a disguise. It is bizarre that the role of officer and gentleman should be played by him hidden under the name of his mother. How did he go about it? Did he change his name by deed poll? Did he falsify anything that might identify him? It is evident, partly at least, this move came from mimetic envy – or at least a desire to follow in the footsteps – of Lawrence of Arabia, who after his glory years joined up as Aircraftman Ross.

Piling Pelion on Ossa, Alec continued to write throughout the war to his friends and sign himself as Alec Guinness; none mentioned him as Cuffe, so he must have told those serving with him that Guinness was his stage name.

Was there no end to the oblique and evasive nature of this strange man? The leading English actor who had hobnobbed with the king of Greece in the royal box, had swapped chit-chat with a future queen of England's consort, was now at the other end of the human spectrum in a Dickensian lower depth squalor of naval ratings listed as 'Ordinary Seaman Cuffe'.

Anger exploded when in his eighties he recalled it. He had to sleep (well, rather, spend the night) in Chatham naval barracks bomb-shelter tunnel, which housed up to seven thousand sailors.

Hammocks were slung about three deep and you had to pick your way in semi-darkness through puddles of urine and lumps of vomit. The air was fetid and it took about half an hour to get in or out of the place. Once slung in your hammock a fitful sleep was ripped apart by nightmare cries, resounding farts and endless cursing. Food, in the over-crowded messes, had almost to be fought for, something I refused to do. Often a kind mate would barge his way through the crowd and bring a meal for us both. That embarrassed me so I took to spending a few pennies on chocolate and biscuits at the local store instead of being waited on. At all times you had to listen carefully to the Tannoy system in case your number was called out, summoning you to a ship. That was something we partly dreaded, as it would mean leaving England and family and really facing up to the war; but a ship – even an old, rusty, greasy

merchantman with one feeble gun – would mean escape from
this nineteen-fortyish version of Dante's *Inferno*.

My Name Escapes Me

Actually, was it all that bad, or did it reflect mainly Alec's
mood later? He recollected this in anger, but defensively, because
he had been attacked in the *Spectator* letter columns by a crew
member who was envious of his late-life luxury cruise, as evoked
in a previous article, on the RMS *Mauretania*.

When he first joined up as an enlisted sailor Alec was passed
A1, the doctor curious about his ability to expand his chest – four
inches – which Alec explained as the result of his voice training as
an actor. Drafted as an ordinary seaman to HMS *Raleigh*, a shore
establishment near Plymouth for basic training, he was selected
more or less straightaway as a potential officer but, as in other
branches of the services, everyone had to undergo basic training.

Among his intake was another young actor, Peter Bull, who
had just been confined to hospital for eight weeks after a bad
accident to his ankle occasioned by carrying a sailor piggyback in
the gym which had resulted in a blood clot. Bull, born in 1912,
was twenty-eight when he and Alec met up in the navy. He came
from a high-caste family – his father Sir George Bull was Conservative MP for Hammersmith and later Mayor of Chelsea – and
had been to school at Winchester. As the fifth and last son,
'he was the only gay one,' according to Sheridan Morley, Bull's
godson, 'and his mother's pet'. He possessed that inherent class
authority to which Alec responded, but it was accompanied by a
campness, an eccentricity and an original sense of humour. 'Bully,'
Morley told me, was 'something of an experimentalist who would
veer from stable live-in relationships, often with younger men, to
occasional ventures into the rough trade.' Like Alec, he had been
an actor since 1933, and recently in management had put on a
'provocative' play titled *Adults Only* which took place in 'an
educational settlement in a Lancashire town'. I tried, without
success, to discover its content, but I think one can roughly guess.
Bull joked of his joining the senior service, 'I had better make it
clear at the outset that the sea was not in my blood. And I took
bloody good care that my blood was not in the sea.'

He and Alec were vastly entertained by naval snobbery. 'It was seriously rumoured that the lighting of a cigarette from another rating's cigarette was a breach of behaviour.

'One of my small pleasures was to steal up behind one of my windier companions and hiss: "Got a light, chum?" From the reaction you might have thought I had proposed blowing up the Admiralty.

'Once I even got the steely reply: "You don't say chum, here. You say *old man*".'

Alec had once turned down Bully's offer of a part. Now Bully and he shared whispered jokes on the parade ground, such as that Madame Katina Paxinou, the famous and large Greek tragedienne had, with a coarse suggestiveness, been 'torpedoed'. Bully, said Alec, was a 'great giggler. When we weren't stamping around the parade ground we gravitated towards each other . . . one of my closest friends.' Usual discreet Alec understatement, similar to Osbert's 'a very dear friend of mine'. 'Everyone always knew Alec had a promiscuous side,' Morley said. 'My father Robert told me first Alec and Bully possibly had a sexual affair, Bully was in love with Alec all his life, but Alec never came out. Nor did Peter, like my other godfather Sewell Stokes (who was Isadora Duncan's last lover and with her when she strangled herself with a scarf); Cyril was also very closeted.'

The naughty ambivalence, the constructive deceit, continued to be attractive to Alec. Bull also dabbled in the occult; later he owned a share in an astrological emporium in Kensington High Street. He possessed a gaiety of heart which made Alec laugh a lot; reliable as he was, there was something spontaneously anarchic about him. Whenever he could, in his subsequent film career, Alec asked for Bull to be cast as well. His two most recent film appearances, he confesses in *I Know the Face But* (1956), one of his accomplished series of memoirs – the title itself has a very Guinness flavour – have been in Guinness films. 'Doubly-windy,' he frets about his scene in *Oliver Twist*, 'to appear with close friends, and even Sir Alec Guinness, who is kindness itself on the set, sometimes reduces me to a quivering jelly by his own perfection. I always feel if I am inadequate it will disturb one's personal relationships.' *The Scapegoat* was the second, 'a wonderful experience, taking me to France for three weeks . . . and a lunch party in the studio, which lasted nearly a week, in which I had to eat gorgeous pâté for hours . . .' Bull grew with age to become enormously fat and greedy; he liked to eat three lunches.

Back in 1941, recovered from his blood clot, Bull had to start training again in Alec's intake and became Deputy Class Leader under a 'Scottish Laird of great distinction', named Algernon Ross-Farrow, aged thirty-eight, a volunteer with a weak heart who subsequently left the service. The trio of older trainees (Bull twenty-nine, and Alec at twenty-six the youngest) survived this parade-ground onslaught on their sensibilities. Alec again winced at the irksome conviviality of the ordinary beer-swilling mass of humanity in close proximity to which he was flung without ceremony, complaining there was hardly a quiet corner to which he could retire and read.

The companionship, and more, of Bully apart – they were moved to different stations and did not meet again till May 1943 at Djidjelli harbour, in Algeria where on leave 'that kind of thing' took over – Alec was on his own. (It is reasonable to assume that in Algeria they enjoyed the day and night life together with probable ventures into the rough trade.) Yet in a different compartment of his mind Alec had strong feelings of loneliness and the sense of painful separation from Merula and six-month-old Matthew. It seemed doubly grievous to be taken from the family he had just started when this gave him the most security and comfort, stripped from the accoutrements of his early, even rarefied stardom. He had, it must be established by now, the psychological requisites for a spy or one who leads a double life. He was able to keep different activities (and different personae) in separate, water-tight compartments. Away from England he also enjoyed a certain relief. He was relieved of the terror of having to perform and in particular of first nights. Yet here were other terrors, more real. This was a continuous performance in what he called 'the longest-running show I have ever been in'.

Merula continued acting – she was with the Young Vic at first for a while when Alec was at sea. 'I suppose I was obsessed by acting,' she said in a possibly unique interview she gave in 1992: 'It was something one could bury oneself in. However, there were awful difficulties in having a small boy and going on tour. I thought to myself that it was no way to be a professional actress and I gave it up.'

She could, Laurence Olivier told Sheridan Morley, have been an outstanding actress. She settled down in the handsome old farmhouse, with its grand music room designed by Lutyens where she still practised her ballet steps at the barre (all through life she retained the posture and poise of a dancer). She wrote an ABC for her nephew Christopher which was published in 1941 and applauded for its 'mischievous humour' by the *Times Literary Supplement*: 'Wholly delightful,' the *Spectator* agreed. She followed this with several more illustrated books, then took up painting, attending classes in Chelsea, and began exploring the making of needlework pictures. She, too, continued to correspond with Edith, whose favourite she remained.

Edith in 1941 won a court case for libel in which the defendant claimed the Sitwells had little talent and had been claimed by oblivion, only 'remembered with a kindly, if slightly cynical smile'. At another time she wrote to Alec that she was hoping to be given a house in Bath. 'It is very like a Chekhov play, the idea of a house in Bath. Either one will go on talking about it for ever, and not buy it, or will buy it, and not have the money to live in it.'

Alec discovered when he spent some time at sea as an ordinary seaman and then subsequently attended Lancing College and HMS *King Alfred* in Hove for officers' training, that he preferred his former life as an ordinary seaman, although he must have given to his fellow sailors 'a queer impression of aloofness or shyness or Puritanism'. He found the officers' code of getting drunk dull, expensive and unnecessary. His individuality, he came to feel, was more respected as an ordinary seaman and he commented, 'I don't think the officer class (if such a thing exists now) is so tolerant.'

He had plenty of time to himself. He tried to write a book, an adventure story written from the heart, which, in a letter written towards the end of October 1941, he promised to send to Sydney Cockerell. He also read avidly, particularly Dickens, and was on *Bleak House*.

Sydney Cockerell, whom Alec had met in Cairo, had, as the curator of the Fitzwilliam Museum in Cambridge, built up its collection into one of the finest in England. He was also a connoisseur of people. A servant disciple of Ruskin, a one-time friend and companion of William Morris, Cockerell provided direct links to the greatest writers of the age: he knew Shaw intimately on a literary level, while he had once visited Tolstoy in central Russia just to be in his company for half a day.

While waiting for his shot at a commission Alec served on a variety of ships and felt himself lucky that he was not posted to the Far East for the duration of the war. The solitude gave impetus to his literary ambitions. For a spell he was on shore duty at Inverary, on Lock Fyne, where he passed several months as a sentry in a box on the seashore. He savoured the solitariness and quiet, and on fine moonlit nights the line of the hills and mountains. Here, he told Cockerell, he was able for the first time in his life to meditate, although adding fairly characteristically that he couldn't think much: 'I've a fairly addled brain and am stumped for knowledge whenever any problem presents itself . . . Actors are so hopelessly undisciplined emotionally – this new life is a tonic.'

He was able to see Merula and Matthew on weekend leave every two months or so. Passing through London he would look up old theatrical friends. He met Osbert Sitwell in the Wigmore Hall, who commented to Edith how smart he looked in naval uniform. 'He [Osbert] knows about these things. He was in the Guards,' said Edith. On another leave Alec even found time to record for BBC Radio, in February 1942, the fragment of Menander's newly discovered comedy *The Rape of the Locks*, in which Peggy Ashcroft played a part and so did Alec's old friend Martita Hunt. His mind continued turning to church matters: he was reading widely if unmethodically in St Teresa of Avila, St John of the Cross, the Curé d'Ars and Charles de Foucauld (the Catholic mystic priest whose martyrdom in the desert was to influence T. S. Eliot when he came to write *The Cocktail Party*).

During the war Merula and Matthew lived mostly at Ockley near Michel and Chattie. The London leases of the Salaman estates had started running out, while the servants had left to join up. Michel did the housekeeping. He would come down from London with all kinds of exotic food.

Alec was proud that Cockerell had told him about picnicking with the Tolstoy family in the apple orchard. They had been sitting or lying in the long grass under the trees drinking black tea and eating cucumber spread with honey. Tolstoy took them to the 'billiard' room where the table was hidden under thousands of unopened letters. Even so, Cockerell managed to come away with a copy of a letter written to Tolstoy by 'the late Grand Mufti of Egypt' (as he had told another correspondent more than thirty years before, in 1907). Tolstoy must have opened some of his letters.

So it was that Cockerell became for Alec an authority, a mentor, the representative of a higher civilized spirit to which he needed to refer. But Cockerell was ruthless and a 'scrounger of genius', as someone called him, who had turned 'a pigsty into a palace'. He was not a formally religious man, but as 'a man without any set creed', as he described himself, this 'bearded infidel' became an important part of Alec's search for a spiritual centre to his life. Alec, as someone who had suffered too much inner toil, as well as material and emotional insecurity, sought serenity and peace. This allied him deeply to the Tolstoy whom Cockerell defended to Dame Laurentia McLachlan, the Benedictine nun who was dubious about Tolstoy's religious values:

> Tolstoy is a man who has lived with the principle *Homo sum humanum nihil a me alienuum puto* (I am a man, I think nothing of man alien to me) – and he was now after immense struggles and wrestlings arrived at that serenity of mind and indifference to worldly annoyance that comes only to the very wise and the very simple and the very religious, and not always even to these. One has only to meet him to feel that he lives on a different plane from most of his fellows – a plane in which love of family and love of God prevail – though what God is . . . he told me he did not know.
>
> *The Man, the Infidel and the Superman*

In view of what we know about Tolstoy's treatment of his wife and family, perhaps the nun was more accurate than the humanist who defended him, while Cockerell was something of a fake.

Even so, Alec wrote to Cockerell only 'occasionally' (he reported that Cockerell in his published collection of letters, *The Best of Friends*, used 'two or three' letters – in truth Cockerell printed nine letters from Alec). Published in January 1956, the *Times Literary Supplement* said of it: 'Old-fashioned ideas of privacy have largely crumbled under the bombardment of what is euphemistically called publicity.' It is rather ironic, perhaps, that

Guinness should have been prominently associated with it, revealing himself as 'the possessor of a serious and searching mind'. Cockerell replied to Alec's letters with telegraphic answers, 'like the Lord's Prayer written on a postage stamp'. Again, Alec was using this very public form of correspondence in an autobiographical way, as an exercise in the artistry of self-diminishment. On the surface the letters were eminently civilized and virtuous in their search for values. But they were not entirely the genuine, humble outpourings of a simple, unassuming person.

In the spring of 1942 Alec came back to the south coast, to HMS *King Alfred* in Hove, where he trained for his commission and 'just about' scraped through. Do we have to believe the craftily channelled modesty? Not entirely, because he was adhering to and fulfilling an idea he had of himself. He passed his selection board because he spoke up with insincere enthusiasm for an officer whom the admiral in charge of the evaluating board had enjoyed seeing in a play. (But remember there was no cause for the admiral, not having before him his right name, to know him. Alec does not tell his reader this.) This was a game of later years. The officers knew that before them stood a young man who had served nearly two years in the navy, but did not know that he had played leading roles at the Old Vic and in the West End and led a famous theatre company on a foreign tour. Alec was perfectly sound officer material, as was the more outrageously 'camp' and extrovert Peter Bull. The latter with tongue in cheek claimed that he passed officer selection because he produced the divisional concert, although he went on to command a whole flotilla of landing craft. It might be claimed that Bull became a forerunner of *The Full Monty*:

> The lowlight of the show was my strip-tease, which I maintain got me through my finals. Some years previously I had laughed loud and long at Tony Beckwith's performance in a Gate Theatre Revue in which he had suddenly had to take the place of a burlesque dancer and take all his clothes off. I realised that a sailor's uniform was ideal for a similar act and I made my first entrance to the strains of 'She's My Lovely', dressed in full uniform with a gas mask on and webbing equipment. Out of the latter I produced cartridges which I threw gracefully at the offices in the front rows. I

slowly stripped to my pants and then coyly retired behind a
screen . . .   *To Sea in a Sieve*

In his light-hearted account of his wartime years in *Blessings in
Disguise*, Alec performs in counterpoint with *To Sea in a Sieve*,
Bull's vividly humorous description of life in a landing craft. The
commissioning of Alec as Sub-Lieutenant Cuffe meant that he was
now posted, in early summer 1942, as first lieutenant to a tank
landing craft on Loch Fyne.

After three months, further promotion followed. He crossed
the Atlantic in late 1942 on the *Queen Mary* (eight were squeezed
into a cabin designed for two) to take up command of a brand-
new landing craft built to carry two hundred troops, which was
nearing completion in a naval dockyard near Boston. The work
was delayed for some weeks and when Alec revived some former
theatrical friendships, notably with Gladys Cooper and Peggy
Webster, he found himself being approached by Terence Rattigan.
Visiting New York to help mount the American production of
Flare Path, his play about a bomber pilot which had opened in
London earlier that year, Rattigan asked Alec to play the lead in
New York, a part which required outer insensitivity and inner
vulnerability (the means by which Flight Lieutenant Graham
ultimately, yet unconsciously, salvages his marriage).

With the British Ambassador in New York pulling strings, in
an unusual move the Admiralty granted Alec eight weeks' leave –
he was, he said, the 'only available actor with an English accent'
– and after three weeks' rehearsal and a week's try-out run *Flare
Path* opened on 23 December at the Henry Miller Theater in
Manhattan. Alec reported in *A Positively Final Appearance* from
first-hand observation that most evenings, after rehearsal, Rattigan
spent going to the theatre and particularly to the ballet; here, Alec
confirmed with titillating delicacy of expression Rattigan 'suffered
an acute *coup de foudre* for a tough young dancer. The young man,
in his innocence and straightforward manner, hadn't a clue about
the hot desire he had arisen.' Rattigan then smuggled the dancer
in to one of their rehearsals. The dancer was astounded there was
no music, he 'could hardly conceal his boredom but did seem
genuinely astonished by our capacity to remember lines'.

'Do you say the same words at each performance?' he asked

Alec. 'In much the same way,' Alec replied, 'as you do the same entrechats.' 'But we have the music,' the dancer said.

Alec might refer discreetly to Terry's homosexual activity, but it may be assumed that he too gained some advantage from the new dawn of sexual freedom as experienced by many in New York at that time, which had become a paradise for homosexuals. The war itself, too, was a liberating factor, with the large concentrations in one place of military personnel: 'A chief petty officer in the navy told of the eye contact that very soon alerted him to the presence of other homosexual men,' writes Colin Spencer in his *Homosexuality – A History*. 'Very quickly you had a vast network of friends.' The navy, traditionally, was the service of homosexuality, as Kenneth Williams humorously reported not very long after the war in his diary: '20 Jan 1953. Delicious story about an Admiral coming across an example of traditional *flagrante delicto* twixt two matelots and saying "If you chaps can't give this sort of thing a rest, I shall have it cut out altogether . . ."' Note: 'this sort of thing'.

Not only were straight sailors the providers of 'rough' sex for money with homosexuals, but there were 'always straight men who engaged in certain ritual behaviour after sex with a queer, designed to reinforce their difference and their "masculinity". These were men who ridiculed the queers and after sex generally beat them up.' (There is an example in the Jack Nicholson film, *As Good As It Gets*.) When Bully and his live-in partner were beaten up in Chelsea, as happened in a well-publicized case later in life, one assumes there had been prior contact between the pair and their aggressors. One forms the impression that in Alec the activity kept occurring, but he excluded himself from the identity. Was he one of those 'who committed homosexual acts throughout their lives, opted out of labelling themselves and merged with social convention and the idea of the masculine'?

'It seems to be another case of an English hit destined to be an English miss,' wrote Robert Coleman of *Flare Path* in the *Daily Mirror* in late December 1942, while George Jean Nathan, the doyen of New York critics commented, 'If the play has so much as even one happy, one redeeming feature, it has eluded this critical cunning. The author's purpose and intention is to pay tribute to the valour of the Royal Air Force; what he achieves, so trivial being his equipment, is something that rather puts that admirable body into a ridiculous light.' What Eleanor Roosevelt had written up in her column as 'a true and moving picture of the RAF' folded after two weeks. No one remarked on Alec's contribution. Had the play been a triumph, and his own performance hailed as outstanding, the history of his war might have taken a different turn.

Rattigan, in low spirits, became an RAF rear gunner. Alec reported back for duty two weeks early in January 1943 to join his LCI(L) 124 which, smelling of paint, diesel oil and coir rope, was ready on its Boston slipway. Then began his 'wild adventures', as he called them, as officer in command of a landing craft, a ship which, for its notorious unmanoeuvrability, always 'left its mark' on other ships in sea trials, lost its anchor or bent lamp posts from the quays to which it was tied. 'Tin Can' and 'bloody menace' were epithets generally applied by the crews of other ships. He 'juddered' his way to Norfolk, Virginia, then Bermuda, zigzagged the Atlantic and in sixteen days reached the familiar Mediterranean. He had a Geordie coxswain: 'a regular RN, very robust, downright, trustworthy and likeable. He would often advise me on some course of action – and probably very tactfully – but I rarely grasped a word he said. Not wishing to offend him by asking him to repeat everything slowly, I got into the habit of replying, "Very good. Let it be so!"'

Hosts of landing craft were converging on the Mediterranean for the monumental invasions of 1943–4. Bull wrote that on taking command of a landing craft, he had 'five collisions in the first three days' so he 'got to the stage where I solemnly prayed for the weather to keep us in port'. Peter Copley reported meeting Bull in Glasgow at this time where Copley was acting with his wife Pamela Brown. In the classic dilemma these craft presented to their commanders, Bull confessed to Copley, 'I don't know how to get it under the bridges . . . and I daren't ask.'

*

Alec docked at Djidjelli, a port west of Algiers, where they practised for invasion and here, shortly after, was joined by Bull, who now commanded a bigger landing craft anti-aircraft ship with seventy marines on board. They spent much enjoyable spare time together for, as Bull said, 'Alec's presence . . . was a life-saver.' He wrote in his book: 'It was nice sending signals to each other with "Repeat Nervo and Knox, Donald Wolfit and Phyllis Neilson-Terry," on them with impunity.' Although disguised as he was as Commander Cuffe, the actor Alec Guinness, like Lawrence of Arabia, did not pass unnoticed.

Together they made one trip together worthy of note (both wrote it up) when 'Lieutenants Bull and Guinness' (or Cuffe, as it should have been in an accurate account) were 'excused duty' to visit companions of old in an all-star company headed by Leslie Henson, Vivien Leigh and Beatrice Lillie, which was playing at the Garrison Theatre in Bougie, halfway between Djidjelli and Algiers. When Bull and Guinness reached Bougie they were too late to see any of the performance, which was packed out. They were confronted by Binkie Beaumont who told them that he would take them round backstage after the show. They spent twenty minutes backstage, but then became depressed as they wondered how on earth they would get back to their ships.

Who should rescue them but Vivien Leigh, flattering and cajoling an admiral into sending them back in his staff car. Even so they arrived late and had to join their craft by motor boat. This hardly qualifies as a significant event, and if you stripped the personages of their celebrity – the unrefusable, forward appeal of Vivien Leigh in her Scarlett O'Hara persona – it would hardly be worth recounting. Yet it fills two pages (roughly one per cent) of *Blessings in Disguise*. Alec remained notably absent from the event, while Bull demonstrated a keener and fuller recall of the way Vivien behaved, and of the niceties of rank. All in all, commented the eternally sunny Bull, 'I got about quite a bit, though most of the time was spent by the swimming pool, watching the passing trade and pretty riveting *that* was.' The inflection of the sentence tells us the kind of trade.

In other words, even in autobiographical narrative, like Osbert Sitwell, Alec kept his distance. 'I, Alec Guinness, do not matter,' he reiterated, 'and I cannot possibly be of interest to anyone.' At the same time he conspired and colluded with the reader/spectator in being interested in Alec Guinness, as if he would like to report on himself without being seen as being there, as if he would somehow like the reader/spectator to be enthralled. No one needs or deserves to show himself as keeping a secret unless he wants in the first place to attract the attention of the person from whom the secret is being withheld.

This was a crucial part of attracting an audience. This facade of secrecy was not a true desire for secrecy, for it would easily have been possible for Alec not to act, to become genuinely a nobody, had he really wished rather than have a *partial* wish for it which he was, instinctively, converting into a magnetic professional ploy and, later, a major and genuine part of his attraction. The deliberate form of his own secrecy, as created by Alec, was really just as strong a demand for attention as the most aggressive or extrovert of showmen might have displayed.

In time Alec's secrecy became more aggressive, the flip side of an intense desire to show off, compounded of shame and guilt over that desire. As Ronald Harwood observed in *Dear Alec*, 'This trait may seem to some an affectation. To the outsider, it may be incomprehensible that anyone, especially an actor, so famous and acclaimed, should for a moment doubt his own importance or, professionally, so lack in confidence.' Yet to the actor himself this affected diffidence felt genuine. Here was the conundrum. Why? Because there was always the deeper secret to be hidden, the deeper duality of nature to be feared, as witnessed in recent years in senior politicians.

Alec's own account of his naval service carried this eerie sense of absence to an extreme. While Peter Bull remained at the centre of *To Sea in a Sieve*, Alec, who would appear willing to write about himself – he submitted accounts of his war to *Penguin New Writing* and offered a description of grounding his craft on Sicily on 9 July 1943 to the *Daily Telegraph* – remained evasive and unsure of expressing himself directly. It was an exercise in angling and directing the spotlight away from the central figure in the narrative, while making the reader always aware he was present. He tantalized himself also, but his one saving grace, or blindness, was that he never became self-conscious about any trickery employed.

The Guinness of the letters to Sydney Cockerell wrote of his reading the lovely 'filigree' work of *Hooker's Laws of Ecclesiastical Polity* (in ten volumes, a little unlikely), and *The Screwtape Letters* of C. S. Lewis. As he sat curled up in front of an electric stove listening to a furious wind, he thought of John Gielgud. He had seen his performance as Macbeth in a mask-like make-up in January 1942:

> The press has attacked Gielgud's Macbeth for lack of soldierly qualities – they've quoted 'Bellona's bridegroom,' etc. They seem to have some notion that fine fighting-men look like prize-fighters, and that Macbeth must above all suggest a great eater of beef. Actually Gielgud manages to suggest great physical activity and alertness. My limited observation of first-class soldiers and sailors makes me think they are more inclined to be like that than the heavy type. *The Best of Friends*

Alec still recognized so much of Gielgud in himself and still had ambitions to play those great parts, such as Macbeth and, once again, Hamlet, in which English actors dreamt of making their name. Close to his heart also were his literary ambitions. He spent his spare time writing his novel. This gave way to adapting Dostoevsky's *The Brothers Karamazov* for the stage. Meantime, his search and need to find himself and to find God continued. Cockerell expressed the idea to him in terms comparable to those he used to Dame Laurentia:

> Tolstoy and Dostoevsky were both men seeking God and their novels are a record of their search. Dostoevsky went further and in *The Brothers Karamazov* he presents us with a world which has found its centre in Christ. Tolstoy never found peace and died in a last frantic effort to escape from a world in which he could no longer believe. But this makes the search for God all the more moving . . .

But now some action! On 9 July 1943 higher command ordered Alec to embark two hundred soldiers from a troopship on a very small island west of a lighthouse on the south-eastern tip of Sicily, and in the disorder of the wind and the high seas, he failed to receive a signal to delay his landing on the sea coast by one hour. He knew exactly where to go because he and Bull, some two or three weeks before the invasion, saw on a slide at a top-secret tent briefing in North Africa a scratched number indicating the height of the lighthouse near the invasion beam ('183 or something') taken from submarines. Later, on board his own vessel, Bull worked out from the *Mediterranean Pilot* the landing place as Cap Passero, Sicily. 'A woeful lack of security,' Alec called it. 'It was a terrible burden to carry.'

They listened to a senior army officer 'of great charm, elegance and gentleness' briefing his junior commanders: 'Tell your Jocks we don't want any prisoners. When Gerry comes running with his hands in the air crying, "Kamerad! Kamerad!" tell your chaps to stick in the bayonet and finish him off.'

Alec had no such encounters. Charging ahead, but still unaccountably accompanied by other landing craft who presumably had also not been informed of the change of plan, his craft ran ashore on a narrow sandy beach from which his soldiers disembarked without opposition. The whole non-event of this landing provided Alec with a perfect scheme or prototype of an anti-heroic little-man-caught-in-the-middle-of-big-events – ideal for his form of deadpan, throwaway humour. It was capped by his turning the tables on an angry commander RN who asked him why he had arrived early on the beachhead, whereupon Alec (naval officer Cuffe?) reproved him in his best West End manner by pointing out that, when a curtain is advertized to go up at eight p.m., it goes up at eight and not an hour later. This was indeed a fitting instance of how not only Guinness but also Peter Bull, when delivering his account of these years, managed to reverse any kind of expectation or reality that one or other of them was in command of one of His Majesty's fighting ships. For such humour to work there had to be an authority or higher command. The figure of authority who failed to command fear could no longer be a butt of humour.

Still, there was another side to Alec who, when writing up his landing, reflected, like Hamlet failing to be stirred by Fortinbras marching to war, on its dullness. 'Many other ships,' he remarked in an article in the *Daily Telegraph* in August 1943, 'had as uneventful a time as I did, but there were yet others – and maybe they did not. But on the whole, it was as if the Italians wanted us to come, and only made a little resistance to avoid being clouted over the heads by their German brothers.

'How dull, how dull all this is. And yet, presumably, it's a good-sized page in the history books already.'

Alec, in the words of Voltaire's *Candide*, 'cultivated his garden'.

For the previous two years he had prided himself on his 'floating library' of forty or fifty volumes, glowing against the pale grey paintwork of the bulkhead: 'Shakespeare, Dostoievsky, Tolstoy, Jane Austen, Friedrich von Hügel [the Catholic theologian and philosopher], Eliot, Saki, Disraeli, Plato, Max Beerbohm, Graves and company, and even an unread paperback thriller . . . My little library used to cause joy to a few visitors, but more often pained or languid surprise. "Nothing sexy? Anything funny? Got a good 'tec'?"' One day when his ship was confined to Naples harbour with a wire round the screw or a dirty filter, a friend lent him a copy of Joyce Cary's *The Horse's Mouth*. 'I accepted his gift with alacrity . . . I imagined to myself a few happy hours of relaxation while the crew welded, hammered, painted, scraped and generally clattered about the resounding iron decks of my forlorn L.C.I. (L).' But this was not to be. After a dozen or so pages he wearily snapped it shut.

> The flicks of colour that Cary jangled before my eye (a man is sick of colour after two years in the Mediterranean and longs for the glaucous line of Sussex Downs), together with the short, knotted sentences and the facetiousness, made me restless, if not downright ill-tempered.   *My Name Escapes Me*

Landlocked in Naples, Alec met up with Bully again. Asked by Anthony Quayle, then serving as an ADC at headquarters and known then and later to be a stickler for form, if he would come to dinner with the American admiral in command, who stayed at the Ciano/Goering villa, Alec asked if he could bring Bully along. The admiral was shy and quiet: at the long table he sat at one end, Quayle at the other, Bully and Alec facing each other across the middle. Both misbehaved, getting very drunk and in a state of near giggles. Bully discovered the chairs were on castors and when the admiral didn't catch a remark Bully whisked himself round on wheels, to appear by the bewildered admiral's side. Alec did the same. After dinner the admiral retreated to his paperwork. Quayle led the unsuspecting pair into the exotic gardens of the villa down to a Gothic folly constructed by Goering. Quayle, who had disliked Bully all evening, encouraged him to climb the steps and open the oak chapel door whereupon the step gave way and the ghoulish figure of a giant red-haired monk sprang at him. This

'Alack, what heinous sin is it in me / To be ashamed to be my father's child.'
– *Merchant of Venice.*

Above, left.
Andrew Geddes.

Above, right.
Alec as a child.

Right. Merula and Alec's
engagement picture while
playing Jessica and
Lorenzo.

'Indeed, the truth was I did not like the "myself" I could see and hear.'
– *Seven Pillars of Wisdom.*

Alec, Merula, and Matthew.

Peter Glenville.

Peter Bull as Sgt Buzfuz.

'Look here upon this picture, and on this.'
– *Hamlet.*

Above.
At the time of
The Ladykillers.

Left.
Michael Noakes's
portrait.

Alec the writer; *insert* – Merula in old age.

'Tis a naughty night to swim in.' – *King Lear.*

Clockwise from top left:
Osric, with Laurence Olivier;
Apothecary, with John Gielgud;
Abel Drugger;
1939 *Hamlet*, with Hermione Hanner;
Fool in *King Lear.*

'I have a strange infirmity which is nothing / To those that know me.'
– *Macbeth*.

Above, left. Macbeth with Simone Signoret.

Above. 1951 Hamlet.

Left. Shylock.

'Some people transmit, he thought . . . Some people are intimacy itself.'
– *Smiley's People.*

The d'Ascoyne family.

Herbert Pocket.   Fagin with John Howard Davis as Oliver.

'Le vice anglais?' – 'Not flagellation, not pederasty . . .
It's our refusal to admit our emotions' – *Deep Blue Sea*.

Left. Lt Commander Cuffe R.N.

Below. Ransom (far left) in
The Ascent of F6, with Frederick Peisley,
Arthur Macrac and Ernest Hare.

had been part of Goering's seduction kit to frighten the fräuleins and offer himself as comforter. Bully screamed and nearly fainted; Quayle was satisfied.

On the first day of 1944 a violent Adriatic storm brought Alec near to death and his vessel close to extinction. They were sailing in idyllic conditions to evacuate women and children under cover of darkness from an island off Yugoslavia when he fell asleep and awoke with the sensation that some terrible end was about to overtake them. A hurricane from Egypt and Libya whipped the sea into an ungovernable fury. They were blown about all night and for most of the following morning were almost out of control, expecting wreck at any moment. Alec asked himself, on the deck of the ship when the storm was at its height, 'Why on earth was I wearing a collar and tie?'

The scene was as vivid as the moment in *Hamlet* when the Ghost provokes Hamlet into calling up 'angels and ministers of grace' to defend him. Light flowed around the ship's rails and hawsers like a bluish brandy dance on a Christmas pudding, until the sight of the ship became dizzying. This was a phenomenon caused by the storm, but a Glaswegian crew member bawled out, 'Is it spirits?'

Alec did not know if he would emerge alive from this moment of terror. He emphasized the passivity, as if he was still at heart that small boy dangled over the bridge by his stepfather, the 'captain'. For Bull a similar moment came in Valletta harbour when German aircraft bombed and strafed his ship. For actors of imagination these were formative events which remained with them and to which they referred again and again in performance, and finally in print. Bull wrote later, 'I have a habit of comforting myself on first nights by trying to think of appalling experiences during the war, when terror struck from all sides, but the windiness felt on the Italian beachheads and elsewhere was nothing to compare with one's panic on that evening of 3 August 1955' (the first night of Samuel Beckett's *Waiting for Godot*).

When faced with extinction the thoughts that Alec expressed in his letters were, first, what would become of his wife and son, and how would they survive? Second, how would Merula cope with the burden of caring for Agnes? He answered to himself that she would not have sufficient money, for Merula's pension as a naval widow would be small. Here was some insight into what was still his deep preoccupation. The responsibility for his mother was forever with him, with the shame and embarrassment it might and could continue to cause.

It was further symptomatic of Alec's desire that life should be unified and whole that, while most people would have dismissed the storm as an event of an imperfect, even randomly malignant natural event, Alec should see Hamlet's 'providence in the fall of a sparrow'. He felt relieved when there was no enquiry into its cause or his own handling of his ship. The notion that he could not be blamed for its being written off subsequently – as it had been when he eventually limped into Temoli harbour on the eastern Italian coast – seemed hardly to have crossed his mind. It had triggered off the guilt and shame residual in his being.

The next six weeks or so were spent in a state of unpleasant recovery – two weeks' leave in Malta followed by an office job until they found him a new command. The shock of the storm took time to wear off. He felt ill mentally rather than physically. As a tonic to recovery, he walked in the sun and wind. His crew was dispersed.

During 1944, in a new landing craft, Alec ran supplies to the partisans in Yugoslavia. The tension of war slackened and he had more spare time to work on his Dostoevsky adaptation, and also on his plans for the post-war period. In August 1944 he confided to Cockerell that he had received an invitation to play with the Old Vic Company at the New Theatre. Boredom, frustration, the dreariness of separation from those he liked tormented him more and more. In the heat he and his new ship's crew sat about in shorts and dark glasses and listened to the sea slipping by – sipping iced water to pass the time. In such conditions he finished his adaptation of *The Brothers Karamazov*:

> I say finished – that is, the play *exists* and *could* go into rehearsal tomorrow, but actually there is still quite a lot of work to be done on it. A playwright friend, Benn Levy, has pointed out weaknesses in the first act, and there is much polishing to be done. However, I'm disgustingly proud of myself for having completed the play – I so rarely finish what I start.

He and his fellow sailors made toys for Greek children at their ports of call on the way to Yugoslavia. As Cockerell wrote to *The Times*, copying directly from Alec, the following were words of a well-known actor in the RNVR 'who has changed the part of Hamlet for that of the commander of an unnamed vessel, perhaps HMS *Pinafore*':

I've even made a large woollen ball myself, which caused a great deal of amusement among my more masculine friends. We happen to know a wretchedly poor Greek convent, where eighty small children, all orphans, are cared for. The very best that can be done for them is done, but it amounts to practically nothing – they are more than half-starved. Many of the babies are red-raw because they have to be washed in sea-water, fresh water being so precious that it can only be spared for drinking. None of them has ever known a sweet or seen any sort of toy. The proud possession of the children was a small ring of steel which could be rolled along the floor – not even a tin to beat with a stick, for every tin is required as a cooking utensil, and all sticks are fuel.

A naval officer I know happened to have a wooden yellow duck on wheels on board; it was an intended Christmas present for a niece in England. He presented it to the convent. It caused stupefaction! It was received with wide-eyed silence and gaping mouths – and then solemnly led by a daring four-year old out into the street. In absolute silence all the children followed it, and soon a regular procession was started, with old men and women, soldiers, priests, everyone, and they all followed the yellow duck through the main street of the town. Someone found a Union Jack and hoisted it on a pole. A tattered dirty drummer appeared from somewhere, and a fiddler with a squeaky fiddle. They played, almost unrecognisably, 'God save the King'. The yellow duck, a hideosity, was led like the Trojan horse back into the convent. And so we make toys for them now.   **The Times**

The Times ran this letter in a prominent position. It was also highly personal. Alec identified with those Greek children, recalling the emotional deprivation of his own childhood. So the year of 1944 drew to an end. The Allies were established on the continent and in the rear of the forward thrusts the theatre companies began to assemble among the 'poys and the luggage', as Shakespeare calls the rearguard of invading armies in *Henry V.* Alec languished on, riding out the Mediterranean swells, some-times with five-day leaves as escape. On one such leave he visited Rome, where he paid homage to the spirit of Keats. He found the terrible inscription on the tombstone disturbing:

> This grave
> contains all that was Mortal
> of a
> YOUNG ENGLISH POET
> who,
> on his Death Bed,
> in the Bitterness of his Heart,
> at the Malicious Power of his Enemies
> Desired
> these Words to be engraved on his Tomb Stone
> Here Lies One
> Whose Name was Writ in Water
> Feb 24th 1821

Also while in Rome he met Pope Pius XII, whom he found gentle and decisive and blessed by a ravishing smile. The Pope spoke of God, at the same time raising his eyes and arms, which made Guinness realize how simple and beautiful such a movement could be. For the first time he felt that he had seen a saint. Yet he was not, or so he said, enamoured of the Roman Catholic Church.

Pictures of Guinness (sorry, Cuffe) in uniform, later during the war, reveal a lean and even gaunt-faced Royal Navy sub-lieutenant with a toughened air. The senior service had been a wearing, weathering experience. The sea was no beautifier. There was a close connection between the many violent transforma-tions to which the sea was subject, and the individualism of the man who managed his ship. As a child in Brighton, he had always found the sea 'good and sufficient company'. In such a very English role he succeeded.

If Alec's theatrical background in the 1930s had stood him in good stead, his years in the navy equipped him in a broader way to play world leaders and heroes such as Disraeli, the Cardinal in

The Prisoner, Colonel Nicholson, Lawrence of Arabia and even Freud and Hitler in such a way that they became real people. He had doubly guarded and developed his sense of loneliness and destiny, and had experienced at first hand heroism and the need for resourcefulness. His wartime years were very different from those of theatrical stars ten years older. Gielgud had spent the years feverishly and wholeheartedly working for ENSA (the Entertainments National Service Association) under Basil Dean, acting in such plays as *Blithe Spirit* and *Hamlet* in order to keep up civilian and service morale; he continued to bathe in adulation: he accepted homage as his due. While Alec was clinging onto his directionless landing craft in an Adriatic storm, Gielgud was staying with the Mountbattens and falling for the flowered shirts in Colombo: 'I am determined to buy two or three to startle my guests,' he writes home to his mother Kate. 'They look so decorative and comfortable provided one has narrow hips. It's curious that though the men have so many of them long hair and some done up in buns at the back of their heads they never look a bit womanish – and you could never mistake their sex as one so frequently does when women wear slacks or uniform in England.'

On 5 June 1945 Alec was back in Southampton, waiting for his release from the navy, and, having applied for four months' leave to play Bob Acres in *The Rivals* with Edith Evans, full of high expectation. He was also loath to lose the comfort, the security and the command of being a naval officer. By now, after long years of service, the role of naval officer Cuffe and Alec Guinness had fused into one and the same person. One of the few photographs of himself allowed by Alec in *Blessings in Disguise* was of him in uniform. He had been proud of being captain of a ship with a small group to command. When he arrived back in Liverpool, he met Judy and Tyrone Guthrie at the Adelphi Hotel. They, as former alter ego figures, castigated him for his grand and British manner, and ascribed it to his uniform. They didn't, he felt, realize he had grown up. But had he really?

Shortly after, in another incident, a colleague recalled Alec arriving at the New Theatre to see Laurence Olivier. The big surprise was that he wore uniform. Not the well-worn uniform of a long-serving officer. But immaculately turned out 'like a tailor's dummy'. He wore white gloves and carried a cane, a black walking stick. 'It all looked so new,' Peter Copley told me, 'as if he had dressed up to play a naval officer. Perhaps it went back to the time everyone was telling him, "Don't be an actor, you have no appearance, nothing . . ."'

Playing the part of a naval officer had been a difficult assignment. As Commander Cuffe he had survived and kept his anonymity. In later life when honoured with an invitation to an Admiralty banquet Alec found little had changed.

> When I arrived the Flag Lieutenant (for it was he) greeted me with 'So glad to see you!' and what I took to be a pleased smile of recognition. He invited me to see where I would be sitting. 'You are here,' he said, 'with Mr So-and-so on one side and Admiral So-and-so on the other. Opposite you, Alec Guinness, the actor.' 'Ah!' I said, 'a Doppelgänger!' But he didn't get it.   *My Name Escapes Me*

Even later Alec expressed the wish that after his death his ashes should be scattered at sea (this was not carried out).

Friends who had known Alec before the war and toured in Europe with him noticed the change: 'When he shot to stardom,' Stuart Burge told me, 'he threw up a lot of defences. He disappeared into a different life – he resented the intrusion. Friends found him aloof.' Perhaps he was to assume the role of Menenius Agrippa, the consul he played in *Coriolanus*, who mediated between the plebeians and the patricians. He now had a different set of friends: those to whom he could remain distant, see on his own terms, although he was friendly, affectionate and giving towards them. Among these more and more numbered the strangely half-real non-intimates, friends with whom to share his new power and celebrity. A circle became a court.

Changed, too, since the war, was theatre-land itself and its formal conventions. These had required younger members of the profession always to wear a tie when they came through the stage door, and never to be seen carrying parcels in case they might be confused with tradesmen. Outwardly, at least, actors were respectable and close to their audiences, indeed they were role models of rectitude and sober living, maintaining their morality even as the 'unfrocked priests' to which Alec likened them. 'Things that went on', 'What people get up to' and 'That sort of thing' – bland phrases covering a host of hidden but not very widely practised activities – had no currency in the public mind and went unexplored. Sybil Thorndike expressed shock at one of the Motley designers, Margaret Harris, designing a brassiere as part of a costume. Alec thought the best nights were always Thursday because the carriage trade was in and most of the stalls wore black tie. On Friday they would go away for the weekend. So there were feelings of elegance, of going out, that gave the occasion a little extra, even though this audience was no more intelligent than people sitting in their raincoats in the gods reading the *Evening Standard*. Experienced actors and actresses (the feminine form was retained, as in gods and goddesses) were always called Mr or Miss: 'It was always Miss Evans and Miss [Elizabeth] Bradley, never their Christian names.'

11. We May Rehearse Most Obscenely and Courageously

Alec had been much involved with Dickens and *Great Expectations* just after the war began. He had left the navy with his adaptation of *The Brothers Karamazov* in his pocket, and with a greater love of Dickens from his reading. Like a delayed gift, one might say a resurrection, from those two experiences, there had come along late in 1945 the film of *Great Expectations* to launch him on his film career.

In reinvoking the horrors of his own early life, the deprivation of taxing manual work, the constrictive atmosphere of small rooms, the taunting claustrophobia of being dubbed 'common', Dickens had dared to express some of the grotesqueries the past had caused in his imagination. The novel of *Great Expectations* is dense with ghosts, with secrecy, with darkness, yet it is that very weight which gives it its quality of exhilaration and comedy. Alec's revenge on his own past – or if not revenge, purging – was to be more subtly sophisticated, more gradual but perhaps in the end more complete. So he did not play Pip, this role fell to John Mills; he played Herbert Pocket as he had at the Rudolf Steiner Hall. It was characteristic that he should have been closely connected to *Great Expectations* as adaptor, and even more closely related in human terms to what the work embodied, yet *not* play Pip, the main character who, like himself, was a self-made 'gentleman' and whose values were formed in the darkness of his early life. Alec liked to quote Trollope's comment on Dickens: 'It has been the peculiarity and marvel of his power that he invests his puppets with a charm that has enabled him to dispense with human nature'; in some ways this might apply to himself and his ability or need to escape from himself.

David Lean, the director of *Great Expectations*, had not been strongly drawn to Dickens, knowing only *A Christmas Carol* before being taken by Kay Walsh, his actress wife, to see the Guinness adaptation at the Rudolf Steiner Hall in 1940. During the war Lean had directed Noël Coward in *In Which We Serve*, the moving propaganda story of a ship at sea; its tense, epigrammatic style made it seem like the epitome of all war films, as it represented the conflict between personal feelings and a sense of duty to one's country. After the war Ronald Neame, who had also seen the pre-war *Great Expectations*, wrote a script of it for Lean to film. Lean became friendly with Alec and this friendship blossomed in an exchange of lively and courteous letters. But Lean was a difficult man; brought up a Quaker he was unlikely, temperamentally, to see eye to eye with Alec in the long run, although there was no clash between them during *Great Expectations*. At no time did he show himself to be enthusiastic at the prospect of Alec Guinness in this film. When he was planning *Great Expectations* his preference, bordering on a craze, was for Ralph Richardson, whom he was to direct later in *The Sound Barrier*.

Lean and Dickens were well matched. Lean found himself responding to the extravagance of imagination and he fell in love with the subject, as he had to do in order to make a good film. Guinness's Herbert Pocket was, as it should be, entirely charming, completely credible. Pocket, knocked down by Pip a number of times, bears no animosity. He 'seemed so innocent and brave'. He had, says Pip, 'a frank and easy way with him that was very taking. I had never seen anyone then and I have never seen anyone since, who more strongly expressed to me, in every look and tone, a natural incapacity to do anything secret or mean.' Considering this statement, to give Pocket's name in order to remain secret was a strange irony. The rhythm, the tone of Pocket's dialogue might also be that of Alec's own. 'It is not the custom to put the knife in the mouth,' he instructs Pip in the manners of eating ' – for fear of accidents – and that while the fork is reserved for that use, it is not put further in than necessary. It is scarcely worth mentioning, but it's as well to do as other people do.'

As the pale young gentleman, Alec's ears were pointed, his eyes shone with eagerness, his mouth curled up at the corners. Exhilaration was the keynote of his performance. He was so popular with the public, when the film opened he became a pin-up. But he was

Alec as Richard II in a contemporary drawing (1947)

frightened of overacting in his first film role, although he knew he was terribly lucky to be doing something he had first done in the theatre. 'I was very nervous and self-conscious,' he later remarked. 'I hated my wig. I didn't want to say it wasn't as good as the wig I had in the theatre as it hadn't got the sharpness to it . . . and it was all a bit softened.' At one point when he had to laugh uproariously he felt he was in danger of being exaggerated. Lean took a break in the film, led Alec aside and said to him, 'Let's rehearse without the cameras rolling.' He told him some stories and Alec started laughing. But Lean cheated, for the cameras had been rolling all along.

Alec would, in time, develop a unique way of measuring a performance during the making of a film: his stand-in would come over to him after he had rehearsed a scene and say, 'I loved the way you did that, Alec.' What a sweet and generous comment, Alec would respond. Then some instinct would tell him, 'Oh, no, that was noticed, it must come out.' He would rely a great deal on the stand-in's praise as a signal that something needed to be stripped away immediately.

The scriptwriter of *Great Expectations*, Ronald Neame, was a big fair man with a boyish character who had been originally a cameraman. His compact, judicious script and Lean's natural sympathy for Dickens's instinctive montage made the film extremely successful in somewhat the same way as *Les Enfants du Paradis* became popular in post-war France. Both films expressed a return to traditional national values, especially those of humour. Both films expressed joy in dark times.

*

For most people the immediate post-war period may have a been a time for celebration, but Alec's way of marking the return to civilian life was to immerse himself in two of the darkest and most gloomy masterpieces of European literature. For these he teamed up with the twenty-year-old Peter Brook who had just left Magdalen College, Oxford. Brook tried to enter the secret service in 1943 but the Medical Board would not grade him, so instead he read languages and became president of the Oxford University Film Society for which he directed a film of Sterne's *A Sentimental Journey*, an enterprise frowned on by the college authorities, and for which he was fined five pounds for neglecting his work and almost sent down. Directing became his first and only love: 'I want,' he said at the time 'to be a vampire of the outside world and at intervals to give back the blood I have drawn out, in some creative form. I want to change and develop, and dread the thought of standing still.' To Kenneth Tynan, three years his junior – who had, unlike Brook, positively manufactured his low medical grading in order to escape conscription – Brook was already a hero fit for the wildest fantasies of a sybarite and an aesthete: he looked edible, like fondant cream or preserved ginger.

Brook and Alec were a contrast. Alec was now a hardened and quite bald ex-naval commander of thirty-two. The works they elected to do together while Alec waited for the Old Vic season of 1946–7 were Dostoevsky's *The Brothers Karamazov*, and, a month later, Jean-Paul Sartre's *Huis Clos*, his powerful study of the proposition that 'Hell is other people'. Imbued with the feelings of a Frenchman who has lived through the German occupation of France and maintained his spirit of liberty, Sartre's play became a flag bearer for the new, popular philosophy of self-fulfilment, or selfishness, known as existentialism, in which it was the responsibility of each individual to forge their identity through their actions, resisting the definitions of others, but if you were sensible you became a communist.

They rehearsed in May and June 1946. Brook was wasting little time after taking his finals in launching himself into a triumphant West End career. They used Alec's own sea-sprayed adaptation of *The Brothers Karamazov*, even though it was somewhat loose and unwieldy. Alec elected to play Mitya, the parricide in whom the Karamazov family sensuality had become a devouring fever. It was hardly typecasting, but it seems that Alec's interest in the work and his desire to play Mitya came to some extent from his continuing preoccupation with his own illegitimacy. The character exorcises repressed feelings of anger or bewilderment over an unknown father and a negligent mother and to a great extent the novel absolves Mitya, or at least finds in him redemptive or saving graces. It was this factor that attracted Alec.

Mitya's defending counsel underlines how as a father old Karamazov was a misfortune which it was impossible for the impetuous Mitya to survive:

He is wild and violent, and we are now trying him for that, but who is responsible for the circumstances of his life? Who is responsible for his having received such an absurd upbringing in spite of his excellent propensities and his grateful and sensitive heart? Did anyone teach him to be sensible? Did he get any proper education? Did anyone love him ever so little in his childhood? My client grew up by the grace of God, that is to say, like a wild animal. He may have been eager to seek his father after so long a separation. Remembering his childhood as though in a dream, a thousand times perhaps, he may have driven away the horrible phantoms that haunted his childhood dreams and longed with all his heart to justify and to embrace his father! And what happened? He was met by cynical sneers, suspiciousness and attempts to cheat him out of the money that he claimed belonged to him ... at least [he] saw his father trying to entice away his mistress from him, his son, and with his own money ...

The love for a father who does not deserve such love is an absurdity, an impossibility. One cannot create love out of nothing, only God can create something out of nothing. 'Fathers, provoke not your children to anger,' the apostle writes from a heart burning with love.

Alec in his quest for personal integration through his acting must have found himself very close to the feeling in these lines: his father had created shame in him. They had had no relationship: he had felt himself rejected even as he needed to express that love which a son has for his father. Mitya offered no relief or solution. The careful, anecdotal way Alec distanced himself when he wrote later of the production tends to reinforce my impression of this alienation from his feelings. He strove outwardly for effect, and in spite of his adaptation being directed with a ferocious rhythm by Brook, he could not reveal anything at a deeper level about the soul and character of Mitya. He was still using his acting – for the present, that is – as a form of self-defence. Although he might choose to explore roles that touched upon inner preoccupations, he would embrace them intellectually rather than commit himself to them. Those who recall this production have expressed surprise that he ever came to play the part. They found him excellent at times, but inconsistent. To some he gave the impression that he was suffering a prolonged attack of anxiety.

Kenneth Tynan, now at Oxford, found the tedium bottomless. He wrote to a girlfriend that he had seen 'Peterkyn's' production of the 'Bros Tara [*sic*]' in Hammersmith. It was visually brilliant, he said, with Valk [Frederick Valk played old Karamazov] 'huge and hirsute, bellowing and pricking at folk with a big avalanche of beard and voice, swallowing up Mr Guinness' heady nail-biting at each bounding syllable'. James Agate, respectful but lukewarm, deleted from the first draft of the article, he tells us in his diaries, the quip 'Alec Guinness is good for you!' He also struck out a reference to the effect that Ernest Milton's Father Zossima was twin brother to Hermione Gingold's King Lear. It was just as well he did for Alec, who had persuaded Milton to play the part, had grown terrified that Milton would receive bad notices.

What possibly endeared Milton to him was that the older actor's feelings were as confused as his own. This was around the time Milton asked him round to sample his Lear, and both of them ogled the young Richard Burton, who was also present. Alec would probably have been far better in *Karamazov* realizing, in a complete way, the character of the saintly Alyosha, yet it is a fairly common propensity in the incomplete personality that he or she invariably chooses to grow by attempting something he or she cannot achieve.

As Garcin in *Vicious Circle* (*Huis Clos*) Alec, with shaven head and playing opposite Beatrix Lehmann and Betty-Anne Davis, excelled, but the portrayal of lesbianism meant that the play failed to pass the Lord Chamberlain's criteria of censorship. It could only be staged before a club membership. *Huis Clos* is Sartre's best play, written before his plays became merely vehicles to carry his ideas. As it had only three characters and one set, Sartre may be said to have innovated the small cast 'chamber' play which became a common phenomenon, for reasons of economy if nothing else. The geographical location impressed Alec: it was set in 'enfer' and its three characters were condemned to live there for eternity. The statement 'Hell is other people' ('L'enfer, c'est les autres') admirably summarizes the atmosphere although it was (or so Sartre claimed) misunderstood (it is 'other people that are important in ourselves and in our understanding of ourselves'). Garcin is a self-portrait of Sartre, a man alienated from others, someone who is a prisoner of himself rather than of those close to him: Alec was subtle enough to make the crucial distinction intellectually, but could he in real life? The concentration of emotion in *Huis Clos* worked effectively: it was Sartre's most actable play, and he wrote it, on his own admission, for three friends none of whom he wanted to feel had a bigger part than the others; thus he deliberately constructed the piece so that no one could leave the set. This was ideal for Alec, he did not have the burden of 'carrying' the play on his own shoulders. Above all, it gave him the opportunity to play a character in essence who was like himself, someone who nursed a secret shame that distanced him from others.

Although the Sartre play, opening in July 1946, ran only briefly the production and its performances received wide acclaim and provided Alec in particular, showing in close-up such vulnerability and passion in his face, such torture in his soul, with many tempting offers to appear in films. According to the *Daily Mail* in September 1946 Alec turned down four Broadway opportunities: to play opposite Ruth Chatterton in *Second Best Bed* and opposite Elizabeth Bergner in a three-play repertory season.

As Alec shot rapidly to celebrity it was his off-stage wit and engaging personality, his notoriety almost, that counted almost as much as his actual stage achievements, which were minimal, but highly rated. Although he said, 'Essentially I'm a small part player who's been lucky enough to play leading roles for most of his life,' he did not rise in leading stage roles but in the powerful medium of film which came to dominate the post-war entertainment industry. His first roles in the following Old Vic theatre season at the New were, with one exception, supporting ones, and his first major-minor role, the Fool in *King Lear* was cut to 'just twelve lines'. He was, he said, to be 'given a total variety of parts for these two seasons, because I have no idea where my talent lies, if it exists anymore'.

One of Olivier's few truly moving moments as Lear in this mainly histrionic and unfeeling performance was, as singled out by Alec in his Westminster Abbey memorial address for Olivier in 1989, when he spoke the speech, 'I'll pray and then I'll sleep.' (It related, for Alec, to how Olivier turned to him in later life for spiritual advice):

He knelt, centre-stage, facing the audience and made no movement.

He created an awful stillness. It was a speech that appealed to his sympathies, his conscience and his religious sense.

He had been brought up a High Anglican in a clerical household and I don't think the need for devotion or the mystery of things ever left him.

Despite Alec's generosity towards it Olivier's Lear was by all accounts poor: Sybil Thorndike, his eloquent early admirer, said simply that he lacked the stature. He never attempted to play the part again on stage for it demanded an understanding and a spiritual self-awareness that he did not have (he played it later in life on television, conveying the pathos of the old man cracking up, but little more). Many critics considered Alec's Fool the best they had seen. He acted it with a clown's white face and wistful eyes. He showed a dejection anticipating the tiredness of his witty thrusts. Philip Hope-Wallace, the *Manchester Guardian* critic, remarked upon his 'sad, bilious loyalty'. Guinness restored the Fool, wrote J. C. Trewin, to his proper place, 'wry, quiet, true, with a dog's devotion; when at last he slipped from the play we felt for a moment that the candle was out.' The actor Harcourt Williams wrote in his Old Vic memoir, 'It was an epitome of all the wisdom in the world falling in stray shreds from a clown's chalked face. It had the beady eyes, the questioning eyebrows, the comedy and pathetic inability to cope with life that was once Grock's [the clown]. It had that strangeness too, which, Bacon tells us, is to be found in all excellent beauty.'

'I made a critical success, I believe,' Alec later told Alan Strachan the director. 'That's because, I believe, the Fool in *Lear* has sixty lines and Larry Olivier wisely cut them down to thirty [at another time Alec had said 'twelve'] so that you couldn't get bored with the doggerel that goes on, and also I was always in his light wherever he went on stage.' He stole the show from Olivier – and Olivier never forgave him for it.

Alec told me that he had difficulty in finding the right image for the Fool: 'One has to be careful of one's own psyche with certain elements in Shakespeare.' He described how one night he had a visit from the Fool. It was shortly after he was demobbed.

He went to a party and then home. He fell asleep, but woke up in the middle of the night and had a waking dream. 'The Fool was sitting at the end of my bed. He had a dead white face and he spoke in a certain voice.' He would tell the others at rehearsal that he had seen him. At one rehearsal in particular there was a sort of click in his brain and he 'took off' – or 'maybe it was a sudden awareness that a pin-drop stillness had descended'. Perhaps because of these visitations Guinness's Fool lived longer in the memory than Olivier's Lear.

During the November week when *King Lear* played in Paris at the Sarah Bernhardt Theatre Alec and the company stayed in the railway hotel next to the Gare d'Orsay (now the museum). It was here on the fifth floor Ralph Richardson, playing Cyrano on an earlier tour, had threatened to kill Olivier by picking him up and holding him over the hotel balcony. Alec's room filled with smoke as engines left or arrived. At *Lear*'s opening, six policemen had to guard Olivier from a hundred shouting and singing women. They partied with the Duff Coopers at the British Embassy and one night, as all seats were sold out, Olivier placed the legendary Gordon Craig, for whom they could not find a place, under the little humped roof to the *trou du souffleur*, or prompter's box. On his first entrance Alec spotted this second Lear – angry-looking, eyes swivelling from side to side in an old handsome white face surrounded by a halo of white hair. Eyeing Craig, not sure which one to address, he spoke his first line, 'Can you make no use of nothing, nuncle?' Before Lear ended, in January 1947, Alec had been named as Olivier's successor to run the Old Vic.

The Fool, as played by Alec, was a miniaturist's part: so what should this Nicholas Hilliard among players attempt next but the foolish young Bisley, a nondescript role in Priestley's *An Inspector Calls*? The author himself marvelled at his performance: 'He had only to walk upstage, his back to us, to give us a further display of the character of this thoughtless youth.' Priestley felt Alec's distinctive quality as an actor was undervalued both by critics and by the public: 'They tend to respond to publicity, fuss, showmanship,' he wrote, 'and these are not what this modest but dedicated man is offering them.' Alec would have been ideal casting for the role of the Inspector, but Richardson, also perfect as the ghostly caller, was there first to play the enigmatic policeman. One evening

Richardson commented that Alec's patent leather shoes squeaked horribly: 'Try water'. Alec did nothing, but next performance when he rushed in to change into these shoes he found them in a bucket of water where Richardson had stood them. 'I squelched noisily through the last act and then missed two performances through near pneumonia.' 'Oh, have you been off, I didn't notice,' said Richardson later, never alluding to the shoes.

Alec next played De Guiche in Guthrie's production of *Cyrano de Bergerac*, during the rehearsals of which confrontations between Guthrie and Richardson were continually expected but never quite happened. Once Richardson – who was forever harassed by Guthrie, 'For God's sake, Ralph, play the scene! Play the play!' – stopped rehearsal and came to the downstage edge of the stage, 'peering gimlet-eyed from both sides of the great Bergerac nose up to where Guthrie stood'. 'I was brought up to find my lights,' he said, 'And I'm finding them and for the first time in your production. So . . . don't call me a bloody fool, old cock . . .'

Alec's own performance was a small study of a bitter and self-critical aristocrat: he looked like a portrait by Van Dyck, but once again he emphasized the icy interior of a man displeased with himself.

He acted after this what he has often described as his favourite role – he repeated this somewhat odd assertion as late as 1992. This was the part of Abel Drugger in Burrell's production of *The Alchemist* which opened just before the beginning of the big freeze-up on 18 January 1947. Not only were there big cuts in the fuel ration – electricity was cut off for five hours a day – but coal and wood supplies were scarce. Ben Jonson's comedy was a hit, with George Relph's Alchemist matched by Richardson's Face (the well-known photograph of Richardson bears similarities to Alec, as if Richardson stole something of Alec for his make-up). Although the company was shaky on its words before it opened, there was no doubt that *The Alchemist* showed it at its peak.

Alec's Fool in *Lear* was fondly remembered by audiences. At his opening line as Abel Drugger, 'I have played the fool myself,' the audience clapped. This gave him the spark, he said, for Drugger. In contrast to his Fool Alec wore little make-up for Drugger, the innocent gull of a tobacconist who is deceived by Face. The essence of a comic victim, Drugger has few lines, but they give the actor an opportunity to create on stage a whole being. Alec saw that this was one time in his life when he was putting himself in danger: 'He's such an extraordinarily innocent character. I felt as though I could go on acting him all my life and never escape from him.' Was he again scaling himself down to the size at which as a child, neglected by his father, he felt himself comfortable and secure?

Tynan, who was now beginning to review plays in letters to his friends, grasped the essential quality of Guinness. This was far from playing Drugger as David Garrick had, by inflating the role into much more than Jonson intended. Alec made the most of the limited opportunities available, but expanded them from within:

> Mr Guinness manages to get to the heart of all good, hopeful young men who can enjoy without envy the company of wits . . . His face creases ruddily into modest delight, and he stamps his thin feet in glee. In a later scene, he demonstrates a very rare gift, that of suggesting the change that comes over a man when he is alone. Drugger is commissioned by Face to bring him a Spanish costume as disguise. He trots away and returns, shyly clad in its showy cloak and hat. Waiting for Face to answer the door, he begins to execute timid dance-steps under the porch. He treads a rapt, self-absorbed measure with himself, consumed with joy. Then Face appears: the pretence is over, he recognises his intellectual master, and, not regretfully or pathetically, but smartly and prosaically, he sheds his costume and hands it over.   *Alec Guinness*

'Timid dance-steps' became a motif in some of Alec's later stage performances.

Was this the secret of Alec's magnetism, as Tynan claimed? 'He can seem unobserved; he can make every member of the audience an eavesdropper on a private ceremony. His art is the art of public solitude.' Tynan understood the suspiciousness of the lonely illegitimate child who wanted to be observed and loved in his privacy – and therefore no longer alone – because he, too, was illegitimate. The empathy was entirely unconscious. Neither man knew that they shared the stigma of illegitimacy.

*

In 1946 the Redgraves, that is to say Michael Redgrave and his actress wife Rachel Kempson, with their small children Vanessa, Corin and Lynn, moved to a fine house, 1 Chiswick Mall, which they bought for £12,000. Alec, Merula, and Matthew now lived around the corner at 7 St Peter's Square, one of the narrow tall houses built for the victorious generals of Wellington's army in the early nineteenth century. They were renting.

Merula, in those austere times of rationing, one day triumphantly produced a duck she had found in Hammersmith market. Alec did not think in its plucked condition it looked much like a duck and the cooking smell was unpleasant as was the meat inedible. It turned out to be a seagull.

More fortuitously she picked up a puppy, a skinny, dying little Alsatian runt whom, against all odds, she revived, renamed Tilly, and who became their domestic companion for the next nineteen years.

Corin and Matthew became close friends because, after a short attempt by both sets of parents to integrate them into the state system of schooling, they joined a small group that was privately taught, and then, with this group no longer functioning, they were tutored, just the two of them, by a Miss Holly at the top of the St Peter's Square house.

Matthew was slightly younger than Corin, who recalls the house being particularly suitable for the Guinness temperament. 'He had a colossal dignity about him, quite awesome, he would sit in a high-backed leather chair and address you in his even-toned and measured voice.'

Corin Redgrave never thought of Guinness as a spiritual person, but found him uncommonly decent and kind. He showed his care, and, as his son's best friend, Corin remarked on how he went a long way to find out what you liked, or he would be there to meet you at the station from a train, demonstrating an extraordinary courtesy. Corin found Matthew extraordinary too: innocent, of open nature, he seemed like one side of the actor in essence. His father, Corin believed, may have been too much of a disciplinarian, and had too high an expectation, picking him up on small details in front of a friend, which used to make him feel embarrassed.

Remembering how his own father was fascinated by Guinness

as an actor, Corin confessed he was himself; he heard stories about how Alec's inventiveness on the set, for instance in *The Three Sisters* in which Michael Redgrave also appeared, used to land him in trouble. He had a certain difficulty in reconciling this fastidious father – who banked at Coutts before it became fashionable to have a merchant banker – with the shiny bald head, the moon-faced smile, the comedian of genius.

Corin also identified closely with Guinness and with his son because his own father was deeply reclusive and shy. But Guinness was also different for he had 'the qualities of a great mime, and his face could assume any shape'. Later Corin felt Alec became much too associated with 'quasi-spiritual' parts and never achieved the quality he showed earlier in his career. He saw something very different in him.

Like himself in many ways, Corin felt it had been hard for Matthew. 'It is hard for the child of whom great things are expected, but harder by far for the one who is adorable and sweet and of whom no one expects very much,' wrote Michael of his youngest child, Lynn. All three Redgrave children were affected by Redgrave's ambivalent sexuality, the demon with which he and his wife wrestled for fifty years. Many will recall rumours that turned out to be true that Michael was bisexual, while he confessed as much indirectly in his autobiography, 'Always it returns to this question of split personality and I cannot believe it would be right – even if I had the will-power, which I have not – to cut off or starve the other side of my nature.'

Like Alec, Redgrave had joined the navy; the night before he left he spent with Noël Coward, one of his lovers. Throughout the years there were one-night stands, quarrels and tearful, remorseful scenes with Rachel Kempson, while on two occasions male lovers lived in a studio at the back of Redgrave's home. While Alec's homosexual or bisexual proclivity was, compared with Redgrave's, considerably scaled down (perhaps on a par with the smaller parts he played on stage) it was for Corin also undoubtedly present, so he identified with Matthew. Corin, much later when playing Coward's *A Song at Twilight*, described the fictional writer's role when he publishes his self-serving and dishonest autobiography, saying, 'The play is about Somerset Maugham . . . Coward chose to write about a man who, unlike himself, could never come to

terms with his own homosexuality. He is hurt by it. He feels he
carries some sort of torment . . . his play is about the withering
effect upon a human being, and a creative human being at that, of
having been forced, obliged, so he thinks, to live all his adult life
under a cloak of concealment.' (*The Times*)

Alec gave parties in his rented home in this illustrious square.
Peter Copley played character parts in these Old Vic seasons. He
recalled for me, 'rather a drunken party at which Redgrave, swore
and drunkenly upbraided Alec for not being funnier as Aguecheek
before the war'. Copley mentioned Rachel's calming, soothing
voice trying to talk reason into Michael, before he himself could
not refrain from a forced exit to vomit in the loo. Writing to
apologize to Alec he received a charming note which put him at
his ease. Copley also spoke to me of Alec's sexual passion for John
Garley, another Old Vic actor who was married to June Brown
(Dot in *EastEnders*) for seven years. How close they became Copley
did not know, but he remarked on Alec's 'hot sexual pursuit of
Garley', and, when on tour, chasing him down the hotel corridor
in his pyjamas. This side of Alec fuelled much theatrical gossip
current at the time, and it was widely known he was, and
continued to be, a closet homosexual. Yet the precise, meticulous
'stickler for form' side of Alec kept this side under wraps and in
order. Keeping a lid on it drove him on relentlessly in his
profession. No wonder, perhaps, Alec disliked Maugham so, when
he met him with Edith Sitwell, for Maugham represented a side
of himself he did not wish to confront (and Maugham was
viciously nasty about his wife Syrie and his lifelong love Gerald
Haxton).

Matthew, after the conversion of his father in 1954 to Catholicism, on the suggestion of Peter Glenville was sent off to Beaumont College, the Catholic boarding school, a move which Corin
regretted because he lost touch with him. Corin heard Alec talk of
Shakespeare, but he had never heard him mention religion or
spiritual matters, so the conversion came as a surprise.

In the early 1980s Corin, a committed Trotskyist in this period,
wrote to Alec and asked him to open a training shop in Brighton
for unemployed youngsters. Alec agreed. 'Well, I'm not political,'
Alec said. 'One assumes he is a Conservative,' said Corin.

The press, hearing of this, latched on to this tale about

Guinness with a vengeance – the famous actor-knight mixing with Trotskyists – and Alec reeled with shock. But, having given his word, he still did not withdraw and he publicly opened the shop. 'He was admirable,' said Corin, 'and he gave the training shop quite a large sum in cash.' Most of all Alec left on him an impression of decency.

The outcome of Alec's relationship, or non-relationship, with Garley is not known, although the young actor, who had no children with June Brown, met a tragic end. One is ready, perhaps too ready, to suspect this might have had something to do with his sexual identity. Was he the unwilling keeper of some secret life, perhaps with Alec, that we will never know about? June Brown has told the story of his suicide 'for the first time' more than once in the press, but refuses to elaborate Alec's role. John was an actor, she said, whose career was going badly (he was, she said, 'touched with genius and supposedly the best actor of his generation'). He became depressed about his future and could not find work. He imagined his health was failing, and he feared he had inherited a mental illness from his father. This was completely untrue, existing only in his mind, asserted Brown, but even so it got to the point where he talked of killing himself.

Admitting she was wrong in thinking that those who talked about suicide were the ones who never did it, June Brown told how one day she was visiting her sister when she had a premonition that she had to go home. 'The moment I got to the front door I knew something was dreadfully wrong. When I went inside, I found my poor husband lying unconscious by the gas fire. He was still just alive and [I] immediately called an ambulance. He died in hospital four days later.'

If Alec had an involvement with Garley closer than the much-discussed pursuit, this must have preyed deeply on his thin-skinned self and created a heavy guilt.

There now fell on Alec a great, tormented kingly role with a flawed personality and an identity crisis mirroring his own. This latter part of my statement would have been unimportant to him and unrecognized by him. But the escape into the character of King Richard II is the translation that awoke and channelled his mimetic desire.

Without a thaw almost until April, the hard weather continued into 1947. Conditions backstage at the New Theatre became appalling. For evening performances Alec had to make up wearing his overcoat. The washbasins were frozen. Rehearsals had to be scrapped. Firmly on the celebrity circuit, Alec was bidden to meet Clement Attlee, the prime minister, at a 'bunfight' at 10 Downing Street which was attended by sixty elderly ladies in velour hats and coupon clothing. Balancing a teacup and saucer in his hand he leaned against an open door which felt as if there was someone crouched up behind it. He eased the door a bit and a rather squashed prime minister emerged from behind it. Alec thought he must be hiding from the 'more serious ladies who had calculating eyes on him'. He mumbled an apology and fled.

Perhaps the postponement of *Richard II*'s first night was fated. Ralph Richardson, who directed and played John of Gaunt, and Guinness had similarities of background but these served more to set them apart than to bring them together. The closeness of background appeared in numerous ways. Each had been abandoned or neglected by his father and suffered a strained or constrained upbringing and single-child relationship with his mother. Both had money and privilege somewhat vaguely in their backgrounds: neither had any serious professional training. Neither had a degree or higher qualification. Both had had to start earning their living at an early age. Each possibly saw mirrored in the other elements of insecurity and fear in himself which neither wanted to confront. Both were fiercely anti-psychological.

Both, above all, were imaginative actors, who brought the vulnerability and pain of their upbringing to bear in their work. Richardson had primarily a poetic quality, Alec almost the opposite, exposing as he could a kind of quintessential nakedness of thought, but both in their best work drew on the marrow of themselves. Both were reticent yet modest, egotistical yet convinced that they were not in the showy first division (which for them meant Olivier and Gielgud). Both were, in one sense, the more exciting actors: they were guardians of the secrecy of life. They believed that, as a quality, mystery was far above explicitness, suggestion far above overt display.

But in *Richard II* Richardson was in charge, alas. He was enjoying everything, at the peak of his fame. During the run of *Cyrano* he had been knighted, even before Olivier ('I should have been the fucking knight,' was the latter's response); backstage they would now call Ralph 'Sir-rano'. As a result, he never became engaged in the anti-heroic aspirations of his junior. When Alec asked his director what kind of a Richard he had in mind he got the answer, 'I'll tell you, old fellow,' and snatching a beautiful Venus pencil from the table Richardson waved it in Alec's face: 'Like that. Sharp and slim, that's what we want.'

'I don't know how to play a Venus pencil,' Alec remarked. 'I've been asked to play Piccadilly Circus by Michel Saint-Denis and that was easier.'

The shared closeness of background did not extend to a good working relationship. Michael Warre, the actor and designer, reported that Richardson's ideas about the setting were just as vague: 'I have a strong feeling that the set should be all wood . . . You should be able to go in and out of it.'

'Permanent?' inquired Warre.

'Perhaps we could change it from time to time . . .'

'We must have an upstairs for Flint Castle and probably for the lists too . . . this is leading us towards a formal structure . . . which is Elizabethan,' pointed out Warre.

'Why not?' said Richardson.

'Costumes?'

'Why not Elizabethan structure . . .?'

'With fourteenth-century costumes?'

The most important thing for Richardson was that it should be made of beautiful wood and the actors should handle it lovingly. Through this set ('a maze of pillars and posts . . . possibly the most impractical that man ever devised' – Kenneth Tynan), Alec had to track the insecure ego of his protagonist:

> Thus play I in one person many people,
> And none contented.

None *were* contented. The performance became as much Guinness's identity crisis as it was King Richard's, but Alec did not see it like that at the time, although he must have understood how Shakespeare was dramatizing his own self-consciousness, a necessary stage in his evolution towards the writing of *Hamlet*. The physiological shadow of himself, yet close to history, Shakespeare's

Player King, who was bewildered and lacked understanding of himself. The tragedy of Richard was not quite a tragedy because the King enjoyed, with aesthetic pride, his own decline. Likewise Shakespeare seems always to be watching himself and taking note. Alec, at very much the same stage in life, explored this whole perception of Richard with considerable skill and intelligence but from the outside.

Guinness was possibly still under the influence of Gielgud when he rehearsed with Richardson. Later he called his perform-ance a 'partly plagiarized, third-rate imitation'. Many people, when *Richard* had opened, thought it bad because he played it against himself, wanting to play it like Gielgud. Yet he was growing aware of the problem of his identity as an actor (very bound up as it was with that of the person).

A subtle actor, Richardson the director remained fairly untouched by all this subtlety. The production secretary who was taking notes from Richardson found that he kept on saying unrepeatable, dreadful things for her to write down – using for him the appropriate method of dictation. These consisted of blistering comments like 'bloody awful' or 'ghastly', which she had to repeat back to Richardson when he asked airily, 'What did I say about Alec?' – all impressions of the performance having vanished from his mind. Perhaps a photograph of the newly knighted Sir Ralph, in double-breasted suit and holding a hat, staring somewhat madly the other way from a timid, costumed Alec summed up the style of his direction.

When it opened, the critics failed to grasp what Alec was trying to do. Some said he had no voice, others that he had no tragic emotion or instability of mood, that he projected surface melancholy rather than the flame and agony of tragedy. Yet it was hard, others noticed, to dismiss it as a failure. The intelligence behind was unmistakable, for Alec *had* captured the quickness of brain, the need for secrecy, all those inner qualities of genius that he himself refused to believe he possessed in common with Shakespeare (and Shakespeare possessed in common with Richard II and Hamlet). As Lionel Burch wrote in *Picture Post*:

Guinness's conception of Richard of Bordeaux was of a man always capable of standing ... a little apart from himself and looking at himself. The man outside observing the man within – but both men resident in different worlds. Private worlds indicated by private jokes which started at the corners of Guinness's mouth . . . some people might find this inter-pretation too cynical and insufficiently 'poetical' for their pre-conceptions. To me it seemed the true apocalyptic link between this cat-and-mouse king's tweaks of sadism at the beginning of the play and his twists of masochism at the end of it.

Birch might have been writing later of Guinness as George Smiley.

Harcourt Williams noted Alec's facility for altering the quality of his appearance without the aid of make-up. This he attributed to the muscles in his face: 'One dreads to take one's eyes off him even when he is not speaking for fear of missing some flitting shade of thought.' This was not a big stage, histrionic quality, but the attribute of a film actor.

As for the director, he stole the show. Richardson's collarless costume as John of Gaunt made him seem to Alec like a large, bearded Peter Pan; as in history, the uncle dominated the nephew: Richardson instructed Alec, 'Never come within six feet of me on stage, old cock,' with the result that he would huddle up with Bushy, Bagot and Green. His failure to blaze meant, one critic said, 'The other characters seemed to take on a corresponding importance, and a beautiful study of the dying John of Gaunt proved the dramatic highlight for the connoisseur of acting.' Richardson *was* wicked.

After this production they would meet again socially, but never again appear on the same stage and were hardly together even in the same film. Richardson never again acted together with Olivier after these New Theatre seasons, but he did with Gielgud. Olivier never acted with Gielgud, although Gielgud did lead a company at the National Theatre when Olivier was in charge. Alec simply never acted on stage again with any of these three great actors with whom he had begun his career. Why not? – a good question. Answer on first page of *Blessings in Disguise*: 'Enter EGO from the wings, pursued by fiends. Exit EGO.' Were they the fiends?

Alec next played in the John Burrell productions of Shaw's

Saint Joan and Gogol's *The Government Inspector*. In the first he was the Dauphin, a nobody whom he played with hands hanging in a slightly abnormal position and a lack-lustre eye reflecting a numbed mind. In the second, he was Khlestakov, the Inspector, the nobody mistaken for a somebody, who then tries to live up to it. At least he was moving on from the Olivier–Richardson season which had become a 'hot-bed of false noses'.

He ended this round of Old Vic involvement with Menenius Agrippa in *Coriolanus*, in which John Clements played the title role. Here, as the veteran peacemaker, Alec transformed himself into a stately old man and captured the best notices, but he failed to satisfy the Old Vic's éminence grise, Harcourt Williams, who commented that Alec deservedly won rich praise, but he wondered if he was not carrying an intellectual approach to his work further than was wise. In reaction, said Williams, 'from over-emphasis and false sentiment he exhibits a cold reserve which seems to prevent a scene from catching fire'. This was a justifiable comment. Alec finished playing at the Old Vic in May 1948, by which time he was filming with David Lean in *Oliver Twist*.

12. Queer. Well – So What!

Outwardly the man exhibited the cold reserve of the ex-naval officer, but inwardly the turmoil continued. As before, sometimes the guardedness crumbled and the inner weakness showed. Here, in one remarkable incident, Alec was lucky not to find himself publicly exposed.

An intimate, if not lover, of Alec's was Peter Glenville the director, who for the next ten years or more was his closest theatrical colleague. Although he said Alec had a complicated nature, Glenville's own nature was almost as multi-faceted, so perhaps it was as much a comment on himself.

Peter was the son of the Dublin-born comedian Shaun Glenville, who played pantomime dames and toured with Fred Karno – Shaun had made his first appearance in Dion Boucicault's *Arrah-na-Pogue* at the age of two weeks, and he was described in the Irish press as a 'howling success'. His mother must have been a no less confusing or interesting case for the study of gender sexuality. She was Dorothy Ward, a famous Principal Boy. Again, like Gielgud, Glenville would seem to have found in his lifelong attachment to his mother an emotional stability which brought him confidence and openness in fulfilling his gay agenda. Dorothy Ward said of Peter once when asked, 'Why wasn't he married?', 'Where could he find a wife with whom he could discuss a script like me?' Douglas Warth, a *Sunday Pictorial* writer of the 1950s who wrote a series on 'Evil Men', once asked in those distant innocent days what men did together. Glenville, who was not at all discreet, organized for him to watch through a keyhole, as graphically expressed by a colleague to me, 'himself and another man fucking'. That same colleague believed that Glenville's role as old friend in Alec's sexual life would mainly have been that of 'procuring'.

At Stonyhurst College, Glenville had sung successively first treble and first bass in the choir, played first violin and first flute in the school orchestra, been president of the debating society, and for ten years winner of every elocution prize. In 1935, as part of the fashionable acting set at Oxford which included Terence Rattigan, he played Hamlet for the Oxford University Dramatic Society in the first ever student production directed by an Oxford fellow, Neville Coghill. After attempting to follow in Gielgud's footsteps, serving in the war, then playing Prince Hal to Robert Atkins's Falstaff, Glenville emerged in the post-war years as a successful director.

Glenville and Alec had met in the 1930s: 'my very close friend' and 'my brilliant friend' Alec calls him, and as we have said at some early time it was likely that as well as being friends and confidants they had an affair. In future years Glenville would direct Alec more than anyone else.

In 1947 Glenville was in Liverpool, directing *The Human Touch* by J. Lee Thompson and Dudley Leslie when he invited Alec down to see it as a possible West End vehicle for him. This was a play about the young Scottish doctor Dr James Simpson, who discovered chloroform in 1847 – an admirable romantic portrait according to the prints, and a demonstration of man's unconquerable spirit. One night Alec committed his by-now famous indiscretion and was arrested for homosexual soliciting. Quick-wittedly he concealed his true identity by calling himself Herbert Pocket. Maybe a bit rash, but presumably he thought that in Liverpool he would not be recognized from the film (no wig, no top hat). The joke was on him. We place the incident in Liverpool. Sheridan Morley mentions it as such in his biography of Gielgud. The story, still with Alec giving Herbert Pocket as his name, has equal currency in theatrical circles as taking place in Brighton, which Alec visited frequently. He did not act in Liverpool at this time, even in Old Vic tours, which never visited this city, although he did tour extensively with the company.*

---

* I made two trips to Liverpool attempting to find a record of this incident. On the first I searched microfiche copies of Liverpool newspapers for the relevant years. These helped to establish which theatrical companies visited the

Simon Callow, speaking to me of Alec's bisexuality and this incident, has always found Alec similar to Charles Laughton. Callow first met Alec in the mid 1980s, after he had written to compliment him on his book about acting: 'I think he admired gays like myself who were open about it and unashamed – he liked participation in gay gossip.' In his biography of Laughton which Callow subtitled *A Difficult Actor*, he relates how the actor, during rehearsals of a play in which the character he plays murders a rich young relative and then has to live with the secret, came home and told his actress wife, Elsa Lanchester, 'that he had a homosexual streak in him which he occasionally indulged'. A young man with whom he had had sex for money was harassing him for more, a policeman had become involved and he was due to appear before a magistrate.

Elsa Lanchester was not too bothered, what with her permissive nature and Bohemian circle, but she did ask, 'if he had had sex with the man in their house? He had. Where? On the couch. Very well. Get rid of the couch.'

Nothing more was said and the magistrate dismissed the case, which was not reported.

But Elsa had been shocked to the core that it had taken place in their house, and she went deaf in both ears for a week. As Callow reports, 'Her awkward, *joli laid*, madly talented husband was *queer*. Well – so what! On with the party! But nothing, of

---

city and when. I also consulted the *Liverpool Post* library, but without success. I established a few periods when Guinness could have been in Liverpool. On the second visit I submerged myself in the City Magistrates Courts (1 and 3) records, 1946–8, which gave a fascinating and utterly different crime profile of a vanished age. In this immediate post-war period there were few offences of 'gross indecency'; only two entries I could find referred to 'the abominable crime of buggery', while rape, and sex offences with minors, seem almost non-existent. Theft, drink-related crime, husbands deserting wives and families and leaving them on the parish (sentence: six months), desertion from the forces and illegal gaming were prevalent. I was very hard-pressed to find cases of males consorting indecently with one another, usually in Selbourne Street or Williamson Square. Women kept virtually a clean sheet. There was little or no evidence of the legal persecution of homosexuality, at least in Liverpool. I cannot claim my searches were exhaustive, or produced conclusive proof one way or the other.

course, was ever the same again . . . the deception is what hurt so deeply.' In time the boy incident 'proved to grow into a great wall – never mentioned, but distinctly *there*'.

There is no evidence to suggest anything like that happened between Alec and Merula, or even that she knew at all. One assumes she knew and that Alec never told her. It would be surprising if she had never guessed, especially when most of us could so visibly, or at least superficially, detect signs of a homosexual proclivity in Alec's camp manner and interests. And she must have heard *something*.

Glenville, a highly influential figure from his Oxford days onwards, remains unknown. Sheridan Morley, who knew him better than most and visited him in Mexico, describes him as a practising, well-adjusted homosexual, with a Mexican boyfriend, who lived between New York and Mexico. He proved impossible to contact. Before his death I wrote to him several times but he never replied. He promised to contribute a piece to Alec's seventy-fifth birthday Festschrift, but it never appeared. The impression Glenville gave to the world was that he was at ease with himself, open and not at all riddled with guilt like Alec about his gay inclinations. According to Gide's very Gallic classification of homosexual men into three classes, the first who is in love with young boys, called a pederast (in which class Gide put himself); the sodomite, whose desire is for mature men, and the invert, about whom Gide had little favourable to say (he assumes the role of a woman and desires to be possessed), it would seem Glenville was mainly 'pederast' and 'sodomite'. Gide, himself a Protestant and the most influential married homosexual in French literature, wrote that these definitions are not always clearly distinct and there are transferences from one to another.

It has been suggested that Merula's possible lesbianism turned her away from having more children. Edith Sitwell, often accused of being a lesbian, forged a strong attachment to Merula – certainly there was something steely and male in the photographs we have of Merula as she stands stalwartly by Alec's side. There was speculation about this among some people, although I do not believe it was true.

'She must have known,' is the consensus among friends and colleagues, 'but turned a blind eye.' Alec was fearsomely discreet and meticulous in his separation of one side of his life from another. Merula would not have seemed to be the inquisitive type and would have behaved like the mother who overlooked the naughty behaviour of her child. Or maybe, in time, she became his chaperone. 'It's still adultery,' Beerbohm Tree's wife is reported to have warned him when she caught him in flagrante delicto. As for being caught by the law again, Alec must have known the risks, so however huge the temptation, the pressure he felt against this from the deterrent effect of having been caught and punished helped him to resist. He would not be the first to turn the force of a temptation into a power to do good and produce work of quality. ''Tis one thing to be tempted . . . Another thing to fall,' says the Duke in *Measure for Measure*. But there would be detractors who would say his conversion to Catholicism constrained and limited his acting, and that never again did he dare and show such danger and sheer breathtaking elan as when he had played Herbert Pocket.

What could Alec have been looking for in men? Was it for a father, some element of manhood he felt he lacked and would receive in some wild and shocking concentrated dose? Was it possession of romantic looks he hungered after – union with the beloved? Or was it for risk, terror, the sheer thrill and excitement to relieve the pressure, the inner demand built up by his attachment to secrecy (but to show he was a rebel too)? Was it a need for sexual pleasure which would pass? Probably a combination of most of these.

Laughton could wonderfully, as Callow showed in his biography, embody decency in a part, while both he and Alec, with their versatility, eschewed classical acting and gravitated towards the movies. As a result they graduated from Eminent English Character Actors into fully-fledged world-famous personalities. Norman Mailer, when he worked with Laughton, wrote of him, 'I don't think I ever met an actor before or since whose mind was so powerful and fine'. Gore Vidal would say the same of Guinness.

In Laughton's case the homosexual streak lingered, even grew and intensified. The boyfriends came and went as Laughton attached himself more to activities that could be pursued in their company – contemplation, painting, reading out loud, teaching. 'Many of these activities could be pursued in the company of handsome young men who would also – sometimes for a small consideration – have no objection to being made love to.' Did it, in Alec's case, continue like this?

Another question lingers, unanswered. Did Merula know? It is also possible that she did not, for they now led such distinctly different lives, although Alec always looked forward to returning to his home, which in time became more and more important to him. His bisexuality was a town pursuit, and she was a country girl. Alec, master of so many aspects of life and art, was as we know a master at keeping his life in separate compartments.

Alec and Laughton had known one another since Alec's early performance of Hamlet, when Laughton came round to visit him in his dressing room. 'He invited him back to his flat in Gordon Square for the sole purpose, it seemed, [a question mark here, perhaps, on the part of Callow, who reports this] of reading, first of all some of Hamlet, then a great deal of King Lear. This last, says Guinness, "was an illumination".'

*

'He does not like to do imitations – he *is* the person – he thinks like they do,' Angela Fox observed to me of Alec. No part better illustrated this, and offered escape from ontological insecurity and fear of discovery than Alec's next. Alec wanted so much to play in more Dickens that he asked Lean out to dinner to try to convince him that he should act Fagin in his forthcoming film of *Oliver Twist*. It was the only time in his life, he said later, that he 'wined and dined' a director with a specific part in view.

'You think in terms of types,' Alec told Lean. 'You won't find what is inside other people.'

Lean, unconvinced ('He's going to be covered in crêpe hair and it'll look awful'), made him audition and do a screen test. Alec in fact demanded the test, which was described as only 'quite good' by one party – while Robert Donat who tested for the role of Bill Sikes was 'terrible'. 'I got mine by the skin of my teeth and Robert didn't,' reported Alec later. 'Of course I was bowled over by it and Alec got the part without another word,' said Lean. Not much diversity of opinion here.

During shooting in 1948 Alec would arrive in Pinewood at 5 a.m. or 5.30 a.m. to be made up. The make-up evolved from

George Cruikshank's drawings of the old Jew. Stuart Freeborn, the make-up man, had experimented with new plastics, enlisting the help of ICI to achieve flesh-like materials that were not only supple but semi-transparent, so that one could see the blood vessels. So intent was Lean on achieving the right appearance for Fagin that he had Freeborn try out numerous variations on Alec: at one time, said Freeborn, 'Fagin looked just like Jesus Christ'. Lean sent the filmed tests off to the States for approval. It was only because Freeborn could manage to make the PVC (polyvinyl chloride) into a very soft, foam-like exterior that he finally achieved the right effect with the nose. America said 'no' to the nose. 'To hell with them,' Lean responded.

Even though Freeborn made a wax mould of the nose he modelled for Fagin, and then made a cast – and then evolved a technique for enabling the melted plastic to dry at different densities – it took three and a half hours each morning to make up Alec. Three and a half hours multiplied by fifty-two days is a considerable amount of time to spend sitting still: 'I won't speak; I shall be very quiet; you need all your concentration', Alec told Freeborn, who pushed tiny rolls of cotton wool into the nose to absorb the perspiration. The crews and set-up came to know the Fagin face so well that one day, when Alec was not required for filming and he wandered on to the set as himself, he was perturbed to find no one recognized him.

As he became better known examples of this kind of story multiplied. One example was of Alec and Gielgud lunching together one day in York. A waitress asks them to sign the tablecloth. 'I'm sure she doesn't know me from Adam,' says Alec. 'She'll be very disappointed if I sign my own name. I shall sign Jack Buchanan.' He does and thrills the waitress (apparently).

Yet one might still become impatient at mentions of Alec's facelessness, for even in those far-off days most people recognized him at once. Indeed, Alec had an outburst – 'I am so tired of them saying I have no face' – for he had from the start a distinct face, even if it was – and this was crucial – easily transformable. As someone pointed out, if we were to cleave him down the middle we would find an angry man parading around with the placard: Recognition Now. He was more easily and instantly recognizable than many others including Marlene Dietrich,

William Holden and Laurence Olivier. It was simply that his image became that of having no face because he could impersonate others so well.

The impersonation that finally emerged in *Oliver Twist* was masterly. Alec brought to Fagin's harsh, rasping utterances a pantomime gentleness of movement, while the apocalyptic mood of Lean's direction was underlined by the music of Arnold Bax. But the exaggerated traits of character were still enough to provoke accusations that his portrayal was anti-Semitic. 'That was, I believe,' said Alec later, 'about the only time since the war when the Russians and Americans united in protest. [In March 1950 *Oliver Twist* was banned by the American Film Industry's Production Code; seven minutes – consisting almost wholly of close-ups of Alec – were cut before it was allowed to be shown in the US.] They all walked out, I'm told, when the film was first shown in Vienna. It was *so* ridiculous, because we fell over backwards to ensure even that the word "Jew" shouldn't be mentioned. I really don't think the film did any harm. I must say that after it came out here, Jewish taxi-drivers used to greet me *most* affectionately and refuse to let me pay my fares.'

But in New York, where soon after the film opened he was playing in *The Cocktail Party*, a hostess at a party said to him, 'I wonder you dare to come. I'd rather give my children prussic acid than let them see your picture.'

What did Alec learn from *Oliver Twist*? Lean taught him to perform the same action identically from take to take. Being neat and liking precision, he found that Lean reinforced his taste for understatement and simplicity. Lean steered him through the new world of cinema and turned him from grimacing his way through a role to relying on thinking. Then, as much later, Alec never minded playing thoroughly evil people, whom he found more interesting to act than good ones. They had to be evil, not weak. 'I don't like playing weak characters because I suppose I'm frightened of my own weaknesses.'

But what about acting Shakespeare himself? Caryl Brahms, literary partner of S. J. Simon, later of Ned Sherrin, met Yvonne Mitchell at this time, imperious beauty, highly talented classical actress. The actress had been reading *No Bed for Bacon*, the Brahms–Simon skit on Shakespeare, and she told Brahms, 'You should send the novel straight to Alec Guinness; he would be the perfect Shakespeare and it would make a perfect film.'

Brahms wrote to Alec: 'Dear Mr Guinness, I am sorry to burden you with one of my own books, but if you would leaf through it you could do so much for one character, Shakespeare.' Alec answered at once: 'Dear Miss Brahms, I could never forgive you for telling my public that I have a face like a dispirited haddock.'

Recoiling from this rebuke, Brahms, in consulting her cuttings book, found she had called him this; but she also wrote, in reviews of his work, about his Fool in *Lear*: 'See, where the marvellously swift and dramatic gesture of tightening of the noose of rope sends him to his rendezvous with death'; of his Richard II, that with his 'little nervous twitch of a smile that came and went and said all that needed to be said about this, the weakest of the English kings'. She later commented that Alec played (in *All's Well*) the King of France 'and probably his wheelchair too'. Of Alec's own favourite role, Abel Drugger, she had written that he carped 'Heartbreakingly like a very young monkey at the end of an organ-grinder's string'.

Fortified with such recall, she wrote to Alec, 'Dear Mr Guinness, Just which are you disputing: "dispirited" or "haddock"?' A few days later her telephone rang and the cultured voice announced, 'This is Mr Haddock Guinness. Would you be free for lunch on Thursday?' At the subsequent lunch he introduced her to the avocado.

Ealing turned down Alec's subsequent suggestion to film *No Bed for Bacon* (cynics might add that it was finally made in 1999, called *Shakespeare in Love*).

13. Floodlit by Moonlight

Alec was approaching thirty-five. He often said how much he hated being in his thirties, and he was right in the middle. Wanting more control of his life and himself, he agreed to take over the direction of a play when the director fell ill. It was a difficult time for him, this year – 1948. While his film career, with offers and projects, burgeoned, the theatre began to look more and more as if it could get along without him.

And the Guinnesses had no more children. Why? Matthew was now eight, just at the outward reach of needing or hoping for a sibling. Many – legion – were the wives of serving officers and men who, separated during the long war years, rejoined their spouses during victory euphoria with spontaneous conception and 1945 and 1946 were bumper years for births. With Alec's new-found earning power – he complained bitterly about poor wages pre-war but never expressed gratitude or relief at his fiscal fortune – (as Woody Allen said, 'Money is better than poverty, if only for financial reasons') – he could have supported a household bursting with kids.

Merula, too, came from a large family and her experience of it had been positive. So what went wrong? Had he become impotent? Did he no longer want to sleep with Merula? One suspects it was Alec's desire of keeping his family small and tightly within his control at the peak of his career that might have stopped Merula. This is strange because one might have thought, being the lonely single child of his mother, he would not have wanted to inflict this same condition on Matthew. Stranger still, why should he copy his own mother? He never once, as far as I can tell or remember, expressed any regret at not providing a brother or sister.

The family Alec acquired was, it seemed, definitely for Alec and not for itself, and this possession of a family was perhaps to harden as well as extend, in time, to members of his profession who are in a sense like a large family. Alec was a film star and while his expressions or posturings of humility were genuine, this was not the whole story. Sometimes humility was an expression of his guilt, a kind of negative narcissism, sometimes it was genuine. As Angela Fox again so aptly said, Alec 'doesn't behave as if he has made money – but he has learnt to behave like a duke: everything is perfection and everything taken with deadly seriousness.' This is not the attitude of a family man, but a stickler for rules and etiquette – except, perhaps, when he feels like breaking them himself. Strong echoes here of Proust's Baron de Charlus.

Ronald Harwood who had a cottage near where the Guinnesses were soon to move in Sussex said how much Alec hated Christmas and was always ill-tempered at this period of the year; it seems that his bursts of ill-temper toward Merula could have stemmed from his sense at being let down or neglected by his mother. He had to get his own back somehow at the woman who had taken the place of his mother in his life, so he could be 'cruel and sharp', while Merula would suffer it patiently. 'She has that thing of absorbing the venom for herself,' said Harwood.

On one occasion when the Harwoods dined with the Guinnesses Merula burnt the meat. She came from the kitchen and stuttering – she did have a slight stutter – announced this: 'I'm awfully sorry the beef has burnt.' Alec cruelly mocked her, 'I'm awfully sorry the b-b-beef is b-b-b-burnt!', although he later apologized.

While Harwood felt uncomfortable in Alex's unpredictable company, Angela Fox said he was sharp, imperious, 'a complete prima donna, very charming one moment, an absolute bitch the next'. To Merula he was unpleasant in front of guests and publicly dressed her down, 'Oh Merula, what the fuck do you mean by giving us this fucking shit, how could you be so bloody stupid! . . . it's foul.' Fox praised her: 'She does not flinch or turn a hair. Next minute he would say, "You must come and see Merula's pictures. She paints like an angel."' Sheridan Morley was amazed that however many times you met Alec with Merula or with his son, he would insist on introducing them formally: 'This is Merula, my wife, this is my son Matthew.' Other actors recall during visits a terrible row between Matthew and Alec where Alec did not in any way control his anger.

Alan Bennett, in calculated mild disloyalty only months after Alec's death, wrote in an extract from his diary published in early 2001 in the *London Review of Books* how Alec treated Merula as if she was just an appendage. He said he bought several of Merula's needlework pictures, only to have Alec thank him 'as if I were doing a favour to him'. He was always 'Nervous she would show him up or show herself up . . . Merula was, for instance, a superb cook and when I first stayed at Kettlebrook would produce meals which Alec would then apologize for – behaviour which she took in her stride, knowing it would pass.'

The contradictions extended to his social behaviour outside his family. At least he was consistent. Fox told me, 'At a party he will stand in the corner like a pale or white ghost or *plinth*.' My daughter noticed that at a Garrick Club party to which we were invited Alec sat near the doorway of this ornate, spacious room entirely alone, saying nothing to anyone. 'He always tries to sit alone at a communal table,' said Harwood of his behaviour at lunchtime at the club. 'He's not amenable . . . it's like asking a ghost to come to dinner. It's his tortured temperament, he tries very hard to deal with it.'

How the angered, injured small boy liked, needed – in spite of discharging resentment on those he loved or liked – praise, is illustrated best by Ronald Neame. When Alec played Gully Jimson, the disgusting, seedy egocentric artist in *The Horse's Mouth* in 1958, Neame noticed how Alec, the producer and star of the film, grew more and more withdrawn during filming. In the end he asked what was the matter. Alec told him everyone wanted to act at some point in their lives, usually between the ages of ten and fourteen. Little girls pranced around like grand ladies, small boys pretended to be cowboys. But when they grew up they went off to be pilots, accountants, dentists and so on, but the actor always had that part of him that never got beyond fourteen.

'An actor has to be praised, encouraged, and every so often, spanked. I have been working on this film for days, putting everything I have into it and nobody has given me as much as a hint of a compliment.' Neame protested, 'But, Alec you're the producer and the star. We've all been far more worried about how we seem to you.' (*Sunday Times*, 2000). This incident goes to show how in his life even with Merula Alec had never really gone beyond his insecurities and resolved them. In his art, as he had begun, Alec remained a loner. He needed her so much, and possibly this need drove him to make such comments as (in *My Name Escapes Me*) 'Merula is likely to chip in only to kill the point of any story I may embark on.'

At the end of her life, apparently when she was dying, Merula talked with recollected dread and horror of the number of frocks she, a country girl, was obliged to have, the amount of changing that went on and the difficulty of dining in gloves. She did not lead a very happy life in St Peter's Square, and like many a film star's appendage (he felt he was obliged to lead a film star's life), she learnt all too bitterly that film actors were not real actors: 'A lot of the time what acting is about, is meeting someone's eye,' Tom Cruise has said. He should have specified 'film' acting, but does he know there is any other kind? Michael Caine has declared, 'Film acting is not so much acting as reacting, doing nothing with tremendous skill.' What both these actors omit to say is that working in films leaves one with a large surplus of unused energy: it makes minimal demands for an exaggerated reward. Film actors have no control over the creative process or shape of their role. Not properly tested, they have time for everything and it is little wonder, perhaps, that those who are successful so often destroy themselves and those near to them.

*

Still in its temporary home at the New Theatre, the Old Vic Company in 1948 was in crisis when in September Alec began directing *Twelfth Night*. In spite of the two Dickens films stage ambitions were still much to the fore. Olivier and Richardson had been sacked as directors of the Old Vic, while John Burrell, their co-director had fallen ill. Alec, having been coached to succeed them, had, as an actor, proved to have neither the power nor the stature. To fill the gap in policy and continuity, he had been given this popular comedy to direct.

The production had not from the start been his. He had taken it over because John Burrell was absent. He worked with Burrell's cast as well as the sets that Burrell had approved, neither of which he liked, nor would have chosen himself. He put his stamp on it by subtly grafting on to Robert Eddison, who played Feste, much of his own vision of the melancholy fool. Alec saw Feste as the centre of the play and in love with Viola, as someone commented, 'like a consumptive prince in exile'. Cedric Hardwicke, whom Richardson had dispatched from Hollywood as his replacement while he made the film of *The Heiress*, played the most gentlemanly of Belches – a 'whisky-and-soda man'. According to Donald Sinden, who was cast as Sebastian to play the twin to a Viola whom he closely resembled physically – only to find her pull out and be replaced by Jane Baxter, who was four inches shorter and utterly dissimilar – Alec's production was 'very distinguished and saved the Old Vic's reputation'.

Alec underlined the melancholy side of everything in the play, transposing the first two scenes, which made Donald Wolfit when he saw the production 'apoplectic'. The reviews cottoned on to the fact that Alec had put Feste, played by Robert Eddison, at the centre of the action, interpreting him with a hard-edged sadness (and why indeed, one asks, did Alec never play Feste in his long career, except that it is the natural clown who wants to play tragedy?). This centring of the play on Feste was, everyone agreed, at the expense of Viola and the sentimental plot. But Alec and Viola did not get on, while Peter Copley, who played Aguecheek, observed that Alec 'seemed to have a strange understanding of other performers' (by this he meant a lack of understanding). He took Baxter, a successful West End actress, also of considerable beauty, and explained to her in long discourses of great complexity, which were completely above her head, the metaphysical niceties of love. 'What *was* he talking about?' Copley said it reduced her to tears, and 'Was it really relevant?' Copley remarked on this element of cruelty in Alec, and that he was clearly not aware he was reducing Baxter to impotence. Not surprisingly her notices were poor.

Popular and commercial though *Twelfth Night* proved, it did little to help Alec's disenchantment with himself in the role of classic stage actor belonging to one of the great English theatre companies. He had shown himself that he was not a director of Shakespeare. He had asked the Old Vic for four varied and contrasting parts to show in what direction his talent lay, but the strong answer had come back: in four different directions.

Or, perhaps, in any direction he was given or chose to take. He would not act again in a permanent or semi-permanent company performing a classical repertoire. With *Twelfth Night* he parted for good from the stage-acting peers of his generation. This was nearly his twentieth encounter with the plays of Shakespeare, yet only a few of these had resulted in more than a costly expense of spirit. Yet during this time Alec continued to capture hearts and cement his reputation as a leading film actor. He quickly became known as the man who could disguise himself as often and as variously as he wanted, yet even here there was dispute about whether he disguised himself in these roles, or actually 'became' them. What engendered this new phase was his happy coincidence with the rise of Ealing.

The 'studio with team spirit' – six acres of dull tarmacked drive and studio in West London – Ealing Studios had opened in 1931 and had churned out historical romance after historical romance, largely under the direction of Basil Dean who resigned in 1938 and ran ENSA throughout the war. Since then the studios had been run by a Birmingham-born Jew, Michael Balcon, who had already created the reputation of Alfred Hitchcock with *The Thirty-Nine Steps* and *The Man Who Knew Too Much*, and of Robert Flaherty with *Man of Aran*. During the war Balcon had nurtured a group of young film-makers who began mostly as editors, many of them with Oxford or Cambridge backgrounds. The directors included Charles Frend, Robert Hamer, Charles Crichton and – from Brazil via France – Alberto Cavalcanti. Balcon produced several war films, whose uncompromising documentary exactness had roused Churchill's wrath, but were praised by high-ranking service personnel enough to escape banning. T. E. B. (or Tibby) Clarke, the war reserve policeman turned scriptwriter whom Balcon discovered, wrote *Hue and Cry*, the first film of a distinctive Ealing style: this tale, set mostly in London, of street urchins who eccentrically capture a criminal, established what Balcon called 'The new story-documentary technique . . . which I believe is going to be the most important trend in the cinema from now onwards.'

Documentary trends apart and in the words of the popular adage, 'Everyone at Ealing is a character,' here was the productive paradox at the heart of the studio's achievement. For its head, this autocrat or benevolent dictator whom some called rigid and puritanical, ruled in the traditional manner of a Jewish patriarch, and formed a group of technician-based film-makers who stayed together for fifteen years so that, quite unusually for the cinema anywhere in the world, they maintained a unity of style. Balcon was admired because he had already taken a lot of chances, and after the war came Ealing's big chance. As Charles Crichton, director of *The Lavender Hill Mob*, told me, 'The war made a lot of difference: for a while American films were invisible. It was a period of emotional stress and this stress came out more in the comedies than in the war pictures. The comedies were more sincere – more human, more warm.'

In the first film that Alec made for Ealing, *Kind Hearts and Coronets*, directed by Robert Hamer, he played the whole of the D'Ascoyne family. In this black comedy of murder and intrigue of a typical English-gentry vintage, the monsters of arrogance and cruelty were bumped off by a rather effete murderer, Louis (Dennis Price), who dealt a good hand in ruthless epigrams such as 'Revenge is a dish which people of taste prefer to eat cold.'

Hamer had a first in mathematics from Cambridge; fair in complexion he had a 'buttoned up' manner; his small face has been described as 'like a clenched fist'. He first offered three of the family roles which he, together with John Dighton, had scripted. Alec then suggested, 'If you want seven or eight people to look like me, why don't I play them all myself?' Hamer agreed: if three why not eight; he persuaded Balcon to let Alec play the whole family.

Hamer and Alec got on well. 'We talked the same language. We laughed at the same things,' said Alec. *Kind Hearts and Coronets* was shot on location at Leeds Castle in Kent, whose lack of size and grandeur at first upset Guinness, Michael Relph, art director and associate producer, told me, in spite of its air of hereditary privilege and its position in the middle of a lake. Douglas Slocombe, cameraman on many notable Ealing pictures, pointed out how meticulous Alec showed himself in his preparation, how he would arrive every morning at six to start being made up, and how his memory was exact.

The split-screen trick shot when Alec appeared as six D'Ascoynes in contiguous church pews at the same time had to be shot in an old-fashioned way. The lens was laboriously shuttered and finely adjusted to open in part for each new impersonation. It took three days at Ealing to shoot the requisite number of fifteen-second shots, while at any moment the composite picture could have been ruined if Alec had not complied with the technical complexities of the placings.

On set one day Alec told Douglas Slocombe how Matthew, now aged seven, snatched up a crucifix which his father had brought home, stared at it in a very puzzled way, then suddenly grasped it by the shaft, held it between thumb and fingers, parallel to the floor and made arabesques in the air with it, like an aeroplane, to the accompaniment of a 'zooing' sound. Alec told versions of this over and over again. For example, to Timothy West, he and Matthew were in the garden together weeding when they had found this old plastic crucifix. 'What's it for?' Matthew had asked. 'These things are made,' Alec replied, 'so we should remember this man called Jesus who was crucified.' Whereupon Matthew picked it up and 'zooed' round like an aeroplane. (I was told by Paul and Joy Scofield that this episode happened between Jill, Merula's potter sister, and Matthew. Alec appropriated it.)

When they were staying on location in Kent, Alec, with his co-stars Joan Greenwood, Valerie Hobson and Price, would play 'the Game', an entertaining pastime of association and memory first made popular by Noël Coward. Each player had to repeat everything said by another player and this could run to sixty or more inconsequential words or ideas which had to be recalled in the order they were said. Robert Hamer had a phenomenal memory: he could read a column upside down in the *Daily Telegraph* and repeat it verbatim. Alec could surpass even Hamer.

Alec later identified his real-life models for one or two of the family whom Louis bumps off. An elderly admiral had once reprimanded him for wearing a scarf over his uniform on an icy day on a Scottish loch and ordered him to put on a collar and tie (which he was already wearing). Alec said he watched the admiral depart through his 'quizzes until he was as small as a mosquito', rehearsing to himself Hamlet's lines to Polonius about the actors, 'Let them be well used; for they are the abstract and brief chronicles of the time: after your death, you were better have a bad epitaph than their ill respect while you lived.' While he was

playing the senior officer D'Ascoyne going down on the bridge of
his ship his mind had jumped back 'to that cold morning near
Inverary. I am ashamed to say it now, but I had my little revenge
and it tasted sweet.'

Kind Hearts and Coronets, released in mid-1949 and one of the
most successful films made at Ealing, became a comedy classic. It
also brought hitherto undreamt-of acclaim to Alec, but a new
complication: fragmentation of character into multiple impersonation. In the eight speaking parts, one non-speaking part and a
portrait in oils he displays different aspects of the same physical
and mental constitution. The key to his immersion in each role
was that he could disguise himself not only physically but mentally.
But here, to explain Alec's reservation, were only eight Abel
Druggers in the same film. Versatility, the knife-thrower becoming
the dog-trainer, the juvenile later returning as the senile old man,
had long been in the music hall and circus tradition. True
psychological complexity remained with the murderer. Or, as Alec
himself put it, 'False noses are too easy.'

Although *Kind Hearts and Coronets* established Alec as the
most gifted character actor in England, he dismissed the roles as
thin stuff – 'Pretty cardboard'. What happened in the darkness
after each D'Ascoyne snuffed it – the mysterious limbo in which
Alec could transform himself into something quite new – became
more intriguing. Who really was he?

Peter Sellers, besotted with admiration for Alec when he saw
this film, began his lifelong hero worship of Guinness, to which
he added a fair measure of envy (and Schadenfreude, when Alec
was not at his best). When he met Alec over lunch he felt he had
been with a demure, one-man rep company. 'You cannot believe
how quiet this man is,' his biographer Roger Lewis reported him
as saying, 'He's shy! He's got a switch inside. He turns it on, and
another person pops up!'

The multiple role-playing stole the show, and in falling short
of the complexity demanded in the murderer, Dennis Price,
according to reliable witnesses, failed to make subsequent progress
as an actor. While Louis murdered the D'Ascoyne family, the
screen success of Alec as the family of his victims became the
instrument of Price's own destruction. For while Price might have
expected a lot of praise for playing Louis, Alec stole the show.

Price, a highly sensitive being, felt rejected and suffered from being overshadowed; he eventually committed suicide. 'It's mythology,' Alec said of this overshadowing. 'I revered Dennis. I so badly wanted him in *Tunes of Glory* that I put up the money to buy him out of *Heartbreak House*.' Alec also paid for Price's memorial service.

T. S. Eliot, whom Alec had met on several occasions through playing in *The Cocktail Party* and who had, as Alec remarked, 'a surprisingly coarse laugh', later disapproved of *Kind Hearts and Coronets*. Eliot believed it immoral to make a funny film about murder. Maybe he was right and the breaking of taboos has done untold harm, but his warnings about cultural decline had little effect at that time or since.

That the director was of commanding importance to the success or failure of a film was demonstrated by the one outright failure Alec suffered in this early batch of Ealing comedies. Just after *Kind Hearts and Coronets* he played the part of a journalist in Charles Frend's *A Run for Your Money*. Frend was an integral member of the Ealing team. The two films he made with Alec, *A Run for Your Money* (1949) and the later *Barnacle Bill* (1957), failed to ignite, although Alec enjoyed Frend's easy raconteur wit and his compendious knowledge of pubs and beer. Like many Ealing figures Frend was known as a 'character'. The contrast between his working self and his social self was remarkable; a colleague has described how, when on the studio floor, Frend became eaten up with nervousness and self-doubt, and as a result fierce and aggressive towards actors and crew alike. He was his 'own worst enemy' and gravitated towards subjects of tragic dimension, if not tragedies: *The Cruel Sea* was one, *Scott of the Antarctic* another.

After his visit to Liverpool where he had stayed with Glenville, Alec opted for *The Human Touch*, which opened at the Savoy Theatre in February 1949 and ran for five months. John Laurie played the disbelieving antagonist to Alec's fanatical young Scot, who 'was dressed in an elegant black overcoat'. Although Alec was described as unsuitable for the role – 'I could not believe the doctors could ever have thought Mr Guinness mad' wrote *The Times* reviewer – it was popular with Alec's new-found following. Queen Mary attended one performance 'wrapped in dark fur with a voluminous stole'.

Alec's next role was closer to his heart in his search for a deeper meaning in life and an integrated self. He had first read Eliot's early poems when he was seventeen. He became an instant admirer and subsequently bought each new work as it appeared: 'Sweeney Among the Nightingales' from the 1920 *Poems*, with its obliquely exotic South American background (his father Andrew Geddes was a South American banker), was his favourite. Sweeney himself was the 'coarse average man', while the poem's ending, Alec rather oddly believed, had some of the best lines in the whole of literature:

> And let their liquid siftings fall
> To stain the stiff dishonoured shroud.

Alec took delight in pointing out 'liquid siftings' meant bird droppings. Although the Sitwells knew Eliot, Alec doubted their assertion that as a young man he used a pale green powder to make himself look more interesting.

In early 1939, when Alec arrived back in London after the Old Vic tour of the continent, he heard that *The Family Reunion* had been published that day. He managed by the afternoon to buy a copy: 'All I can say is that I sat up that entire night reading it twice through with intense excitement.'

His first personal contact with Eliot had come when, as an ordinary seaman in naval barracks, he heard him talk on the radio. Struck by what Eliot had been saying, he wrote to him at his publishers Faber and Faber and received a reply in which Eliot recalled seeing Alec play Hamlet before the war. Once again Alec ambitiously sought contact with one of his heroes to confirm and develop some aspiration in himself. We identify this as the mimetic envy which drove his life, a trait Kenneth Tynan also possessed, although with far greater effrontery. Alec later pointed out how that talk of Eliot's contained 'words and phrases which cropped up in *Little Gidding*, which he hadn't at that time written'.

When, in the spring of 1949, Henry Sherek, who had been spreading the word among his friends that Guinness was 'the best actor in the world', asked him to appear in *The Cocktail Party* at the first Edinburgh Festival, Alec waited anxiously for the daily half-dozen or so sheets of the text to appear, 'hot from T. S. Eliot's typewriter', sent round from Sherek's office. He was thrilled to be one of the very first people to read a new work by Eliot, and he 'used to have the pages spread out on the floor at home anxiously and [was] cliff-hanging for the next batch to come the next day. Oh I loved, loved it as a play!'

During rehearsals his admiration for the poet, his senior by twenty-six years, deepened further. Later, he found himself in Eliot's company on one of the liner *Queens* crossing the Atlantic:

> I found him a man of immense good humour with a richly warm laugh and he loved his dry martini and had no, not a shred of arrogance. [Notice this puts a different construction on the 'coarse' laugh.]

As an example of Eliot's modesty Alec cited his behaviour at rehearsal one day when Alec, in the course of delivering his lines, said to him, 'Oh Mr Eliot, haven't I said this speech before, rather?'

> Eliot looked at the script and said, 'Oh yes, you're quite right', and he put a pencil through sixteen lines without a qualm and a little later in the day I said I cannot get from here to cross the stage . . . and there'd have to be a pause. And he again took the script and wrote four superb lines, they just flowed from him which enabled me to do the thing I wanted to do . . . The only other person I've come across who can do that is Graham Greene who again has the same masterful hand at seeing his own possible mistake and helping the poor wretched actor.   **BBC interview**

One has to remark that this example of humility did not in future years affect Alec's own treatment of younger playwrights such as Simon Gray and Alan Bennett.

The Cocktail Party expressed something of Eliot's fear, which he shared with Shakespeare and in particular Hamlet, that to enjoy love was to destroy it. Alec was often playing against the bent of his genius; like him, but as a dramatist, Eliot was not an explicit artist, rather one who modelled much of his dramatic craftsmanship on the indirect, thwarted action of *Hamlet*, the supreme play of inner life. It was therefore perhaps to be foreseen that Alec would triumph as Harcourt-Reilly, the Harley Street psychiatrist who becomes Eliot's arbitrator of love and wrecked marriage, and the authoritative voice in *The Cocktail Party*. The temperature of the piece never soars very high, but in this production there was a powerful current of feeling beneath the surface, similar to that in *Hamlet*: 'I have that within which passes show.'

Eliot had based the missionary zeal of Celia Coplestone on the life of the religious visionary Charles de Foucauld, who had fired Alec's enthusiasm some years before while he was serving at sea, by his mysterious power of holiness. Born to wealth and social position, Foucauld practised as a priest in the Sahara, living in a stone hermitage and giving medical aid to tribesmen, until he was killed in 1919 by marauding Arabs. While *The Cocktail Party* was somewhat rigged with forced and theoretical ideas about the love of God versus the love of man, Irene Worth as Celia brought an inner sensuality to help clothe Eliot's words in flesh, while Alec himself tapped the hidden depth of feeling with a kind of sinister potency. Worth described the impact Guinness had on the play and on her own performance:

When I, as Celia, had the good fortune to play the 'break-up of the affair' scene with Robert Flemyng ... Robert's performance had been so profound that he had prepared the ground for the great 'consulting room scene' to follow. Alec Guinness then said 'Yes', and brought the house down ... When the couple left, Alec lay down on his own consulting room couch and put a handkerchief over his face. The telephone rang, he answered it and said, 'yes'. I don't know what alchemy he used. I often watched him from the wings before my entrance. There was nothing to see – only Alec at the telephone and the audience laughing with delight. His brilliance defies explanation.

After the laughter, Alec prepared a stillness for my entrance which made it possible for us to play the ensuing scene sitting, without a move, until it ended perhaps twenty-five minutes later. His stillness allowed Celia to pour out her heart. His stillness was like the stabiliser of a great ship. Alec's love and knowledge of the sea are not wasted. His stillness was like the sea. **Dear Alec**

Later Alec did not speak highly of this production or of the one he himself did at Chichester in 1968, which transferred to

London. E. Martin Brown, the director on the first occasion, proved himself on Eliot's wavelength although he had no great theatrical sense. He directed it, so Alec said, as a smart drawing-room comedy of the 1930s although Alec was probably 'more Sinister Street than Harley Street', as someone at the time teased. It did more than justice to the play: it became the touchstone for the short post-war revival of poetic drama. It had a powerful influence on Alec's subsequent conversion to Catholicism. Alec's performance fascinated Harold Hobson, who, on the death of James Agate, had assumed his mantle as critic of the *Sunday Times*:

> On the surface Guinness was light-hearted and playful, but fundamentally he was immensely serious in his treatment of the psychological problems presented to him by the Chamberlaynes' guests, and by the Chamberlaynes themselves. It is to one of these guests, Celia Coplestone, that Harcourt-Reilly, like Hamlet showing his mother the two pictures of his father and his uncle, compares the life of domestic utility with that of dedication. On the one hand:
>> If that is what you wish,
>> I can reconcile you to the human condition . . .
>> Learn to avoid excessive expectation,
>> Become tolerant . . .
>
> Which is to be compared with the life of sanctity and martyrdom:
>> There *is* another way, if you have the courage . . .
>> The second is unknown, and so requires faith.
>> The kind of faith that issues from despair . . .
>> You will journey blind.

Hobson described how this was beautifully spoken by Alec.

Celia rejects the ordinary humdrum domesticity for the way of martyrdom (bizarrely devoured by ants in some savage country, an idea Eliot copied from Michael Innes's *Appleby on Ararat*). However it did not, 'for all the beguiling fascination of Guinness's voice . . . for a moment make me believe that Eliot believed in the glory of martyrdom'. Hobson admired, but did not feel himself conquered.

Alec, by virtue of the choice of this Eliot role, may have been on his way to becoming the martyr himself. That he was aware, perhaps only at an unconscious level, of the importance of this choice, was registered by his purchase, with his first week's salary, of the gold vest-pocket watch which he had once imagined he might inherit from his father. This signified he had earned some money that counted.

He carried the watch during the performances of *The Cocktail Party*. And what did he have engraved, on the inside – and not on the back, so it would be a private gesture to himself – but Hamlet's 'The readiness is all'. This was recognition by Alec himself that he had 'arrived'. The success took everyone by surprise, so there was no London theatre available for it until May 1950. Just before Alec departed for the opening at the Henry Miller Theater, New York, he could afford to unbutton himself just a little. He did this in a talk given in Oxford to the university dramatic society. The report in *Isis* on 20 October 1949 remarked that offstage Alec looked most unlike an actor:

> . . . almost shy in his self-effacement, and one could well believe that he was so upset when bullied once by Mr Gielgud that he lost his voice. To recover it he visited an elocution specialist, an old lady, who we feel must have looked like Margaret Rutherford in a character part. Muttering about doggie-woggies, she hurriedly pushed young Guinness on to his knees and made him scramble about on the floor barking 'Bow wow'. The treatment was unsuccessful. Next he saw an actress, who seized hold of his upper lip and said in a toneless South Kensington voice, 'My dear, it's quite flat – no good to you at all. You might as well get rid of it.' Mr Guinness still has the lip, and seems to find it useful.

Alec talked about acting, striking out in a direction very different from that of Olivier, Gielgud and Richardson. 'An actor needs a slightly mystical approach to the stage, for after all you can't force a character on yourself; you must absorb it into every pore.' He told his student audience that actors were born and could never be made, and that four months was long enough to be in 'Rep' for 'inevitably this week's character study suffers from that of next week's'. But, he added, twenty years' experience was necessary before one became an actor. This *Isis* reporter added – tartly or tactfully, one is not quite sure which – 'The exception proves the rule, for Mr Guinness himself has been acting for fifteen years.'

On the liner taking them to New York, Alec and Irene Worth rehearsed in the corner of a vast lounge. When he raised his voice to demand 'What had you believed were your relations with this man?' Alec remarked that copies of the *Ocean Times* were lowered in many an armchair. In New York (and he gets the date wrong, something an alleged 'diarist' should not do) he and fellow members of the cast, summoned to a supper by the famous society hostess Elsa Maxwell, found themselves 'set up' for a TV commercial advertisement. As Alec lifted his fork to pierce the turkey on his plate someone yelled 'Cut', the lights went out and their hostess shouted 'Don't touch what's on the table. Your food is in another room.' When they realized their buffet had been plastic, outrage followed and the *Cocktail Party* guests left.

After the short New York run of thirty performances which began in January 1950 Alec had to leave because of film commitments. In New York *The Cocktail Party* became a sell-out: Brooks Atkinson in the *New York Times* called the play 'verbose and elusive drama that had to be respected', while another critic said 'American playwrights should go home and break up their typewriters.'

On his way back to Southampton Alec met Beatrice Lillie, with her lover John Phillips. Alec knew her from North Africa, but her only son had been killed in the navy in 1942, and as a result she drank heavily, especially so on this *Queen Elizabeth* crossing, when she tried to manoeuvre Alec erratically round the dance floor; later when displaced from her and her friends' deckchairs by two other passengers who claimed them as theirs, Lillie took off into flights of drunken invective, called the passengers 'Teeny weeny assholes' and 'two old anuses'. 'You get the steward. He's called Eric. Whenever we meet we always have sex whatever the weather.'

When the pair, whom it is hard not to feel sorry for – Alec in his account finds Bea Lillie's coarse abuse of them amusing – said they would fetch the captain Lillie told them 'great', she had slept with the captain every time she crossed the ocean, maybe forty times in all.

The operative interest in this anecdote and similar ones is that

Alec relishes the extravagant behaviour of an eccentric middle-aged woman who has 'lost it'. He is uninhibited in his flaunting of a woman's outrageous sexual behaviour, as if he needs to purge its threat, while he is modest and inhibited about similar manifestations in any man. Is it Martita Hunt once again, and even, behind her unmentioned in the shadows, his mother Agnes? The traffic of cab drivers dropping in for sexual favours, the hampers of smoked salmon and quarter bottles of champagne, stirred his imagination into grotesqueness and Dickensian exaggeration.

Last Holiday, Guinness's next film, was a more typical Ealing film than *Kind Hearts and Coronets*; while not altogether a success, it was more prophetic of Alec's future development, both on and off the screen, as well as being revealing about the human condition of being Alec Guinness. In *Last Holiday* Alec played the first of his 'little men' on screen and demonstrated his capacity for ordinariness.

J. B. Priestley's characteristic but wayward script tried to draw a social message out of a man dying of an incurable disease. This stopped *Last Holiday* from being the more interesting film it might have become had the story been developed more subtly. Priestley felt that London critics missed the various depths of irony as 'they shrugged it away'. As George Bird, Alec in double-breasted pin-striped suit and under sentence of death from 'Lempington's disease', attempts to enjoy his last weeks in a 'high-class' seaside hotel.

It seemed that only Alec could convey with magnetic power that special melancholy of the anonymous man holidaying alone in a run-down quality hotel. Unaffected in every way by the illness, Bird withholds his secret from the women and other characters to whom he becomes attached, and gains the power, love, and social distinction he previously could never enjoy. Bird finds out the diagnosis is mistaken, but dies anyway – in a car crash on the day of his reprieve.

Priestley commented, 'The scenes were not shot in chronological order, which meant that Alec had to be ready every morning to present his young man at some different stage of his development, jumping forward or backward in time. And this he did beautifully.' For the first time, he showed the ability to convert the screen into an intimate, private means of communication, as if revealing something special to each member of the audience. But still he watched and withheld.

Last Holiday was the prelude to five films made in quick succession, interrupted only by *Hamlet* at the New Theatre. The first of these was *The Mudlark*, occasioned by his Edinburgh and Broadway success in *The Cocktail Party*, and in it Alec impersonated his first historical genius: Disraeli. The high point of the film is the moving speech Disraeli makes in Parliament, punctuated by a long, dramatic silence, which, commented producer Darryl Zanuck, is one of the most effective moments of silence in film history. Since the script had not called for it, Zanuck asked Alec later on how he came to think of it. 'I didn't,' Alec told him. 'In the middle of my speech I forgot my lines – dried up.'

This was Alec's first Hollywood picture, directed by Jean Negulesco, although much of it was shot on location in England. Prestigious and successful as it was at the time – Alec won the *Picturegoer* Gold Medal for most popular actor and the film was chosen for the Royal Command performance – it sank in mid-Atlantic condescension. *The Times* called it a 'hybrid'. The photograph images of Alec's Disraeli make-up remain potent.

The Cocktail Party did open at last in London in May 1950, without Alec in the main role, but with Rex Harrison. Alec's evasiveness makes it hard to detect this fact in any of his three books, but he was upset, for the production enjoyed a long run while he, either from previous contracts to make more films, or from not being chosen for the Savoy Theatre production, missed playing the role intensely, all the more so, as he told me himself, when it had been promised to him.

His next two films kept him busy and both became Ealing classics. But his hunger to succeed definitively in a serious stage role, together with the identification he felt in particular with Eliot's Harcourt-Reilly fuelled his resentment, which in turn contributed to the most spectacular failure of his career, which followed these two films.

The first, *The Lavender Hill Mob*, was as far from the pretension of Eliot's new poetic drama as could be imagined, and it became part of folklore. Alec played the devious, bowler-hatted Mr Holland who seduces Stan Holloway's Pendlebury, a manufacturer of cheap souvenirs, turning them both bank robber. For this picture Alec was paid £6,000 (to Edith Evans's utter amazement when he told her of it). 'It had to be written and rewritten,' said Tibby Clarke, 'eleven times before it satisfied all concerned – and a really good climax eluded me through three or four versions.'

Alec spent several days with the script, weighing up each line and making illuminating suggestions that would never have occurred to Crichton, the director, or Clarke. 'I see Holland as a man given to handwashing gestures,' he pronounced. 'Anyone who usually does that is on the plump side so I think I ought to be slightly padded . . . we should somehow point the incongruity of a person like Holland seeing himself as the boss of a gang. It might be a good way to get the right effect if he were to have difficulties in pronouncing his R's.'

Guinness could become over-meticulous, recalled Crichton. He would hate having any pre-ordained moves; he would never allow a double to walk in the distance for him, although once in *Oliver Twist*, when Alec was off for some reason, Lean had made up as Fagin and, doubling for Alec, been filmed walking down a street. One day they were filming the scene at the kiosk at the top of the Eiffel Tower. Alec had not been called until later. A double was standing in. There was only one position for him to stand, and an assistant had put down some marks: 'For Christ's sake,' said Crichton, 'take those marks away. If he sees those it'll be a disaster.'

Alec's performance, if not revealing of his deeper self, had complete relaxation, together with an element of the commanding absence he somehow managed to place at the centre of some of his best film performances. Here was the elevation of Ealing's 'little man', the quiet rebellious type who was to find his apotheosis in Alec's next film and its best directional exponent.

*

'An Ealing comedy – we know . . . Sir Michael Balcon's jolly gagmen have established a style,' wrote Kenneth Tynan, who deputized for Milton Shulman on the *Evening Standard*, about Alec's next, much more significant film:

We know that there probably will not be a hero – or that, if there is, he will be slightly comic if not downright weird: that we shall not spend much time in the boudoir or the country-side: that we shall see a good deal of the Civil Service, the police force and the small shopkeeper: and that the theme will be the bizarre British, faced with yet another perfectly extraordinary situation.

The writing will be crisp and astute (Ealing all but invented scripting as a full-time profession in England) and nobody will rupture a blood vessel to make us laugh. Ealing offers an exceptional middle-class man's view of the middle-class. The novelty is to find a film studio with any point of view at all.

For his new director, as Alec wrote, 'The enemy was always lurking behind the portals and façades of the hierarchy. In short he is an artist, and like all artists wants his own way. Rightly.'

Up to this point Alexander Mackendrick had led a wayward, even erratic career. Born in 1912 in Boston, Massachusetts, he was repatriated when he was seven to Glasgow, where he lived with his Calvinist grandfather. His mother was an alcoholic who walked out on him and became a Catholic convert: 'Frankly, I preferred her when she was a tippler,' said Mackendrick later, who felt injured by her desertion and maintained a lifelong aversion to religion.

Lonely and unhappy as he was, Mackendrick nursed, in spite of his mother and albeit grudgingly, some moral feeling and when, after a brief spell at Glasgow School of Art (which he left without a degree), and outstanding work at J. Walter Thompson's on 'Horlick's continuity ads', he landed the job of directing *Whisky Galore!*, he brought to the Ealing comedy a special preoccupation which work with Alec deepened. The directors and crews at Ealing were notorious drinkers and would 'repair' after shooting to the Red Lion opposite the studio gates. Set on the whisky-starved Hebridean island of Todday, on whose rocks a cargo boat carrying 50,000 cases of spirit vital above all to Ealing, *Whisky Galore!* seethed with moral ambiguity. The way people saw things, their modes of perception, came to the forefront as the hopes for intoxication in the subversive part of the community overthrew the structure of authority. The innocent rejected what they could not see; the experienced blinded themselves.

This thematic depth was important to *The Man in the White Suit*, Mackendrick's next film, which was based on a play by his cousin Roger Macdougall, and further developed by John Dighton, of *Kind Hearts and Coronets*, and by Mackendrick himself. Alec, portraying this highly eccentric inventor Sidney Stratton, was surprised to find, on the first day of shooting, pinned on a board in the studio a sort of strip-cartoon Mackendrick had sketched of his intended shots for a scene. Although they were, as he thought, 'admirably and vigorously drawn', he was put on the defensive, for they signalled rigidity of approach, something of which he had a horror.

Stratton invents an artificial fibre of such perfect qualities that it threatens the livelihood of millions of textile workers. In that threat there is a disintegrating factor at work – as in *Whisky Galore!* – what the playwright Samuel Beckett identified as 'the principle of disintegration in even the most complacent solitudes'. As Charles Barr, a chronicler of Ealing wrote, 'Outside Mackendrick's work, how many British films have intelligence as a central concern, valued in the characters as it is expressed in the organisation of the film?'

When Mackendrick adapted Macdougall's play he 'took Roger's hero and gave him a minor role, and pivoted the whole story around a secondary character, the one played in the film by Alec Guinness, to make a new story entirely'. This was a remarkable discovery of Mackendrick – 'that there is a character you need in a play, but don't need in a film because the camera takes over from him. It's Enobarbus in *Antony and Cleopatra*, it's Horatio in *Hamlet*. The camera becomes that character who holds it all together – the viewpoint character.'

The imaginative breadth of *The Man in the White Suit* was Faustian, beginning with the Dickensian 'Coke Town' landscape of smoky chimney and grimy back-to-backs: scientific discovery was destructive, the work of the devil, and Mackendrick imbued the atmosphere with a kind of uncertainty bordering on catastrophe, a mind-at-the-end-of-its-tether or stop-the-world-I-want-to-get-off atmosphere. The documentary style was where it began. The nightmare was where it would end.

Alec felt it was an exemplary picture. The film was completed in fifty-nine days. He and Mackendrick shared a concern, even an obsession, for detail. Both were painstaking in establishing the comedy in precise detail. The solid carpentry of imparting information and laying fuses was what both enjoyed most.

They also relished the private joke, the comically enriching closeness between the textile town Stratton throws into confusion and the world of Ealing itself, which had a strong enough identity to be satirized. The mill-owner's paternalism, for instance, owed much to Michael Balcon's benign presence being manipulated by subversive noise-makers. Philip Kemp notes in his biography of Mackendrick that 'Guinness borrowed traits from a young studio technician whose innocently self-absorbed air he had noticed.' The noise of Stratton's invention created particular delight. Obscene bubbling sounds which the sound supervisor described as 'like breaking wind in the bath'. Kenneth Tynan, in his review (which failed to pin down the unique quality of the film), called it 'chortling and burbling . . . like a sort of plumber's zither'.

When the invention causes strikes and the strikers pursue Stratton in his gleaming suit of the imperishable textile through claustrophobic alleys, the film deteriorates into hysteria. Alec's innocent and blinkered quality made Stratton glow from within and generated a rich comic sympathy. In fact there were many obnoxious qualities about the inventor but the story was built so that the audience was predisposed to side with him. Alec conceals the scientist's obsession by spending much of the time trying either to hide himself or his clandestine research from the rest of the characters. Privacy and a quality of mind were at the core of his attraction, yet the overall effect turned more and more into the Buster Keaton vein.

Alec did not care for some aspects of working at Ealing, especially that the studio was, he thought, more geared towards serving the needs of technicians than those of the actors:

> They rather thought actors got in the way of things and they were always trying to get me killed. I remember on *The Man in the White Suit*, I had to climb down a wire rope. I thought it looked dangerous. 'Nothing to it,' said the technicians. 'It can withstand a tension of ten tons – so it will certainly hold you.' I said I had some experience of wires and ropes in the Navy during the recent hostilities and I wasn't so sure.

I climbed down just the same. The rope snapped. I fell. All they said was, looking a bit surprised, 'It shouldn't have happened.' But they didn't say sorry. That was the way it was.

Philip Kemp: *Lethal Innocence: The Cinema of Alexander Mackendrick*

14. I Live for the Day When I Can Twist Harold Hobson's Crutches round His Neck

Guinness told me in 1989 that he had nothing 'imaginative or even sensible to say about Shakespeare', and that he could not possibly be described as a Shakespearean actor, having appeared in only 'three' of his plays over the previous thirty-seven years (this takes one back to 1942). In fact, he had appeared in six Shakespeare plays since the end of the Second World War while the Hamlet he played in 1951 was his twentieth encounter with Shakespeare's plays. This, his second attempt to play Hamlet, opened in May 1951 at the New Theatre and was disastrous. The failure of this production was critical to what subsequently happened to him and seminal to what he did. For the rest of his life he appeared in only two Shakespeare roles in England, two in Canada and one on television. The modern Hamlet he had played with Guthrie in 1938 when aged twenty-four had in his view been ridiculous: 'water off a duck's back'. This time he was thirty-seven.

Backed by the flamboyant showman Henry Sherek, he displayed an uncharacteristic self-confidence in masterminding a new production of the play which was as large and mysterious and elusive as himself; he cast the rest of the characters himself and he dared to play the title role.

In the *Spectator* of 6 July 1951 Alec recapped that he had seen nine previous Hamlets, once again crediting that of Ernest Milton as the greatest: 'When I came to play Hamlet for the first time, in 1938, in Guthrie's modern-dress production at the Old Vic, I was merely a pale shadow of Gielgud with some fustian Freudian trimmings, encouraged – he will forgive me, I know – by Guthrie. I list these things, as I believe they are important in the way of tradition and as showing how an actor can react against the traditional and yet be steeped in it and love it.' Alec had recently read the essay *On Hamlet* (1948) by Salvador de Madariaga, which convinced him of the necessity of having a Spanish designer to show him how much Elizabethan England was influenced by Spain. He engaged Mariano Andreu. When it came to the set design he still had the nightmare Richardson production of *Richard II* on his mind. His was a reaction against permanent, semi-permanent and realist sets in Shakespeare, and above all, of a stubborn dislike of raised acting areas:

> Rostrums, apart from cluttering the stage, tend to produce a one-foot-up, one-foot-down sort of acting which I find peculiarly dispiriting. I have very few conversations on the stairs in my own house, and see no good reason for making God's gift to an actor – a flat square stage – into something like the entrance to the Athenaeum.   *Spectator*

The casting of *Hamlet* indicated perhaps a wayward eye: it was just as well that he had had no hand in casting *Twelfth Night*. He gave the heavy roles mostly to actors who had little experience in Shakespeare (e.g. Walter Fitzgerald as Claudius; Robert Urquhart as Horatio; Ingrid Burke as Ophelia; Lydia Sherwood as Gertrude). This last was perhaps the oddest casting of all because she was thin and nervous, not at all voluptuous, sexy or motherly. He relied on some intuitions about the casting, based on whether he felt those he chose could become real in the parts. He did not do badly in picking Alan Webb for Polonius, yet in general his perception of the ability of his cast to deliver finished performances was naive.

For Rosencrantz Alec selected a twenty-three-year-old newcomer, Robert Shaw, who was playing a page in *Much Ado About Nothing* at Stratford-upon-Avon. He went round to his dressing room after one performance, humbly introducing himself, 'I'm Alec Guinness,' to the unknown actor.

Shaw never removed his feet from the dressing-room table or stopped provocatively rocking back and forth in his chair. The arrogance provoked Alec, and Shaw's handsome looks, in what now had, according to colleagues, become a pattern, stirred passion within him. Shaw agreed to play the part for twenty pounds a week, an almost unheard-of sum then for such a small role. His Rosencrantz had a sinister appearance with a black patch over one eye. Alec wooed the young actor and several times invited him back to his house, also helping him to a small role in *The Lavender Hill Mob*. Shaw became another of Alec's serial infatuations, with no reciprocation, but provoking comment from others.

The most eccentric piece of casting – as if Alec was willing self-destruction – was that of Kenneth Tynan as the Player King. Alec had seen, in January 1949 at the Rudolf Steiner Hall, Tynan's notorious Oxford production of *Hamlet* (in which Tynan acted the Third Player Queen). John Schlesinger and Robert Hardy had also been in this production. In what seems like a fit of wildly extravagant behaviour, Alec wooed the young critic to appear for the first time on the professional stage.

Was it so extravagant? Perhaps the two men were drawn to one another because of the – as yet undeclared – secret each sensed in the other. Both were illegitimate. Both shared a preoccupation with *Hamlet*, at whose centre was a hidden impostume or boil. Tynan, besotted with theatrical illusion of all kinds, had long been obsessed with the play and its leading role, which he had acted at his Birmingham grammar school.

The two men met in the White Tower restaurant. Invited there by Alec, Tynan wore 'bright green from top to toe'. Alec found him very amusing, slightly 'startling' was the word he used. Something about Tynan struck Alec as especially attractive: something, perhaps, of his own, preoccupation with the narcissus mirror-image. Alec noticed that, when animated, Tynan did not seem to stammer, so he was not much bothered by this. He was used, anyway, to stammerers, for he said, at Ealing Studios, 'pretty well everyone stammered. I think there was a great fashion at that time – it was considered rather elegant.'

Alec wanted Tynan as the Player King to be rich and ornate: as Tynan said later, 'I, an attenuated twenty-four-year-old, was alarmed at the prospect of playing a robust and bearded tragedian.' Alarmed he may have been, but Tynan leapt at what he thought was the offer Alec made him at lunch, so that on 15 December 1950 Alec wrote in reply to him saying he had not actually made him an offer but had only asked him if he would be interested in playing the part. Alec stated firmly that he was not in a position to offer parts as he was not the management, though he sincerely hoped Tynan would agree to play the part. He suggested Tynan badger Sherek for further information.

Alec also engaged Frank Hauser, a young BBC producer with whom he had recorded Jean Anouilh's *Antigone* for radio, in which Alec acted the Chorus, Peter Ustinov Creon, Denholm Elliott Hymen and Mary Morris Antigone. Hauser had written and asked Alec if he wanted an assistant. He said yes. Later they lunched at Le Caprice where Alec told Hauser that, 'You may want to resign when I tell you that I have cast Kenneth Tynan as the Player King.' In fact Hauser, who had been at Oxford with Tynan, knew his acting and had respect for his ability, at least to play old men – Tynan had played the Old Judge in *Winterset* and Holofernes in *Love's Labour's Lost*. Hauser himself had never directed a stage play before, so he probably felt in good company.

Rehearsals began for the opening at the New Theatre (it opened six months after Alec lunched with Tynan, so time for preparation was never a problem). The idea was that Alec should 'block' the play, that is supply the moves, and then hand over to Hauser. But did not Alec believe, in accordance with the ideas of Guthrie, that actors should not write down predetermined moves, as Gielgud would have wanted to do? If he did, he did not follow the principle. Alec arranged for a great plastic ear to be made for the Player King to be poisoned through, to be worn over Tynan's own ear.

At the first few rehearsals Alec propounded some of his ideas. For instance, as he wrote later, 'I followed Granville-Barker's advice and did not drop the curtain, as is usual, at the end of the "Rogue and peasant slave" soliloquy. Now this seems to me to be the only daring, original and exciting thing we did in the whole production, and it escaped the critics' notice.' (At another time he found something else 'the only original thing'). In place of the customary thudding curtain, he pointed out, the audience got: '"To be or not to be" within a minute and a half, followed by the "nunnery" scene, followed by the social ease of "Speak the speech" – in fact, they get the greater part of Hamlet's character stripped bare before them ... And all in the space of about fifteen minutes.'

After this he took a back seat and invention seemed to wane. The inability of Alec to commit himself to sole direction adversely affected not only the production, but also his own performance. There was criticism that Andreu, who lived in Biarritz, had little time to adapt his gouache designs to the needs of the actors. In the last week of rehearsal the insecurity became palpable. Tynan demoralized everyone. Each morning he would arrive at rehearsals dead tired and try to get into psychiatric analysis of the characters. Alec was worried about him: it was all a bit light, he was 'a bit bored', he commented politely.

One night Alec lost his temper with one of the others in the cast and they had a screaming row: 'I remember Ken was very near me. Suddenly he was nodding vigorously. I felt he would have much preferred the whole thing to be played in high emotion.'

Tynan kept silent. Alec had his way. It was his production and his Hamlet, and carried the stamp of his own emotions and preoccupations in every way. It restrained and repressed the feelings. Towards the first night it tapered away and diminished altogether.

After the first run-through, when Hauser gave the cast their notes, Alec said to him crossly, 'You've said nothing to me'. 'I thought you understood,' replied Hauser, 'you were magnificent.' 'He thinks I am so bad I am being left out,' said Alec, as if to someone else. Hauser for the first time realized that, in the theatre, silence invariably conveyed disapproval.

The first night was something of a fiasco. Tynan was told by Alec about his spiritual preparation for the moment the curtain rose:

> He [Guinness] arrived at the New Theatre far too early, and killed time by strolling round the corner to the Garrick Club. After glancing at the newspapers, he was about to leave when his eye fell on the new bust of Forbes-Robertson, standing on its pedestal in the entrance hall. Ever a hostage to superstition, he looked about him and, seeing no one, reached up on tiptoe and touched Sir Johnston for luck. Duly consoled, he made for the door; and then noticed the bust of Irving. Warily, compulsively, he touched that too. These things going in threes, he thought he had better do the same for Shakespeare. The pedestal proved too high for him. Undeterred, he dragged up a heavy club chair, climbed on to the seat, and, wobbling, achieved his object. Having appeased the fates, he

> sauntered back to the theatre, where the fates quickly showed
> him what faithless harpies they are.
>
> *Alec Guinness*

As many have observed, on first nights Guinness's confidence was
invariably at its lowest ebb; he was never the kind of actor who
rose to the chemistry of first-night hysteria and glamour. Normally
he developed a crippling pain in his knees and back.

But this Hamlet far exceeded in torture everything he usually
suffered. The new electronic or computerized lighting board in the
New Theatre went mad, and the lighting for the Elsinore battle-
ments became that of the Court scene, and vice versa. *The Times*
said in its review that the lighting had first-night nerves; someone
remarked backstage that Guinness was calm, but his reply was,
'It's the calmness of despair.'

There were boos after the curtain came down. 'It was my fault.
Don't blame yourselves,' Alec told everyone after the final curtain.
'I gave up in the first act.'

Alec did not receive good reviews and was deeply hurt and
shaken by the whole experience. Tynan later wrote that it became
'Hamlet with the pilot dropped.' He called it a self-inflicted
wound. This was a fair diagnosis. 'I made a balls-up of Hamlet,'
Alec confirmed in person to me. 'I did it out of revenge . . .' (This
was, he said, for Rex Harrison playing *The Cocktail Party* in
London, which had been promised to Alec.) 'I was sick every
night. I retched every night. I was overcome with nausea.' Hamlet
could take its toll of good actors. In 1969, for example, Nicol
Williamson stopped one of his performances and said, 'I can't go
on – I am simply exhausted, and I'm not giving my best. In fact
I'm fucked . . .' and then walked offstage.

Tynan benefited most from the bad reviews; Beverly Baxter
wrote, under the banner 'Worst Hamlet I have ever seen' that
Tynan 'would not get a chance in a village hall unless he were
related to the vicar. His performance was quite dreadful.' But
Tynan *was*, in an obscure and mysterious way, 'related to the
vicar'. He asked for celebrity and he got it. He was much criticized
for making so much critical capital out of the fiasco, for shortly
afterwards he joined the *Standard* and a year later ousted Baxter
from his post: he also wrote anonymously a damning review of

Hamlet in *Harper's Bazaar*, described by Frank Hauser as a 'virtuoso piece of treachery'. Alec complained in a gentlemanly way when Tynan further wrote a 'hysterically frank letter . . . I felt he should have come to the management'. In his response to Baxter's review in the *Evening Standard*, Tynan said, 'I am quite a good enough critic to know my performance in *Hamlet* is not "quite dreadful"; it is, in fact, only slightly less than mediocre. I do not actually exit through the scenery or wave at friends in the audience.'

Hauser told me in 1992 that he continued to admire much of Alec's performance: it was, 'very very exposed, very brave. He played the closet and nunnery scenes ruthlessly, savagely.' He thought the performance had been extremely well thought out: it was a 'remarkable, magnificent performance which never got properly credited but needed a John Dexter to come along and take the whole thing in hand'.

But Harold Hobson had written in the *Sunday Times* that Alec apart, you would never hear of the actors again: the arrogance of this so enraged Alec that he claimed it was the only time he felt like taking revenge against a critic. He repeated this often in his autobiographies. The bitterness continued and in 1985 he wrote to John Warner, who played Osric, that he lived for the day 'when I can twist Harold Hobson's crutches round his neck'. To be fair to Hobson the critic revisited the production in its last weeks, praising at least four of the cast; as for Alec's Hamlet, Hobson wrote that while on the first night it gave no taste of its quality, it was now showing, in the sickening sense of his own insufficiency, moments that were 'almost unbearably moving and beautiful'. This for Hobson, putting his finger on Alec's inner self-hatred, is a Hamlet which 'in its dark bitterness looks upward at the height from which it has been thrown'. Could Hobson have been referring to Alec's rejection by a member of his cast?

On his second viewing, Alan Dent still found that Alec, in his prim and silly little beard, set off looking like Osric. Then he turned his back on most of the fire, passion and poetry. All in all, he judged a poised, serene and all-too-detached *reading* of the part. As for most of the supporting players they were 'if possible' even worse than on the first night.

Except, retorted the later curmudgeonly Alec, for the Ophelia ('Who did go mad'), and several of the others, 'Every single member of the cast became a star of some sort. No one could afford it now.' This he told Osric when they reminisced. The cast included not only Alan Webb and Robert Shaw, but also Stanley Holloway and Peter Wyngarde.

Alec could, with greater self-knowledge, have added that, while he might not have been able to pick the right actor for the right role, he knew how to select other geniuses. 'We knew he was a magnificent actor,' wrote J. C. Trewin, 'but it was not his night.' The *Daily Express* was more blunt in its headline: 'Guinness's Hamlet booed'. Matthew told his father he got chivvied at Beaumont College because of this poor notice, and this upset Guinness: 'You begin to think, "Hey, hey, hey?"' The production closed on 31 July 1951 and lost between £12,000 and £15,000.

Alec's second Hamlet must have marked a turning point in his life, causing him to abandon finally the specifically English challenge of becoming a great stage actor in Shakespeare. The tantalizing or binding power of the event over our imagination comes from the likelihood that Alec, had he known how to marshal and integrate both his force and his intelligence, might have been outstanding. It is the comic spirit that tends towards the enjoyment of disintegration and chaos, and even in 1989, when Alec talked of Hamlet to me, it was the comic discontinuity of the role he saw, pointing out how Hamlet displayed a 'different personality' in each act. He thought there should be intervals between each of the five acts. The many-sidedness of Hamlet possibly dismayed him because he had to confront in it his own unresolved many-sidedness. In real life he possibly was too much like Hamlet to be able to act Hamlet.

Tynan's picaresque Player King ear supplied another image for this great disaster:

Phosphorescent paint had been applied to the crown, the vial of poison and a great plastic left ear which I wore over my own: these glowed in the darkness, and the tableau as the poison was poured took on the aspect of an advertisement for a proprietary brand of rum ... I remember handing the ear over to the stage manager and feeling, for a moment, remarkably like Van Gogh.

Gore Vidal, commenting in *Palimpsest* on Alec's eerie precision in *The Ladykillers*, 'even down to the way that Ken, who was to die of emphysema, stagily held a cigarette between ring and little fingers' – went on to say about Tynan and Alec:

> Ken also, despite – no, I am sure, because of – his lifelong stammer, was the Player King in Alec's *Hamlet*. What was Ken's performance like? Alec sighed. 'He elected to play the part as a Chinese, a curious choice. But then I was bad, too. The only original thing about the production was that I insisted that there be no staircases on the set. I have found in life – if not onstage – that I have *never* had an intelligent conversation with anyone – much less a monologue – on the stairs of my house.'

Just before his death in 2001 John Warner recalled to me Alec accosting Tynan at the stalls bar before a performance, saying to him, 'You've played it Welsh, you've played it Scottish, what are you going to do tonight?'

Warner also remarked on Shaw's insolent delivery of the line 'Will't please you go, my lord?', and the strong sexual overtone of Alec hitting him.

Warner also reported that Alec, bowing to the critics, shaved off his beard for the last week of the run. Hauser deplored this. Stuart Burge believed, he told me, that the whole thing was a big mistake, commenting adversely on the flat stage, the Goya-esque costumes, and on how inhibiting the women's costumes were. Andreu, the designer, was frankly homosexual: he painted porno-graphic pictures of gays coupling. An outrageous example of one of these, bought by John Gielgud, went on sale as part of Gielgud's collection at Sotheby's in 2000.

Although outwardly courageous, extorting his cast with such phrases, after the bad notices, as 'Now we've got something to fight for,' or (in Tyrone Guthrie mode) 'Rise above it', the stress affected Alec to such a degree that he was uncharacteristically open and unguarded in showing how much he lusted unhappily after Robert Shaw, having first seen him as a page in *Much Ado* at Stratford. During the rehearsals and run Alec had remained in crisis over this, even confessing as much indirectly and discreetly twenty-five years later in an *Evening Standard* interview. One night, he recalled, he had slapped Robert Shaw's face when Shaw put a Rosencrantz line too rudely to him, a 'quick temper' reaction on his part:

> It had an impolite edge and Shakespeare hasn't written the comeuppance line and there was nothing to do but crack him across the jaw ... I was very distressed, I'm not given to that sort of thing.

'That sort of thing?' There was more to come. On 9 August 1951, Robert Shaw's twenty-fourth birthday, Alec threw a large party for him at the White Tower restaurant, inviting Shaw's friends such as Barbara Jefford and Robert Hardy, together with former student companions. Speculation for the reason behind such lavish generosity to the twenty-four-year-old Shaw was rife, reported John French in his life of Robert Shaw published in 1993: 'Didn't you know?' Robert Hardy volunteered, 'Alec's fallen in love with him.'

After *Hamlet* closed Alec asked Shaw and Russell Enoch, another actor in the company, to accompany him to Brighton and stay the weekend in a hotel. Shaw himself recalled that there was a frisson in the Old Ship Hotel when Alec touched his hand for a second or two, 'but the "love" remained only a friendship'.

Guinness must have felt rejected not only by press and public for his Hamlet, but spurned and made to feel ridiculous by the object of his intense, if only temporary, infatuation. He was to make sure, however, that never again would there be such a public display of feeling for a man. He had made a fool of himself. Or, as Alec probably saw it, in the revised words Hobson used of his Hamlet, 'He is a Lucifer whose fall is into the pit of his own festering imagination.'

15. I Never Needed Privacy More

'Pain is at the centre of all his characters,' wrote a commentator in *Time* magazine in 1958, quoting Alec's own admission of 'a certain uncomfortable void' at the centre of his life, and of a friend who said of him, 'I would call it Alec's personal abyss. There is this great sense of absence in the middle of him. This lack of identity. One seldom sees a man who lives so intimately with nothingness.'

This pain was at its most intense at the end of July 1951 when *Hamlet* closed. Relief came, at least for the moment, in following the French motto 'reculer pour mieux sauter': but he needed a retreat to *recule* to. He was looking, in the words of his favourite T. S. Eliot, for the 'still point of the turning world' – this turmoil now being mainly of his own self. He desired peace from Barbellion's internal chaos: the dancing star had well and truly disappeared.

Alec had always been a south-coast man; as a child he attended schools in resorts, as if Agnes insisted he should be surrounded with the wholesome air that had attended her brief encounter with Andrew Geddes in the summer of 1913.

> Sea breezes
> Lift up the chemises
> Oh Jeses, oh Jeses.

Later he married Merula, the daughter of a Surrey squire, immersed himself in the world of village greens and picturesque brick and tile-hung houses. In the war he joined the navy, so yet again home was a south-coast haven. It came as little surprise, then, that he and Merula should buy, in 1951, a fourteen-acre field near Petersfield, on the Hampshire side of the border with Sussex, and build for themselves an £11,000 house on it, first as a weekend retreat, later to become their permanent home. The three-bed-roomed house, Kettlebrook Meadows, was designed by Merula's brother Eustie Salaman, who had a practice in Petersfield. Later, in 1962, they enlarged the hall and study by three or four feet: 'One always knew they were too small,' said Alec, 'but when the house was designed there was a limit on space because of building regulations.'

The landscape around Steep Marsh, a hamlet on the edge of Steep, itself a quite small village close to Petersfield, was very gentle. Petersfield, with its fine equestrian statue of William III, had become important as a watering place on the London–Portsmouth road, well inland of course, notable from the twelfth century onwards for its wool market. A mile or so to the north-east rose the ground that contained the parish of Steep, still, at the time they bought the meadow, quite remote with no regular village centre, a strung-out affair of scattered large and small dwellings along the roads or tucked down bridle paths, in dells, or in hidden-away copses. There was something about its inaccessible winding ways and yet its general mildness that appealed strongly to Alec. The beech woods that clothed the slopes that surrounded the meadow where he built his house; the slopes themselves, Butser Hill, Harting Down, and the Hangers – the names might well have been part titles for the *Four Quartets*. East Coker (near Yeovil and more deeply in Hardy's Wessex than Steep) was perhaps its twin, with its enfolding landscape of deep lanes shuttered with branches, dark in the sultry afternoon light of summer hazes, and, above all, its houses rising and falling. Home is where one starts from. Here he could find stillness and quiet: the still point of the turning world.

But, apart from spiritual satisfactions – 'listening to the precious silence, broken only by an intermittent sleepy bird' – Kettlebrook Meadows answered a more basic need. Alec was a very English type: like Wemmick's in *Great Expectations*, his home became his suburban castle with the drawbridge up. Alec some-times felt ashamed not to be living 'out of a clothes basket, with no home', but the truth was that 'not having a home as a child I spent a great deal of time wanting it . . . I *need* my house – the thing itself with its walls and foundations . . . I love the sense that my possessions have been there for years, and that what has been planted has come up in *my* soil.' On their arrival they found only a fine Atlantic cedar and two cypress trees, so they planted four hundred trees – as it turned out, Alec grumbled later, too close together.

Bedales, the co-educational school, was just down the road; Edward Gibbon once had his family home in a nearby village; Trollope had lived several years in another (Alec loved quoting Trollope, for example 'One is patriotic only because one is too small and weak to be cosmopolitan'; or, 'A newspaper should never waste its columns and weary its readers by praising anything'). The cottage of Edward Thomas, the poet who died in 1917, was not far away either. Thomas had written, appropriately where Alec was concerned, about how most intense moments were those of depression, wondering whether 'a cure that destroys the depression may not destroy the intensity – a *desperate* remedy'. Yet what could have been more safe, secure, and a better place to hide from the glare of the spotlight, as well as a haven of the long hoped-for calm, and later the autumnal serenity and the wisdom of age?

Much had to be done. The verandaed, largely timber-built house was constructed at the end of a long tarmacked drive. A five-barred gate, rarely to be closed, was at the main entrance. Here the actor made for himself a territory all of his own: 'His seclusion,' wrote one reporter, 'has created a useful myth, that no such person as Alec Guinness exists behind the many masks.' Certainly his profile as a local resident never became high. J. B. Priestley had a friend who lived near Alec and told him that 'Alec could wander around or attend local functions and yet never be recognized.' But this reflected how Alec, when he did not want to, knew how not to be recognized. The local library could find no cuttings on him in the file: he was never 'written up'. When something happened to him, like a fire which severely damaged the whole lower floor of his house in 1987 there was the shortest of reports: 'They sat in one of our police cars while firemen dealt with the fire. No fuss.' The fire was caused by their French-style Aga overheating. Peter Glenville was staying with them at the time. There was also a smaller fire in March 1955 which Alec attacked with his jacket.

For three or four years after their house was built, Alec with

his film commitments in Ealing still lived much of the time in St
Peter's Square, but by 1954 he was writing to friends, saying how
the house was 'gorgeous' and that they must come down to stay.
Merula, having given up acting and taken up painting, had always
loved horses and they now kept two ponies, two dogs, a parrot, a
horse with one brown eye and one blue and a cat.

Irene Worth, who played with him in Feydeau and Eliot, was
one visitor some years later:

> Alec won't live in the bustle of a city. He and his wonderful
> wife Merula, their son Matthew not too far away, live in the
> country and their love and knowledge of nature is strong.
> There one finds them in their element, without pretension,
> with animals, books, paintings, answering the telephone,
> reading, writing. There are no photographs or paintings of
> Alec standing about.

Coral Browne was another, who described her host as the 'soul
of discretion . . .' and 'a truly formidable, invisible man'. She and
Vincent Price, her third husband, went to Kettlebrook Meadows
on one of 'those rare, halcyon English summer days that erase all
the grey drizzle from the memory . . . The entire house and its
grounds bespeak everything about this generous, adorable and self-
confessed odd couple . . . The idyllic garden . . . owes much of its
charm to the interests, rural hobbies and loving care of Merula.
"This England" in a nutshell.'

Of Alec himself, Coral Browne observed: 'I am not aware of
any troubles that ruffle his serenity . . . However, I have never
known him to laugh volubly, rather a silent amusement, his
merriment contained to a mischievous smile.' When she left the
parting was all too perfect, too:

> Alec waved a farewell to me and I looked back at him framed
> in the doorway. His attire – cardigan and well-worn trousers
> – had been exactly right for this day in the country. But, I
> knew for sure that should our next encounter be anywhere in
> the city he would be head-to-toe immaculate. Mr Impeccable
> poses a constant problem for the likes of Jean Marsh, Eileen
> Atkins and yours truly . . .

Was Coral Browne saying that she was being put on her mettle by Alec almost as a woman would be by another woman? In his manner of celebrating exotic females, Alec saw an incident involving Coral just after the war rather more as a woman than a man might see it: Coral 'muffled in furs, skating on a remote section of the Serpentine ... She was executing an elegant figure of eight when a seedy man slid towards her and flashed himself. Coral continued to skim around, calling over her shoulder, "Put it away at once! You could catch your death of cold." ' Alec's mockery and motives for telling the story would seem to stem from identification with the woman.

Meantime, the gallery of comic upstarts continued to swell. In *The Card*, Eric Ambler's film script of Arnold Bennett's novel, Alec played another, Edward Henry 'Denry' Machin, who rose from humble obscurity to become mayor in a provincial town, while his path was strewn with the maxims of the self-made man: 'The road to success is fraught with hardship; it's the woman's duty to adapt herself to the man.' Some have attributed this choice of role to a desire in Alec to win audiences outside London – he had never done the customary stint in an out-of-town touring or repertory company. Others have claimed that Machin, a man who set out to conquer the world, presented the challenge of a new kind of hero. Certainly the parvenu capitalist was a most unlikely role: Alec invested him with tantalizing ambiguity so it was never clear if Machin's actions were above board or if he was going to be caught as he charmed his way into wealth and prominence. Again he devoted himself to detail. An extra who worked on the film reports (in August 2001):

> One scene required Machin to come out of his mother's cottage and call 'goodbye' to me. After he had done this a couple of times, he noticed that the local extras watching were commenting to each other about it. He – the great actor – went over to them to ask what was wrong. They were reluctant at first but then told him that locally people of that class don't say 'goodbye' but 'tara'. He got them to say it a few times, tried it out and went back to do another shot, now in the film, in which he calls 'tara' the way they taught him.

So once again an Ealing film caught the moral ambivalence of English society in that muddled post-war period. 'What great cause has he ever been identified with?' sneers a political opponent on the eve of Machin's adoption as mayor. 'I think I can tell you,' retorts the Countess of Choll. 'He's identified with the good cause of cheering us all up.'

Beyond Machin, Alec conveyed the philosophy of Mr Sleary in *Hard Times*, who defends the pleasure of the circus to Gradgrind: 'People mutht be amuthed. They can't be alwayth a learning, nor yet they can't be alwayth a working, they an't made for it.' Peter Copley, another actor in *The Card*, commented to me on the continuous alertness Guinness showed to props during the filming. At one point, warned by his co-stars Valerie Hobson and Petula Clarke, he stopped a heavy studio lamp toppling on the heads of the crowd. He was always on the lookout too for opportunities: in the tailor's shop, for instance, when Machin gets promoted, he was longing to pick up and do something arresting with the tailor's shears.

Ronald Neame, the director, after Alec's death, said of this inventiveness: 'There is a scene in which he comes back to his mother, an old washerwoman, with a hat full of sovereigns for her. "I want to play this on the floor lying under the table," he said to me. "How on earth can we do that?" I said. He told me that he would put the hat on his mother's lap, she would scream when she saw its contents, and the coins would fall on the floor, rolling in every direction. Alec would then get down and retrieve them, speaking his dialogue from the floor.'

Alec asked Neame for a special favour: 'that I would cast his young son Matthew to play his younger self. I did, and when Matthew had his big scene to do, Alec was very nervous, making me so.'

A schoolboy friend of Matthew, Thomas Forde, recalled him arriving back at Beaumont with a red wig in addition to his normal red hair. When told to get a hair cut he triumphantly removed the wig.

In April 1952, with commendable courage and promptness after the failure of *Hamlet*, Alec returned to the West End, this time to the Aldwych Theatre under Binkie's management, to play the Ant Scientist in Sam and Bella Spewack's *Under the Sycamore*

Tree. The characters were ants while Alec's character had found out enough about mankind to want to teach his fellow ants to emulate human skills in communication and mechanization, as well as destruction. Oddly, however, the characters talked as if they were insects but did not sport ant costumes. What also made *Under the Sycamore Tree* fall short of a coherent symbolic fable was that it had too much of a sketchy, revue form. But it did give Alec, wrote John Russell Taylor, the chance to dominate 'every scene as the infinitely guileful and adaptable ant intellectual, and even ageing to ninety in the last scene, for which, in looks at any rate, he did the best version of his renowned impersonation of Alistair Sim.' This boosted morale for, while the play was hardly a sell-out, the notices were good, the run respectable and he was back among close friends – Peter Glenville directed, while Peter Bull also played a role.

The Malta Story as an idea for a film attracted Alec because it gave him another chance to play a hero based on the model of T. E. Lawrence. Peter Ross is an archaeologist who, skilled at aerial photography, records the movement of Italian trains carrying gliders which foreshadows the Nazi invasion of Malta. Rommel's supplies have therefore to be sunk. As this juvenile heart-throb it has to be said Alec convinced nobody very much, but it did exorcise for ever the demon of wanting to star as a romantic lead, which he never hereafter attempted. (At the time of *Kind Hearts and Coronets* he had said he wanted to play a straight juvenile – 'Well, *almost* juvenile'.)

The self-deception had reached the end of its tether. During the filming in Malta Alec was clearly very unhappy as other demons of his life seized him. Angela Fox recounted how her husband, awoken one night with a desperate telephone call from Alec, had to fly out next day to rescue him from some legal entanglement with the police following a bout of drunkenness and encounters with rough trade. Fortunately Robin was a lawyer as well as a compassionate agent. Had he been arrested again? It seemed likely – 'he likes the male rough trade,' Angela told me. 'He is the most completely sexually tormented man one knows.' But she added (this in 1986) 'he may have managed to subdue or tame that side of his nature with the help of priests ... In Simon Gray's *Wise Child* the way he came on and did the male strip-tease, that was all *perfect* observation – he knew it, like the priest in *The Power and the Glory*, he knew intimately all the backward and seamy side of life, a deeply tormented man who could rise and be reborn again, reach the spiritual heights.'

*

During the run of *Under the Sycamore Tree* Tom Patterson, a Canadian who was organizing the 1953 Stratford (Ontario) Festival under Tyrone Guthrie's direction, visited Alec in his dressing room between a matinee and evening performance. Guthrie wanted to attract Alec to work with him again. But also he supported his old friend and protégé's ambition to conquer one of the highest peaks – for this reason he told Patterson to offer Guinness Hamlet again.

At their first meeting Patterson, in his account, suggested to Alec a fee of $3,500 dollars, omitting to make any mention of Hamlet. For six weeks of rehearsal and four weeks of playing, the fee was tempting. Alec was interested, but next day, when he and Patterson met for lunch, he received the suggestion of Hamlet coldly and became suspicious that Guthrie was out to show him up: he remarked tartly, 'that a certain gentleman was very good at encouraging actors and quite good too at slapping them down when they became stars'.

Yet he agreed finally to appear although not as Hamlet; the plays chosen were *Richard III* and *All's Well That Ends Well* (in which he was to play the King of France).

Guthrie's account differs from Patterson's. In it, Alec and he read all of Shakespeare's plays. They agreed on *Richard III*. 'Guinness wanted to play it. We both felt that the complicated genealogy, the rather obscure historical background, were probably drawbacks for Canadian audiences but might be offset by the strong thread of melodrama.' The new transformation he could effect upon himself delighted Alec. 'Do wish you were able to come to see me and my wig as Richard III,' he told Tynan in March 1953. He and Tynan conducted for a time this provocative, mildly flirtatious correspondence.

The project nearly collapsed, however, because they still had to erect a festival theatre, even if this was as yet only a huge semi-permanent tent. Only then could they rehearse and act in it.

Funds dwindled and they were unable to meet their bills. But the contractor who was preparing the site had, according to Guthrie, 'decided that the honour of the community was at stake and that, whether he was paid or no, his part in the whole plan would go forward'. The big top of the festival theatre finally went up (and was blessed in a service of dedication by five ministers of different denominations) so they assembled in Ontario for the remaining rehearsals. With his usual meticulousness Alec to the last fought Guthrie over the amount of bloody ooze on the outside of the sack which held the severed head of Hastings. He wanted less of it.

> Rehearsals were always immensely lively, with never a slack or unconcentrated moment . . . Personally I don't think I got through any production with him without a bicker some-where along the line. But he was always the one who made the gesture of reconciliation – usually by some extravagantly absurd and funny statement. But once we had a row which, through my fault, reached proportions whereby we were non-speakers for two days. It all had to do with the severed head of Hastings in *Richard III*. Tony's gesture of reconciliation was to give me, very solemnly, a small brown paper bag of rather squashed cherries.
>
> **address at Guthrie's memorial service**

Guthrie neglected to calculate one unexpected effect, as multitudes came to lurk in the spring twilight outside the skirts of the great tent. On the whole they behaved all right but then (Guthrie recounts):

> a juvenile head would appear under the canvas, momentarily, slyly, six inches from the ground. Then an enormously magnified whisper from outside would reverberate, 'You're sure it was Alec Guinness?' the head would reappear. The actors, led by Guinness, would make desperate efforts to get on with the job. Pay no attention. Go ahead. Over the dialogue would float the enormous pervasive whisper: 'Well, what's he like?'   *A Life in the Theatre*

They solved the acoustic peculiarity of playing in the tent two days before the first night by covering the whole floor with coconut matting. Throughout the day of the first night the cars rolled up: in one rode the Governor General, Vincent Massey. Guthrie's biographer wrote:

> The young volunteer ushers ... moved like naval cadets putting the ship to sea; got people aboard and seated with courtesy. Trumpets blew. The red geraniums were in place round the tent. A yellow pennant – present from Stratford-upon-Avon, England – floated from the top of the tent. A gun fired. The play was on. Guinness took the stage, as Richard III.
>   'Now is the winter of our discontent / Made glorious summer . . .'   James Forsyth, *Tyrone Guthrie*

Alec triumphed in both plays, although in *All's Well* his triumph was subordinate to Irene Worth's portrayal of Helen, a part which Guthrie regarded as Shakespeare's finest female creation.

> I remember [said Worth] the loneliness of his Richard III as he sat, horribly alone, silent, his Coronation train covering the stage, his eyes filled with fear and guilt, his voice, in a rasp, saying, 'I am not in the giving mood today.' I remember his dying, exquisite King in *All's Well*, whom I wheeled about in a wicker bath chair. I hear his gentle voice: '. . . since I nor wax nor honey can bring home, / I quickly were dissolved from my hive.'   *Dear Alec*

The festival as a whole captured a new mood in Canada. It was extended for two weeks. According to the designer Tanya Moiseiwitsch, many people came who had never before seen a stage play. One, Joyce Watt, wrote to me in 2001: 'I hope you have an idea of the thrust stage Tanya designed. At the very end of *Richard* Alec Guinness was sitting on the edge of the balcony (back hump and all) swinging his legs. The image that I will always treasure is the spotlight being on him, and growing smaller and smaller and then – total blackness. The theatre just erupted.' The presence of Alec in Ontario lent prestige and was germane to this new festival which in time grew to become of international importance and as such created a new community. Alec paid tribute to how Guthrie's gifts extended into welding communities together, especially divided ones, as happened in the case of the first season in Ontario, where there were Episcopalians, Presbyterians, Methodists, Catholics, Baptists and 'including also that sect which feels it vanity to wear buttons'. The effect of his six-foot-four striding about and smiling on all had been miraculous: the result became that 'strict teetotallers began to keep whisky and gin in their homes for visiting Anglicans, Baptists – not greatly given to colour – bought and planted geraniums round the theatre, and at the dedication Catholics deigned to join in the Lord's Prayer with everyone else'.

After Guthrie's death, in 1971, the doctor arrived, looked at Tony and said, 'Surprising humility.' Judy his wife replied, 'Yes, surprising humility; but quite tiresome!' The doctor thought for a moment and then said, 'Surprising humility, and – yes – quite tiresome!' Alec added: 'William Tyrone Guthrie. May his noble soul rest in happy peace, in the God he trusted.'

For the rest of his Canadian visit Alec rode about on a bicycle, 'trilby on head and decently clad, moving smoothly and sedately along the tree-lined streets, like a character right out of one of his Ealing comedies'. Not one hopes Professor Marcus, the most intricately evil of his future characters. In August he sat for a portrait by John S. Choppin, a Canadian artist. With the enthusiastic notices and his personal satisfaction at an all-time high, he could withdraw with honour from the Shakespeare stakes.

PART TWO: ILLUMINATION

The transition from tenseness, self-responsibility, and worry, to equanimity, receptivity, and peace, is the most wonderful of all those shiftings of inner equilibrium, those changes of the personal centre of energy, which I have analysed so often; and the chief wonder of it is that it so often comes about, not by doing, but by simply relaxing and throwing the burden down.   William James

Jung thought that the achievement of optimum development of the personality was a lifetime's task which was never completed; a journey upon which one sets out hopefully toward a destination at which one never arrives.   Anthony Storr

Low's cartoon for the *Guardian*

16. The Use of the Impersonal Third Person

Kenneth Tynan researched and wrote his study of Guinness in 1953, before he became drama critic of the *Observer*. Alec cooperated. It was the first and last time he ever did such a thing. As he was still climbing the ladder, he could not, or so it might seem, afford to be secretive and off-putting in the way he became later. Before he left for Canada he allowed Tynan to borrow all his assiduously collected and assembled press cuttings. ('I never read my notices' has a hollow ring here.) Tynan peppered his monograph with long quotations from the many hundreds of reviews of his early performances Alec had collected.

They had last seen each other during the disastrous *Hamlet*. For a while their friendship flourished, so that Elaine Dundy, whom Tynan had married two years earlier, recalled his 'bubble of calm serenity' when she and Tynan visited him at St Peter's Square, 'with his beaming boy face. You live well – good for you!' she remembered thinking in the spacious and stagnant Regency square, with Merula and Matthew, two dogs, a Siamese cat and a grey parrot. Here, as Tynan wrote,

I have seen him make many outlandish faces; describing perhaps, a rehearsal mishap, maliciously observed and not for publication. 'And so,' he will cry, acting it out, 'one came capering on, one pranced across the stage, with all *this* going on' – a wild waving of the arms – 'and all of a sudden one felt terribly silly, because . . .' He pauses to cover his mouth and chuckle. The use of the impersonal third person is characteristic. It brings us back to where we started: to the persistent, ubiquitous anonymity of Alec Guinness.

Elaine Dundy recalled that he was quite without the usual actor's mannerisms: 'No stories about how we should have or didn't, or might have played that part.' Tynan recently had completed a television directors' course and they discussed the possibility that Alec should appear as Winston Smith in a television adaptation of Orwell's *1984* which Alec had been 'horrified' to read. But he also, he told Tynan, felt it was 'fearfully formless and consequently often monotonous and repetitive'. He would be fascinated to see what Tynan would make of it as a script, as he was anxious to do a really good television play – while, as he said, 'I've never appeared in bright blue in the Oxford Street stores.'

Even allowing for the rigours of his film work, Alec was prepared to spend several Sunday afternoons with Tynan 'discussing whatever horrors about me you want to know'. Whether or not he revealed his illegitimacy to Tynan we do not know, for Tynan remained quiet on this subject, while otherwise (untypical of his later manner, not of his earlier quality) respectful towards whatever Alec may have told him in confidence. I suspect he did not, however, for in view of how Alec did reveal it later, in terms of a wider public it still remained a secret: as Chesterton wrote of Dickens, 'He never talked of his nightmare but kept it deadly silent . . . the unbearable but impersonal shame.'

When he was nearly seventy Alec would grumble at certain aspects of the book, for instance at a mistake in it about his 1938 Hamlet: 'I wish he'd just checked up.' It's hard to detect this mistake now, although he seemed not to have liked Tynan quoting Agate, and wished he had quoted Ivor Brown's review instead. The book was – because it was about Alec Guinness – 'in a sense as dull as ditchwater', although 'highly readable'. At the time he confessed himself enormously pleased with it, for he thanked Tynan (on 29 October 1953) for writing such a worthwhile and, as far as he could see, honest book about him. He suggested another side of his personality which luxuriated in the praise of others and which he was soon to eradicate more or less entirely, for he described the book as being like a long and flattering session with a fortune teller in which his ego could bask delightedly. He affectionately hoped Tynan and he would meet soon, pull the world to bits and put it together again in happier colours.

What a sigh of relief Alec must have experienced, his secret life intact, when he returned from Canada via New York, beaming happily while Matthew looks quizzically at the camera, and Merula shows a fixed, dutiful smile. He may have regretted his long absences from home on filming assignments, for as he confessed in a public statement, 'I did warn her from the beginning that it might be a bit lonely for her some of the time. She is wonderfully self-contained, but it does get a bit lonely for her with the house to look after and the dogs.'

No cover could have been more successful for Alec than that of the happily married man. As well as a cover it was also true, he *was* happy with his family and more than anything did not want to leave or lose it. It did not solve the tension that lay behind the secret, which continued, nor the tireless work needed to maintain the complicated set of constructive deceits that hid the inner man.

'Is this not perhaps,' wrote C. Kerenyl, 'the secret of every true and great mystery, that it is *simple*? Does it not love secrecy for that very reason. Proclaimed, it were but a word; kept silent, it is *being*.' By this point in his life Alec had learnt much about the essence of mystery; to be silent about his bisexuality or about wife and son or other personal matters, was not, in his case, a concealing weakness. It went beyond, being part of the big game, the supreme artistry of not being who you are. It became the essence of his being, making him feel wanted and secure in ways that frankness and openness never could. The mystery was acknowledged. He made the point that it was there, concealed in an anonymity or ambiguity which gave it power. The game beyond the game. And it was, of course, in *being* that the power and quality of Alec as an actor lay. In *being* rather than doing. If not in doing nothing, then in trying to do less and less to establish the life of a character, and giving the appearance of life.

Tynan had written that if Alec had been wanted for murder and his description circulated an enormous number of people, all of different aspect and build, would have been marched into police stations across the land. On his return to London from Canada Alec must have felt relief he was not a wanted or hounded man, as John Gielgud became that autumn. Sheridan Morley describes admirably in his authorized biography of Gielgud the impact of this exposure on Gielgud, how he contemplated suicide, its diverse effects on his friends and colleagues, and how the reaction of audiences was the reverse of what Gielgud feared. Nevertheless, in spite of the subsequent Wolfenden Report leading to the repeal of laws criminalizing homosexual activity between consenting adults, Gielgud continued to feel shame, not at what he had done, but because he had been found out. As Kenneth Williams wrote in his diary on Friday 23 October 1953 (all three, Alec, John Gielgud and Williams had similar tiny, meticulously formed handwriting, using ever, it would seem, grammatically precise, uncorrected English):

> It appears in the papers that Sir John Gielgud has been arrested on a charge of homosexual importuning. He described himself on the charge sheet as 'a clerk of Cowley Street with an income of £1000 a year'. Why tell these kind of lies? Of course, this is clearly a case of persecution. Poor fellow.

I have not found what Alec felt about the arrest for soliciting in a Chelsea public lavatory of the actor to whom he said he owed everything. I suspect he said nothing. As he had had a similar experience, or so we believe, the public consequences and exposure of which to his large admiring public he had managed to avoid, he must have felt both relief that it was not him and threatened that it could have been. What if the incidents in which he had been involved had, at the same time, become public knowledge?

Alan Hollinghurst in his novel *The Swimming Pool Library* in 1988 sets out to capture the risk-taking excitement and sensual allure of these ultimate gestures of anonymity and sex without responsibility. Kenneth Williams in his diaries and letters, and Ned Sherrin in his novel *Scratch an Actor* ('Scratch an actor and you'll find an actress' – Dorothy Parker) on the other hand disclose the futility and sadness of such encounters.

At the time *The Swimming Pool Library* was published Alec called in one day at the Heywood Hill bookshop, where he was a frequent customer, and asked for a good new novel to read, whereupon the sales assistant recommended he buy it. The next time Alec was in the shop the same assistant asked innocently whether he had enjoyed the book. Alec abruptly replied, 'It was disgusting. I threw it in the dustbin!'

Hollinghurst's novel leaves little to the imagination, especially such passages as, 'He rolled over, feet swinging above my head, and snuggled down beside me again . . . putting off the looming fuck. My cock did look thick and threatening between his thighs, nudging its head up under his balls (etc. . . .)' But I am surprised Alec did not see their lighter side and that they did not appeal to his sense of the ridiculous. Perhaps they touched a repressed but still raw nerve. Plenty of the love that dared not speak its name 'now seems to be the love that never shuts its gob', in the words of Tom Utley in the *Telegraph*. If Alec took against you, as Ian Richardson said of him, 'It could be rather chilling'.

When Alec made *Father Brown*, his next film with Robert Hamer, the director of *Kind Hearts and Coronets*, it seemed like a return to the circumference of character acting, a new disguise, another of the thousand faces. But, 'In Father Brown,' wrote G. K. Chesterton, 'it was the chief feature to be featureless. The point of him was to appear pointless; and one might say that his conspicuous quality was not being conspicuous.' It sounded ideal casting, but Alec unfortunately did not achieve invisibility so well as he did with later roles such as George Smiley.

The attractive feature for him about Chesterton's character was his concern with the spirit. Father Brown was modelled on Monsignor John O'Connor, a venerable Irish priest, who received Chesterton into the Catholic Church. 'The great miracles are too big to see and the small ones too numerous to count,' Mgr O'Connor famously said. Father Brown roots out the criminal in any situation because he has identified within himself the criminal instinct which we all possess, and which used to be called by most people 'original sin'. 'No man's really any good till he knows how bad he is, or might be . . . till he's squeezed out of his soul the last drop of the oil of the Pharisees; till his only hope is somehow or other to have captured one criminal and kept him safe and sane under his own hat.' The same sympathy provoked the observation attributed to Sir Thomas More, who, watching a murderer being led off to execution, reportedly said, 'There but for the grace of God, go I.'

In the film Father Brown voices his mission: 'I want to help man . . . to cure him of the sickness of his soul', but this became secondary to the detective work. Self-identification led him to the murderer – in other words detection had become a creative process

similar to that of a writer or indeed an actor. As the script of the
film indicated, 'I try to get so far inside a man, I move with his
arms and legs.' There were, in short, strong and distinct similarities
between Chesterton and Alec.

Yet Alec confessed himself dissatisfied with this film and one
can see why. Although Father Brown is horrified by the secret and
shameful knowledge that every one of us is capable of crime, Alec's
portrayal remained a matter of harmless externals, while he was
always owlishly visible. He failed to penetrate the man more than
superficially. Alec, in his autobiographical search for truth and
identity, had not yet the 'readiness' to take up full residence in the
spiritual centre of a role. Typically he blamed himself. Yet he was
wrong to blame himself for not achieving the full stature of
Chesterton's conception: this was more probably the fault of the
director and other elements in the film, such as the semi-farcical
script with its Chaplinesque chases. He remained peripheral to the
depth of Father Brown: as the reviewer in *The Times* commented,
this film gave Guinness only 'half a chance and Mr Guinness takes
that half even though he cannot turn it into a whole'.

Years had passed since Alec had been anticlerical and 'shuddered' with superstitious dread when he passed a priest or a nun.
Like Agnes, his mother, he had always been receptive to quasi-
mystical or spiritual experiences. One night during the filming of
Father Brown, which was shot in a village near Mâcon in Bur-
gundy, an incident spun him in the direction of conversion to
Rome.

He had finished filming. It was pitch black and still robed as a
priest he began the walk of a mile or so back to where he was
staying. Over twenty years later he told a reporter:

It was absolutely dark. I heard little footsteps running after
me. Suddenly I felt my hand taken by about a seven-year-old
boy, who walked with me all the way back to the village
swinging my hand and chattering. I only caught little bits of
what he was saying. I didn't dare utter a word in case I
frightened him with a foreign accent or my clumsy French.
I remained absolutely silent, and eventually he squeezed my
hand and disappeared, and I thought it was simply marvellous
that a child in the kind of dark, in a dark lane, will run up to

a man, because he's dressed as a priest. And it totally changed my attitude ... I don't base my religion on that but it's the attitude. No, I think it's marvellous that a small boy has confidence ... I've always looked back on it as a magic moment.   *Evening Standard*

It was still to be some three years before Alec fully embarked on Catholicism. He was thirty-nine years old when he played Father Brown; as he later told a friend, as a way of life and an answer to his fear and insecurity, 'The years between thirty and forty are the worst. You have got so far, and you are struggling to reach the very top, finally to arrive.'

Alec was edging more and more towards conversion to Roman Catholicism. This became evident in his next stage role, which many believed represented the peak of his acting achievement. The leading role of the Cardinal in *The Prisoner* by Bridget Boland supplied parallels with Alec's own early life, either consciously or unconsciously, although without Alec's cognizance of them as such. The play was dedicated to Alec, and in it he achieved a quality of identification and spiritual conviction which has rarely been surpassed on stage or film. The secret weakness of this prince of the Church is the truth about his background which he has concealed. How had Bridget Boland picked on this? Did she work it out unconsciously from being a close friend and near neighbour of Alec in Hampshire? Possibly she had.

Boland was a questioning and forthright woman, a brilliant, even pugnacious conversationalist who always had an unusual point to make. Born in Ireland, she read politics, philosophy and economics at Somerville College, Oxford, later becoming a major in the ATS engaged on Intelligence duties. At the end of the war she visited Belsen four days after it was opened up; a lifelong Catholic, she was one-time secretary of the Catholic Truth Society and like the Catholic philosopher Elizabeth Anscombe, who died in 2001, she was a champion of truth. She would, for instance, burst out laughing at the statue of Oliver Cromwell in front of Parliament, observing something to the effect that 'only the English could manage to put that up there – "without which [i.e. Parliament] he [Cromwell] managed to rule for eleven years..."' Her first play, *The Cockpit*, had centred on the problem of Serb and Croat refugees. Awkward and tall, she could suddenly blow up into a temper over the world's injustices.

The Prisoner, the Interrogator, the antagonist, played on stage by Noël Willman,* was attempting to convert the Cardinal from his faith into becoming a supporter of the communist, totalitarian system. What he uncovered as the Cardinal's weakness was his lack of love for his mother and for humanity in general – 'I do not love my mother, I never have' – as well as excessive humility and inverted pride. In fact, or so it emerges in the course of the play, the Cardinal really hated himself with self-gratifying masochism. As a celebrated leader of the Church he becomes revealed as an egotist indulging in secret treachery, an ambitious man who tried to hide away the fact that his mother was a whore; he was intent, above all, on justifying himself to himself – 'to me, not to God'.

The interrogation achieves his spiritual cleansing, his purification, as if the Interrogator, in some clever ironic way, becomes himself the agent of God, and by trying to destroy what is the greatest threat to the socialist, materialist way of life, in fact ends by losing his own faith in that system. 'To do my job,' the Interrogator says finally, 'I had to get so close to you that we were like two sides of the same man talking to each other. And I came to love and pity the other side and hate what I made it do.'

There were many biographical touches buried in *The Prisoner* which suggest that Boland intuitively tuned into her leading actor's complicated soul and was painting in some of the emotional background of his own lacerating experience of family life and deprivation. She gave him the opportunity to reveal to the world

---

* Noël Willman was a Londonderry-born actor and director who specialized in the playing of cold-hearted villains and who was an old friend of Alec's, for they had trained together with Saint-Denis at the London Studio. A homosexual, Willman later befriended Kenneth Williams, and when Williams was having a nervous breakdown he stayed for a while in his flat. With Alec as the Cardinal, Willman as the Interrogator and Glenville as director there must have been considerable interplay of offstage personalities and a pool of sublimated memories and feelings, all no doubt subsumed and channelled into the cathartic confrontation with guilt offered by the play. But here also were three remarkable talents who did not spare their skill and self-discipline in the cause of the production and play.

– but completely disguised in character – that his mother was a prostitute, if not in fact then something very close. Alec at last could portray his own deep emotions about this shame from the inside. Boland was a powerful and intuitional writer who could depict men as few women writers for the stage had done. But a fashionable style, an engaging posture of presentation, eluded her. So perhaps did some of the depth. The manner was direct and brutal: canonical.

There was little doubt that this play resulted in Alec's greatest performance to date. His acting brought to the text an authority and sensitivity which had never until now quite become integrated into the whole work. The Cardinal's shame, his darkness, his sense of guilt and sin, his aspiration towards the good, above all his faith, all became convincing, and worth quoting:

> *Interrogator:* What were you hiding? Why were you
>   ashamed?
> *Prisoner:* Unclean flesh.
> *Interrogator:* Yes. Yes?
> *Prisoner:* My body of her flesh and blood.
> *Interrogator:* Your mother.
> *Prisoner:* Filth of her filth, me at the root of it, her lust.
> *Interrogator:* Behind the Fish Market. A prostitute?
> *Prisoner:* Not even for money. A whore. Not even for money,
>   for lust . . . Remembering the smell of the woman who
>   bent over you to try and kiss you good night. Where,
>   before I was born or after it, would I find a heart?

The Prisoner ends far from glorifying God or even establishing the heroism of the unidentified Prisoner. Like the many statues of the 'Unknown Political Prisoner' in vogue in the early 1950s, this prince of the Church bears a somewhat grey if universal identity. The progress of Boland's play is towards the man's disintegration – a peeling away of his defences before his shame. His punishment could not be worse: release on medical grounds to face the world he accuses himself of having betrayed. His explicit confession: 'That I am the son of my mother, and my whole life a fantasy to hide me . . . I prayed for forgiveness, but I knew I had no heart.' The phrase 'my whole life a fantasy to hide me' is especially telling, as it plays another variation on the theme of Alec's life.

The Prisoner ran at the Globe Theatre and then was made into a film. London audiences, although they respectfully attended, viewed it ambivalently. Communism was the bogey, for sure, but persecuted Catholicism behind the Iron Curtain was rather a remote and unknown quantity, while a large proportion of English society viewed Catholicism with as great misgiving as they viewed communism. The spirit of serious English theatre was left-wing and pro-Brechtian, while priests were more often than not treated as objects of obscene derision, or as props of a decaying order.

Yet the impact which *The Prisoner* had on those who saw it, or saw the film, came from the uncanny realism of Alec 'confessing', at one level removed and in emotionally safe circumstances, the shameful background of his own life (and if not the actual truth, then the feelings he had about it). Subsequently Alec was supposed to go to Broadway with *The Prisoner*, but this fell through because he could not stay in New York more than four months due to the films he had contracted to make.

The film of *The Prisoner* proved an unequivocal triumph. Peter Glenville, who had moved to America, again directed faultlessly. Ralph Richardson once said, after his taxing role of Peer Gynt, 'It's a funny thing about acting, I have nothing to say about it at all which is a bit odd because one does take such immense trouble to try and find the character, to create the character, that it is rather as if the memory vanishes. Perhaps it's rather a painful experience, really, and one forgets pain very easily, thank heavens.' I suspect this was also Alec's feeling about the Cardinal. If that moving sense of isolation that he created on stage, and that still presence in prayer and remorse, were absent in the film, the close-ups of Alec's face on screen more than made up for them. His expressions, and the underlying passions they represented, registered the effect Jack Hawkins as the Interrogator had on him as he peeled away the priest's layers of defence, not so much by tormenting his flesh as by undermining his sensitivity and revealing the impure motives for his vocation. Some triggers of the guilt may not have been entirely convincing, but with its evocation of the mother's 'unclean flesh' the film reached a tragic dimension that it never lost.

And so Alec placed before us the naked soul of a prince of the Church driven to desperation: 'I wanted to justify myself to myself

... To me, not to God ... I succeeded. I can serve ... But I can't care.' Playing without hairpiece or any other form of disguise Alec sacrificed neither ordinariness nor humbleness, but suggested depth and greatness. 'Try not to judge the priesthood by the priest,' the Cardinal tells the young prison guard after his humiliation, echoing St Peter's denial of his master before the cock had crowed three times.

He also eschewed sentimentality, embracing simplicity. The acting was inimitable with nothing spare, nothing excessive, giving away the actor. 'I wouldn't,' as we have quoted him saying, 'go to a psychoanalyst in case he revealed something and said, "And that is the springboard for such talent as you have." I would feel it was just that, was it, instead of having something almost magical ... like an empathy with animals, something you can't explain, something tucked away inside.'

Here, for once in his life, and definitively, was the undisguised, naked Alec. He describes later staying in Bridget Boland's flat in Rome but he never mentions *The Prisoner* in *Blessings in Disguise*, nor in *My Name Escapes Me*, although in *A Positively Final Appearance* he momentarily recalls Bruges as the film's location. With *The Prisoner* there was no disguise and no hiding place. Italy banned *The Prisoner* as being anti-Catholic. The Archbishop of Westminster, Cardinal Griffin, authorized Alec to quote him: 'This is a film which every devout Roman Catholic should see.' It had a warm reception in the US where it was voted the best foreign film of 1955.

17. The Criminal Mastermind

Unlike Richardson, who turned down the part of Vladimir in *Waiting for Godot* and regretted it, Alec never expressed regret over not playing Estragon, the other tramp, which he was offered. He told a colleague he did not warm to the idea that Vladimir and Estragon discuss the possibility of getting an erection if they hang themselves, nor to having to drop his trousers in the final moments. But it had been Peter Glenville who had first optioned *Waiting for Godot*, together with Donald Albery, although in the spring of 1955 Glenville moved to New York and relinquished his part of the option.

I have found no trace of Alec's views on Beckett, although I suspect they may have accorded slightly with those of Bully, who played Pozzo in the first English production, and who relished with disgust the effect acting in Beckett had on him. 'I noticed,' Peter Bull wrote, 'that my friends were clearly mortified at having to hear my lines and Bob [Robert] Morley had thrown the script from one end of his garden to the other.'

Bully opened in *Godot* on 3 August 1955. He described the tribulations of performing in a play whose ambiguity has challenged the efforts of academics to explain it. He found the people who liked Godot alarming – 'they either sat spellbound in respectful silence or laughed their heads off in such a sinister way that the actors thought they must have forgotten to adjust their costumes . . . and it didn't help me in my portrayal to learn that Pozzo represented Fascism, Communism, Lord Beaverbrook, Randolph Hearst, Mussolini, James Joyce or, rather surprisingly, Humpty Dumpty.'

Towards the end of 1955, Bully transferred in *Godot* to the Criterion Theatre, Piccadilly Circus. Alec was now rehearsing the role of Boniface in Feydeau's *Hotel Paradiso*, again under Glenville, who returned from New York to London to direct it. As Glenville explained, the characters in the play were 'straightforward types, without over-subtlety or complexity'. It must have been a relief for Alec after the soul-baring of *The Prisoner* to find himself in the intricate, ordered world of farce.

The rehearsals were 'hard and gruelling', as Glenville outlined the conditions for making *Hotel Paradiso* a success. 'There usually comes a moment when the actors cannot believe that such scientific hard work will ever induce laughter at all. There can be no rewarding conversations between director and cast about the mood, the inner motivation, or the subconscious. This necessity for precision work is like the making of a Swiss clock.'

The discipline and hard work brought solace to the highly strung star of the *Carry* On films, who joined Alec in *Hotel Paradiso*. Kenneth Williams lived at a continual pitch of tension over his identity. Just before he was asked by Peter Glenville, on Alec's suggestion, to take the part of Maxime in *Hotel Paradiso*, Williams wrote in his diary that his 'nerves are almost at breaking point – footsteps behind me in the streets get me so I am screaming inside – I'm watching for people to stare and hating them – I want to talk aloud with myself, but there's always people there ... I have *never* needed privacy *more* and I have none. I'm weeping a lot too ...'

However, once in rehearsal for *Hotel Paradiso* his angst miraculously evaporated and when in mid-April they had opened, Williams reported his friend Peter Eade had come to see the show: 'He says not to worry about it [the sense that Williams was playing Maxime badly]. Small part but I acquit myself well. That's consoling, I was beginning to feel a complete fraud.'

Hotel Paradiso opened at the Winter Garden Theatre in May 1954 just prior to *Look Back in Anger* at the Royal Court Theatre. Two years before, Anthony Armstrong-Jones, then a twenty-four-year-old freelance photographer, had photographed Alec in his Pimlico studio. 'Uncle Oliver recommended me' – he meant Oliver Messel, the designer – and Armstrong-Jones, later Lord Snowdon, was surprised to find Alec was as nervous as himself, a nervousness that showed in the slightly wooden, self-conscious portraits.

Armstrong-Jones arrived at the photocall at the Winter Garden

Theatre and took a remarkable picture of Alec as Boniface with mad, staring eyes. This was his first commission for *Vogue* and over the next forty years he went on to photograph Alec more than any other actor: he complained on that first occasion that he had to work from the stalls with a long lens and because it was a weak shot had to do a rescue job on it:

> I wanted a close-up of Guinness's head to avoid showing he wasn't in costume. So I blew up a section of the negative, using an 8mm ciné camera lens in the enlarger – if I had blown up the whole negative it would have been twenty-foot square. It came out grainy and flat. I then put potassium ferrocyanide on the whites of the eyes to bleach them, which made it almost into a caricature.   *Dear Alec*

Alec made his first entrance in *Hotel Paradiso* sharpening a pencil, slicing away at it with his penknife until he had nearly walked over the footlight into the laps of the audience. Only then did he become aware that anyone was watching. The critics in their glowing reviews talked of Alec as 'letting his hair down' as Boniface, but that was not at all his way when he played the character Glenville called 'the timid husband with a roving eye'. As Glenville explained in an introduction to an edition of the play, 'Any attempt on the part of the actor at comic elaboration or subtle undertones will disrupt the pattern and rhythm of the play.' Tynan, his mind still full of Alec, wrote of his 'exquisite stealth' as Boniface; 'the chubby, crafty little fellow obsessed by an urge to break out and show the world his mettle'. 'When Alec had hidden from my husband inside the chimney,' wrote Irene Worth, who played Marcelle, 'and returned, quite black with soot, he said, "It's me, Marcelle," with such concern and reassurance to me that the audience began to laugh louder than ever. I shouted to him, over the roar, "Shall I wait or go on?" He shouted back, "Go on!" We did.'

After one performance Alan Brien, the critic, visited him backstage, observing him emerge from the character he was playing:

> As we talked he held in his hand a cloth-faced wig-rest upon which someone had lightly pencilled some vague human

features. Between sentences he removed his toupee, his eyebrows, and his moustache and transferred them to the dummy. Then he picked up a towel and wiped off the rest of his make-up. I forgot what he was talking about. But I stared in amazement at the man with the face as blank as a balloon who was holding in his hand an exact effigy of Alec Guinness as a Frenchman. *Daily Mail*, 7 March 1958

In the middle of the run of *Hotel Paradiso*, after a dull matinee, Williams wrote to his friend Annette Kerr, 'I have just come back after my first entrance. Not a tinkle, or a laugh. Charming! The girls and I were practically hysterical. The being of the play is *always* in the auditorium. It's *their* lives we are rehearsing, and their tears we cry. So when they're too lethargic to enter into it, there's really nothing the actor can do. Those actors who say a dull audience is a challenge and all that crap know nothing about the theatre.'

Alec was now an object of admiration for character and comic actors, especially Williams. There was widespread belief that he was the greatest comic actor in the world, 'and I don't except Chaplin', as Tay Garnett, the experienced Hollywood director expressed it. During the run Williams was rehearsing in a sketch with Jimmy Edwards and Zsa Zsa Gabor at the Palladium for the Night of a Hundred Stars, finding Gabor was 'buggering up' the whole thing because she had no idea of comedy, or so Williams told Alec. At the evening performance Alec, Williams said, 'suddenly hissed at me, "Zsa Zsa Gabor to you too" and I laughed of course.'

Jokes and sudden unbuttoning apart, Alec in his role as leader of the profession provoked awe. He started taking out his cast regularly to dinner; for instance on 25 May Alec 'took us to dinner at the White Tower. It was all very sycophantic indeed,' reports Williams. This was to become a frequent ritual. Aged forty-two, Alec outshone his younger colleagues, especially if, like Williams, they were full of complexes. Williams writes to a close friend (after performing with Alec), 'For various reasons, an actor decides – subconsciously or otherwise – that his own identity is not the right one. Always assuming that he has got one. This may be through genuine thought, or through sheer lack of faith in his own ability.

So, he decides to identify himself with someone else – or something else. It may be Gielgud, it may be Olivier, it may be Guinness. Whatever it is, the accent is on purloining. The result is imitative, derivative acting – patchwork personalities – woolliness – uncertainty – and a complete lack of INDIVIDUALITY.'

As an actor, Alec had none of these problems. He was now well-defined, which is the opposite of invisible. He was distinctive and personal, which is the opposite of anonymous. He liked to pretend he was anonymous, because it suited him and gave him power; Tynan colluded with him in this game. This game was all about image.

With Kenneth Williams, Billie Whitelaw played a juvenile in *Hotel Paradiso* on the provincial tour. Williams said they were both dazzled by the Malmaison Restaurant in Glasgow. Whitelaw suddenly launched into an hysterically enthusiastic account of *Picture Post*: ' "They have a fascinating article this week on this Dutch community in Staines ... They've managed to preserve their own cultural traditions, even clothes! All the women wear Dutch caps!" – failing to observe the full stop before adding hastily, "on their heads, I mean". Alec smiled unperturbed and mercifully ordered for us . . .'

Williams relates how Alec manoeuvred him upstage behind potted plants because he did not want the audience to notice he had left his flies undone. Alec was the exaggerated soul of generosity towards his understudy, at first omitting to thank him for taking his place for two performances, then sending a gracious note and a crate of whisky. On being informed whisky was not the understudy's drink, he changed the bottles to gin. Was it fear or desire for love that made him entertain at his own expense, and bestow such lavish gifts?

In the spring honours list of 1955 Alec was made a Commander of the British Empire. A month or so later he descended into the lowest circle of criminality in the film *The Ladykillers* at Ealing, again with Mackendrick directing. This became Mackendrick's best film to date, some say his best ever, although he went on to Hollywood to make *Sweet Smell of Success* with Burt Lancaster as the venomous columnist J. J. Hunsecker, and Tony Curtis as the sleazy showbiz press agent, Falco.

The Ladykillers was Mackendrick's last film for Ealing and when he directed it Ealing had passed its prime, and was soon to be sold off to MGM, although still run by Balcon. His scriptwriter was William Rose, an American expatriate who told Mackendrick of a dream he had had one lunchtime when they were drinking in the Red Lion. Rose, from Missouri, had dreamt a whole film: 'complete' and 'original'. It was, Rose told Mackendrick, about five criminals 'who lived in a house with a little old lady and she found them out. They decided they had to kill her, but they couldn't and so they all killed each other.' When Rose outlined the idea to Michael Balcon, Rose recalled Balcon watching him with those strange hooded eyes all during the telling, 'never taking his eyes off me – just once in a while glanced at Sandy [Mackendrick] as if to say, "Is it just he who has lost his mind, or have you both lost your minds?"'

Rose's 'dream', as developed, at least partly borrowed from *The Amazing Dr Clitterhouse*, a popular 1930s comedy-thriller play, had the gangsters posing as a string quartet. In the US film of *Clitterhouse* they were led by Humphrey Bogart and called the 'Hudson River String Quartet' – the film also had a character called 'The Professor', played by Edward G Robinson. Kemp, in his biography of Mackendrick, described how the crucial casting of *The Ladykillers* came about, the part of Professor Marcus being originally intended for Alistair Sim. But Balcon stepped in: 'We're making money with the Guinness films, we're on a run of strength there. It's got to be Guinness.'

Alec read the script and told Mackendrick, 'But dear boy, it's Alistair Sim you want, isn't it?' They assured him it wasn't. With Alec Mackendrick cast Cecil Parker, Herbert Lom, Peter Sellers (who played the Teddy Boy plus the voices of Mrs Wilberforce's parrots), and Danny Green, an ex-boxer. As the old lady, again in the face of opposition, Mackendrick cast the seventy-seven-year-old Katie Johnson, who had played countless tiny roles of old ladies but never had a big part in her whole life.

Sellers, according to himself, watched Alec during the filming like a kestrel. He admired his Fagin, Herbert Pocket, Disraeli, the d'Ascoynes (he would impersonate the Reverend telling Dennis Price about his west window), Henry Holland and Sidney Stratton. As his biographer writes, 'The Guinness whose magic operated on Sellers was the one whose imagination (like Shakespeare's)

could encompass saints and sinners, the restrained and the grotesque. (Sellers, however, thrilled by the amorality of the artistic
impulse, made the mistake of applying it to his private life, and
this is what undid him.)'

Sellers, apparently, did not much admire Alec's performances after Professor Marcus, for Peter's deep frivolousness and
impatience, his need for instant pleasure, were worlds away from
Alec's modesty and quiet. He 'used acting, along with his transient
enthusiasms for a variety of women, religions and residences, as a
means of exploring, in a way that was almost detached – *entranced*
you might say – all the misshapen madness that loomed inside
himself.' Others would say that he was just a bloody-minded,
selfish sod.

'We'll never be able to kill her, Louis,' Alec's Marcus says to
Herbert Lom. 'She'll always be with us, for ever and ever and ever,
and there's nothing we can do about it.'

Mrs Wilberforce's innocence is absolute; the evil of the criminal gang wavers in squeamishness. Rose explained to Mackendrick,
'In the worst of men, there is that little touch of weakness which
will destroy them.' In fact, in Alec's academic professor of dislocated mental genius, there was plenty to redeem the deformity.
Mackendrick observed how Alec worked on the character: 'He has
a strange habit of working from the outside in. In the early stages
he's very much a putty-nosed character, working off gimmicks,
funny voices and so on. But then he gets it down and discards the
inessentials and finds the core of the character – even when he's
dealing with a comic grotesque.' The real-life model for Alec's
Professor Marcus had also a strange personal reflection, especially
as that model had just written a book about Alec.

The first idea Alec had was to play Marcus as a cripple – with
a dislocated hip which was, as Mackendrick says, 'quite gruesome
but horrendously funny'. He discarded this because the 'boss'
(Balcon) would never stand for it. Alec sulked – 'and went and
looked out of the window. And while I was talking about the
script he was snipping away with a pair of scissors, and he made
some paper teeth which he stuck in, then turned around and
grinned at me.'

The portrait which developed – 'snaggling teeth, lank hair,
trailing scarf, the cigarette between second and third fingers' (not

fourth and fifth, as Vidal reported) – grew to become, so Mack-endrick said, 'an absolute personal portrait of Kenneth Tynan'. Alec would naturally disclaim any such intention. 'I think I had in mind the wolf in Red Riding Hood. When I first saw myself in make-up I remember saying to Sandy, I look remarkably like an aged Ken Tynan; perhaps I'd better smoke cigarettes the way he does. But that was it. Nothing really deliberate.'

Or, one might add, conscious. But, unconsciously or consciously, and one suspects the latter, this was Tynan to the core. Exaggerated though it was, the role grew into what might be described as a cartoon of the naked psyche (or 'gestalt') of Tynan, perhaps in a kind of (completely unintentional) revenge on him for writing his book. In some way, albeit at a slightly ridiculous or even ironic level, it had to be a reassertion of control, of power, over the biographer. Here, anyway, was Alec's own private biography of Tynan, and, curiously enough, it revealed something accurate about the brilliant although often misguided mind of Tynan, whose eyes, described by one of his friends, with their 'Whites above the pupils, dart right into the farthest recesses of your psyche, the hollow cheeks crease into the shape of a stylised gargoyle, and more fangs than one had believed possible fight like maenads to jockey themselves to the front.'

Buck-toothed and macabre as he is, Professor Marcus lives and makes us laugh because the portrait Alec gave the audiences was rooted in the reality and observation of Tynan. The criminal mastermind was endowed with eccentricities both disconcerting and reassuring – kindness, intellectual scrupulousness – which were as much part of the comedy as the terrifyingly large teeth. To Elaine Dundy, Tynan's wife, there remained no doubt that Alec was playing Ken. 'They admired one another tremendously.'

So it became an affectionate, ironic and many-layered portrait of someone who had by now become something of a caricature himself – an immature, nightmarish person at his peak but, as he always had been, operating at one remove from reality. This showed, for instance, when Tynan wrote a review of his old hero Orson Welles as Othello, rubbishing him as an amateur 'Citizen Coon', then next moment inviting him to a party and expecting him not to react in an unfriendly way. Alec, himself alert to the treachery of the brilliant mind, immortalized it in his depiction of

Professor Marcus in a comic and harmless way. Beneath the surface of the portrait the spirit of G. K. Chesterton breathed: a diabolical visitation by a man who believed increasingly in the existence of the devil. Alec might even have quoted Chesterton with an unconscious reference to Tynan: 'St John the Evangelist saw many strange monsters in his vision, he saw no creature so wild as one of his own commentators.'

They filmed *The Ladykillers* in North London in the vicinity of King's Cross Station: with its image of a decaying England, its genteel horror, its Dickensian scale of character – and of good and evil – it mingled mirthfulness and icy macabre. These drew a wide following and the film became a commercial success. In America, however, critics failed to register its subtleties. It was compared unfavourably to *The Court Jester* with Danny Kaye, yet it did very well at the box office.

Further commentaries on the allegorical impact of *The Lady-killers* followed in time: a historian of Ealing Studios regarded the gang as the post-war Labour Government, who with their facade of civilized behaviour, radically set about redistributing wealth. A *Times* essayist in 1990 found it recorded the vanished charm of 1950s London. Sellers's biographer called it a masterpiece of fairy story-telling as well as 'one of the great railway movies . . . the steam trains are the film's dragons . . . the house a bit of broken gingerbread.'

In a scene cut from the first print, when Alec as Marcus makes his inspection of his rooms he listens to Mrs Wilberforce wittering on about her previous lodger, 'a Mr Proudlock, who did nothing but stare out of the window and collect engine numbers. ("And, what," Guinness said, exasperation eventually getting the better of him, "did Mr, eh, Proudlock *do* with the engine numbers he collected . . .?" The pointlessness of the hobby is a glimpse of Hell.)' (Roger Lewis, *The Life and Death of Peter Sellers*)

Mackendrick left Ealing, the studios were sold off to the BBC and Balcon took his Ealing entourage with him to Boreham Wood under the wing of MGM. Balcon was joined by Kenneth Tynan, who became script editor in spring 1956 to a studio he described as a kind of 'outsize Anderson shelter' in a corner of the Metro lot. Later Tynan advised on two of the poorer Guinness films, *Barnacle Bill* ('not a very good idea of T. E. B. Clarke, for whom work had to be found') and *The Scapegoat*. When he left Ealing, disgruntled at what he had not been able to do, he complained of Ealing's reluctance to deal at all seriously with sex, social problems or politics. He felt it had 'made' no actors of any significance, except for Alec.

On 2 September 1955 Alec flew to Hollywood via Iceland; during the flight his berth in the Scandinavian Airways plane collapsed so that he found himself hanging head down with his legs suspended in the air. 'I was so afraid of disturbing other passengers,' he told a reporter, 'especially the rather irate lady in the next berth, that I stayed in that position all night.'

Grousing about the world in old age, Alec harked back to what, for him, was more recognizable about the world in the Fifties. He had seen an old friend, Clifton Webb, playing an RNVR lieutenant commander in *The Man Who Never Was*, and recalled how Webb gave a glamorous birthday party when Alec first arrived in Hollywood to play Prince Albert in *The Swan*, his debut as an international film star.

He relished this career from the start, although distanced himself from it, deprecated it and deprecated himself in it. He loved the giants, the ghouls, the fairies and the monsters and saw in their larger-than-life dimensions both the raw material for gossip, which he loved to retail as, like Tynan, possibly some form of celebrity compensation for his illegitimacy and resentment. After all, to mix with celebrities while on the road to becoming himself was as much to reflect their light while measuring oneself against them and becoming as good as they were. It was only to take him three more years to have his photograph on the cover of *Time* magazine, with six pages of text singing his praises.

Thanks to his apprenticeship with Gielgud, his absorption of the three theatre gurus of the 1930s, Komisarjevsky, Saint-Denis and Guthrie, he had more knowledge of the craft of acting than many of those big, mainly empty Hollywood personalities. Moreover he had, from a film's point of view, one asset few of them, whose looks and little more were their brand names, possessed. The infinite and subtly variable – and photogenic – Guinness face.

The character he assumed in *The Swan* was that of the visiting actor, the correct, even icy bridegroom in this film adaptation of a play by Ferenc Molnár. Grace Kelly played the other half in this comedy of royal marriage, her last film before her retirement and 'correct' own royal marriage to Prince Rainier of Monaco. Her character falls temporarily for a beguiling tutor played by Louis Jourdan before realizing her duty. John Russell Taylor wrote:

> Knowing Guinness as we do, we are not surprised that he makes no attempt to pull the text out of shape by winks and nudges and sly twinkles at the camera to indicate that really, whatever everything else he does and says may tell us, he is really every princess's dream lover. It is a brave tactic, but not one which suggests future Hollywood stardom – or even any noticeable desire for it.

Alec and Gielgud liked to try to prick Noël Coward's conceit. Alec recounts that at this Clifton Webb party he found Humphrey Bogart and 'Betty Bacall' as well as Coward (to you and me 'Betty' is Lauren Bacall but Alec likes to share the familiarity with us). Alec as the new boy here, earnestly in talk on the sofa with some 'blond young man' who has been working hard on his pectoral muscles, is told by Bogart to shut up because Coward begins entertaining with his light voice at the piano: 'He looked across the piano at me with a sweetly pained expression. There was no doubt I have blotted my copybook.'

A week later Alec is at another, identical party and again Coward plays, but this time Bogey strides over to Coward and tells *him* to shut up as they had had enough of him last week. He 'swiped' him across the shoulder, Alec says.

A more powerful Hollywood anecdote from this period records the death of James Dean. To go back to the beginning, Alec says it was on his very first night in Hollywood, and perhaps he still felt somewhat upside down from his travel experiences on Scandinavian Airways.

> I had arrived off the plane, and I'd been met by Grace Kelly and various people, but I found that I was alone for the evening, and a woman I knew telephoned me and asked me out to dinner ... We finally went into a little Italian dive and that was full, so we were turned away. Then I heard feet running down the street, and it was James Dean. He said, 'I was in that restaurant when you couldn't get a table and my

name is James Dean.' He asked us to join him and then going back into the restaurant he said, 'Oh, before we go in I must show you something – I've got a new car', and there it was in the courtyard of this little restaurant, some little silver car, very smart, all done up in cellophane and a bunch of roses tied to its bonnet, and I said, 'How fast can you drive this?' and he said 'Oh, I can only do 150 mph in it.' I asked if he had driven it, and he replied that he had never been in it at all. Some strange thing came over me, some almost different voice and I said, 'Look, I won't join your table unless you want me to, but I must say something, please do not get into that car because if you do (and I looked at my watch), it's now Thursday (whatever the date was) ten o'clock at night, and by ten o'clock at night next Thursday you'll be dead if you get into that car.' I don't know what it was – nonsense, so we had dinner. We had a charming dinner, and he was dead the following Thursday afternoon in that car.

John Russell Taylor, *Alec Guinness*

Alec was right. The Force was with him. He travelled back to England by sea, on the *Queen Mary*. An early example of the paparazzi snapped him bald. 'My wig is in my trunk and I am not supposed to have pictures taken without – it's part of my contract.'

18. Peering into the Darkness

About the time he acted with Alec in *Hotel Paradiso* Kenneth Williams summed up the unhappy position of the homosexual in English society. He wrote to his actress friend Annette Kerr whom he found so sweet and understanding that he once thought of marriage to her. The marriage would never work out, she told him, when they considered sharing a flat, because 'her smalls in the bathroom were inevitable'.

Williams was, he told Annette, 'FORCED to try to understand why homosexual writing has such a self-pitying Masochistic flavour, worst of all the Oscar Wildean "each man kills the thing he loves" philosophy so adolescent and fatuous in itself.' He goes on in a statement which relates to an unrealized potential in Alec. 'And the reasons are not hard to find. We have created a situation in society where more and more homosexuals are encouraged to regard themselves as persecuted. They band together and become gregarious as a result, and create freemasonries of their own, in countless industries and organizations. Automatically this leads to a falsification of ALL values. The corruption is obvious. Of course the creative homosexual SEES the trap and tries to avoid it. If he succeeds he often only becomes a lonely, bitter person, pouring his frustration into his writing. Seeing himself as the proud, tortured soul, who is unable to declare his love for the beautiful, but alas, normal young man, and killing himself as the result.'

English theatre in the 1930s had been dominated by a freemasonry of actors and directors such as Williams had described which resulted in certain attitudes to style: cool, passionless, unthreatening acting from women, for example. One can see Alec shared some of these tendencies, such as the fastidiousness over clothes and hygiene, but most of all he strove, in his complicated yet pragmatic self, towards full integration. He escaped the traps of hysteria and any sense of persecution. He did not blame society. He looked towards another goal. Whatever dilemmas he had over who he was, Alec chose another path. Religious conversion.

A true believer in Christianity, such as Alec was to become, would consider not that he chose God and Jesus to follow, but that he had been chosen. That archetypal conversion of St Paul was not Paul's choice. It happened to him. It is easy to question or niggle at Alec's conversion if you are intent on finding loopholes in it. Psychological causes, reductive reasons such as that it brought him emotional security, that he found a mother at last, that he could hide his secret shame in God's forgiveness, and so on can be advanced.

Nevertheless, conversion in any person's life is an action with consequences as fundamental as the most mortal of sins, such as murder or adultery, and on an equal basis with getting married, becoming pregnant, choosing a profession or even dying. Many who have written about Alec's conversion do not take it seriously, considering it perhaps on a par with joining the local bridge club or acquiring a timeshare holiday home in the afterlife.

The signs, in Alec's own deliberate steps towards conversion to the Roman Catholic faith, were clear ever since he was a young man. As a schoolboy he had sung hymns with images of twilight or geography, Greenland's icy mountain – either melancholy or rumbustious. When confirmed as an Anglican in Holy Trinity Church, Eastbourne, by the Bishop of Lewes, he had realized with a flash of insight that he had never really believed in God.

He befriended Cyril Tomkinson, an Anglican priest, who told him as Hamlet he crossed himself incorrectly, and later he stayed with him in Bristol for four nights during the Blitz. Tomkinson and Ronald Howard, headmaster of Hurstpierpoint College were, according to a correspondent of mine, 'an item' although at this time 'absolute discretion was obligatory'. Tomkinson, who told Alec that 'many of his lady parishioners had lesbian tendencies', plied Alec with Algerian wine fortified with port and tried to make him, during his stay, confess to him. Alec found him 'entertaining, witty, eccentric, rather old-maidish in a naughty way'. Also in the early years of the Second World War, on one Sunday morning, he had risen in the dark to bicycle to church for Holy Communion; but again his enthusiasm for Anglo-Catholicism felt to him, in spite of the effort he made, in decline. On the other hand he had 'odd, almost mad, phases of near-psychic experience, too'; once, in his search for a meaning in life, he sought enlightenment among the Buddhists. In 1945 there was the leave weekend spent in Rome when he met Pope Pius XII; commenting how he felt for the first time in his life he had seen a saint. Another time he wandered into Brompton Oratory, London. Spotting a screwed-up piece of paper at the feet of the statue of St Anthony, and overcome with curiosity, he furtively snatched it up, read it and returned it to its place. He felt humbled by the simple plea he found. 'Please, St Anthony, help me to find work.'

As he neared forty, certain professional and personal threads were pushing him towards a more extraordinary outcome to the crisis of middle-age than many people experience. Already, playing Father Brown in France had provided the strange mystical experience when he was mistaken for a real priest by a child. Then Matthew, aged eleven, was struck down with polio and paralysed from the waist down. Walking back from filming in Hammersmith one day, Alec dropped in at the Catholic church and made a negative bargain with God; if Matthew recovered he would never put an obstacle in his way should Matthew wish to become a Catholic.

Matthew did recover and this was when, with Peter Glenville's urging, they decided to send him to Beaumont School near Windsor, a Catholic school. At the age of fifteen Matthew did choose to become a Catholic. In the meantime the conversion of Alec proceeded slowly: in 1955, having by now played in the stage success of *The Prisoner*, Alec visited a Trappist monastery where he took a retreat.

Along the way Alec experienced cold feet about conversion. John Russell Taylor identified, none too sympathetically, this feature:

> It is well-known that in virtually all his major roles, and indeed major successes, Guinness has got cold feet somewhere along the way, and begged and pleaded to be released from

his contractual obligations. So much so that it became a ritual, not perhaps to be taken totally seriously, even by himself.

Taylor went on, 'Though he is an Aries, he should be a Virgo, since it has to be rape every time, with someone else taking final, formal responsibility.'

'Rape every time' is an extreme charge. But Taylor was pointing out that Alec's professional character seemed more often than not like that of a victim. Is this true or false? There had been a sacrificial feeling about the last time he played Hamlet. It certainly seemed here as if he had been offering himself up to be mauled, inviting the world to participate in tearing him apart and causing him pain.

The failure of *Hamlet* had resulted in a general lowering of confidence. He abandoned a number of high-flying theatrical projects involving figures as variously distinguished as Edwige Feuillère and Tallulah Bankhead. He renounced his ambition to play King Magnus in *The Apple Cart*, a role for which he lacked the Shavian brazenness or panache, yet could have imbued with irony, poise and regal nonchalance.

Yet the sense of failure may well have contributed to or hastened his conversion. If he was a victim, he was now becoming ready to embrace the Christian idea that the greatest and most important man of all was powerless in his moments of victory. The readiness was all. And at least, in this production of *Hamlet*, he frivolously consoled himself, he had crossed himself the right way round.

Conversion takes many forms. Some of these, as described in the sceptic William James's *Varieties of Religious Experience*, are sudden and dramatic, impulsive and compelling – one's whole future life becomes revealed in a flash and the path which is to be followed is illuminated. This had sometimes seemed to happen sometimes to Alec during these years of uncertainty when he had not yet fully committed himself. In the middle of one afternoon he was walking up to Kingsway, for example, 'When an impulse compelled me to start running, with joy in my heart and in a state of almost sexual excitement.' He ran until he came to the little Catholic church (St Anselm and St Cecilia) which he had never entered before. 'I knelt, caught my breath, and for ten minutes was lost to the world.'

It was typical of the man's ever watchful intellectual censor that he should have to justify this deranged – or so he called it – zeal some few lines later, by saying that Ronald Knox, the eminent Jesuit, also had such extreme lapses and had found himself running on several occasions to visit the Blessed Sacrament. He needed authentication, in his virtues as in his vices. 'And so I hide my weaknesses in great reputations,' said the Michel de Montaigne he was so fond of quoting.

Alec secretly received instruction in 1955 and was confirmed privately by the Bishop of Portsmouth early in 1956. The day of his conversion, 24 March, was sunny and hot; the ceremony took place at St Lawrence's Church, Petersfield, with Father Henry Clarke officiating. One might raise an eyebrow at his godfather, Peter Glenville, who now shared his bed with a younger man in New York, and would be considered by the Church as living in a grave state of sin. In the *News Chronicle* of 31 March 1956, under the somewhat disparaging headline 'Guinness turns Catholic', Alec spoke out a little cagily about playing Father Brown and the Cardinal: 'My research work for the parts certainly made me go into the subject of Catholicism a bit more than I had before.'

The inference behind the answer could have been that there was something rather dark and shameful about becoming a Catholic, and that Alec's 'excuse' was that of being an actor and so he could not help it. Nearly thirty years later, on the first page of *Blessings in Disguise*, he would write, 'Poor, rich, exceptionally brilliant Peter Sellers never seemed to get himself sorted out' – in other words, 'There, but for the grace of God, go I.' When he had confessed to his superior officer in the navy he was an actor, 'You automatically got the sneer.' An actor, again from *Blessings* is usually no more than 'an assortment of odds and ends which barely add up to a whole man'. Catholics, like actors, in those days were seen as a bit beyond the pale, decidedly outside the mainstream.

Alec, sincere as he was, joined up at the highest level of Catholic snobbery, again needing authentification. When he came to write of other conversions and fellow Catholics it was of the upper-class literary figures such as Evelyn Waugh and Edith

Sitwell, rarely of his old Catholic housekeeper at St Peter's Square whom he cherished and supported in her old age and who maybe had, in her way, as strong an influence over him as the grand old roués of conversion such as Waugh and Sitwell. One feels he tended to feel a bit superior to Irish priests and Irish Catholics and view them a little as the peasantry. Yet in Alec's paradoxical way his was a sincere conversion and it had a sound intellectual resonance which was to last. He enjoyed, too, and identified with the retreats – the stays in convents or monasteries, the mysticism of the profound Catholic thinkers – and of course the formality and sensuousness of the ritual.

In *The Cocktail Party* as in Eliot's other plays, as well as implied if not stated in much of his poetry, a single moment of choice confronts the main character. It stems from, or is closely related to the Either/Or philosophy of Kierkegaard, himself a profoundly religious philosopher. Eliot's plays are true to life and coherent because, in spite of their restricted scope, they were based on Eliot's own experiences, and these experiences shaped themselves into a pattern on which the poet continually drew, repeating it in many forms.

Central to Eliot's experience and constituting the main formative experience of his adult life was his acceptance of Christianity. From the time he wrote 'Gerontion' (1920) and *The Waste Land* (1922), until *Ash Wednesday* (1930), this gradual commitment – sometimes fluctuating, at other times seemingly attainable – provided the main inspiration, in the widest sense, of his existence. In *Ash Wednesday*, after passing through what mystics call the dark night of the soul, as well as after reflecting in other works that terrible, arid, post-First World War despair and nervous exhaustion of society, he celebrated his sense of recovery, his turning towards life.

There are parallels which can be drawn between Eliot's 'voices' and Alec's faces – the man, to his own annoyance, described as of a thousand faces. So, perhaps, just as Alec, twenty years later, after a similar experience of war, could find no identity at the centre of himself, and therefore of his acting, so also had Eliot only found a society of displaced, homeless individuals whose spiritual desolation was compensated for only by their need for stimulus, multiplying 'variety / In a wilderness of mirrors.' In picking the

right words for the situation, the poet could be said to be mapping
the unknown, and of course Eliot's words on the poetic method,
in *East Coker*, are well known. But actors also make and define
their culture, and therefore help or hinder people to control the
world in which they live, or worse, encourage them to coarsen or
destroy their culture by what they choose to play. At the same
time actors, such as Alec Guinness, have in their real lives had
an influence on the world in which they have become the most
influential mirrors held up to nature.

To some extent every religion has at its centre – and before it
can become real to the believer – an act of conversion. Eliot's own
entry into the Anglican Church happened at roughly the same
age and over the same span of years as did Alec's and therefore
we may view it as a similar emotion-maturing process as well as a
firming up of intellection conviction. If *The Waste Land* was,
as Alec said, the 'last great poem Eliot wrote before he became
a Christian', *Ash Wednesday* marked his acceptance of the will of
God. If you listen, as I have, to Alec's reading of this poem which
was broadcast in March 1974 (or to his later recording of the *Four
Quartets*) you can understand how he identified with the finality
of the emotions in the sense Eliot conveys that he has renounced
something. He had made up his mind so that he would never,
from that time forth, go back on this decision.

But there was more to it than that. Eliot, although he became
an Anglo-Catholic rather than a Roman Catholic, underwent, or
had undergone, also during the time of writing *Ash Wednesday*,
a profound change in his literary method and aspiration. This
came as an effect of his reading Dante's Divine Pageant at the
end of the 'Purgatorio'. The scene where Dante for the first time
re-encounters Beatrice, wrote Eliot, in his essay on Dante,

> belongs to the world of what I call the *high dream*, and the
> modern world seems capable only of the *low dream*. I arrived
> at accepting it, myself, only with some difficulty . . . poetry
> not only must be found *through* suffering but can find its
> material only *in* suffering. Everything else was cheerfulness,
> optimism, and hopefulness: and these words stood for a great
> deal of what one hated in the nineteenth century. It took me
> many years to recognise that the states of improvement and

beatitude which Dante described are still further from what the world can conceive as cheerfulness, than are his states of damnation.

Eliot may have been writing of Dante, but he was perhaps talking about himself. And it was not long before, having travelled a long way from *The Waste Land*, he could move on to celebration of the Christian martyr Becket in *Murder in the Cathedral*:

> Ambition comes when early force is spent
> And when we find no longer all things possible.
> Ambition comes behind and unobservable.
> Sin grows with doing good . . .

In Alec's case the 'high dream' he could now begin to enjoy as a result of his conversion was his greater ease in making those public transformations, those leaps, into men of genius, those notable leaders of heroic figures, instead of the 'little men you do so well', as Gielgud had described them. He could identify on a higher plane, at the same time having a strong enough sense of himself to which he could return. It is perhaps also important to make it clear that Alec's conversion, similar to Eliot's, in a way even imitative of it, was not an emotional conversion.

Both had, by the time of this crucial moment, their own processes of work under control. Eliot defined his own, in *Tradition and the Individual Talent*, as a 'continual self-sacrifice, a continual extinction of personality'. Both became, as Christian converts, essentially explorers in the world of inner experience, while still, of course, rooting their paradoxical observations in the external world:

> Those to whom nothing has ever happened
> Cannot understand the unimportance of events.

Contemplating Alec's conversion now, after his death, what I find almost alarming is that in a man who claimed to be private, who flaunted his anonymity like T. E. Lawrence, the conversion should have been so high profile. If it had happened today I should not have been surprised to see it featured in *Hello!* magazine. 'Famous English actor converts to the Roman faith.' At the same time the article would have pointed out that we were looking (in *Big Brother* style) at the conversion of a 'very private man'. It could make one suspicious that there was this public aspect to Alec's Catholicism, its 'This-is-me-with-the-Pope' aspect, as if above all he sought to be accepted, to belong to a respectable and established church but to be seen doing it privately. He could simply have done it and told no one. This is why I suspect a little the many stories of Alec's munificence and charity and well-meaning actions towards others – one always knew or heard about them. Fine. There is no reason why one should not, except that he felt a need to make it clear that he did not want it known who the benefactor was. (But somehow it was clear that everyone did.) And yet, it has to be said, even so, complicated as he was, he was not that kind of hypocritical person that the public awareness of such actions might suggest.

The same with his conversion. When you think of it, the mimetic desire stirred up in Alec by another's conversion – the ceremony might have come out of *Hotel Paradiso* and been written up by Feydeau. The crown jewel in Alec's collection of pre-war Gothic celebrities had experienced a renaissance in the 1950s, much fêted on her trips to America for her Byzantine clothes and her loony, medieval majesty. Unworldly as she was, and capable of getting lost in her own garden she had, in the year Alec played in *The Prisoner*, been made a Dame Commander of the British Empire.

Edith Sitwell's high honour coincided with a decline in her creative powers as a poet, her increased bitterness over brother Osbert's attachment to his lover Horner, and Horner's infidelity and cavalier treatment of Osbert. Regularly the trio toured America, where Edith savoured the joys of the dry martini and Horner those of the American homosexual underground. With a tendency to paranoia, an increasing dependence on alcohol prompted her to write in August 1955, 'My life in America and since I got back from America has been *one long hell* . . . and I have been able to settle down to nothing excepting over-work, and becoming a Catholic (which I became on Thursday).'

Unlikely although it may seem, the influence of Edith's conversion over Alec was apparently strong. It was grandiose, with Father Caraman performing the ceremony, Evelyn Waugh in attendance as her godfather, Alec and several poets as acolytes and hangers-on. They lunched afterwards at the Sesame Club. Waugh described it as a banquet – 'cold consommé, lobster Newburg, steak, strawberry flan and great quantities of wine'. Edith was confirmed two months later at Farm Street in front of a large invited audience, the cream of Catholic London, including Lady (Christian) Hesketh, who was Edith's godmother. Edith may have, as she wrote to Father Caraman, achieved a sense of happiness, safety and peace 'such as I have not had for years' but she quickly became an 'eccentric' Catholic, attending Mass irregularly, although she continued her confidential relationship with her confessor. She had, wrote Kenneth Clark, 'experienced imaginatively, not merely intellectually, the evil and misery of the world and has overcome that experience by the conviction . . . that all creation is one under the Divine Love'.

Another commentator on Edith's religion, Stephen Spender, wrote (of Eliot) that his smugness in taking shelter in the Catholic view was irritating (Eliot was high-Anglican, a sliver away). 'It's all right on paper, but in practice Catholics can only get through the day with the help of aspirin or whisky. They have acute neuralgia, most of them; and those that do not are hypochondriacs.' This dismissal of Catholicism was widespread among a liberal elite.

Merula became a Catholic a few months later, when Alec had started filming *The Bridge on the River Kwai* in Ceylon (now Sri Lanka). It came, or so he claims, as a complete surprise to him: 'I had no idea she was receiving instruction. If I had known I would probably have opposed it, for fear she was doing it only to keep me happy.' In his posthumous appraisal of Merula, Alan Bennett paid tribute to her nun-like devotion to Alec. 'The truth was that she made him a nicer, less awkward, more accessible person but even after sixty years of marriage she still found it odd that they got on and that she could cope with his fussing and over-propriety.' What practical effect did Catholicism have on both of them? 'Deep down, our faith has made a great difference to our lives,' Alec told the *Daily Mail* in 1959. 'Merula takes some cripples out in the car once a week. And I don't swear as much as I used to.' A frivolous but suitable response. A year later he would muse (in the *Standard*) that Catholicism 'seems such an eminently reasonable way of living; it is so sensible. The very opposite of the puritanical.'

Alec always felt that actors had an affinity with priests – 'unfrocked' priests, he called them, 'because clearly they were not priests, nor had they a sacramental role to play, yet there was still something priest-like about them, a sense of evocation and a sense of ceremony'. He believed that his fellow actors Olivier and Richardson possessed these qualities, and now several priests came to be numbered among his personal friends, among them Father Caraman. Alec, naturally, considered himself unworthy of the company of the other distinguished Caraman converts – part of the elaborate good manners of his constructive deceit? He reflected later that it must be quite a burden to 'carry' that lot in his mind. He found Father Caraman sweet natured, very sophisticated, as well as extremely determined. The sweet nature was not something that had struck me. In Rome for the canonization in 1970 of the forty English and Welsh martyrs, Father Caraman showed his determined spirit, so Alec wrote in a letter to Angela Fox. It was his job to present Pope John Paul II with a pair of doves, but having done this he felt he would like to have them back and breed from them. But the Pope had also taken a fancy to the doves. Caraman won – after three days of negotiation and, it was rumoured, by expressing himself rather sharply in Vatican high quarters.

Later still, at Easter 1994, a day after his eightieth birthday, Alec rejoiced in his attendance at Pope John Paul II's Easter Mass, held amid thunder, lightning and pouring rain outside St Peter's. In *My Name Escapes Me*, Alec celebrated the aspect of high farce worthy of an Ealing comedy ('A thousand white, starched coifs, which half an hour before looked like a great aggressive Armada, went limp and the nuns fell silent without a shot being fired'), followed by impressive dignity (His Holiness's voice, 'the most beautiful and dignified speaking voice I have ever heard').

Let us rest for a moment or two in Alec's conversion, in the peace and comfort it brought to his restless and searching self. It conferred unification.

It may come gradually, or it may occur abruptly; it may come through new intellectual insights, or through experi-ences which we will later have to designate as 'mystical'. However it comes, it brings a characteristic sort of relief; and

never such extreme relief as when it is cast into the religious
mould.   **William James,** *The Varieties of Religious Experience*

Would the conversion prove lasting? Many priests remained for
Alec essences, their influence absorbed through the words they
had written – chief among them Teilhard de Chardin: 'The
incommunicable part of us is the pasture of God'. Conversion
enabled Alec to come to terms with the disablement, the withdrawal of promised glory everyone feels in growing up, but which
in his case was extreme.

> When Paul asked the Lord to remove 'the thorn in his flesh'
> and heard 'my grace is sufficient for you', he was making
> a discovery that we still are far short of: that the weakness,
> the wonkiness, the wobble in one's life is due precisely to
> the glory's withdrawal and *therefore* is the place for grace's
> entry. 'Where I am weak, there am I strong.' The strength
> works in the weakness primarily 'to stop us boasting', but
> because the strength is the secret, the ratio of the weakness.
>   **Sebastian Moore,** *Let This Mind Be in You*

Alec would have agreed. But what would happen now to his
acting, and would he still continue to feel conflict over the thorns
in his flesh? Pope John Paul II calls man the visibility of the
invisible – meaning God. Alec's visibility became only too evident
in the following months of 1956.

Punch's cartoon for the lookalikes in *The Scapegoat*

19. Some Further Visibility of the Invisible

Pierre Boulle, the French author who paradoxically created the exemplary British army officer that became Alec's most famous film role before Obi-Wan Kenobi in *Star Wars*, wrote that 'Perhaps the mentality of the Japanese Colonel, Saito, was essentially that of his prisoner, Colonel Nicholson.' Captain Clipton, who observed Nicholson, came to the conclusion (in Boulle's novel on which the film was based) that the individual characteristics making up Nicholson's personality – his sense of duty, observance of ritual, obsession with discipline and love of the job well done – could not be better described than by the word 'snobbery'. Nicholson was a perfect example of the military snob, a type 'which has gradually emerged after a lengthy process of development dating from the Stone Age, the preservation of the species being guaranteed by tradition'.

Boulle continues in a vein which was important to Alec:

> Clipton, however, was by nature objective and had the rare gift of being able to examine a problem from every angle. The conclusion he had reached having somewhat calmed the brainstorm which certain aspects of the Colonel's behaviour caused him, he would suddenly feel well disposed and recognize, almost with affection, the excellence of the CO's qualities. If these were typically snobbish, he reasoned, then the argument needed to be carried only one stage further for the noblest sentiments to be classified as such, until even a mother's love would eventually come to be regarded as the most blatant sign of snobbery imaginable.

Snobbery, defined here as an almost princely sense of being set apart, had become part of Alec's early determination that no one should know who he was. This had been confirmed and deepened by the years in the navy. The pressure on him to conceal remained more powerful than any other feeling he knew. At the same time he had cherished and nurtured a sense of virtue, of being in the right, to gain necessary self-respect. And now, with conversion, the greatest terror of his life had been overcome, or at least contained: the concealed shame of his various secrets was at last safe, either to be discontinued or confessed if a lapse occurred. He could afford to be more personal, reveal more of himself and his vulnerability in the new film he was about to make, his third with David Lean.

It only goes to show how film directors, even those rated highly such as Lean, have perhaps as a component of their ability blindness and stupidity, and then fill with self-denial when found out. That Lean should not have perceived straight away that he should cast Alec as Nicholson is with hindsight inconceivable, but true. But then, although it is claimed otherwise, often the best things happen entirely by default, as much with the subjects made as with the actors chosen. Lean insisted he never offered the part first to Charles Laughton, the reason being that Laughton's bulk would have sunk the role into self-pity. His wife Elsa Lanchester recalls it differently: Laughton agonizing over the offer and turning it down because it entailed travelling to Ceylon. Another version of Laughton's rejection involved his unfitness, making him too expensive to be underwritten by insurers.

Lean's first choice had been Laurence Olivier: 'Why should I go to Ceylon to play a martinet when I can stay at home and act [in *The Prince and the Showgirl*] with Marilyn Monroe?' Given the thousand and one biographers and journalists and photographers who would have been starved of material had he gone, it's probably as well he didn't. But Lean's (and producer Sam Spiegel's) avoidance of the obvious choice for the role had not stopped here. Third choice had been Noël Coward. Well he would, as he had in Lean's *In Which We Serve*, have portrayed the snobbery, he would have exuded frigidity, and he had even a hint of oriental inscrutability about his eyes. He was unlikely to suggest that quality Boulle conveyed of agape, or disinterested love for his fellow men. In his case it was hardly disinterested.

Lean and Spiegel, unlike the French author, thought of the colonel more as an obsessive, someone in whom eccentricity and a mad sense of duty finally won over the extreme brutality and stupidity of his Japanese captors.

In the end they had to settle for Alec. He was not at this point a pukka world film star, little more from *The Swan* than a 'visiting Hollywood actor'. Perhaps piqued at being fourth choice, Alec added his own refusals to the heap of rejections. He told the columnist Godfrey Winn in 1970, 'I refused the part three times.' Perhaps once for each of the previous actors Lean had approached. Lean set Spiegel to work on Alec (or perhaps he did not by now mind who played it). Alec told Spiegel he was wasting his time trying to convince him, but Spiegel's power of persuasion was such that 'At the end of it, I was asking him, "What kind of wig will I be wearing?"' Even afterwards Alec claimed Nicholson was never his favourite part (but then, being the 'Duke' as Angela Fox called him, he was likely to turn against anything which made him a lot of cash, as he did later when he repudiated *Star Wars*). It only showed how much he identified with Colonel Nicholson who would have disdained the vulgarity of raking in a fortune.

Kwai took a long time to make: shooting (ten miles from Colombo) ran from October 1956 to May 1957. The bridge itself, 425 feet long and 90 feet high, consumed 1500 large trees, cost a quarter of a million dollars, and took five months to build. At first Lean told Alec that he wanted him to play a character who, if he sat next to him at dinner, he would find a complete bore. 'You're asking me to play a bore?' answered Alec tetchily. Alec found out about Laughton and remarked that Lean was 'hoping that Charles Laughton was going to play it' and that, 'far from liking his own performance [he] was over the moon about William Holden,' who was cast as the American guerrilla detailed to blow up the bridge. Holden had secured a much better contract than Alec, a fee of £300,000 and ten per cent of gross receipts paid at an annual ceiling of $50,000. Subsequently the film's receipts were so great the company invested Holden's share and paid him out of the interest.

Lean and Alec had the biggest clash of their careers together during the making of *Kwai*. Lean had taught Alec a great deal about film acting. Alec, as he himself said, had earlier been 'like putty in his hands . . . He had a brilliant eye for visual detail . . . I'm very *neat* as an actor. I do things rather precisely . . . David was very keen on actors being able to do things *identically* from take to take. If you aren't careful, the spirit can go out of your performance.'

The trouble stemmed from the degree of control both men wanted over Alec's performance. Lean wanted control for what he called 'the will of the film', in other words the obsessive nature of the protagonist. Alec wanted creative flexibility and space – and the scope to behave spontaneously. Lean's intention was to show that the military ethos on both sides, the Japanese and the British, was equally mad. He wanted a humourless performance. In his view Nicholson was a nut and Alec had to play him as a straight nut. This was a rather coarsening departure from the subtle and universal theme of Boulle's novel, namely that both commanders are intent on 'saving face'. Another significant departure was the blowing up of the bridge, which doesn't happen in the book. Said Boulle, 'For three years I fought them over this change. In the end I gave up.'

Not only was Alec bound to invest the part with some of his subversive humour, but with his deep instinct for reserve and self-preservation, he also shied away from intensity. The screamingly obvious neurotic was more than likely to end up, as played by Alec, as underlyingly reasonable. He took delight in avoiding the obvious and in circumventing expectations. And so Alec's Nicholson became real, filled out with observation of himself: that he had been fourth choice was only a first indicator of the muddled perception of Lean and Spiegel, for at times during *Kwai* Alec so failed to do what Lean asked of him that Lean felt his film was being undermined.

In one specific moment Spiegel found Lean beside himself with frustration. This was the moment – subsequently viewable as perhaps the most affectingly ironic moment in the whole film – when the bridge was completed and about to be blown up. Nicholson reflects on his twenty-eight years' service: 'I don't suppose I've been at home more than ten months . . . I wouldn't have had it any other way.' But there are 'times when you are nearer the end than the beginning'.

Alec played this obliquely, away from camera: 'It was pretty good torture for me. David wanted me to finish this long speech just as the sun tipped the tops of the trees on the horizon down the river.' They spent five consecutive sunsets getting it timed to the exact second. Alec complained it was 'like doing it backwards'. And, 'I never got a word of thanks.' Nicholson then inadvertently drops his officer's baton in the river.

Spiegel said that Alec so refused to do what Lean asked of him that Lean 'literally shed tears'. In fact it proved that the undermining comedy of dropping the stick fleshed out the unbuttoning moment. The moment was worthy of Mackendrick at his best. But Lean disliked it. Spiegel acted for an hour as go-between to settle Alec's and Lean's differences. 'I couldn't totally believe in the man,' said Alec later. 'I knew it was a good part, I knew the naval equivalents, a bit thick between the ears, a bit blunted . . . I wanted a bit more send-up and humour.'

Lean went on record as saying that 'Alec is one of the most fantastically knotted up men I know.' This rather vague insult would seem to have been true of himself. Alec was seriously complicated but not knotted up, which suggests seized up with neuroses, while self-knowledge continually flashed like lightning once had around his landing craft, illuminating parts of himself, if not the whole. Alec knew that, although he cut down the humour, ultimately Nicholson needed to awaken the sympathies of the audience, tilt them strongly towards himself and traditional British grit and obstinacy. His blinkered and humourless humour was merely the background 'humour'; his not allowing his officers to work on the construction of the bridge alongside their men was narrowly upholding the letter of international law, but had a wider significance. That the whole centre of dramatic effect should revolve around whether or not officers did manual labour may be unthinkable today. But in his portrayal of Nicholson's refusal to be broken, Alec suggested limitless inner strength and broadened the conflict to make it universal. This mirrored his own inner way of being able to make human his blinkered snobbery, his fixed ideas and his infuriating contradictions. As such he becomes the symbol of British discipline and achievement in adversity. What Alec was also able to show in his portrait of Nicholson was an affecting humility, as in Eliot's lines:

> The only wisdom we can hope to acquire
> Is the wisdom of humility: humility is endless.

The striking moments of *The Bridge on the River Kwai* retain their appeal over the years. Alec's slightly shifty eyes cloud sometimes with unspoken emotion; sometimes, after devastated hope, a smiling pride breaks through pain. Sometimes the pain was actual. Saito (Sessue Hayakawa) struck Alec so hard his nose bled. 'I'm bleeding for my art' said Alec as Hayakawa apologized. The story tension was reflected in bad feeling between the English and Japanese casts.

Alec has told how after his humiliating punishment in the suffocating tin kennel, he based the half-blind, staggering glide of victory with which Nicholson crosses the parade ground on the way Matthew, attacked by polio, used to walk. He conceded that at this moment it was Lean's 'strength of imagination' which lifted him up to the necessary exaggeration. 'It's in rather a different scale,' he said, 'a larger scale than mine ... I thought I'd gone over the top.' Lean took him behind the camera. 'What sweep it had: I could see how extravagant I could be.'

Elsewhere expression of masterly hidden feeling irradiates the flat, officer-code dialogue: to lines such as, 'You're a fine doctor, Clipton, but you've a lot to learn about the army,' Alec brought the dimension of Nicholson's whole existence. The colonel grows from being an inflexible British officer intent on saving face into the representative of order versus chaos, civilization versus barbarism. He echoes Ulysses: 'Take but degree away, untune that string, / And hark what discord follows.' Yet Alec's performance, remaining within the limits of Nicholson's mind and physique, remains the opposite of showy or theatrical.

It seemed Alec may well have deliberately kept or needed the temperature kept high by others during the filming of *Kwai* to draw on this extraordinary, unearthly power. He attended Catholic Masses, for sure, during the filming. On Christmas Eve, in a rare admission, he had been to midnight Mass in Colombo, greeted at the convent chapel by a young nun who resembled Audrey Hepburn and was 'even more beautiful'.

By the end of the filming period he and Lean were both upset and parted without saying goodbye to each other. He had never been happy and after the making of the film said he was exhausted for several months, which may well be believed. But with *Kwai* Alec achieved the status of international film star. His performance won him an Oscar as the best film actor of 1957. Charles Laughton commented that he never understood Nicholson when he read the script, but did when he saw Alec play him. Olivier would not have captured nearly as well as Alec that sense of loyalty arrived at through suffering with his men. On Sunday 22 December 1958 Noël Coward noted in his diary that he was now fifty-eight and that in the previous week Sam Spiegel gave him and the theatrical company he was touring with a private showing of *The Bridge on the River Kwai*: 'Really satisfying. I rather wish now that I had done it.'

The film won seven Oscars. Fifty million Americans saw it and it grossed $20 million. Later it was reckoned that it had been seen by more people throughout the world on television than any other film made. *Time* magazine devoted its cover and six pages of text to singing Alec's praises. 'One of the most expert living masters of his craft,' ran the article, 'he ranks with Olivier, Gielgud and Richardson as the big four of English acting, and he is recognised as the most gifted character actor of the English-speaking theatre.' This echoed Ivor Brown, the theatre critic who, in 1954, in *The Way of the World*, wrote, 'All that can be said of the most eminent is that they have their particular excellence, Sir Laurence Olivier his persuasion of voice and rich poetic quality, and Sir Ralph Richardson his truth of common humanity in its humours and bewilderments, while Alec Guinness ranges over the multifarious oddity of mankind and drily etches the ludicrous and drives into the heart of the pathetic.'

Time also compared Alec to Chaplin – the actor whom Alec did not like. Alec had made seventeen films, some of them, according to him, 'pretty lousy' partly due to having 'contracts to fulfil'. He regretted not being his own master: 'It's a great mistake, the frightened thing of seeking security.' He disliked having no final control over his own performance – and often seeing something that he had been relying on disappear, so that he would have conceived the whole thing differently had he known. Yet he took film making very seriously.

Achieving such fame and status as Alec now had did not make him unduly exult or feel triumphant. But it did allow him for the first time to reveal in public what he had carefully guarded as a personal secret. He could, he felt, let at least one cat out of the bag. But was this to solve or further to increase the mystery? As a guarded secret it no longer had potency. Besides, there was another to take its place. Here was the beginning of the meticulously controlled striptease of self Alec was set to perform for the rest of his life.

> His absence of identity is an official fact; no record of his birth exists. Last week Alec cautiously made a statement on the subject to a *Time* correspondent: 'My father generated me in his 64th year. He was a bank director. Quite wealthy. His name was Andrew. My mother's name was Agnes. He was a handsome old man, white-haired. A Scotsman. I saw him only four or five times. I was taught to call him uncle, but I suppose I always knew he was my father. **Time magazine**

It was a factual error on the part of *Time* to say 'no record of his birth exists'.

Was this revelation of Alec's illegitimate birth the solution to what *Time* quoted an actor saying about Alec, namely 'the best-kept secret of modern times, a sort of one-man Tibet'? The article was undoubtedly true in its assertion that Alec's 'essential gift is not for creating characters, but existences'. But what were the other secrets which lay ahead and still had to be revealed? One secret at least which had come out was that Alec had entered the Roman Church. Had the master of the blank canvas really given way to acknowledge the greater master of the blank canvas? Of all the actors she had known, said Angela Fox – and she had known many and the greatest – Alec came the closest to being God.

Since just before his conversion Alec's acting had been growing in the direction of a fuller inner life, moving beyond the creation of character to that creation of existences. But, as if harking back to the golden age, the state of man before the Fall, he still had a nostalgic desire to return to playing Abel Drugger in *The Alchemist*, at one time entertaining the dream of making a film of it. He was inclined to be dogmatic about acting, he told Peter Copley in a seven-page letter written in 1961, while he could never quite sort out what he felt about it. His dogma changed with lightning rapidity and now and then he comforted himself by thinking perhaps he could remain fluid, and that in middle age his experience of life had crystallized and given him definition.

Actors *had* to grow up as people. He was still remarkably faithful – and so would remain – to Hamlet's philosophy that the readiness was all, but to that readiness or desire for balance had now been added, perhaps as the effect of his conversion, a sense of sin, a sense that most people had what he called a 'list'.

This was why he was not at heart a method actor, because deep down he felt he could not put himself at the centre of his acting; reduce, that is, everything to himself. He had to go out to other people. Above all, he had to show imaginative sympathy with the character he was playing. He envied young actors their relaxation and assurance, and he wished he had had this quality twenty years before instead of his shy, inhibited, and above all frightened and over-careful 'niggly' self.

These thoughts were formulated to Copley after he won the Oscar for Colonel Nicholson. The inner man was different from what the world now celebrated as a success. He had become fond of quoting G. K. Chesterton; never more did he need, in the flowering of what others would call worldly success, to hold onto Chesterton's famous dictum that 'the Church is the one thing that saves a man from the degrading servitude of being a child of his own time.' Yet what had Hamlet called the actors to Polonius, but 'the abstract and brief chronicles of the time'? Here was the dilemma that the life he led constantly presented to Alec. 'After your death you were better have a bad epitaph than their ill report while you live,' Hamlet went on. How could you avoid 'degrading servitude' if you chose to be an 'abstract and brief chronicle of the time'? It was Shakespeare's problem, as well as Alec's and, like the actor, Shakespeare had continually to play Russian roulette with his soul.

There was now another element introduced into his acting. He disparaged it, but it was inevitably there. His Catholicism. Just as Graham Greene had said of himself as a writer, Alec was not a Catholic actor, but an actor who happened to be a Catholic. Catholic writers and actors were not in the English tradition (as they were in the French, as with Paul Claudel and Jacques Copeau). Cyril Cusack, much admired by Alec and himself an Irish Catholic, if a rather alcoholic one, explained how Catholicism came to function in Alec's acting: 'Somewhere amid the elaborate Guinness scenery lurks a spiritual watchman, somewhere a brand of Catholicism that was to flare through the portals of the Farm Street church.' It had been there in his Hamlet, noted by Tynan as 'a touch of the headsman, judicious and inexorable'. The powerful presence, to be switched on and off at will. The ability, as well, to keep separate life from art.

*

From November 1954 to the spring of 1960 Alec worked only in films, returning first to his old friends T. E. B. Clarke and Charles Frend in the twilight days of Ealing. In *Barnacle Bill* Alec acted as he had in *Kind Hearts and Coronets*, six different roles, all of them seafarers, including an Elizabethan explorer and an ancient Briton, as well as the nautical down-and-out of the title becalmed by seasickness to the end of a pier. This was a lacklustre extravaganza.

Next he played Gulley Jimson in Joyce Cary's *The Horse's Mouth*. On Merula's suggestion Alec wrote and organized this in 1958. He overcame an earlier dislike of the book. The artist hero Jimson – in Joyce Cary's mannered prose – looked back to the heroes of the Ealing films. But it was not the nondescript clerk or salesman, or even the modest inventor who was the creator of subversive anarchy, but the egomaniac painter himself. The film wears a somewhat monotonous air today; authority is weak, while the 'creative spirit' has moved depressingly downmarket (as Alec might have said). Ealing presupposed a world where the boss, however much he might be sent up, had real authority. Yet the film, by virtue of Alec's commitment, was a work of integrity: close to the novel, its strengths and faults emerged as being almost the same, and much dialogue remained unchanged.

Unfortunately, for everyone the comic obstreperousness of the part failed to ignite, for the anarchy of Gulley's mind was more appealing on the page than was the physical expression of his ego in the film. Seeing his artist's models made flesh does not work. They were as lifeless as the society caricatures in Harold Pinter's recent adaptation of Proust. Alec as Jimson was not entirely convincing: as character impersonation, with white hair, unshaven stubble, gravelly voice, Jimson only sometimes caught the imagination and lifted off into the realms of delight; but, 'Merry, rowdy, droll in one of the most exciting and searching character portraits to be found on the contemporary screen,' said the *New York Herald Tribune.* The New York reception was fantastic.

In the New Year honours list of 1959 Alec, now in his forty-fifth year, and only a few months short of completing twenty-five years as an actor, had received that knighthood from nowhere. Almost immediately the pressed dubbed him 'The Knight from Nowhere'. Even about the timing of this recognition there could be noted a meticulousness, a precision which Alec could not shrug off modestly with his long account of how he quelled an anti-British riot in Mexico City when sent there by the Foreign Office to restore British prestige at an international festival.

Anti-British feeling was running high and the embassy expected to be stoned, because British arms were being supplied to the reactionary Batista government in Cuba. As the sole British representative, Guinness laboriously learned a speech in Spanish which he delivered in a packed auditorium to 7,000 hostile people, and was subsequently applauded and mobbed. They screened the unsuitable *The Horse's Mouth* and with the crowds yelling 'Alecco Guins' the Brits became popular, relieving the embassy siege. Alec believed the knighthood was his reward for this, but it was, although meant sincerely, one of his poorer efforts at modesty. At this festival he had received a script of Evelyn Waugh's *The Loved One*, in which the great Spanish film director Luis Buñuel had a hand.

Shortly after his arrival in Mexico Buñuel sent him a note inviting himself to coffee at Alec's hotel the following morning. Buñuel arrived at noon, 'full of amiability and chuckles. He kept removing his glacé-mint-type spectacles to wipe tears of laughter from his eyes.'

'I am a very happy man today,' Buñuel told Alec. 'I have just been to the screening of my last movie, for the critics. It is good I think. They all congratulated me. How did you like the music, I asked. Mm – mm – wonderful, they said. The music was truly *wonderful,* they said.' At this point Buñuel took off his glasses again and mopped his eyes. 'I promise you there is not one note of music in the movie.'

Alec took his new position as a knight of the theatre very seriously; he was now a senior officer, as he had been in the navy, and while he might send up himself, he didn't like others to joke about it. Some years later John Bird, standing in a queue with him for sandwiches at the counter at Fortnum and Mason, noticed they were served first and good-humouredly teased, '"You got served first because you're a knight." He went absolutely puce.'

Daphne du Maurier had seen Alec as the Cardinal in *The Prisoner* and sent him the manuscript of *The Scapegoat*. He liked it. It offered double identity in the same story, a lookalike shy Englishman and French immoral aristocrat, the latter tricking the former into taking over his wife and possessions and then running off in his skin. When they met, the authoress found Alec very compatible with her. He resembled her father, Gerald du Maurier, the debonair leading man. Alec commented that she seemed to suffer from the same shyness as he himself did.

But not according to Gore Vidal, who with director Robert Hamer wrote the script.

> Daphne was unconsciously condescending to me, and so I came to know what an experienced butler must feel in a stately home. I was, she would say to others, 'the hack from Hollywood', which was not too far off the mark, and she was *la belle maîtresse sans merci*. With Alec, she was adoring, even, horribly, kittenish. Alec was her father yet again, but also . . . also . . . *incest*, anyone? Alec treated her with ineffable charm during their interviews. He also managed to keep at least one large piece of furniture between them. If he could, I think he would have brought Merula, his wife, to our meetings and let her play the sofa to the romantic lady from Cornwall.
>
> *Palimpsest*

Du Maurier became the film's co-producer with Alec and with the control she had over the film had already overturned the wish of MGM to have Cary Grant in the main double role. Alec chose Bette Davis to play de Gue's mother, but they did not seem to click. She was his opposite. 'My price for putting my name on that marquee is £200,000, and ten per cent of the gross. They're seeing thirty-seven years of sweat.'

The film was shot at the château of Semur-en-Vallon, but Robert Hamer was continually drunk. Alec had chosen Hamer, who had directed *Kind Hearts and Coronets*. Vidal writes:

Robert and I got on beautifully. He was droll and cynical and hopelessly in love with the actress Joan Greenwood, easily the best comedienne of the time but not, she had told him solemnly, made for love. 'I am too small ever to be entered.' Robert actually believed her. But then he was on something like methadone, which he would absently spray down his throat from time to time. Daphne's ears must have heated up whenever Robert and I got on the subject of her novel. We invented scenes of such obscenity that not even the theatre at Charenton would have put them on. We also spent a lot of time reading her prose aloud, savoring the rich tautologies, the gleaming oxymorons, the surreal syntax.

Vidal also told me, 'I think Alec was flattered until [Daphne] began her monologues to all of us on Alec as the reincarnation of Gerald du Maurier' (her father). Because of Hamer's problem – ('gone back on the booze which I, out of loyalty to him, told no one'), Alec had been handling most of the direction. Now he listened to her carefully. Vidal tells me (he mentions my request in *Palimpsest*, his memoir), 'Poor Alec, in her presence, became very still and soothing, like an analyst with a potentially dangerous patient.' His later version runs:

> Alec, a very literary man, was not only patiently tactful but treated her with all the skill of a slightly edgy psychiatrist soothing a potential werewolf at dusk. Certainly she was in absolute heaven with Alec, and he reported to me that she had told him, several times, the entire story of her life and how she felt guilty that she had so let down her military hero-husband, 'Boy' Browning, some sort of royal courtier, recently dead. 'He would do everything for me, I nothing for him in his palace life.' She lived for her art.

On du Maurier, Alec later commented, 'I was fond of her and after the film we used to meet from time to time for a meal. But I don't think I ever felt I knew her well.'

But even with Vidal and Hamer's script, the story remained cumbersome and complicated. In her memoirs Bette Davis blamed the failure on Alec's influence: 'He cut my part into shreds so that my appearance in the final product made no sense at all. This is an actor who plays by himself, and in this particular picture he plays a dual role, so at least he was able to play with himself.'

Alec's behaviour off the set, Vidal commented to me made him 'always a joy, the intelligence acute, malice serene, sense of absurdity alert when game's about.' What would the aristocrat *wear*, Alec had asked Vidal. Tweed, had suggested Vidal, he was an anglophile. 'Tweed? Mmm. Yes. But boiled first. Yes. Yes. *Boiled* tweed.'

The Scapegoat fared no better with the critics than Graham Greene's *Our Man in Havana*, which Noël Coward, who starred in the film with Alec, said was a good script, directed by Carol Reed. Alec and Merula, who was otherwise absent from these long filming engagements, visited Firefly in Jamaica to stay with Coward before filming began. In Havana Coward stayed with the Guinnesses in the Miami-American. It was just a few weeks after Castro had wrested the city from the control of the corrupt Batista. People were being rounded up and interrogated. On his way to the gents' lavatory in the Miami-American Alec jolted a fat man who was loading his revolver, whose bullets spilled on the floor and rolled off towards the *pissoir*.

English supporters of Castro were also in Havana. Kenneth Tynan, whom Alec met in his hotel bar, suggested to Guinness he might like to join him at the Fort that night at one a.m. when a Castro firing squad was due to execute a pair of sixteen year olds. Alec's most recent contact with Tynan had been his participation in the *Observer* playwriting competition which the critic had organized for his paper in 1957 and 1958. Guinness and his fellow judges had awarded the prize to Errol John's *Moon on a Rainbow Shawl*, which had then, in a production by Frith Banbury, failed to attract critical favour.

'A boy and a girl,' Tynan gleefully told him. 'I thought you might like to see it. One should see everything if one's an actor.' Had Alec gone along to the execution, perhaps his participation would have ended up being recorded in a piece that Tynan was writing. Alec refused however. Tynan's widow Kathleen later said that Alec misrepresented Tynan when implying, in *Blessings in Disguise*, an unhealthy voyeurism in Tynan's attendance at the execution.

Alec and Merula walked the streets, among thousands of 'bewildered Cubans and surrounded, for protection only, by hirsute armed policemen'. Merula went to have her hair done: 'I was the only woman client,' she told a reporter. 'All the other chairs were occupied by Castro's boys, with their guns slung over their shoulders. They all had their beards in curlers. The girls serving these heroes were in ecstasies. But Alec and I could not fail to see the tumbrils going by.'

One day they were hustled, together with Graham Greene, into a car and driven off to meet Castro in a remote hideaway. But, after ninety minutes of waiting for him, he had still not turned up. On another occasion Alec did meet the dictator: he was sitting in a small cafe in Havana drinking black coffee when Castro unexpectedly passed through this old *quartier*. Alec was taken outside into the square to meet him. He found Castro surrounded by small boys who brandished daggers at him – bodyguards unobservable from a distance. They held a brief unremarkable conversation in English.

Alec spent time in Havana with Ernest Hemingway, who had a house in Cuba, and who found Coward's chatter at dinner inane, and expressed an urge to hit him 'if he wags that silly finger once more'. Not a comfortable man to be with, Alec thought, commenting later that his self-inflicted death did not take him entirely by surprise.

Alec also encountered Ernie Kovacs, who struck him, in a Goonish way, as 'just about the funniest man I have ever met'. He dreaded working – playing the part of the chief of police – with the 'toffee-nosed Brits: Sir Carol Reed, *the* Noël Coward, Sir Guinness . . . but you're the one who laughs with me, not all those American broads and clapped-out bores.'

Although Coward left the filming in Havana with a glow of happiness and had loved working with Alec and with Ralph Richardson who 'although slightly boring, is a dear', when he saw a private showing of the film he felt that Alec played the whole thing in too minor a key. '. . . A faultless performance,' Coward wrote, 'but actually, I'm afraid, a little dull.' The reviews agreed. Much later Alec laid the blame for his performance on Carol Reed, who wanted him, he said, to play Wormold straight, and not as Alec had envisaged him, as a shambling Ealing comedy middle-aged man with worn shoes who had bits of string in his pocket. What he meant, but expressed tactfully, was that Reed had inhibited him, and should have left him to play the part as he saw fit.

Alec's world of conversion, his visits to Rome, his withdrawal to a Trappist monastery, his quiet, persuasive love of Latin litany, seem at this point in his life rather remote. On 15 January 1960 he told the *Evening Standard* he had just turned down half a million dollars to play Christ in a film, saying he would not do it for a million. He said that his bank balance was 900 pounds (although he had just paid 25,000 pounds' income tax). He had already turned down the opportunity to play Gandhi, telling director Gabriel Pascal, 'I think it should be played by an Indian.'

He may not have had much in the bank, but any disguise he chose now to put on was eminently bankable.

*

In 1960 Alec returned to the theatre with a vengeance, hungry to tread the boards again, something he tended always to do gently and softly. This time a lifelong obsession, which had several times in the past briefly opened then closed again, could now fully flower. Here was a part he could, in Bette Davis's words, play 'by himself, unto himself'.

At first *Ross*, Terence Rattigan's biographical play about Lawrence of Arabia, did not seem a promising venture. Rattigan's love story *Variation on a Theme* had just been ill-received by the critics, although it had, like the fringe satirists, the intention of 'blowing up' the establishment. The reason for this play's failure, said B. A. Young, Rattigan's biographer, was that 'Terry had written with his heart rather than his head ... He could not write convincingly about love between a man and a woman, because this was something he had never known at first hand.' As a teenager, Shelagh Delaney had seen *Variation* on tour and wrote *A Taste of Honey* in a few days because she reckoned she could do better.

'A human personality is many-sided,' Alec once declared, indulging his later-life penchant for slightly pontifical pronouncements (which could still be true), so that one has to be 'sufficiently balanced to know which side to bring out in a given situation – when to be reckless, and when to be cautious, when to be critical and when to be understanding, when to stand firm for one's rights and when to give way a little'. (undated letter to Peter Copley)

Such truisms delivered with his utter conviction and quasi-religious authority overawed those who were beginning to sense this new Magus aura he carried. Like Alec, Rattigan's Lawrence was a very complicated, many-sided character. He had begun life in a film script, which, when the money was withdrawn from the film (in which Dirk Bogarde was to play Lawrence), Rattigan promptly salvaged and simplified.

In the play Rattigan concentrated on a 'dramatic portrait' rather than on the events of Lawrence's life: as he had worked immensely hard on the film narrative, perhaps the figure of Lawrence that emerged was not entirely clear and determinate. The dramatic centre of the play is Lawrence's torture when captured by the Turks; although understated in Rattigan's treatment, offstage Lawrence is subjected to homosexual rape. Rattigan's implication is that Lawrence found in this a secret pleasure.

There was no factual evidence for the rape, and definitely none for Lawrence's enjoyment of it. Herbert Wilcox, the film producer, recounts in his memoir *Twenty-Five Thousand Sunsets* that when the five-foot-three-inch Lawrence himself brought to him his book *The Seven Pillars of Wisdom*, wanting to make a silent film of it, he described the homosexual advances of a Turkish chief, and 'how in desperation once he fought him off with what he called a "knee-kick", which resulted in the chief being uninterested in homo- or any other form of sexual activity for a week or so, and the author being scourged and tortured for his attack.' But there was a good reason why Rattigan should want to create his own version of what happened to Lawrence, and of what Lawrence felt, especially in the new pre-dawn of sexually ambiguous characters and the relaxing of stage censorship over references to homosexuality. The Wolfenden Report had been published in 1957 although the government had not yet acted on its recommendations. Questioned by a much later interpreter of Lawrence and after showing a reluctance to talk ('he wouldn't give an inch'), Alec told Simon Ward, that 'Der'aa [the location of the rape scene] didn't happen.' This being so, one might place a question mark over Alec's involvement with this particular piece of make-believe. It comes back, I believe, to Alec's desire to avoid truth: it would be unlikely that Alec would have participated in any play about Lawrence which set out to find the truth about the rape. That kind of investigative animus never turned him on.

Alec studied the role with immense care. The script was, as one commentator said, 'tight and fast as a fibre-glass racing car'. Twenty-one years before, Auden and Isherwood had based Michael Ransom, their hero in *The Ascent of F6*, on Lawrence of Arabia whom Alec at that time was able to impersonate easily, 'by chucking a towel over my head and twisting a tie into a sort of burnous'. He still felt Lawrence was a fascinating enigma. Avoiding the central truth, he pursued the details of his subject like a biographer. He had by now letters by Lawrence on the walls at Kettlebrook. He went to see Sydney Cockerell in Kew, who was now bedridden in his ninety-third year. Cockerell told him that Lawrence was a 'terrible fibber' who when asked why he bothered to lie replied 'because my lies are more interesting than the truth'.

Other friends of Lawrence to whom Alec talked, such as Siegfried Sassoon, Robert Graves and David Garnett, gave Alec highly coloured views, tainted, he thought, by their jealousy over his friendship: 'like schoolboys who had a slight crush on the captain of the cricket team'. He walked like a duck, someone else told Alec, toes turned out, arms stiff at his side, straight down the middle of the road in the dusk. Alec found this useful. But later, when taxed with sharing an intense privacy with Lawrence, he camouflaged himself by saying he did not feel a great affinity with him: 'I don't think I had a great deal of personal sympathy.' He quoted Cockerell about him being a 'terrible fibber'. Back to the hiding game.

When it opened on 12 May 1960 the exact power of Alec's impersonation amazed critics and public alike. Herbert Wilcox, who had bought the film rights of *Ross*, boasted that he saw it eighteen times and 'never once lost the illusion that I was seeing and hearing Lawrence himself'. Franco Zeffirelli was 'overwhelmed'. It was, he said, 'wonderful, fantastic, one of the greatest emotional experiences I have ever had in the theatre. I went three times.' Donald Wolfit, the great romantic actor-manager, declared a more circumspect view. He wrote to Ronald Harwood, his dresser and later biographer:

I set myself to do a theatre round. 2.30 'Ross' at the Haymarket where I saw some of the worst settings (by Motley) and some of the worst acting I have ever seen at the Haymarket. Dear oh dear – but Guinness redeemed all as I told him afterwards – it's a film scenario of a play, four good scenes. But the climax was buggery, you know.

Maybe Wolfit saw a poor matinee. An occasional night Alec liked to 'break out' – to redress the balance. He straddle-walked across the stage after the famous understated scene in the blackout, giving an extreme impersonation of someone who had been violated. One can well believe that, if not actually on his face, then somewhere inside him was a grin.

Noël Coward responded to this masterpiece in a sour manner. Alec looked very like Lawrence, he wrote in his diary, and played it well enough, but there was something lacking: 'He has a certain dullness about him and his big moment seemed contrived. He also wore a blond "piece" which was too bright and remained blandly intact after he had been beaten up and buggered by twelve Turks.'

Caryl Brahms, linking the mysterious alter ego of Alec with the Lawrence he played on stage, recalled she had met the latter in the reading room of the British Museum in the 1930s. 'He did not look unlike Sir Alec Guinness: more often and longer in the open air, maybe, and even more detached; more sturdy than was Sir Alec in those days and more compact than he is now. Not perhaps a man of fun, but evidently a man of impulse.'

She bungled the chance of having tea with him. That was, she wrote, 'Lawrence of Arabia, who had no time for journalists; and no time for women; and as for women journalists . . .'

About Alec's performance in *Ross* she wrote in her memoir *Too Dirty for the Windmill* that he seemed to be most things that we believe the legend to have been, in a performance in 'which his extraordinary technique was informed and governed always by his heart'. Still in search of T. E. Lawrence or Alec Guinness (they had by then so coalesced that Brahms could not have said which) she went backstage 'to see him – or, of course, him. Or was it them? "Will the real Mr Lawrence please stand up?"'

There were two Americans and Ned Sherrin already in Alec's dressing room. 'Forgive me, but do I know you?' Alec asked them.

'No, sir.'

'Then how on earth did you get in?'

'Easy! We gave the stage-door keeper ten shillings each.'

'Only ten – I'd have thought I rated higher than that,' said Alec, a saddened man.

'Each,' they reminded him. And left.

Ned Sherrin told them an anecdote about Lawrence, D. H. and Lawrence, T. E.. Edward Marsh had lent T. E. the unexpurgated copy of *Lady Chatterley's Lover*, which T. E. returned, saying he had felt privileged to read it, with the comment that he could not understand 'all that fuss about the sex business', as 'he'd never met more than half a dozen people who cared a biscuit for it'.

Alec, keen as ever – the master capper of other's anecdotes – told of an encounter between Marsh and Lytton Strachey. Marsh had received and read Rupert Brooke's early poems and, charged with excitement, rushed from his flat to a neighbouring Bloomsbury bookshop where he met Strachey, the 'one man in London whose voice might in moments of stress hit a falsetto an octave above his own'.

'A new poet,' Marsh panted. 'His work is *steeped* in beauty!'

Only a superb technical comedian, commented Brahms, could have pitched Marsh's 'steeped' so high that it sounded unbeatable – and then judged Strachey's pierced answering shriek so that it topped it:

'STEEPED!'

Brahms's verdict on the play was 'an unwriteable play well written, an unactable play well acted, an undirectable play well directed'. Later Victor Spinetti, Sherrin tells me, used to do an unforgivably funny and grotesque imitation of 'Sir Alec Guinness after being fucked by the Turks'.

Ross ran for 762 performances, although Michael Bryant took over after the six months that Alec would only ever commit himself to. During the run Alec again visited the bedridden Cockerell in Kew. On 2 June Cockerell wrote in his diary that Alec came that day at noon and stayed an hour. 'He was absolutely charming, as he always is. He brought a mass of beautiful roses and kissed the top of my head when he said goodbye.' Cockerell presented Alec with his old Arab cloak in which he was shipwrecked in the Gulf of Suez in 1900 and which he had once lent to Lawrence. Later Wilfrid Blunt, Cockerell's biographer, seeing the huge bunch of pink roses, asked jokingly if they had come from the Pope. Cockerell gave him a second guess, but Blunt could not find the right answer, so Cockerell told him.

The period from six to ten weeks was the period Alec felt most happy during any play's run, 'when I am at my least awful'. Alec did not play Lawrence in New York eighteen months later, when it opened at the Eugene O'Neill Theater, but John Mills did. In June 1960 the normally reticent Alec revealed to the English press that two years earlier he had turned down an offer of £500,000 from a brewery company in America to introduce thirty-nine of their half-hour shows. Alec told the *Daily Telegraph*, which described him as 'the one star of the British screen who can be guaranteed to bring in the audiences in any part of the world', that he would have despised himself for accepting, and referred to his working in his youth, and against his will, as a copywriter in an advertising agency. He said he would 'rather die in the gutter than go back to advertising'.

He had appeared in the five-hundredth edition of the BBC radio feature *Desert Island Discs*, during which he recalled he had played Macbeth at Sheffield when he was twenty-five, and would like to play it a second time. He pulled a cheque from his pocket and said, 'Thirty guineas, not bad.'

20. Lesser Expectations

Alec's acting now and increasingly in the future seemed to move in the direction of, in Michael Caine's words, 'doing nothing with tremendous skill'. It was this ability to take people in, through the force of his personality, as well as the acting skills he had acquired, which grew with age. As with his parts, you feel, so with his life, he still had the ability to 'break out' into rebellious behaviour, the rebel, the misfit, the outsider were able to trigger his imagination as much as the dames and knights, albeit eccentric ones, of the Establishment. In personal terms he was arrested by human foibles and weaknesses as much as grandiose gesture and ceremony. The detached and humble attitude he personally assumes – this is what he conveys in the theologically entitled *Blessings in Disguise* – is that of the parish priest.

He describes the actor at various times as a kind of unfrocked priest who celebrates mysteries, concocts rituals and convinces audiences they can see things that aren't there. It is a muddled metaphor, but it sounds good and carries weight and self-importance. You cannot analyse it however – 'Unfrocked?' For what, for some misdemeanour? The actor does not concoct rituals, does he, he performs in plays written by someone, not himself, which he interprets. 'Celebrates mysteries.' That much is true, although this hardly applies much to actors playing in Ibsen or Shakespeare. Convinces audiences they can see things which aren't there? Well, again, props, disguises in make-up, all these have a tangible reality, and one of Alec's greatest skills was the concrete accuracy of his impersonations. It was no accident that he was married to an artist and had joined a family whose talents lay in the representational field.

The word music of 'celebrates', 'concocts' and 'convinces' is what creates the power of this particular utterance. However calm and docile he might seem on the outside you sense – even in this sentence of his – some impatience and strong contradiction lurking beneath. 'Unfrocked', for instance, suggests dismissal and rejection, 'concocts' suggests falsity, 'convinces' itself has a spurious possibility. In fact, this is a dangerous, not to say immoral, attitude to the actor, the kind of attitude that caused the Church to condemn plays, by making audiences believe that they were true. It explains why Alec became a film actor more than a stage actor, because in the theatre you cannot take people in, and the pleasure of going to the theatre is that your emotions and feelings are raised in the consciousness that what is happening is art, is the imitation of action, not the real thing. This explains why Alec never excelled in conventional dramatic parts. He had to take in himself entirely, become the role he was playing, invest it with his personal life. He had this uncanny ability to *become* rather than to create: he took on strange shapes and forms and lived inside them. These were the gargoyles he was, increasingly, to take on in the future: Berenger in Ionesco's *Exit the King*, for example, Mrs Artminster in *Wise Child*; or their opposite, the eminently cool reasonable voices of authority, the gurus.

While most people were transfixed by Alec's performance as Lawrence, some were scathing. The insanely jealous Peter Sellers, hopeful his great idol would fall, had gone to see it with Wolf Mankowitz: 'Probably the worst performance ever given by Alec Guinness', reported Mankowitz. 'After being buggered by the Turks, he walked across the stage with a waddle that came straight out of the world of the Goons. Sellers and I both thought this was an absurd play and an absurd performance – and Sellers was happier than I'd seen him for a long time. This capacity for doing a *Kind Hearts and Coronets* – he was always coming back to that, always jealous of that film.'

During the run of *Ross* Alec, who collected the Evening Standard Award for Best Actor in 1960 for a performance that impressed most people, was on call to Ronald Neame for further scenes to finish what many consider one of Alec's very best films. *Tunes of Glory*, adapted by James Kennaway from his own novel, was directed by Neame. The Acting Commanding Officer 'Jock' Sinclair, claimed Alec on at least one occasion, became his favourite film role, and 'perhaps the best thing I've done'. Cast against type – Alec had first been approached to play Sinclair's disciplinarian replacement (John Mills did this in the end) – Alec rose magnificently to the task of crushing this stickler for form in a conflict which was, as in *The Bridge on the River Kwai*, a conflict between two sets of military virtue.

The duel is to the death. Sinclair wins. 'Whisky for the gentlemen who like it – and for those that don't, whisky' sums up his easy-going, paternalistic attitude to the battalion. It became, Alec said, madness to cast him as a drunken, heavy, boorish Glaswegian up from the ranks; but, 'for all my reticence, now and then I like to take a big breath, and semi-explode'. Note the 'semi-'. There were no fireworks in the passion scenes with Kay Walsh as the Colonel's pet; these were not very sexy.

Alec's profane, rabble-rousing appeal shows in the delight with which he got his teeth round phrases such as 'a piece of cherry cake'. He fired scorn at his Eton- and Oxford-educated butt, making, by comparison, the film of *Look Back in Anger* seem arch and dated. Alec captures the nature of an unreflective egotist with superb self-assurance. My favourite moment is when Sinclair notices in the mess how one of his junior officers is inept at smoking: 'Go on, laddie, smoke it, smoke it!' exhorts Sinclair. 'Draw it in like a man!'

During the shooting, with the need to restore balance in his mind so that Jock Sinclair did not tip him over too far into coarseness and self-gratification, Alec would, after filming, talk far into the night about Catholic faith to John and Mary Mills. This became so affecting to the married pair that, according to John, 'Mary and I were within an inch of becoming Roman Catholics.' If a young Jesuit priest who had spent ten years in the Gobi desert had not many years before 'flung himself at Mary (she was seventeen at the time) and bitten her lip, we would, with Alec's enthusiasm, have embraced the faith'.

Tunes of Glory is a superbly watchable film, but it was made in the age of the Cuban missile confrontation, pacifism, and the anti-Vietnam war movement. It was almost not made. The script began by being turned down by every major company. The heroes of the hour were Castro and Che Guevara. Another cultural star was Chairman Mao with his 'Thoughts'. Old-fashioned British military

'He was a great leader of men; he was able to reject intimacy without impairing affection.' – *E.M. Forster on T.E. Lawrence.*

Above. Garcin in *Vicious Circle* with Betty Ann Davies and Beatrix Lehman.

Right. Ross.

'Every story's the story of one man's war – the setting, the battlefield is only incidental.' – *The Prisoner.*

Left.
The Prisoner.

Below. Alec with Pope Pius XII, Merula in the background.

'When people cease to believe in God,' said Father Brown, 'it's not as if they believe in nothing, but rather the case that they will believe in anything.' – *Father Brown.*

Father Brown.

With the Abbot of Subaco.

'I'll show you what a man should be . . . strong, tender, and terrible in his passion.' – *Hotel Paradiso.*

Above, left. Boniface in *Hotel Paradiso*, with Martita Hunt.

Above, right. With Grace Kelly in *The Swan.*

Left. With Daphne du Maurier attending to a wound during the filming of *The Scapegoat.*

'Colonel Nicholson's a model of dignified behaviour. A born leader, that's how he struck me, sir.' – *Bridge on the River Kwai.*

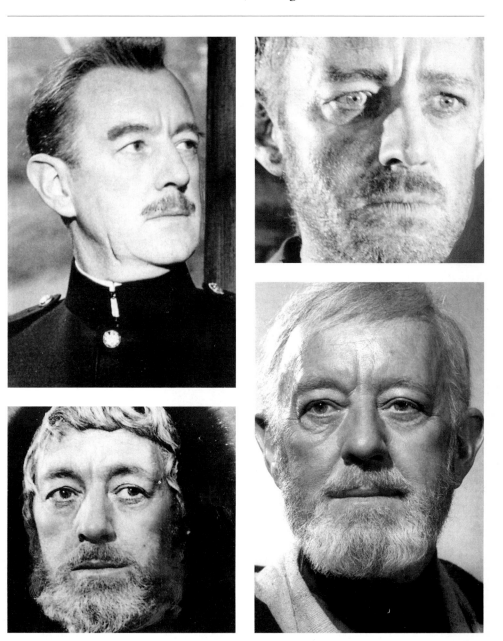

Clockwise, from top left: Jock Sinclair, Nicholson, Obi-Wan Kenobi, Marcus Aurelius.

'Can't you see I've had enough of it, locked away like one of your harlots in chains, my needs suppressed.' – *Wise Child*.

Left. Dr Wickstead in *Habeas Corpus* with Joan Sanderson.

Right. Mrs Artminster.

'I invested my life in institutions – he thought without rancour – and all I am left with is myself.' *Smiley's People*.

'I'm accustomed to be complimented as the – ha – Father of the Marshalsea.'
– *Little Dorrit*.

Left. Old Dorrit.
Below, left. Charles I.
Below, right. Hitler.

virtues were swept away in what Macmillan called 'the wind of change'. Such a wind was not yet affecting Alec.

On 12 January 1960 Alec, who rarely showed any political passion, saw the front page of the *Guardian* filled with a cartoon by Low. This depicted a spectral figure by a blackboard, against a cemetery of endless crosses, instructing a crowd of youngsters. 'Alas! a New Generation,' ran the caption. There had been an outbreak of anti-Semitism and Nazi-like slogans which the government had done little to counter. Alec felt that Low's cartoon should be made into a large poster and placed on hoardings throughout the country, 'which has always boasted of racial evil, "it couldn't happen here".' He wrote to the editor that Low's cartoon should be seen daily by a larger public than the *Guardian* normally reached.

This apart – and recovering from a ten-day sojourn in a private London nursing home for the removal of varicose veins – Alec's career was pointing him in an international direction. On the eve of the worst confrontation between East and West since the war, Grigori Kozintsev, the Russian film director who some five or so years later became known through his four-part *War and Peace*, mentioned him in the context of making a joint Soviet–British film, 'providing a common subject of interest for the Russian and British public could be found'. Could such a subject be found?

Not very much later Henri-Georges Clouzot, the French film director, announced that he had agreed to make his first English-language film. Clouzot had made *Le Salaire de la peur* (*The Wages of Fear*), his harrowing study of fear, and, more recently, the macabre *Les Diaboliques* in which Simone Signoret had acted. The principal player had been named Alec, his part that of a painter living in Paris after the Second World War. *The Horse's Mouth* had impressed the French, and they were arranging settings of a Modigliani studio, a Parisian police station, an art gallery, and a cheap Montmartre nightclub. Who would he be now? It sounded most unlikely. Shooting was scheduled for the spring of 1962, 'after Sir Alec had completed two other films'.

These two other films were *HMS Defiant*, in which he played another naval captain, and *A Majority of One*, a frivolous Broadway success by Leonard Spigelgass which was transferred to the screen with Alec as Koichi Asano, a Japanese diplomat who has a holiday affair with a Brooklyn Jewish widow. Alec was no more convincing in the role than Cedric Hardwicke, who had played it on stage. Rosalind Russell played the widow, while it was her husband who produced the film and she who had persuaded Alec to do it. With a running time of over two and a half hours it received dire notices. Alec and Merula did not much mind. With a fee of £70,000 they rented a bungalow in a rough, fir-lined cul-de-sac which was sex-idol Laurence Harvey's love nest. The decor was white everywhere, which blinded them, but they enjoyed the turquoise kidney-shaped swimming pool with under-water lighting. Alec claimed he only ever saw ten minutes of the film, but loved the critic who had described his Japanese business gent as 'me with ravioli stuck on my eyelids'. *A Majority of One* did not stem the offers of more of 'the Great Inscrutables', which now became something of a flood. Gandhi headed this list, for David Lean was hard at work setting up this project as a suitable follow-on to *The Bridge on the River Kwai* and, as with *Oliver Twist*, he undertook the most exhaustive work to make sure his casting was exact.

I have described how David Lean and Alec fell out so heavily over *The Bridge on the River Kwai* that Lean did not want to work with him again. However, Lean wanted him for Gandhi, a project he had to abandon. Legend, if so it be, has advanced the colourful notion that Lean had already started shoot-ing Robert Bolt's version of the Lawrence of Arabia story with the tall, gangling romantic Peter O'Toole playing Lawrence as a self-deceived mystic, when Sam Spiegel, the film's producer, announced to Lean that he had cast Alec as Prince Feisal. Alec, seven years earlier, had already considered himself too old to play Lawrence on screen when approached by another Hollywood producer. According to Andrew Sinclair, one biographer of Spiegel, Lean stopped work and said he was leaving the picture:

Spiegel fell to the ground, the apparent victim of a heart attack. Rushed away to the hospital he was put in an oxygen tent. The stricken Lean visited him, offering to give Spiegel anything he wanted, anything, if it would help him to recover. Spiegel immediately revived and smiled and said, 'You're so nice. So we cast Alec Guinness.'

True or not as this anecdote may be, Alec as Feisal was a near-perfect piece of casting. It became one of Alec's most impressive film roles. In it he displays his wholehearted and unreserved admiration for a gentleman, and his disdain for the self-centred virtues of Lawrence, who had once been an idol of his. He shows again his uncanny genius for penetrating the mind of a foreigner, this time a wily Arab who has a code of honour in many ways superior to that of Lawrence.

Although the slant on Lawrence is historically unsupportable, *Lawrence of Arabia* captures the romantic image of the man with a breadth of vision and a sense of style which make the picture remarkable. Lean creates a nuttiness to match his own obsession with such figures, and it took him three years to achieve it; but in an oddly contradictory way Alec's performance emerges as the touchstone of sanity, gentleness and balance. Maybe this is the boring quality of maturity, yet it is one which Alec could make significant and above all gripping. Feisal is intricate and complex and different – apart. A portrait of someone whom the ordinary Englishman, who identifies with Alec, would distrust, yet Alec also brings to him an ordinariness, an innocence, which makes him wide in his appeal. For a similar intelligent portrayal of an Arab leader, and his relationship with an Englishman, one has to look to Saladin in *The Talisman* by Walter Scott. Scott had a similar gift with words for character impersonation.

During the filming Alec was, according to Sian Phillips, enjoying a hilarious time staying at the hotel Alfonso Treci in Seville with his co-stars. At one point O'Toole writes to his wife that he encountered Alec wandering in a Seville street suspiciously early one Sunday morning. 'Confethione,' Alec said to him and passed on. Do the Spanish go to confession before Mass on Sunday? I wonder.

In late 1961 Alec was telling a friend that in December he would be taking a two-week holiday, then he would be off to Spain in January, and that this would be followed by a year's exile in Hollywood and Spain for a Fred Zinnemann picture. This last film never materialized. He then turned down the role of an ageing homosexual kidnapper in Bryan Forbes's *Seance on a Wet Afternoon*.

In August 1962 MGM took over an eighteen-room miniature

castle outside Madrid for Alec and his family, completely staffed from chauffeur to scullery maid, while he played, in *The Fall of the Roman Empire*, the part of Marcus Aurelius, a performance the *Telegraph* described later as 'warm and foxy'. 'Perfect junk,' Gore Vidal called the film, but the only Roman film he had seen that was accurate in appearance, designed by someone 'who knew what the city looked like at the time of Marcus Aurelius, played by Alec Guinness, "in all those flowing robes" as he put it, "and swirling clichés".' That same year also saw Alec in retreat for a fortnight in the Benedictine Santa Scholastica in Rome, sleeping in a monk's cell in a wooden cot and eating simple food.

A few years on, in 1965, he was to be defended by Roy Jenkins, then home secretary, who remarked during a speech that Alec Guinness was not responsible for Britain's formidable crime wave, and that Guinness's Ealing films such as *The Lavender Hill Mob*, *Kind Hearts and Coronets* and *The Ladykillers*, which had been named as glamorizing crime, contained 'such an element of fantasy it was difficult to think they could be constructive to criminals'.

In the summer of 1966, as Alec himself reports in the *Spectator* in 1987, he was in Paris filming *Hotel Paradiso* with the old-timer Douglas Byng in the cast. Walking in Saint-Germain-des-Prés one day he spotted this figure, straight out of his early love for the outrageous bygone age of the music-hall stage, sitting at a little table outside Les Deux Magots. Byng, a familiar dapper figure in a grey homburg hat, had once been Boadicea, Queen of the Keni, Flora McDonald ('bending the bracken with young Charlie Stu'), and another dozen dames. 'Gay Paree,' the old queen who had also run a homosexual nightclub in London, told him hopefully. 'This is the spot to watch the cruisers.' Alec would seem not to have been tempted.

For the next thirteen years Alec gravitated back to and remained mainly on the stage, playing ten leading roles, while his dozen or so film parts, with the notable exception of Hitler in *Hitler: the Last Ten Days*, were minor or leading supporting roles. On the eve of his fiftieth birthday his power and influence (if largely concealed and refused acknowledgement by himself) had grown immense. Peter Sellers had once called him a demure one-man rep company, i.e. playing all the parts. Now he had become, in a sense, a one-man National Theatre company, because the weight of his opinions and the fact that he could virtually play any role he wanted had brought him limitless authority. But he was, in quite a strange way, to opt for commanding absences more than commanding presences.

*

In the ten years Laurence Olivier ran the National Theatre, from 1963 to 1973, Alec was approached several times to play important roles. He was offered Danton in Büchner's *Danton's Death*. He was invited to play Shylock in *The Merchant of Venice* (*before* Olivier himself played the role in Jonathan Miller's memorable production). After 1973, when Peter Hall took over direction of the National, Hall was extremely keen to have him play Prospero. But Alec still did not want to become involved. He had parted company with the institutions of his country's theatre when he left the Old Vic in 1948 and he never returned. He was the outsider who looked sometimes as if he was at the very core of power. Again it would seem that he knew himself, for he was the outsider with a pervasive power and influence, even when he was not there.

Alec was apolitical in a somewhat studied way. In the early 1950s he had sat twice on the Equity Council and, each time, said he had felt useless and tongue-tied. He described himself in a letter to Peter Copley as 'having no political convictions other than an old-fashioned brand of liberalism – I do not enjoy the situation of fence-sitting, which it seems to me I am so often involved in'. He wrote an anti-nuclear sketch for Tynan who was organizing a Sunday night political review at the Royal Court. This was, as Alec told him, a 'clownish mime thing', while Tynan responded with a sweet and flattering reply telling Alec how well he wrote, but that the piece as such did not work.

'In Eternity,' wrote Sir Thomas Browne, another of Alec's most admired writers, 'there is no distinction of tenses.' *Exit the King*, the absurdist play by Eugene Ionesco – the Romanian exile who wrote in French and who locked antlers with Kenneth Tynan in a ferocious but gentlemanly dispute over whether the theatre should be political or not – was an attempt on Alec's part to do something very different. It was the nearest he came to performing in an avant-garde play.

Alec declared: 'When you look at the performers I most admire

– Eileen Atkins, for instance – you see it's all done from the inside. You have to change yourself, alter your personality, to be the part. Of course that's far more difficult and it can be dangerous. You're playing about with your individual soul.'

What did he mean, in this context, by 'individual soul'? Did he mean that which might for ever be damned, or saved for eternity? Did he mean that unique sense of oneself? Or did he simply mean the rational self and the ability to hold on to oneself? Backing as he did continually into the limelight these anxieties possessed him constantly, although he played games with them. They gave the sense that at every minute of his life man was dicing with death. At the time of *Exit the King* (and having missed out on Godot) Alec thought he was showing his sympathies were 'entirely with new methods of putting over stories and characters'. It gave him the opportunity to work again with George Devine, to whom he had not entrusted any direction of himself since the days of *Great Expectations* at the Rudolf Steiner Hall. Devine, a touchy figure, was at the very height of his influence, for the Royal Court Theatre had, with the advent of Osborne, Pinter, N. F. Simpson and Wesker (playwrights in whose stage plays Alec never once appeared), become the new powerhouse of the English stage.

Devine and Alec had met professionally when both had been filming in Arnold Bennett's *The Card*, directed by Roland Neame. Devine had ruined a scene ten or a dozen times by drying. Alec had taken Neame aside and asked him to pretend to shoot another take without running any film and for this take he (Alec) would dry to restore Devine's confidence. They did this: Devine's reaction, according to Alec (who told this to Irving Wardle), had been instant derision: 'Ah,' he said, 'it even happens to your great film star!'

Devine chose Eileen Atkins to play the part of Juliette opposite Alec: she did not expect to find him in 'an avant-garde theatre like the Court . . . it didn't have film stars, it was for dedicated grubby actors who didn't care about money or fame'. There was at once an argument between director and actress over the age Devine wanted Eileen to play Juliette: she wanted to play it her own age, which was about thirty, while Devine, on the principle that Brecht often expressed, namely that young actors play older characters better than older ones, wanted her to act about sixty, with a funny walk and a grey wig. Alec – who had endeared himself to Eileen by asking her to drop the 'Sir' – further won her gratitude by supporting her against Devine when the latter wanted her to leave the cast:

> George has told me what he said to you this morning and took me to one side. I think he's wrong and I've told him so. I think you're going to be very good indeed – and you're quite right, she should be young. So it's agreed you're not leaving. All right? *Dear Alec*

She stayed in the role and learnt a great deal about stagecraft from Alec, which she felt was ironic when she had thought of him as a film star, although he said he saw little difference between acting on stage and on film:

> In *Exit the King* I was required to wheel him in a wheelchair for half the evening. It was the first time I was aware of finding the lights on stage because it was my responsibility to get the chair with him in it into the correct position each time. There were also tricky technical things when he had to start to fall and I had to push the chair under him at just the right moment without giving the back of his legs a whack. Alec would rehearse this business meticulously and I found I enjoyed the discipline of getting that chair in exactly the right spot all the time. George rather left me alone and Alec would occasionally, very tentatively, give me a note which I always found to the point and very helpful.

Alec confirmed what Eileen said. Devine did not give him a word of encouragement throughout the production. This annoyed him. Devine was sensible, a bit schoolmasterly and dispiriting, clapping his hands to get people back to work. Alec believed that having directed Rex Harrison at the Court the previous month Devine harboured suspicion of star visitors. When Alec wanted, as he sometimes did, to send up the whole play during rehearsals, Devine was intolerant. Compared to Guthrie, Alec told Wardle, Devine was both lumbering and too meticulous.

Exit the King opened at the Edinburgh Festival in the summer of 1963 and ran for a short while at the Court. Peter Brook came to see it and conveyed in no uncertain terms his feeling that the whole production sagged and could have done with a lift. But Alec's performance was much applauded.

After the rarity of the absurd, a descent into documentary coarseness. Alec's uninhibited impersonation of Dylan Thomas, which opened in Toronto in January 1964 and played on Broadway at the Plymouth Theater, enthralled packed houses for six months. *Dylan*, by Sidney Michaels, was a subject of dramatic possibility, but it was treated as little more than a series of flippant jokes interspersed with pathos. With Peter Glenville once again directing, Alec's performance won him the 1964 Tony Award for best actor, but he spoke the naked truth when he said it came easy to him. 'Of course, it's not really Dylan Thomas at all that I am playing: just an exaggerated Welsh version of myself if I had tow-coloured hair and drank a lot. I have no reverence for Dylan, or anything like that. He wasn't my kind of person at all. People go on about his voice, but to me it was the voice of a bombastic curate. I really have no interest in the man.'

Too true; and perhaps for Alec it was too easy to let himself go, but far more subtle and demanding for him to reach out to what he would like to be: to attempt to embrace the true quality he felt to exist inside him. As *The Times* critic wrote, he was 'not only giving us Dylan Thomas, but is able to stand aside and watch himself, adjusting his performance as if in a mirror. Every movement, every gesture is so real that competent portrayals by his fellow actors sometimes seem stilted beside him.' One might add, in the wry tone Alec himself made his speciality, 'I'm amused by people who stand apart and look at life; maybe I do that a little myself.'

Alec had found over and over again that as an actor it was not good to indulge himself, let the performance 'truth' hang out. Just think of the numerous, self-indulgent characters he could have played, but with his unerring instinct and the unintended enhancement of his own reputation, did not.

Two films followed *Dylan* in quick succession, neither of them especially distinguished by Alec's performance. In *Situation Hopeless but Not Serious* Alec played Herr Frick, a mild-mannered but crazy German who keeps two captive allied soldiers as pets after the end of the Second World War, 'playing on their belief that the war is on and they are surviving only by the virtue of his protection', according to John Russell Taylor, who judged that 'The subject was promising, and Guinness's support from Robert Redford and Michael Connors was solid. But Gottfried Reinhardt, who produced and directed, appeared to be undecided about whether he was dealing with an Ealing-type comedy or a kinky psychological drama.' Need more be said?

For *Doctor Zhivago*, which followed on rather too quickly from Lean's point of view from his masterly *Lawrence of Arabia*, Alec was attracted, this time with Lean's reconciled and happy enthusiasm, into a major minor role – a narrative device – that of General Yevgraf Zhivago. Alec did not at first respond to the script, but Lean persuaded him that the role was both subtle and warm: 'Don't let's argue about you being a bore. I seem to remember we've had that one before.' Lean later told Alec he was too old for the part and looked terrible. He got his revenge. The result was grey and colourless, and Lean and Alec reverted to their former mutual, although polite, antipathy.

The years 1966 and 1967 were by no means Alec's best. One might say, rather, that they were his worst when he gave mediocre, forgettable-to-disastrous stage performances, a film version of a successful Feydeau play which was quickly shelved, and a couple of mediocre film roles, one of which, that of Major Jones in *The Comedians*, had some redeeming features. These years and those that followed did give the lie to Alec's frequent assertion that he lacked courage in his choice of roles. Some could be described as risky, others, to say the least, foolhardy.

I always feel audiences never much mattered to Alec, there was no great sense of rapport, but rather he inspired rapt attention and expressed irritation – sometimes extreme – at bad or unruly behaviour. He provoked admiration, applause, laughter, yes, but not that spontaneous warmth and love that other actors might command. Mystery, a reserve of power, a withdrawn energy, could always command attention and there was the sudden relaxation of this, the rich warm baritone guffaw that Alec could produce, the fruity look or sly sidelong aside. But never equality, always a lofty, patrician attitude.

The satirist John Bird who in 1973 acted with Alec in *Habeas Corpus* noticed he would walk to the wings at the front of the stage before a performance and peep through a hole where you could see the audience. Here, quite arbitrarily, he would make up his mind as to what kind of audience was in. 'Oh,' he would say, 'there's a ghastly-looking woman in the fifth row!' Or, 'They're all Finns tonight!' He would then play to what he believed the audience to be: if weak, for example, he would underperform and not try very hard. He kept his distance, and reciprocation was not part of the game.

The great comic actor, such as Alec was and forever remained, has insecurity as the element in which he lives, for the laughs are generally on him, which make the comparison of Alec with Sellers, or the assimilation of Kenneth Williams's brilliantly expressed sense of inferiority in his diaries and letters, so germane and relevant.

Alec's next stage appearance was as Von Berg in Arthur Miller's new play, *Incident at Vichy*. Miller's reputation was at a low ebb and, according to Peter Wood the director, the play was based on a false premise, that of arresting the fake Jew (the non-Jewish character, played by Alec in an ash-blond wig, a courteous, civilized Austrian prince who heroically sacrifices himself). To make the whole accusation more credible, so that the audience would swallow the notion that a blond non-Jew could be rounded up, Wood placed another blond Jew (played by Dudley Sutton) among the prisoners.

It still did not work: altogether not a happy experience, says Wood, who found Anthony Quayle, who played the Interrogator, a difficult man. 'Whatever you asked him to do, he would look at you and question. Other people's moves too.' Because there was no woman in the cast the men competed with each other, macho behaviour became the order of the day. Alec was 'all too relenting . . . it could have done with unrelenting: Alec went along with it.' Finally, 'The play was a diagram; it's not good.'

Rehearsals before it opened at the Phoenix had not been uplifting. Peter Wood tried to lighten and inject spontaneity into the heavy proceedings by having the cast improvise, recalled another member of the cast. Alec would not play and said frostily at the end, 'Back to the book now' or words to that effect.

Audience contact sunk to an all-time low during the short run. Alec was accused by the critics of walking through the role of Von Berg, and showing such restraint and reticence he was dull. He didn't like this at all and angrily exclaimed at the time, 'Tackling a live audience is like fighting a wild animal.'

Ernest Milton had once, privately for Alec in his front room at St Peter's Square, performed both Lady Macbeth and Macbeth in the scenes before Duncan's murder: 'It was as if blood had dripped on the carpet.' When Alec embarked on this most guilt-ridden of all the tragic roles in October 1966 no such powerful evocation of evil happened. He was now fifty-three and he felt that opportunities to stretch himself in the future might become more and more rare.

'The utter limbo of my Sunday,' wrote Kenneth Williams in his diary on 20 November 1966. 'Even masturbation denied me today, 'cos I caught my cock in the zip fastener and it's quite painful today.' Williams's frustration was heightened as he had just been along to see Alec play his disastrous Macbeth in William Gaskill's production at the Royal Court which seemed something of an anomaly in that swinging era.

'That box set and no props (the lairds bring on their own stools for the banquet) makes nonsense of the play.' Williams attacked the production and told Simone Signoret, who acted Lady Macbeth, why he disliked Gaskill. When subsequently he saw Gaskill defend the production against the bad notices by saying that in Shakespeare's time they played in daylight, Williams grew even more heated. He rubbished Gaskill and his arguments, but went on 'he v. decently defended Signoret by saying there was no English actress who conveyed the strength and the sex. Pity she can't speak Shakespeare, I thought.'

What *had* possessed Alec to turn again to Shakespeare?

'I like a line drawing, a very simple line, it pleases me, I love simplicity in acting. Shakespeare in the end is the Bible ... In the whirlwind of your passion you must beget a gentleness,' is how Alec expressed it. But was it the right approach for one of Shakespeare's great tragic figures? Could Macbeth ever be described as a line drawing?

Gaskill's production was stark and Brechtian, perhaps also unsuited to Alec. There was virtually no set and the lights were blazing and so powerful that, as Alec observed, 'You cannot flick your finger without it seeming as significant as a pistol shot.' But his main difficulty remained that of confidence, the kind of easy confidence he had with *Dylan* eluded him with Shakespeare's tragic villain: 'I do find it hard to trust the flow of something and not be cautious. I'm far too cautious an actor very often or usually.'

He did not regret the lack of lush scenery. He felt that the work he had been doing recently had been lazy work, and that Macbeth was not lazy work: the effect on him was, as one person who talked to him noted, 'Exhaustion had drawn pink lines around those pale lizard-lidded eyes.'

In spite of Williams's sharp tongue Alec greatly enjoyed working with Simone Signoret, towards whom he expressed fondness. She was, like her husband Yves Montand, very left wing. She had a purity about her which he admired. As Corin Redgrave told me, 'He liked actors who had more to them than just acting.' Yet meeting her with his friend Gordon Jackson who played Banquo, Kenneth Williams felt 'in all her conversation she was rather worthless. Willing to talk about Alec Guinness's conversion to Rome in the nastiest way – "He has got himself the nails in the hand and in the head – he wants to be crucified" . . . etc. . . . I told him [Jackson] "I don't like her".'

Scorning the reviews, Alec's worst since *Hamlet* in 1951 – one was sneeringly headed 'Aimez-vous Glam's?'; another said his eyes were 'as blank as contact lenses' – he claimed that he did not read the critics, adding, possibly a little waspishly, 'It must be dreadfully annoying for them. But I learned that whatever they say, nice or nasty, is a distraction.' But Kenneth Williams applauded the way he showed such vulnerability as to become deeply moving, although he claimed Gordon Jackson as Banquo was 'the shiningly best thing in it'. Irene Worth noted the walk Alec assumed on his way to the murder of Duncan as 'frightful, blood-curdling'. The production was sold out before it opened: standing room only. Alec settled for saying that it bore, director Alan Strachan told me, an 'air of civilized controversy'.

Perhaps this was the point at which Alec started to enjoy acting less. He did not look forward to it quite so much. He did not embrace it as he once had, and each part became more and more of a mountain to climb. And he hardly gave the impression that he liked to save himself and store up energy. He filled his time off with pleasures and indulgences as taxing as his work.

21. A Smoothish Face Which
Had No Features

Friendships, social contacts, conviviality and letter-writing thrived in Alec's middle and later years. His extraordinary gift for friendship with women (indeed his non-sexual worship of them) was never better illustrated than by that formed with Coral Browne, who became at this time one of Alec's inner circle.

She fitted the pattern. Once, not liking a luxuriant wig for a part in *Tamburlaine*, she explained to the director, 'I feel as though my face is coming out of a yak's ass.'

A flamboyant, distinguished classical actress during the 1950s and 1960s, Browne suffered 'sort of organized heart attacks in terror' a close actress friend said, on first nights. Judi Dench thought highly of her Gertrude and Lady Macbeth, but in addition to her reputation she was a beautiful woman and an elegant clothes horse, much pursued by couturiers to model their creations. She had great wit and was much quoted. A columnist with a wooden leg whom Coral did not like once entered a restaurant where she was dining, whereupon the actress pronounced, 'Oh, look, there's Radie Harris, with all of London at her foot.' Harris sued for slander and won.

She enjoyed, with her reputation as a tempestuous and sexually rampant woman, a successful marriage to a homosexual actor-agent, Philip Pearman, before he died in 1964 of cancer. Upon his death Coral and Alec became friends; as Alec put it, 'I had always been charmed by her, and I didn't know Philip well at all, but when he died we were playing across the street from one another – I was at the Haymarket and she was at Her Majesty's . . . [Alec was inaccurate about this]. I went over because I thought she might need some human contact. Coral meant a lot in one's life.' Alec then went on patronizingly to excuse Merula for being shy and apprehensive about meeting Coral. 'But Merula said, when she had, "I think she's the most beautiful woman I have ever seen." ('One' might recoil at Alec's tone here.)

Coral next became sexually besotted with Vincent Price, the Hollywood legendary horror movie actor and according to his daughter Victoria in her biography of him 'a possibly bisexual and relentless charmer'. Both were over sixty but this, according to Diana Rigg, did not deter 'their wildly sexual relationship'.

Price divorced his wife, and Coral, by now, like Alec, a Catholic, influenced his subsequent capitulation to the faith. Coral fitted her obscenities in well with her faith. One Sunday morning she was stopped outside the Brompton Oratory by a theatrical 'queen' who regaled her with gossip. She exploded, 'I don't want to hear such *filth*, not with me standing here in a state of fucking grace.'

It seemed Alec, Vincent and Coral were fated to become friends, as each of them was reflected in so many aspects of the others. Before Price, Coral had a sexual affair with the homosexual Cecil Beaton, claiming 'Women feel very comfortable with homosexuals. There's a certain delicacy. We don't want to be pounced on every thirty seconds by some hairy ape.' Her appearance as the lesbian radio producer in the film version of Frank Marcus's *The Killing of Sister George* underlined rumours of her bisexuality. 'Miss Browne was seen grimly twiddling the naked chest of Susannah Yorke, as though trying to find Radio Three,' one commentator noted. Of her reputedly bisexual new husband, who played Oscar Wilde on stage and many a camp horror role, Alec perceived how guarded Price was about his innermost thoughts and feelings. Noting his 'beautiful charming manner', Alec told Victoria Price 'one felt one knew him better than one did'.

Coral became more and more possessive of Price as time went on. It shattered her to learn in the mid-1980s that he was having an affair with someone else. Alec, who knew all about it, did some masterly evasive footwork: 'There was an upset in later years, but I don't know what it was.' He did, of course.

The mixture of elegant hauteur and madcap insouciance endeared Browne to everyone: she was very much an Alec 'type' and when she died in 1991 he said how proud he had been of her friendship: 'one of the really rare people'. Yet one wonders, as with many of Alec's friendships, how deep it actually went and if the rules and proprieties were not carefully observed by the one on whom Alec bestowed his friendship how it might suddenly cease.

Her husband celebrated her for living in 'our hearts and in our minds for the laughter she brought to a too-often troubled world'. But she shocked and stunned everyone, for after having forever complained how poor she was and how expensive everything cost, she left over one million American dollars and three million pounds sterling. Price apparently registered trauma and felt betrayed because she had never told him how rich she was. Deceptions, double identities, and the artistry of not being who you are were part of the era.

Browne had also been one of Alan Bennett's 'dearest and most gossipy friends' according to Alexander Games, biographer of Bennett. Before she died she sent back to Alec all the letters Alec had written her. Alec quoted in a memoir from one of these letters in which he had made a teasing remark about Bennett. Browne told Alec that she was sending them back 'for you to do with them what you want. What we *don't* want is for Alan Bennett to get hold of them and knock them up in a play.' Bennett had at this time been seriously unhappy with Alec for not agreeing to act Proust in his *102 Boulevard Haussmann*. He had Alec very much in mind, but probably Alec had qualms about a role which might have encroached upon his own identity, giving him a public image a little too close to the reality for comfort.

If Coral Browne often viewed Alec as 'another woman', as pointed out by the solicitor's notes on my first typescript, what are we to make of the portrait painter Michael Noakes's perception of Alec in middle age? Alec was fifty-six when Noakes started to paint him in 1970. This was a daunting assignment because, showing what Stuart Freeborn, the make-up artist on Alec's David Lean pictures, pointed out, his face, basically, was very ordinary: a 'smoothish face which had no features in any overall development . . . not an outstanding face in any way'.

But just under the skin (and as George Lucas was to find revealed about Alec in an unusual moment during the filming of *Star Wars*) there resided this amazing musculature of imitative skill. Alec was able to get 'so well into what he was going to do', that with just a 'small amount of movement he was able to convey the greatest amount of emotional feeling'. Of all this, Freeborn thought, Alec had been extremely aware.

How does a portrait painter paint what lies just beneath the skin? How does he convey the invisible gesture and the unspoken word of which Alec was the master? And how does he paint that power which, in the actor's face, lay in the control of movement? Further, considering the sitter, who should the ontologically insecure Alec *be* for the portrait? Actors are usually painted or photographed playing somebody else. That is how people want to see them.

Both painter and subject must have exercised considerable thought on this problem. Noakes noted how Alec could merge into a background, yet, when he wanted, summon up a powerful presence. He reported later in his essay published for Alec's seventy-fifth birthday, that Alec talked to him a great deal during the sittings; the subjects he raised were his illegitimacy, which he had known about at an early age; and his decision to become a Catholic, giving the painter, who was also a Catholic, a sense of privilege (because, as Noakes said, this was before he wrote it up in *Blessings in Disguise*, so he felt complimented 'that he chose to tell me about these important factors in his life'). But by now, as we are well aware, these were well-known 'public' subjects so Alec was not really being revealing. If you have told a reporter from *Time* magazine your secret, you are not really granting all that great a privilege to your portrait painter by telling him exactly the same thing. You are merely conferring on him the flattering illusion of intimacy.

In fact, there would seem from then on to have been, between artist and his sitter, an interplay of intentions. Noakes relates that Alec (who was quite possibly trying out autobiographical material he was to use later in *Blessings in Disguise*) recounted to him some near-psychic experiences of the early 1950s ('when he was preparing his notoriously disastrous Hamlet'). In his and Merula's bedroom they had a painting by Bernard Meninsky of *Two Irish Girls*, a solid subject of two females in shawls with a background of 'bright green bushes and withered hedgerows', as described by Alec, but which had about it something enigmatic. One night he was 'seized' with a chapter and verse from Luke dinning in his head which, when he checked, he found to be, 'For if they do these things in a green tree what shall be done in a dry?' When he looked at the painting closer he saw that while the greenery of the bushes was bright, the twigs which held the leaves themselves were 'tortured figures', as Noakes put it, so presumably reflecting some extreme state of the painter's soul.

Alec, uneasy at the ghostly M. R. Jamesian effect he felt, removed the painting from the wall. He learned later that this peculiar state of mind about the painting had overcome him on the anniversary of Meninsky's suicide.

The painter's rationalization of this subjective material emerged as follows. Because of Alec's 'busy interior life' he decided to paint him surrounded 'by more space than I would normally allow'. He divided the space between a roughish terracotta floor and a pale azure wall (which had a blue-sky effect and increased the sense of space even more). He dressed him (or both decided this) formally in a dark blue suit, with a slightly short coat which was buttoned up fully and emphasized the chubbiness of his figure. His cuffs show just a little, as does his collar and an almost, but not quite, neatly tied tie in a knot that is just a little too large.

The most satisfactory part – the whimsical touch, one could say – are the shoes and feet. Clownish boots, socks which are flesh-coloured, the same tone as the flaccid fingers, and short tight drainpipe trousers, emphasize the chubby thighs, the sexually neutral crotch. The trousers have a ragged end to them as if they have been cut off at the ankle. It seems as if Noakes wanted to turn Alec into the kind of type Alec followed in the streets, although, 'I can't keep up with people's walk any more . . . I long to play not a tramp, but a down-and-out dotty character . . . My eyes go straight to them because their trousers are always four to six inches too short.'

The chair the painter chose is also peculiarly, although delib- erately, significant to the sitter's state of mind: high-backed, a white-painted Victorian kitchen chair with a very large and dominating back which curves round like a band behind the lower part of Alec's head. It makes Alec look not only clownish but passive, as if the white chair is holding him together, envel- oping him, giving him backbone, but also imprisoning him. The skeleton as well as the cage. The painting is that of a mollusc, a clown without a spine but with a shell; the face is sad, the eyes inward-looking, slightly pained, quizzical, the mouth ambiguous, sensitive, suggestive of that uncomfortable void at the centre.

If there is a secret person Noakes discerned in Alec, it is the, by now, cliché of Lawrence of Arabia. Lawrence liked space around him – that of the desert, naturally. But the space around Alec in the Noakes picture seems to emphasize not so much the busy interior life, but a loneliness, an isolation, and also, curiously enough, the strong sense of Alec as a victim.

Noakes expressed the hope that 'the lone figure would be read as shrewdly observing all that goes on around, whilst knowing that it is all – the heights and the depths – the beating of a gnat's wing'. The figure of Alec in this fascinating and tantalizing portrait conveys an awareness of life's absurdities.

A later view of Alec which Noakes expressed in words suggested a more flamboyant image. The actor was walking down St James's Street. The artist drove past in his car, stopped and offered a lift which was refused. Noakes remarked that Alec wore a large floppy hat (it was summer), and an overcoat and carried a plastic bag in each hand. Again the interplay of intentions struck Noakes as curious. Alec had chosen to be anonymous in his action – travelling on foot around a famous quarter of London carrying plastic bags – yet at the same time he deliberately wanted, with the floppy hat, to be eye-catching. The Lawrence of Arabia syndrome yet again. Noakes probably drew the right conclusion: 'He must surely have taken pleasure from the thought that everyone who glanced at him without a thought would have been tickled pink to have known who he was, had he decided to be less anonymous.' In other words, Noakes was saying, Alec enjoyed his fame, at the same time as wanting no part in it.

22. The Departing Transvestite

In *Wise Child* Alec cross-dressed for the last time. Early in 1967 he had played Major Jones in *The Comedians*, Graham Greene's attack on Papa Doc Duvalier's Haiti. The major had disguised himself for a minute or two in drag 'as a swivel-hipped cook in blackface', but that had been a conventional affair, directed naturally by Peter Glenville. The film was poor. Papa Doc sued the film in the French courts and was awarded one franc damages.

Quite unusually, given that bisexuality and transvestism were now in vogue, the *Daily Express* asked in early October 1967 if a shortage of good parts had possibly landed one of our most distinguished and dignified actors in a situation he regretted. 'I sat on the script in trepidation for a few months,' Alec said about Simon Gray's *Wise Child*. 'No, I thought, not another of those transvestite things.'

Alec was caught irritatedly wondering how to hang up his skirt in the dressing room of Wyndham's Theatre. Rather like Alec with his skirt, Simon Gray, for his first stage play – based on the news story of a murderer called Roberts who, convicted of killing three policemen, had escaped and was on the run disguised in women's clothing – had also found himself with something he did not know quite how to handle. The fashion was for baroque nastiness: Joe Orton set this fashion rolling with a certain style, others climbed on the bandwagon.

Not surprisingly, Alec felt uncomfortable. He had agreed to play Mrs Artminster. He had to appear first on the stage as a trim, grey-haired matron clad in a blue suit and a fur coat. The scene was of a seedy provincial hotel, of the sort he was familiar with from childhood. He had then to delve into a handbag, pull out a small whisky bottle and take a manly swig.

Alec tried to reassure himself: 'Do not worry. I change back into a man in the last moments on stage. That is the trickiest part – playing a man who is playing a woman who is not a woman really but a man. A complicated bit of technique.' Mrs Artminster was much more: an ageing thug in wig, blouse and high heels drunkenly uttering obscenities, trying to 'have it off' with the character Cleo Silvestre was to play and sucked into a sick attachment to a young psychopath (Simon Ward).

Some of it could be carried off in the *Kind Hearts and Coronets* manner; different voices, seraphic smiles – and he was well up to realizing every trick of stage camp. But for what? The intentions of the play eluded him: was it merely black farce, was it vaguely threatening, ambiguity for its own sake? Was it a social play?

He tried to reassure himself by checking out Simon Gray who, aged twenty-nine, had just written several successful television plays. 'We all thought at the time Alec's sexuality was a matter of immense speculation,' Gray told me in 2001. 'I had sent my play to Van Thal, Alec's agent, who turned it down with words to the effect Alec would never do such a disgusting work. I then had sent it direct to Michael Codron, who showed it to Alec.' The subject of the play, transvestism and bizarre sexual passion, was such that Alec wanted 'every possible guarantee that the author himself wasn't a freak'. So Gray, he told me, was invited to Alec's London pied-à-terre for dinner. 'It was, needless to say, an immensely civilized evening, in which we quoted to each other from the poems of T. S. Eliot, he in movingly canonical tones, I in the brisk fashion of a respectably married university lecturer.' Both of them got very drunk: it was fine 'until the moment the door closed behind me, and I tottered down the path, across the pavement, fell into the gutter, and threw up'. Gray had an impression that a curtain twitched in the pied-à-terre and a compassionate face peered at him through the darkness, but this may have been an illusion. 'And even if it wasn't, the sight of a respectably married university etcetera rolling drunkenly in the gutter was probably vastly more reassuring than that sight of a departing transvestite, however sober.'

The reassurance was only temporary. Gray found that the director John Dexter (Alec had insisted on having the very top director, Codron tells me), an astonishing combination of the pragmatist and the magician, revered 'Sir Alec' too much while behaving abrasively towards the other actors. 'Alec expected deference, wanted to be a bishop. Dexter was just brutal.' Gray found himself segregated from Alec; he discovered one thing wrong, which he tried to rectify:

> At the end of the first act my text called upon the character played by Sir Alec, togged up as Simon Ward's surrogate mother, to recoil in disgust from a particularly perverted outburst from the Simon Ward character, and then in spite of him/herself – moved by the Simon Ward character's display of pain (jealousy) – to put an arm around him and cuddle him into comfort, in which image *lights down* and *curtain*.

They were getting the disgusted recoil, Gray felt, but not the pitying cuddle, 'so that *lights, curtain* descended on an image of Sir Alec keeping a morally refined distance from the surrogate child I'd wanted him not to be able to withdraw from'. Oddly enough, Alec had sought advice and coaching before opening in *Wise Child*, he told Codron, from Geoffrey Bennison, a well-known interior designer who lived in Pimlico, renowned for dressing in matronly women's clothes. Bennison would parade on Battersea Bridge for taxi-driver trade: 'They thought they were going home to mother.' That Alec should make this admission to Codron, who was surprised by it, ensured it was seen as an effort, while perhaps Alec also wanted to show that it was foreign to him.

When Gray pointed out this lapse of the mothering gesture to the director, Dexter impassively drew him over to Alec. 'Sir Alec listened with seraphic gravity, and then the two of them retired for one of their canonically artistic conferences. After rehearsals John Dexter came over to me as I was about to head to the pub and put it to me that as we were only a few days off our first (of three, I think it was) previews, Sir Alec would prefer me not to attend any further rehearsals.' Gray ended by disliking strongly the deference shown to Alec.

When it opened *Wise Child* became something of a succès de scandale and ran for six months. Alec's notices were good, some of Gray's not so good. Gray met Alec, said, 'Yours were good, mine weren't.' 'I never see them, I never look at them,' said Alec airily although the notices were pinned up by the stage door and in the Green Room. Merula wrote consolingly to Gray, 'Thank you so much for getting him back' (on the stage).

After one performance, recorded Kenneth Williams in his diary, he went round backstage at Wyndham's Theatre to Alec's dressing room. Williams happened to be rather drunk and in a tizz. 'My hair is in a terrible mess,' he shrieked. 'Alec stroked his bald head. "Oh! I so agree – couldn't do a thing with mine either . . ."' As the run continued Alec's qualms about the modishly shocking piece deepened. 'His initial affection for the piece was,' Gray tells me, 'I suspect, gradually eroded by the reaction of his admirers, who doubtless expected from him, even in his comedies, a touch of the spiritual – failing that, certainly a dash of gentlemanliness. But there was no place for spirituality or gentlemanliness in the character I'd provided for him.'

At an early performance a gentleman of the old school rose in the middle of the first act, shouting: 'I thought you were above this sort of thing, Sir Alec!' and led his family out. ('They came to see *Kind Hearts and Coronets*,' Simon Ward told me.)

Alec insisted on a short-cropped ginger wig under the female wig, presumably for the contrast of butch manliness, and this made him seem even less like himself than when he dressed up as a middle-aged woman. The fan letters had an unsettling effect on Alec, while as Gray pointed out, 'the delight in cross-dressing was an aspect of his confused sexuality'. Fetishists and weirdos wrote all kinds of strange propositional letters to the playwright, so one could hardly imagine what they must have been like to Alec. Ward said he left his own mail unopened – 'I used to open his letters'. Ward believed Alec had misjudged the play in terms of its danger. One close colleague believed of Alec in *Wise Child*, that he 'was totally hooked on Simon Ward', and he couldn't allow or didn't in any way want Ward to be off so that the understudy, Robert Farrant, would have had to play it. Ward, reluctant to admit the pursuit to which anyway he was unresponsive, told me that one night he had tonsillitis and a temperature of 104°. Alec pleaded with him, 'I wouldn't ask anyone but you – but Ralph [Richardson] is in tonight.' Ward performed – with an ambulance standing by.

Sex was no longer camp fun, as it was in the old-fashioned

days of the pantomime dame: it had assumed a murky, disturbing mantle brought on by permissiveness (to become encrusted with new, baroque layers). The innocent vaudeville tradition of cross-dressing had come to reveal itself as an evil monster: 'Sir Alec seems uncertain exactly what proportion of masculinity should show through his Widow Twankey outfit,' wrote Alan Brien in the *Sunday Telegraph*. By his own miniaturist standards this was 'a coarse, slapdash performance'.

Gray told me Alec had loved the rehearsals, and once went off to Harrods dressed in female costume to see what it felt like. 'It was trying for him, a murdering working class bloke putting on the disguise of a middle-class lady.' Gray found Alec had to wrestle with his distaste. Alec was in the last stages of preparation when on one occasion Gray visited him in his dressing room: 'Sitting in front of the mirror, in his wig, skirt, blouse and high heels, dabbing on rouge or stroking on lipstick, his eyes briefly meeting mine in what I came more and more to feel was a kind of reproach.' Gray could see that four months in the run of his play had been quite enough and that this was why he was never mentioned in Alec's volume of memories, 'even though,' Gray joked, 'it's called *Blessings in Disguise*'.

A very different impression emerged for Gordon Jackson, who played Mr Booker. Once Alec was checking all the props in the handbag and he told Jackson, 'You know, Gordon, I may seem rather silly and sentimental to you, but I'm going to miss this old bag – ' and walked on stage. Another time he remarked, ribaldly, before going on, 'Oh! I can't play it tonight, my dear, I've got the curse!' Jackson visited Alec at Kettlebrook where he was taken out to the meadow to see the new pony, called Gordon. 'Call his name,' Alec told Jackson. He did so and the animal dutifully trotted up. Jackson told Simone Signoret this story, who exclaimed, 'That's nonsense! When I visited, the animal answered to Simone.' The trick was in the carrots Alec held.

Angela Fox recalled going backstage with her husband Robin after one performance of *Wise Child*. In the dressing room they found him just emerged stark naked from the shower, and Angela described with glee this strange, pale, forked creature joking and clowning without inhibition.

The stage-door keeper knocked on his door and announced

the name of a theatrical agent who insisted on calling: 'Vere Barker' – 'Oh no, I've seen enough of agents; on no account let him come round,' commanded Alec. 'But, but we're too late,' expostulated the stage-doorman. Alec seized a towel with which to cover himself and in walked an extremely 'gorgeous' black gentleman, the Kabaka of Buganda.

Alec wrote playful letters to Angela claiming he never read the reviews and signing himself off as the *Observer* theatre critic, Penelope Gilliatt – spelt with several extra *t*s. He wrote thanking the Foxes for their delicious suppers, but apologizing for carrying on about Graham Greene's *The Living Room*, and 'delivering ghoulish tales of my dear Martita Hunt'. He didn't sleep a wink as he spent the night thinking up witty and stinging replies to a letter written by the film director Michael Powell to the press.

When, a few years later, Robin Fox was dying from cancer, Alec made to Angela an unusual declaration of his belief in the efficacy of prayer. He believed in prayer totally, yet it remained a very odd mystery. He was at that time, he disclosed, discontented with the Church and what it stood for, and would happily have broken away, and yet the Church had an umbilical cord of great strength and love, while he felt at his least mad and wayward when he submitted to its tug.

This letter prompted Angela Fox to ring Alec and voice her fears about William (i.e. James), and his conversion to Christianity which had really shocked the terminally ill Robin and her. James, now twenty-nine, had after a highly publicized spell as a heroin addict (during which time he starred with Mick Jagger in *Performance*) become, to the shock and horror of Angela and Robin, a born-again Christian. Alec invited the three of them to dinner and subsequently, on a Friday morning, they had a long telephone conversation. Alec advised Robin that he and Angela should on no account mock James in his state of religious fervour and that he should, at this critical moment, be treated with a very special delicacy, which is what they had done at the dinner. He admonished them, hoping that he was not being rude or censorious, not to lose their patience if they received some arbitrary New Testament text flung at them.

For, having been through it himself, Alec knew about the extreme moods that conversion could bring about in one's psyche.

He wrote to Angela of the famous 'enthusiastic' group in the early seventeenth century who ran naked through the streets of Amsterdam shouting 'We are the naked truth' – commenting that in 1970 they had come nearly full circle. He warned Robin and Angela against the dangers of a reaction in James, and how he might become bitter and dismissive of the earlier extreme commitment he had felt. He spoke only from partial experience, he said, for he himself felt he had never gone 'a hundred per cent full hog at anything', although he regretted the extent to which he felt he must have bored the agnostic pants off friends when he had a 'wild Roman mood' on him. Like many present-day English Catholics he expressed an aversion to proselytizing.

Again it was perhaps indicative of how the Church, in Catholic theology the Bride of Christ, had taken the place of the mother Alec could never respect. He wrote that he longed to suggest to James books he should read, as he felt that a sane attitude to Christianity must be grounded in history.

James had been offered two good parts, a tempter and a knight in Eliot's *Murder in the Cathedral,* which was to be performed in Canterbury Cathedral in October 1970 for the eight-hundredth anniversary of Becket's death. Alec hoped that the director E. Martin Browne and the cathedral itself, might prove to be hard-headed, steadying influences.

It turned out Alec was wrong, because, as James wrote later in his book about his conversion, in trying to combine Christianity with acting, 'I only succeeded in becoming more and more frustrated. I wasn't exercising my talents in what I could do best, and I found that Christian drama isn't necessarily an aid to Christian development or even communication.'

The main cause of confusion in the Fox family was the illness of Robin. Their last hope was to take him to a famous cancer clinic in Germany, run by Dr Issel. Alec heard of this one dry and damp Saturday afternoon in November, sitting at his desk with the trees facing him nearly bare and the ground looking as if it was rotting. He swam 'somewhat' in fumes of sloe gin of the 'Messrs Berry Bros' variety, having taken a glass or two at lunch.

He and Merula had spent a disappointing five days in Paris where, on Marie Bell's invitation, they had gone to see her act in Michel Simon's *Le Contrat.* On his return he received the postcard

Angela had sent from Bavaria; he had been impressed by a programme on television about Dr Issel and he looked them up on the map. All he knew of Germany and Austria was a depressing three months spent filming in Munich and a few enjoyable days spent at Salzburg. Once he had got 'fairly suicidal' in Berlin (his sanity saved by the zoo).

He replied, remarking there was nothing sensible he could say about Angela's distress at seeing Robin's deterioration. The Benedictine nuns at Stanbrook Abbey – which he himself visited on retreat, and where the abbess, his friend Dame Laurentia McLachlan, had been the correspondent of Sydney Cockerell – had written asking about Robin, for he had requested them to pray for him. He reassured them that all appeared to be going fairly well. He told Angela that he had written a second time. He vigorously believed something could be done through prayer. No cures, of course. He might have echoed Gandhi on prayer, Gandhi whom he so nearly played on film. 'Without it I would have lost any reason long ago ... It delivers us from the clutches of the prince of darkness.'

Alec also wrote to Father Caraman, who said Mass for both the Foxes. He questioned whether it might be an irritation or a pleasure to Angela to hear of such things, but of course it was the latter. He told anecdotes to cheer them up, regaling them with tales of Waugh, Sitwell and Greene's confessor, and his own recent trip to Paris, describing Marie Bell, the French actress, who met them after her performance dressed as a 'rather stout Vietnamese peasant in mink, with a vast curved hat to match, from which dangled leather thongs'. A leather miniskirt, a rope of pearls descending so low they clicked audibly on the heels of her lace-up boots – in Alec's absurd depictions – completed this apparition of the great tragedienne. It almost made the evening worthwhile. But he got stuck inside her hat while having a friendly embrace. As Angela Fox told me, 'Even in the worst possible circumstances Alec could always make you laugh!'

The Dr Issel treatment turned out to be useless and, as Angela recorded in her books *Slightly Foxed* and *Completely Foxed*, cruel and senseless. Robin, defeated and more ill, and she returned to their home near Alec at Cuckfield where Robin died early in 1971. Angela told me that when Robin's agent partner moved Robin's personal effects out from his office and took his place almost straightaway, Alec, who had left him and M.C.A. ten years before to join Dennis Van Thal, organized with some of Robin's clients a demonstration in protest. Over twenty years later, in April 1994, on the death of Frances Donaldson, Angela Fox's half-sister, Alec wrote again to Angela hoping that she rejoiced, as he did, that James had made such wonderful strides towards life. He had remembered.

*

In 1968 Sir Donald Wolfit, the last out-and-out heroic actor-manager of the English stage died. His younger rival colleagues were uncharitable. Ned Sherrin was producing a television obituary for Wolfit. He approached the knights to contribute. Michael Redgrave was 'ill'; Olivier wouldn't, 'because he was already reading at the memorial service', Sir Ralph was known to hate the man, so wasn't asked; as for Sir John Gielgud, he replied, 'No, I couldn't be so hypocritical, we all thought he was a joke.' Alec's answer was typically Jesuitical: 'I admired him as a film actor, but I have never seen his work in the theatre.'

It was with relief, undisguised, early in the same year that Alec returned to the touchstone, T. S. Eliot. In the meantime he deepened his friendship with Eileen Atkins, who recounted the dream she had:

> An odd thing happened before Alec asked me to play Celia Coplestone ... I'd been in New York for eight months in Frank Marcus's *The Killing of Sister George* and I dreamed one night that I was doing a play with Alec on a platform surrounded by green fields and we were both dressed in evening dress and speaking verse, but I knew it wasn't Shakespeare, and out of the back of my evening dress I had a huge cock's tail and I said under my breath to Alec while we were performing 'Have you noticed what's sticking out of the back of my dress?' and he said, 'Yes, that's perfectly correct.'

To interpret this dream in terms of the confused sexuality of the late 1960s might seem opportune, but there was little doubt of Alec's archetypal force in the dreams of his admirers. Alec asked Eileen to play Celia at Chichester and later they transferred to

London. She found the experience happy. Alec's direction she found firm and tactful: he told her, when she thought she had parts of this very difficult and complex play well worked out, 'Yes, now you know exactly what you're saying but you're spelling it out to us – because *you* know exactly what you're saying you can now gather it up – the audience will understand.' Atkins adds, 'Oh how often have I sat in audiences since saying to myself "Yes, yes, don't spell it out to me – GATHER IT UP!"'

Alec had created the part of Harcourt-Reilly nineteen years before. This time, directing as well as playing, he thought to make the play 'Bloomsbury, literary, tatty'. Harcourt-Reilly would be a 'mentally Herculean figure'. He carried a heavy walking stick and there was a lion-skin on the floor.

There was a reaction against the 'parental' attitude of Eliot, as Irving Wardle, critic of *The Times*, called it. Wardle admitted the true basis of Eliot's stripping away of illusions: ('in this respect at least the play has not dated: Eliot's "hell is oneself" is a truer line than Sartre's "hell is other people"'). As for the performance, Alec played Harcourt-Reilly as a 'white-bearded replica of Freud, and cultivates a manner of grave whimsicality (lying flat out on a tiger-skin in his consulting-room), which seems the most satisfactory approach to a profoundly unsympathetic role'. Wardle praised Guinness's direction which conveyed the spirit of intimate dualogues across the huge open stage of Chichester, and lifted the atmosphere to somewhere near farce. He liked very much the smooth transitions between party chatter and ritual exchanges, 'when the guests whip out their dark glasses as spiritual guardians'.

While playing the profane Gray, Alec had refreshed his contaminated soul with talk of T. S. Eliot; but now he was playing the po-faced Eliot he needed naughtiness if not obscenity. Before one show Eileen had been saying how she liked sexy mouths with the lip rolled back (Steve McQueen, Jeanne Moreau, Mick Jagger). He secretly taped back his upper lip, and then appeared facing upstage at the beginning of the play – they were all facing him – rapidly whipping the tape off before he had to face the audience. Eileen had great difficulty in not corpsing.

Another time she was losing her voice: Alec became irritated by this, being of the traditionalist (correct) view that if you use your voice properly you need never lose it. Eileen consulted a voice specialist called Mr Punt who, to mollify Alec, left him a note saying, 'You must not be cross with Miss Atkins, she has difficulty because all her passages are narrow.'

During the performance that same night Harcourt-Reilly handed Celia Coplestone a piece of paper on which he was supposed to have written the name of the convent she was to leave for. Alec had written, '*All* your passages are narrow?'

When Harcourt-Reilly speaks of the affair Celia had, and the man she had it with, he asks, 'And what does he seem like to you now?' On another night a member of the audience shouted back, 'A cunt'. Alec and Eileen could not believe it. They speculated that the man must have been some poor fellow dragged along to the theatre by his wife, who had then had too much to drink, hadn't understood a word of the damn play, but suddenly – during a moment of illumination after more drink in the interval – it had all clicked.

It was a measure of Alec's dedication to Eliot that *The Cocktail Party* kept running and running: first at Wyndham's, to which it transferred in November 1968, then at the Haymarket (February 1969).

And now Alec signed up to play in a better film role than he had for years: another profoundly spiritual being, but also a victim. The only sadness was that, overall – his performance apart – the film was poor. This was *Cromwell*, directed by Ken Hughes, in which the eponymous role was played by Richard Harris. Alec's film roles, as his stage roles, had in the 1960s been for the most part lacking in substance. He now wanted to attempt 'something impossible', or 'something that would pull the best out of me'.

The role of Charles I, the martyred king, unfurled in an interpretation of history quite unfairly loaded on Cromwell's side. When they filmed in early 1970, and with little help from his script, Alec did manage, with stutter and prancing walk and the variable shading of a Scots accent, to create a memorable existence of the doomed Stuart who, like Colonel Nicholson, thought it his duty to uphold the law. He showed Charles as having a keen sense of humour – more than could be said for Harris's hoarse-voiced Cromwell – and a touching sense of family feeling.

6 January 1970. 'My next stint is to play a chemist – rather a special kind of chemist – the more I visualize the part, the more I

see him with a moustache like this,' he told Godfrey Winn, the journalist. In Steep Marsh at the end of a very warm January under a cool green vine, they lunched out of doors. 'Oh, it never produces any grapes,' said Alec. They ate a quiche Lorraine cooked by Merula.

The chemist came from Bridget Boland's *Time out of Mind*, a project which, although destined for the West End, never left the Yvonne Arnaud Theatre in Guildford where it ran for several weeks. Alec played this rather special kind of chemist, named John, who, beginning life as a medieval alchemist, has lived for six hundred years. Having discovered the elixir of life John finds that death eludes him. Perhaps for Alec it was the ultimate in elusiveness. Matthew also had a part in *Time out of Mind*, as Paracelsus, the scientist of history who figures in John's imagination. Matthew was now thirty and had been acting for four years, mostly in northern repertory companies. He had played a sizeable role in Solzhenitsyn's *One Day in the Life of Ivan Denisovich*, which was filmed in Norway with Tom Courtenay in the title role.

Irving Wardle in *The Times* extremely disliked *Time out of Mind*, calling chemist John a 'crass reptile' and Alec's performance 'seraphic'. 1970 had been a lean and slack year, appropriately marking the end of a decade which for him ended with not so much a bang as, in Wardle's description of John's death, an 'ecstasy of giggles'.

23. New Outlines in the Mirror

Although not yet in his mid-fifties, Alec had slowed down considerably. He had done nothing more in 1968 than *The Cocktail Party*, and virtually nothing at all in 1969 except for the Executioner in a television adaptation of Dürrenmatt's *Conversation at Night*. Flying about as Marley's ghost in the television film of *Scrooge*, directed by Ronald Neame in 1970 he suffered a double hernia which had laid him up for several months.

At the end of the year Laurence Olivier and Joan Plowright approached him to play Shylock at the National Theatre, a suggestion which after meetings and discussions he took very seriously. Plowright was to play Portia and Jonathan Miller to direct. Alec suffered a bad attack of cold feet (was it the emotional weight of Plowright that made him fearful?; or Miller as director?) and withdrew, writing to Plowright a letter she published in her autobiography and enclosing a copy of Samuel Butler's annotated edition of Shakespeare's *Sonnets* to which he would refer when he met me twenty years later. 'I shall not be your Shylock – I have just re-read the play and hate it ... it doesn't interest me as a performer.' Tynan wrote later in his diary (6 April 1975), 'Alec has never worked at the RSC or the National, but at least he has been asked.'

Alec was next offered an extreme test for his objectivity: to give a rounded portrait of Hitler in a film by the Italian director Ennio De Concini. 'Is the disguise right for *him*?' wrote John le Carré on Alec. '(*Him* being himself in his new persona.)' Hitler's moment had arrived.

While he studied Hitler Alec played John Mortimer's QC father in *A Voyage round my Father*. Before its opening in August 1971 Alec sat in at the *Oz* trial, conspicuously anonymous to the left of the dock. During the try-out week in Brighton before *A Voyage* came into the West End, Mortimer felt that Alec was underplaying his role: 'My father was an angry man consumed by inner anger at his blindness and I am not getting any of that.' He, Michael Codron and Alec went and had a fish lunch in The Lanes. During this Alec professed to be astonished at Mortimer's reaction: 'I don't know how you can say this. Haven't you noticed the anger in the breakfast scene in the way I tap my egg?'

This performance, which enjoyed a long and successful run at the Haymarket Theatre, was overshadowed by Olivier in the same role on television. With his direct and vulgar appeal for sympathy, Olivier turned the character into a popular hero, giving a huge and affecting performance rather than a well-observed study of a real person. And perhaps, while Alec's sympathies with the blind, opinionated old lawyer were subject to his just sense of restraint, Olivier had no inhibitions to keep him aloof: he 'blazed'. He loved old Mortimer as he had loved Richard of Gloucester and every other villain he played.

But there was no other actor like Alec to fill a theatre. He was, says Codron, 'cast-iron box office', and on ten per cent of the gross made a pretty fortune. After performances Alec would repair to a Greek taverna in Beak Street, persuading members of the cast to join him for ouzo, retsina, a meal of sorts and an effort at Greek dancing. This would seem, in Alec's words, a strange, rather fey idyll, but supposedly true.

I fondly imagined that one day I would pick up the steps accurately; I never did. The two bouzouki players pitched up the adrenalin and soon people were kicking off their shoes and, if feeling very confident, would dance solo on the tables. For most of us it was staggering in some sort of line and, after a brief demonstration from the patron, we would exhaust ourselves dipping up and down travelling the length of the room and back. On one hot summer night we chained our way out into Beak Street and down as far as Regent Street. Stockings were laddered and socks had to be abandoned. Never a sign of police but faces in passing buses were amazed. Then back to the taverna for a long cold beer.

A Positively Final Appearance

Codron noticed, at this time, Alec was beginning to despair of audiences. One night a woman in the front row placed her mackintosh on the edge of the stage. Mortimer Senior QC, although blind, came over with his stick and tilted it back onto the woman's lap.

Perhaps the same thing, underplaying the anger, was wrong with Alec when he came to film in *Hitler: The Last Ten Days*. The ten days in question were 20–29 April 1945. They started with Hitler's decision that he would remain in Berlin. Alec had spent ten months, or so he said later, researching and preparing for the role. At another moment of recall, this became five months during which he read the historical records and saw all the films.

'My poor wife, my friends,' he said, 'have to put up with every new scrap of information I unearth. So I'm not depressed [by getting inside the mind of such an evil man]. I'm obsessed.'

Was he prepared to strike out and declare *anything* outrageous or histrionic in the man? The Hitler of the script, as well as being the more hackneyed maniac when, for instance, he threatens his own senior officers with execution, has a lot of sympathetic elements. There is also his puritan streak which would recommend him to millions today when he boasts how he stopped everyone smoking. And he loved dogs, as we all know, and could be gracious and charming to women.

For the most part Alec took the line that Hitler was a Gulley Jimson manqué, that he sacrificed his vocation as an artist in order to restore law and order to his country, or, as someone in the film says, 'What a pity for the world you couldn't have devoted your life to art.' You feel quite sorry for the Guinness/Hitler, betrayed by the drug addict Goering, especially when his women, too, turn on him. ('The Germans are a nation of whores: destiny will punish them.')

Alec shows him boyishly moving from foot to foot and, with his extraordinary shy and shifty face, he becomes the moody anti-bourgeois misfit. ('Nature is cruel, so I too must be cruel . . . They want to see me naked in a cage.') When he commits suicide the rest, the real villains of the film, as one might call them, celebrate by lighting up cigarettes and cigars, as if he were a pioneer of ASH and the anti-smoking lobby. (And, of course, his enemies Roosevelt, Churchill, and de Gaulle were all heavy smokers – as was Alec himself to nearly the end of his life.)

Alec spent a great amount of energy and thought in making himself into a close proximation of the man himself. As someone said about meeting Alec off the set, 'I cannot quite account for the tremor of shock I felt when that pasty face, with its hooded mesmeric eyes above the little blot of the moustache, spoke with the amiable, relaxed musical voice of an English country gentleman.'

But this was where the research was important – the face was almost entirely his own. He grew a moustache and 'gradually cut it down from each side. It's now a fraction too narrow – a sort of black postage stamp – but that is in order to make my nose look as broad as his.' He sought out someone who had seen Hitler in the bunker: Gerhardt Boldt, a cavalry captain sent with a message to the Führer who described to Alec elements of behaviour that he copied; how his left arm trembled, his left foot dragged, how he raised one limp hand to his shoulder in a token Nazi salute.

While Alec thought it was his best work to date, when he saw the film he expressed disappointment. It ended up somehow as just another desultory picture and the performance, objective as it was in Alec's new mood of paring away anything superfluous in a performance, seemed to lack love and devilry. Where was the Hitler of Chaplin's satire, Brecht's Arturo Ui in his *Resistible Ascension*, or even Hollywood's big bad wolf? He wasn't there at all. Was this because of Alec's deliberate holding back and desire to do something different? Alec's reflective Hitler could never have swayed eight million people, a man who had, as Alec said of him, 'a great following outside Germany, in France, Italy, Spain, Sweden, Denmark, Norway' . . .

Alec blamed the script: 'The film has been cut by half an hour and cut sensibly but I wish the script could have been cut before we started.' This contrasted with what he was saying during the filming, namely that the ebullient De Concini had a 'touch of genius . . . Hitler, surprisingly, had a sense of humour.' Alec made another ex cathedra statement, an obvious one: 'Let's face it, wicked or evil people are fundamentally more interesting dramatically than good ones. The other day I was asked why I didn't make a nice film about someone nice, like Nelson. I wrote back to say I had no objection to playing Macbeth, who wasn't a particularly nice man either.' A bad reception produces weather-vane moods, for at another time he named Hitler as one of the four or five best performances he had given: 'Although it was dismissed I thought the performance had something.'

Simon Ward, playing a 'pure German youth', confirmed Alec's high opinion. Watching Alec every day for the ten weeks he spent on the film, Ward thought Alec's performance 'extraordinary, brilliant at showing the moral dilemmas of Hitler'. Ward believed the film, which was 'shot very flat', was lost on the cutting-room floor. Invited with his wife to visit Kettlebrook during the filming, Ward remarked that Alec's study behind the drive had a curved window. There was a light on the desk and if you sat at it you would be looking at yourself in a 'widescreen reflection'.

Timothy West's father, Lockwood West, had worked with Alec on the film of *Last Holiday*, and Timothy remembered his father saying how silent Alec was in the studio: 'There was no conversation between takes.' When Timothy spent a few days on *Hitler*, playing a Red Cross supervisor who came to pack up and leave, he found Alec brusque and uncooperative but controlling: 'I think if you could turn away from me here – it would be better, duckie!'

West believes Alec had extraordinary control of the character he was playing, but was not an actor who explored the inner life. What Alec asked himself was, 'How am I going to make this work best?' He was again bringing to famous, well-documented people an exotic life. It was no good, West thought, merely to research well and realize the outward trappings of the character you are playing: this was important, but in addition, 'You have one instrument to play the tune – yourself.'

When Alec came to do some publicity on the Duke of York Steps in Pall Mall, he parked his car in a forbidden place. He was politely approached by an elderly policeman who wanted to book him. 'I was going to pounce on you, sir, but I don't want to end up in a concentration camp!' The Israeli film censor banned the film for representing Hitler 'in a human light without giving expression to the terrible murders for which he is responsible'.

He did not pursue evil in the good man, as Chesterton might have done when, also in 1973, he played Pope Innocent III, a small part in *Brother Sun, Sister Moon*, a film Franco Zeffirelli made about St Francis of Assisi. Olivier had backed out of this role.

Zeffirelli tells how Alec was presented as a giant. 'His first appearance in the film was at the top of a gold-encrusted staircase with gold mosaics. Byzantine, embodying the glory of the Church. When he descended the long flight of stairs each step he took was a coming down to earth, as it were. The glory, the paraphernalia, the accessories fell away. He came down to this group of poor young friars . . . One had the impression he envied them for their simplicity and poverty. There he was trapped in luxury and glory desperately wanting to begin his life again . . .'

The director added, 'I have a feeling Guinness is a bit like that himself.'

Alec worked one week on this film. 'He is very withdrawn,' concludes Zeffirelli. But 'Why should he be pinned down? You see, it's the tip of the iceberg again. The English would call him shy but I don't think he's really shy. He is, from my point of view, the exact opposite of the Latin temperament.'

*

On 3 April 1973, the day after his fifty-ninth birthday, Alec sat at his small writing desk in the sober blue-and-white drawing room of his fourth-floor London flat. He was now studying the part of Dr Wickstead in a new play by Alan Bennett due to open in six weeks' time. In the small hall of the flat were hanging several framed costume drawings of roles played by Merula in the 1930s: the lean majestic Tiger, one from *Richard II*, another from *School for Scandal*. Alec moved to sit in his peacock chair. The silence was punctuated by the soft ticking of a clock. The draught blew open the door of the drawing room.

The day before, he had gone home to Kettlebrook to have the chance to walk around the garden and look at the fish in the pond. But it was pouring with rain. He had a slight gastric infection and felt irritable. Yet he was healthy, although the glowing face was now surrounded by wispy white hair. He was dressed in a dark 'mod' shirt and a blue suit.

He thought that perhaps the title of *Habeas Corpus*, the play he was studying, was a bit misleading because it had nothing to do with legal affairs. It meant, in Latin, 'You must have the body,' a phrase Bennett chose to take literally.

'I play a doctor who is immoral, or is it amoral? He is inclined to interfere with his patients!' Shades of Dr Shipman? we might ask with millennium hindsight.

In a newspaper interview Alec said that he suspected Bennett would be a bit tetchy if he described the play as a farce but it had all the ingredients of a farce. But 'also like a Restoration play, some of it goes into doggerel verse and rhyming couplets. It is unlike anything I've ever been connected with before. The form is rather odd, but it is very funny indeed in places. Music is used but all played by cinema organ. I was a bit scared about being in a sort of permissive play but there are no ordinary four-letter words and no one is actually in the nude.'

Alan Bennett, Oxford scholar, medieval historian and satirical investigator, was just within the pale, only marginally the wrong side of decency. As Michael Codron, again Alec's producer, said, Alec was much happier with *Habeas Corpus* probably because he seemed able, with Ronald Eyre directing, to voice continually his insecurities about the whole enterprise: 'I don't think I'm quite right for it,' he would keep saying, or 'I can't do it, I'm not going to be any good, why did you choose me?' He worried about the Latin title and one day, when they were auditioning an actress for another part in the play he turned to Bennett saying, 'Cold feet'. Bennett was impressed with this new idea. 'What a wonderful title!' 'No, no, no,' said Alec, 'I've *got* cold feet.'

In rehearsal John Bird recalls how struck he was at how Alec would try out anything physical in the way of stage business – such as putting his hand up Joan Sanderson's skirt, or other gestures of lewd or questionable taste – but was deeply fastidious about language. 'Most curious – I wondered if it was something to do with his Catholicism.' At one stage Joan Sanderson's underwear was alarmed: any vibration or feisty movement set it off and policemen would run in. They dropped this idea. Under-lyingly, thought Bird, Alec's lasciviousness was very strong, without affecting the surface.

Codron tells me how Alec suggested he should at the end of the play introduce a little dance of death. He had begun this fashion of a celebratory dance with Harcourt-Reilly in *The Cocktail Party*, and continued it in *Time out of Mind*. Olivier had taken up the idea, possibly in unconscious imitation, in his exultant little dance as Shylock in the National Theatre production of 1970.

Bennett disliked the idea, saying 'That's not my play.' Alec said he would not do the play unless he included it. The dance he produced was, says Codron, 'magical, haunting, just what was needed'. It became an often-recorded, memorable moment.

When they played in Oxford prior to London, Alec had another attack of cold feet. Cutlery fell noisily to the table in the Randolph Hotel as Alec was overheard telling Van Thal, 'I think you're going to have to get me out of this one.' He was prevailed upon to stay. When the play opened in London it received excellent reviews but Alec thought everyone else in the play was good except for him.

During the London run Alec took the cast to dinner at Le Caprice. Bird was joined by his friend and colleague John Fortune, who found himself seated at the opposite end of the private room dining table. Alec, at its head, told the company, 'I've taken the liberty of ordering the menu for us.' The first course, Fortune told me, was 'Marrow bones on a kind of brioche which we had to tackle with long wooden spoons.' Fortune, who was feeling nervous of the occasion, finished it and met Alec's eye. 'And what do you think of that, John?' 'Oh,' stuttered Fortune, 'it's like leukaemia on toast.' Alec, Fortune said, 'looked absolutely glacial at me'.

Alec refused to be photographed for the *Oxford Mail* against a Playhouse backdrop. They took him over the road to the Ashmolean steps, according to Don Chapman, the Oxford critic, but he was 'grumpy and uncooperative. Then a small boy appeared from nowhere and started taking pot-shots at him from behind the slabs and pillars with an imaginary pistol. Guinness's face lit up with that classic enigmatic smile.'

Alec never visited Bird's dressing room except once when he asked Bird, before a 2.30 matinee, looking shaken, 'Oh you haven't got a brandy – could I have a very small brandy?' – excusing himself that it was the first drink he'd had before going on since 1948. Bird gave him one and then Alec told him he had arranged to meet Ralph Richardson at Pruniers for lunch. Richardson was a quarter of an hour late (a long wait for Alec) and all the waiters in frock coats – and fellow lunchers – stared as he, attired in motorcycle leathers and helmet, strode in. After a short while at the table he rose, saying, 'I'm really sorry, Alec, I've got an appointment. I've got to leave' – Alec added, 'I regret to say I was very relieved to see him go. A short while later he came back in saying his motorbike wouldn't start, and would we help him – so we all stood outside on the pavement, waiters and myself trying to get the motorbike to start. I'm completely unnerved by the whole thing!'

Christopher Good, another member of the cast, underlined how well they all got on. 'He couldn't bear how I came into the theatre wearing shorts, I'd always go and say hello. He'd frown – there was a sort of privacy about him . . . He never suggested he was attracted by me (yes, I'm gay). I think this was a problem for him. It was not easy to categorize him . . . But, yes, I think he would have liked to have been free.'

Alec liked, Good thought, to be a centre of fascination. 'He was titillated by the fact of people talking about his sexuality, their speculating, "I wonder which side he was on" – forbidden fruit is extremely riveting. In the balance between the masculine and feminine side things break out – I can't put it into words. What made him a great actor is that he subsumed all this into his work. What he exhibited was so terribly dangerous and interesting. The answers lie in his work, not in who he slept with or didn't. In *Wise Child* he explored a dangerous transvestism.' Yet at the same time, says Good, 'You feel he had to clear it with God – the slate had to be absolutely clean.'

Heinrich Böll emphasized the godly side too in his satirical novel *The Clown*, which won him the Nobel Prize for Literature in 1972:

> For me there were only four Catholics in the world. Pope John, Alec Guinness, Marie [the Clown's wife who has left him because he has taken to drink] and Gregory, an old negro boxer who had once nearly become World Champion and who was now eking out a meagre living as a strong man in vaudeville.

After the more than appropriately titled *Habeas Corpus* closed, in March 1974, Alec and Merula spent a month south of Delphi in Greece, renting a cottage in the broken-down port

of Galaxidhion, inviting old friends such as Margaret Harris, the
Motleys' designer, to share their holiday. (She told me, when I
interviewed her at the end of her life that, 'Alec is a very difficult
man to know'.) Flower- or bird-spotting occupied them, interspersed with visits to the architectural wonders of Delphi, Corinth
and Epidaurus, while Alec kept an eye out for snakes.

Habeas Corpus apart, the early years of the 1970s were desultory
in terms of new projects for Alec, although he read as much as
ever. Approaching the age of sixty, he seemed to be slackening off,
although this may have reflected that nothing very exciting came
his way and that, since the intellectual vacuum of the war years
when he was forced back on his own resources, he had not really
thought of originating any ideas of his own.

He did have the notion to write a play about Jonathan Swift,
which came to him out of a charitable enterprise at Aldeburgh
in which he had read the *Journal to Stella*. Swift's description of
taking a swim in the river at Chelsea during a hot summer had
attracted him. Adapting Swift for the stage seemed a fitting
progression from his three previous adaptations. But if it was
Swift's anger, his bitterness, his darkness and his wit that attracted
Alec, how would he handle these when he came to play them on
stage?

Now, for the most part, he became involved in minor enterprises. Going back to the year 1970, he claimed when talking to a
journalist, he made only ninety pounds and he underlined the
insecure feeling all actors have: 'Each morning it's simply a
question of *How insecure shall I feel today?* One never knows, does
one?'

He rejected the opportunity to play Prospero at the National
Theatre in Peter Hall's new regime (and with Hall directing).
Is it significant that he should never have trusted himself to Hall,
or to Trevor Nunn, while his favoured directors, Lindsay Anderson, Dexter, Glenville, and probably Ron Eyre, were homosexual?
He quarrelled or fell out with well-known noted heterosexuals,
for example George Devine, and in the film world, Lean. The
conclusion would seem to be that he didn't altogether feel comfortable with those whom he could not control, and who might
challenge him. Gay men naturally deferred, and were more sensitive to his wavelengths. He still felt the scars of Macbeth, but

perhaps this was an inexcusable rejection based on wanting to control everything and have, as actors tend to want, everything on his own terms. Hall commented in his diaries:

> Bad news from Alec Guinness whom I had asked to do Prospero, a part he had never played. He has decided he dare not in such an exposed situation as the NT. Funny, everyone always agrees the propositions, and then gets out of them. At least in the theatre. I do it myself. Perhaps we are too anxious to be loved, or perhaps the basic insecurity about our work makes us agree to every possibility as something too reassuring to refuse. Perhaps we only contemplate something seriously *after* we have agreed to do it.

Here was a role in which Alec could have excelled had he been prepared to work with Hall. Was it arrogant pride or overpowering humility that made him say no? Was it sexual aversion and fear? Opposites are sometimes equals. Probably it was just cold feet.

Alec visited Hollywood once more, in 1975, to make his second and last film with his ardent love–hate admirer, Peter Sellers. 'Of the two British character actors who have managed to become sound-era film stars of world renown, one went insane and the other is cordial,' wrote Roger Lewis in his life of Sellers. Alec responded in a letter to Lewis on the subject of the insane one after his death, 'I admired his talent – which had flashes of genius – enormously . . . During the making of *Murder by Death* he had become pretty odd – measuring his caravan with a tape measure to make sure it was larger than everyone else's; deciding his mood by the colour of a stone in his ring . . . I had the impression he greatly feared death but can't actually remember him saying so.'

Sellers had already had one big heart attack, in 1964, which he felt was pre-ordained: 'I do remember one thing clearly, a feeling; a feeling that I would expire, but I wouldn't actually die. I remember there being a sort of large, strong, outstretched arm, pulling – I knew as long as I clung on I wouldn't die.'

Murder by Death was a Neil Simon detective fiction parody in which famous detectives compete to solve a murder. Alec played, in an all-star cast which included David Niven, Maggie Smith and Elsa Lanchester, the blind butler Bensonmum. The final cut emerged as a much-hacked sequence of knock-about gags, but the script had made Alec laugh – 'and not many things in recent times have done that'.

Sellers during shooting submitted the management to extravagant demands: one day he didn't turn up saying he was ill, but David Niven saw him lunching in a Beverly Hills restaurant. While Alec feared Sellers might be, as he cautiously said, 'a little unbalanced', Sellers said of Alec, when interviewed during shooting, 'Lovely chap, but I must say the snoring on the set does rattle the grips a bit.' Even so, snoring or not, Alec became a centre of balance in the film, staring at the world-famous sleuths with eyes that don't see. Unlike Sellers, who played Sidney Wang in 'ceremonial robes and monster-teeth . . . a stick-puppet', Alec was stately and still, 'hieratic'. John Bird, who worked with both, summed up: 'You look at Sellers's work, you think: What is going on . . . there's nothing obvious you can copy and make use of yourself. As with Guinness, it is great acting.'

To the very end, the selfish but doomed Sellers had stayed with the false noses that Alec left behind.

Alec made two television appearances in 1974, as Jocelyn Broome in John Osborne's *The Gift of Friendship* and as Caesar in Shaw's *Caesar and Cleopatra*. The first of these was a largish insignificant part in a not very significant play. In the Shaw, he was cast more as a grandfatherly potentate than a sexy old man, opposite Geneviève Bujold, the French star. They made a strangely incongruous pair without much of the sexual chemistry that is supposed to ignite their wit. While Bujold was not feeling very well during the rushed period of filming, Alec himself became openly fractious. He didn't like his performance at all.

At this time he seems briefly to have begun to consider the idea of writing his autobiography. He owned up to having written three chapters but did not go on. 'I do wish people would stop asking to do it for me.' At fifty he had told the *Sunday Express*, 'I have no ambitions left,' but now he reluctantly admitted to trying to find new classics.

In February 1975 he attended the Queen's reception for the media at Buckingham Palace with several other actors (Ustinov, Finney) and many directors, television channel controllers and the like. He tramped the reception rooms, drank the sweetish white wine and choked on the Lyons pâté. He would rather have been anonymous, or so he said, but he was there. He reflected on the worst moment of his life: when he had been knighted in 1959, the band at the palace had struck up with 'I'm Gonna Wash That Man Right Outa My Hair'.

Now he was sixty-one he (somewhat condescendingly) agreed to appear once more on stage. This was in Julian Mitchell's adaptation of Ivy Compton-Burnett's *A Family and a Fortune* at the Apollo, again produced by Michael Codron, with a first directorial encounter with Alan Strachan and a last and touching acting partnership with Margaret Leighton, with whom he had acted at the New in 1947. The once luscious and much-pursued sex goddess Leighton, with a serious drinking problem and by this time ill with multiple sclerosis, had to walk with a stick. Pretending nothing was wrong he quietly insisted she receive top billing, and moved out of the star dressing room on stage level so that she could make her many costume changes with the minimum of effort.

Alec had first been asked to play the part of Dudley in *A Family and a Fortune* four years before and had read the book with a view to it being filmed. It had been relegated to the back of his mind until he was turning out some scripts to send back to their owners and came across it. Dudley was the hanger-on of the family, one of those misled people who believe they can 'edit' their own lives; as Alec said, a kind of Chekhovian conception with a 'bit more steel tucked into him'. He was amusing, pleasant, had to sing for his supper and was aware of the 'jealousies, and how that he's been hurt and how that comes through'.

People have been critical of how Alec fixed first on the externals of a part, he said at the time, but 'unless I can look like I would like to look . . . then I wouldn't tackle it'. With Dudley he used a wig with a quiff at the back, to catch this most schoolboyish of men in his late fifties. Alec brought out every last shred of irony in the character: it was, Strachan told me, like 'excavating the innards of a crab'.

In May 1975, a month after the play opened, the more mischievous social side of Alec was noted by Kenneth Williams in his diary. Alec asked Williams to play a small joke on some American guests at a dinner party. Rona, the wife of Gordon Jackson, at this time well known for his role as Hudson the butler in *Upstairs, Downstairs* on television, and Williams needed to arrive early and 'had to hide in the kitchen. Rona was introduced as Mrs Rona Trossach, and then he clapped his hands and called out "Hyde", and I had to enter with the tray and the Americans shrieked, "Oh my God, Alec." – I said I thought it was a tasteless piece of vulgarity.' (I worked this obscure piece of business out as follows: Alec was pretending to be Williams – teasing the Americans because they thought – as a theatrical knight – he must be playing the butler.)

Alec then returned to Swift's savage indignation. He called his exploration of the man and his work by the unpromising name of *Yahoo*. Swift's imaginary brute with the form of man had just been used in a speech by Harold Wilson, the prime minister, and Alec believed it had acquired respectability. Apart from it being later adopted, perhaps with unconscious appropriateness, by the largest Internet directory, it was a poor, off-putting stage title. But Alec wanted above all to get away from the received idea of Swift, underline the misanthropist, as well as the literary impersonator and entertainer. He asked Alan Strachan to help him devise the portrait and also to direct it. Michael Codron, who loved 'marriage broking' with Alec ('he liked me because I'm gay,' he says blithely), was to present the evening while Nicola Pagett played Stella, and Angela Thorne Vanessa.

Alec committed himself to the idea with considerable enthusiasm: there were only three minutes, he said, when he was not on stage. A far cry from Abel Drugger. Learning the part became something of an ordeal and he went through his lines with 'a young actor' telling him how once, when he and Merula were on a ship to America, he recorded an arduous part he had to learn on tape in order to play it to himself over and over again. To depersonalize the character he read it in an absolutely flat tone, which he thought would make the learning easier. The result was disastrous: he could not bear to listen.

Although *Yahoo* when it opened drew good audiences and ran successfully for six months, Alec's performance was more *pointilliste* than barnstorming. He did not manage to focus enough on the ferocious side of Swift, while during the long sections from *A Modest Proposal*, for example, 'A child will make two dishes at an entertainment for friends, and when the family dines alone, the

fore or hind quarters will make a reasonable dish . . .', he wanted
to show Swift's human face. This was perhaps impossible in the
context of what Swift was trying to say. The main consensus went
probably with Peter Hall, who wrote in his diary on 8 October
1976:

> Guinness appears to have at the moment a bad attack of
> 'the lovelies'. He seems to me to want, above all, to be loved
> by the audience . . . What we received tonight was a gentle
> half-smiling ironist about as far away from the ferocious
> misanthropic Swift as a duck-pond is from the Pacific Ocean.

Alec in *Yahoo* enjoyed the sense of personal identification with
Swift: he might have been speaking of himself when he relished,
as he said, Swift's 'trick to appear very bland; then suddenly he
has a rage or puts the knife in'. Yet for the most part he was
guarded and evasive. A journalist who befriended Alec at this time
and who prefers to remain anonymous found himself invited to
restaurants – the Mirabelle, the Poule au Pot – and given an open
invitation to go round backstage after performances. The seduction, if such it was, of the much younger man, was very gentle.
Alec would tease, his sexual message would be equivocal. Back
to the Smith Square flat. The friend remarked on the gout chair,
an eighteenth-century antique with a retractable shelf on which
Alec would rest his leg. They both drank a lot, the friend noticed
the bed behind a curtain. The friend, who was married and had
had bisexual experiences, didn't take the sexual implications very
seriously. He felt flattered. Alec's captivating memories flowed
endlessly, the talk was vivid, funny, the intention or unspoken
temptation plain. Soon both of them were very drunk. The friend
felt more flattered, wanted, unbothered by guilt; 'Shall I stay?,
Shall I go?' he asked himself, weighing up whether it was worth it
or not. In the event he left. No consequences, no offence taken, a
card a day or so later arrived, expressing the hope he'd got home
safely, but from now on a gentle cooling of invitations, all very
sensitive and civilized. 'Alec had these gulfs,' said the friend, 'I
don't think he was really being unfaithful to Merula, it wasn't
another woman and one felt, well certainly during the last twenty-
five years, the sex wouldn't be important. It was the intimacy, the
contact and exchange of sensitivity that mattered.' This scenario

repeats often in other forms: a driver, an actor, an old friend. He'd given up the anonymity of it, the casual sex, if such it was, now had an intimate dimension. It did not intrude.

Still much in demand, Alec had also agreed to appear in a dramatization of Evelyn Waugh's *The Ordeal of Gilbert Pinfold* at the Royal Exchange Theatre in Manchester. He recalled how he and Waugh had first met on their hands and knees collecting up hundreds of bangles dropped by an old lady at Edith Sitwell's inauguration into the Catholic Church. But after some dithering he seemed to want to extricate himself from the Waugh. His Hampshire neighbour, Ronald Harwood, who had adapted the novel for the stage, found himself invited round to Kettlebrook one weekend to have dinner with Alan Bennett, who was staying for the weekend and who, it was made clear to Harwood, was working on a new play. Harwood said on his way home, 'I smell trouble.'

The extrication was not at all open. Alec telephoned Harwood some weeks later and told him he had to go into hospital early in 1977 for a hernia operation. Harwood felt that Alec had engineered this second hernia as a way of getting off the hook, whereupon the 'diplomatic hernia' became something of a cult. The operation took place and *Gilbert Pinfold* was cancelled as far as he was concerned, although eventually produced in 1977. About this time Alec was about to be launched into a new, if to him disagreeable, orbit of international stardom with the release of a film which probably became more famous than any other in the history of film-making.

While the last seventeen years or so both on stage and in film had been, by his standards, desultory with some distinguished exceptions, there had been nothing as electrifying as the general run of his performances until, and including, Jack Sinclair in *Tunes of Glory*. Here was the opportunity for a change in fortune.

24. Most of Life Is Lived below
the Water's Surface

True it is, but perhaps depressing to say, Alec's character in *Star Wars*, Obi-Wan Kenobi, the Jedi master, became in the late twentieth century as well-known to much of the world's population as Jesus Christ, Buddha, or Confucius, while his mantra 'May the Force be with you' was quoted more often than any motto or political catchphrase. Alec had served a long apprenticeship in saint-like warriors and authority figures, tyrants and men of genius. Obi-Wan was all these in one, but most of all he was a presence: and then, when disposed of in the script, a commanding absence. The Force came from the actor saying or doing very little. 'These days I get others to do the acting for me,' he observed flippantly.

Two years before, a film script had arrived at Kettlebrook. 'It came through the door and the moment I saw a sci-fi sticker on it I said to myself "Oh crumbs, it's not for me." But I started to read and I had to turn the page.'

Alec compared the script of *Star Wars* to le Carré's *The Honourable Schoolboy*: 'It had vigour and I finished it at a sitting. Was that normal? No, not at all. But it's a jolly good sign. I don't apply any professional "technique", if that's the word, when I read scripts. But if I'm held by them then I think there's a chance the public will be held too. Probably the last time I went through a film script so swiftly was when James Kennaway's *Tunes of Glory* came into my hands.'

He agreed to meet director George Lucas, who was in London, with a view to playing the master warrior Obi-Wan Kenobi. He thought the part difficult because Kenobi was a wholly good character. There was a danger of becoming 'a bit smug, a bit know-all'.

A short man, as short as Alec, George Lucas was very vulnerable, very nervous of people, and shy. Anthony Daniels, who played the robotic character C-3P0, said Lucas carried a little black book in which he wrote everything down. His own part of C-3P0 was full of 'terribly corny lines', such as 'Curse my metal body, I wasn't fast enough,' which were, in an odd way, reminiscent of Victorian children's fiction.

After his first discussion with Lucas, Alec agreed to play the role of Obi-Wan. But subsequently they had a crisis, some weeks before shooting, because Lucas changed the script. In its previous version Kenobi had appeared on page twenty, when he became leader and tutor of a small band of rebels. He led these on their series of adventures that 'culminated in a giant space battle that destroyed the evil empire's principal weapon, the "Death Star", and ended with Ben Kenobi giving everyone medals'.

So Alec described it in oversimplified manner. Obi-Wan, the Jedi Knight, has learned control over mind and body, developed extra senses and the power to alter Force lines in nature and life. The Force is the energy field that surrounds the galaxy and binds every living thing together. But it has a dark side, and unable to redeem his friend and pupil Anakin Skywalker from its evil influence Kenobi engages him in a lightsaber battle, wins it, but the molten pit into which Skywalker falls transforms him into Darth Vader, who unleashes an irresistible power of destruction.

Changing his name to Ben Kenobi, Obi-Wan goes into hiding and after various adventures to save the galaxy, as protector of Anakin's twins Luke and Leia, engages Vader again in combat on the first Death Star. He disarms himself to distract Vader and enable the twins to escape. Vader cuts through him, activating his disappearance and absorption into the Force. Here was the significant plot change. In further visitations as the commanding absence – 'If you strike me down, I shall become more powerful than you can possibly imagine,' he has warned Vader – Obi-Wan lives on, appearing to Luke as his mentor.

Lucas had to inform Alec of this important plot change and, as he did, grew nervous. 'Although Ben is the leader,' he explained, 'I think it might be better if he . . . Oh, like kinda died halfway through the picture.'

Alec was upset. Understandably so. Actors do not want to play a character that dies halfway through the film; nor do they want to be informed of their premature demise over lunch.

Although he remained civil, Alec told Lucas that he no longer wanted to do the picture. Lucas had a major anxiety attack, which led to another long meeting with the actor. 'I went on and on,' Lucas said, 'about how important the change was in order to make the story work. And how important it was to have a powerful actor to play Ben, especially now that he had so much less screen time. As a writer, he was easily convinced.'

As an actor, too, Alec eventually came around. When they began shooting he became much more than an actor in the film: 'an incredible blessing', Lucas was to call it later. The preparation for the filming took on a Herculean dimension: what had endeared Lucas to Alec was that he himself brought the costumes to London to see if Alec liked them, and he came to all the fittings.

Daniels spent six very undignified months preparing for C-3P0, which sometimes entailed 'standing naked in a cold room at Elstree' while they 'F/Xed' his body for its robotic role. When Alec and Merula arrived at Heathrow in 1976 for the flight out to Tunis, where they were to film on location, Daniels first saw him as a grand figure whose limousine drove right up to the plane.

In the course of seeing much of them over the next weeks, Daniels found Alec very approachable, while Merula was 'a living saint'. Alec fussed over whether the young actor was being paid proper expenses and offered to advance him some 'per diems'. They spent two or three weeks on desert location on some salt flats in windy and blisteringly hot weather eating a hotel diet of 'unremitting veal or chicken' – at one point the Guinnesses went down with food poisoning. There were often long waits while the ailing special effects were sorted out.

Incarcerated in metal, at one time having to lose an arm (torn off in a fight), Daniels found the waiting painful, while he was rather embarrassed about the whole restriction of playing a robot. Alec, he said, helped his confidence greatly (he was especially clever at indirectly paying him compliments), while his calm permeated everyone, including Mark Hamill who played Luke Skywalker.

It was, of course, quite clear to others that in his now distant and civilized way Alec fancied Daniels. The image Lucas had of Alec was of him sitting in a chair with a relaxed, approachable elegance, as if on the deck of some exotic cruise ship floating down a celluloid river. As for Alec, Lucas in his power of concentration reminded him of the young David Lean. But, unlike Lean, Lucas did not dictate or impose. During the filming he had little to say although able to sense when Alec was uncomfortable and would walk across and 'drop a brief word in your ear'. Others found him not all that interested in the actors as such: 'Very retiring,' said Daniels, 'he doesn't enjoy directing actors very much. He would invariably say, after a take, "Terrific; can you do it again a bit faster?"'

The heat and the waiting while they tampered with the machines was too much for Daniels, but he stuck it out: then, 'One day Alec blew up . . . Gosh I'm not wrong about the heat,' thought C-3PO. Alec quickly returned to serenity: 'a whirlpool of serenity' was the phrase Daniels employed when talking to me. During the lightsaber fight between Alec and another actor his assailant lost concentration and failed to keep to the pre-arranged numbers with the result that Alec 'hit the wall and the floor. They ran towards him. He was all right but everyone was shocked. It was the fact he didn't lose his temper made me realize how angry he was.'

'His presence,' commented Lucas, 'lent so much credibility that everyone finally believed that giant furry aliens and talking robots made perfect sense.' It was more than a presence, however. Familiarity breeds contempt. The machines such as R2-D2 ('Reel Two Dialogue Two') and C-3PO ('an euphonic accessory') as well as the hirsute monsters, were often treated as they looked, or relegated to a sub-human plane and ignored.

Alec, as Ben Kenobi disguised as the crazy wizard and hermit in the Jundland Wastes, would enter this world of weird creatures and adapt to it, yet he remained well-centred in himself, and kept within his own brief. In this way he helped the cast and the production team to treat the menagerie on the mythical Tatooine as real, sentient beings. He brought to *Star Wars* and its two sequels (written but not directed by Lucas), in which Kenobi returns as a guiding spirit (or as the underlying deity of the Force), its human identity and at a profound level helped the film to communicate its sense of the good (conceived of as an energy source) triumphing over the bad.

During the filming on location Merula, Alec's own saint, spent her time sketching in the local town or market: on one occasion she was drawing a mosque when some of the gendarmerie stopped her, threatened arrest, and wanted to confiscate her sketchbook. She gave them a few pages, but kept her own drawings tucked away.

One moment during the filming became of special significance to the director. In the cramped cockpit of Han Solo's spaceship, Han was at the controls – with Chewbacca, the giant furry alien, next to him, and Luke and Ben squeezed in behind them – as they played a scene during which Chewie had to reach up and hit a switch above Kenobi's head. In one of the retakes Chewie reached up to flip the switch for the 'umpteenth time and accidentally hit Alec right square in the face'.

Alec was unhurt but so taken completely by surprise that he fell out of character. When Lucas looked at the rushes next day in the editing machine he noticed that, studied one image at a time, from the moment Alec was hit his face went through a series of different characters, 'all in a split second, starting with Ben and ending with Alec, with about a half-dozen completely different characters in between'.

Lucas understood more clearly what he called:

the incredible physical nature of creating a character; how a truly gifted actor is so concentrated, so thorough that even their facial muscles are transformed. Like a chameleon, Alec has a lot of different shades, different colours and different characters. Every frame of film from the moment he was hit was a different character . . . until he finally arrived at Alec Guinness.

Alec echoes this, quoting in his *Commonplace Book* the remark made of Verlaine: 'I have seen all the deadly vices march in order across his face and leave it washed and empty for the virtues.'

Speculation about how much Alec made out of *Star Wars* has grown and waned and, like most reports of the earnings of actors, has at times not been based in fact. '*Star Wars* takings are already

$100 million. Sir Alec gets 2% of profits,' ran one *Daily Express*
headline. This was an underestimate. The true figure seems to
have been 2½ per cent of the gross, negotiated at the stage when
the film was running out of money and Alec agreed either to
reduce or waive his fee. Let us say the gross takings were $100
million, then Alec received at least $2.5 million. I was told, on
reliable authority, he earned £12,500 per week until the day he
died and beyond, which is £600,000 per year. Rumour has it that
Lucas, worried as to how carefully Alec might have invested or
looked after the money, phoned him. 'Oh, I've taken care of that,'
Alec reassured him. 'It's in my post office account in Roberts-
bridge.' *The Return of the Jedi* and *The Empire Strikes Back*
were still to come – 'I will do them if the lines are sayable' –
so ultimately the return was even more exceptional. The idea
that Alec more or less overnight had been turned into a multi-
millionaire was true, although strenuously denied by Alec. The
rather reckless spending on friends subsequent to *Star Wars* was
attributed by many to guilt, although not in an unkind way.

'I would keep more, if I went to live in America. But living in
Los Angeles I'd go completely mad.' (Alec momentarily closed his
eyes at the painful thought). He decided to stay in England. 'As
I pop through the stage door every night, I think, "This is what I
wanted to do as a kid: going to the dressing room, putting on my
make-up . . ."' But he did add: 'You'd think Denis Healey [the
Chancellor of the Exchequer] might send one a letter of thanks
for staying. I don't suppose he will.'

Alec was, in spite of all the fuss and exposure, pleased with
Star Wars: 'It wasn't smug,' he said at the time. He was a bit
puzzled at some reactions: 'It's funny how people identify.' One
person, perfectly sane, or so he said, wrote to him, 'I wish to be a
Jedi Knight. I wish to come to outer space.' He wrote back saying,
'I earn my living as an actor at the Queen's Theatre' (where he
was acting again in a 'decent' play).

The play that Alan Bennett had been working on still had to
undergo what the playwright called 'its elaborate wooing process,
like a formal dance', before Alec agreed to be in it. The subject of
this play, *The Old Country*, in which Alec in the end fell in with
Bennett's wishes to play the part of the Philby-inspired Hilary,
was treachery. Treachery was the national obsession. The mood

was for deconstructing patriotism, soon to be followed by the deconstruction of marriage and other traditional structures and rituals, including history itself. Bennett had become consecrated as one of the new high priests of deconstruction. 'The story of Kim Philby lives on in us,' wrote le Carré.

Hilary's brother-in-law Duff, a newly knighted bisexual lecturer of considerable distinction, has travelled to the Soviet Union to persuade Hilary, who defected just before he was due to be arrested, to return to his homeland. He was to be swapped with a captured Russian spy. The pair engage in a massive duel of mind and emotion, but Hilary can no longer feel, can hardly even remember, the reasons that caused him to damage his country so many years ago, while Duff, the interrogator of his motives, has also emptied his soul of principle and virtue: as Sheridan Morley wrote about his father Robert's desire to play Hilary, which subsequently he did in Australia:

> Home to Hilary is where the heart is not; a man with an infinite capacity for melancholy and almost none for love, he lives in a permanently stately home of the mind, the precise geographic location of which has become irrelevant, even to him. It is neither England nor the Soviet Union, but somewhere inhabited exclusively by the survivors of a pre-war education which trained men for a non-existent future and flooded them with the memories of an all-too-distant past.

Bennett shows the thinness of aspiration, the rootlessness of middle-class English society. The characters are discovered 'seemingly in the English countryside . . . but it emerges they are outside Moscow'. This makes for an effective coup de théâtre. For Hilary, loyalty can be bartered without a shred of shame, and crime expiated in a kind of affected cynicism (Hilary is perhaps more like Blunt than Philby). For Duff, life is a game where the self-seeker may win honours for his ego. He is perhaps the new Englishman signalling the launch of the coarse materialism of the Thatcher years that will follow. Neither of them can feel, neither of them has a soul. The method is that of undercutting the comforting cliché: 'We never entirely mean what we say. Do I mean that? Not entirely.' Or, instant character self-assessment: 'I don't bubble over. I have always been at Gas Mark One.' It could sound a bit like a variation on the theme of *The Prisoner*.

This was not middle-Europe, however, but home-counties England transposed to dacha-land. Espionage scandal showed how, Bruce Page wrote in 1979, 'the British ruling orders are a very limited set of fellows, modestly competent in the minor arts of bureaucracy and manipulation, but with a deficient grasp of intellectual method, and a tendency to be shaky on loyalty of any kind.' (*New Statesman*) So here was Alec yet again, perhaps more significantly than in other popular plays of the period, holding the mirror up to nature. As Bennett said later, 'He made it like his own life.'

They rehearsed in Cheyne Walk in Thomas More's Old Church Hall: outside a splendid statue of Henry VIII's chancellor looked down the Thames in the direction of Westminster – as if to anticipate having his head removed soon as a penalty for his integrity. Alec arrived – he had never before worked with the director, Clifford Williams – bearing Russian vodka and caviar. Williams was thrown by this unnecessary generosity and at once felt uneasy – as if it was buying something. The cast included Rachel Kempson (behind whose back Alec would on occasions, in black-joke mood, pull scurrilous faces, as if to say, 'Look at her' – this shocked the director), Heather Canning, Faith Brook and John Phillips, who was playing Duff.

Bennett worried about whether Alec was not underplaying the whole part, and at one point stormed in anger out of the rehearsal, whereupon Alec remarked drolly, 'What's wrong with him? Something I did?'

Williams found it very hard to make a judgement on Alec's performance as Hilary. Alec was not, he thought, an actor he could direct. It was a case of finding 'somewhere for him to perch on' and otherwise, as Williams put it, 'arranging the traffic'. Unlike the directors who fussed about Alec like favourites in a court, Williams, a seasoned RSC director of the Saint-Denis school, held himself back. Alec stuck to his under-energized guns and the performance when it opened turned out as great a success as that of Dr Wickstead in *Habeas Corpus*. Bernard Levin described it in *The Times* as played by Alec with 'an infinite weariness of the soul', while Duff was 'played with no less consummately polished emptiness by John Phillips'. Sheridan Morley later commented on how they hated *The Old Country* in Australia, in spite of Robert Morley as Hilary: 'Where Guinness in London had offered a dry, almost desiccated Hilary, Robert imbued him with a breathtaking sense of loss and a terrible forlorn gaiety.'

There was a price to be paid for this outer projection of inner quintessential treachery. Playing a traitor was like rust eating into the soul. Alec maintained his innocence by being what the director could only describe as 'vitriolic' to Merula when they went out to dinner together.

'What sort of life would it be if I couldn't grumble about the missing coffee-pot, the dangerously exposed electrical appliances, the burned potatoes, the oil paint on the door knob, the barking of her dog, or the forgotten arrival of my train from London?'

Alec would take out the tension on the person closest to him who, while he was being waspish, froze and said nothing. Of course Alec was not really 'under-energizing', he was still seized and active with a secret life on which he kept the lid well battened down. Or nearly so. He would allow nothing to 'blow the lid off his closely guarded privacy' as Simon Callow has put it. But he needed – as who wouldn't? – a few safety valves where he could hiss and bubble in full view of the public. (Men hold, said Montaigne, 'a curious bias against what is close at hand'.)

As a result of the production Bennett noted that Alec was inimitable: 'There has never been a satisfactory imitation of him. Peter Sellers had one, but it wasn't very good.' (Sellers had mimicked the Kennomeat bloodhound as Alec – 'My man always gets my food, don't you, Sydney?'). 'He doesn't leave anything spare for the public outside his acting.'

Tinker, Tailor, Soldier, Spy, the first of John le Carré's Smiley novels in which Alec was cast as Smiley, was filmed in 1978. About that time and just later there were at least two newspaper articles claiming le Carré had based the character of George Smiley on Alec. In the very opening of *Call for the Dead*, le Carré's first novel, published in 1961, Smiley was described as 'without school, parents, regiment or trade', and as 'a traveller in the guard's van of the social express'. So was the idea so fanciful? Could it be that le Carré had enjoyed and studied those extraordinary films which Alec made in the 1950s, and formed the idea of a hero which was a composite – perhaps the essence – of the different characters Alec had played? Smiley and Alec had much in common. But so had the backgrounds of Alec and the author who grew up as David Cornwell.

The name Smiley itself has a Guinness ring – neutral, ironic. Almost anonymous. Like the name Abel Drugger, the minor character Alec played in *The Alchemist* in 1946 and the part he sometimes said he would like to go on playing for ever, for the tobacconist, the character, was almost the opposite of the name. Smiley has little to smile about: 'We are not speaking of pleasure.' Although he far surpassed Drugger in intelligence, and although he was a major, huge character as opposed to a tiny, minor one, they shared one vital characteristic: both were dupes. Smiley was not only a dupe, but somewhere deep inside Smiley was the cuckold, the betrayed, the essential Drugger; above all, the innocent. He was victim and hero at the same time.

Smiley does not stand out in a crowd. Neither did Alec. Smiley was plump, myopic. Alec had to fatten out to play him, gaining several stone in weight, but even so Alec was more and more becoming a short, barrel-shaped man. If Smiley had no lookalike face in an actor of stature – he was a creature of imagination – the famous English spy of MI6, Maurice Oldfield, bore an uncanny resemblance to Alec. Le Carré had no George Cruikshank, whose caricatures would become so embedded in the mind that when Dickens's characters came to be played in films actors and directors would base their impersonations upon his drawings (as had happened with Alec's Fagin). A more complicated process had to take place with le Carré.

Another striking quality which suggests that le Carré might have drawn on Alec's past performances is Smiley's saintly quality, albeit that of the battered or savaged saint. Le Carré claimed that his Smiley novels were about 'national falling standards . . . almost to do with meanness, mutual consideration and gentleness; the shameless adjustment by politicians of their position'. A sense of professional failure may often have stood for a sense of spiritual failure, but there is also a strong vein of the metaphysical in Smiley's isolation.

The superintendent in *Smiley's People*, who looks at the corpse of the émigré Russian general, notices that Smiley, engaged in

similar contemplation, has an oddly moist face. The policeman
sees this as a kind of sympathetic horror in the presence of death
which he knows only too well, so that it becomes for him as if he
and Smiley are sharing a spiritual perception: 'You wondered what
the hell Christ bothered to die for, if He ever died at all.'

Even when the policeman had first flashed his torch on
Smiley's face he had remarked to himself, as if le Carré had Alec
specifically in mind, that it was, 'unlike your face or mine. It was
not one face. More like a history of the human face.' Remember
what Lucas said about Alec's face when Chewie accidentally hit
him. Le Carré, a much more flamboyant artist in words than Alec
was in gestures, went on to a baroque elaboration of the idea. But
the point had been registered.

Saintliness, although in run-down or distorted form, also
pervades le Carré's depiction of the spying service as a closed
order. The jargon in the Smiley novels is often that of celebrants
or self-denying ascetics. Smiley uses the phrase 'distant churches'
to describe those aims in life that people substitute for their
spiritual hunger, their deprivation of the wholesomeness of divine
worship: 'Party', 'Circus', 'marriage', 'children'.

Smiley, too, has much of the philosophy of Chesterton's Father
Brown with which Alec was conversant: to detect the criminal in
the world, first find the criminal in yourself; to know one's
adversary was to know oneself. Victory, when it came, brought
no satisfaction. The image of Father Brown, with his round
'Norfolk dumpling' face, his clumsy hands, and his similarity
to our underground friend, the mole, took us from spying back to
Hamlet's search, also for his own identity. 'Well said, old mole.
Can'st work i'th'earth so fast?' asks Hamlet at the re-apparition of
his father's ghost.

In *Smiley's People*, as in *Hamlet*, religious imagery abounds,
while Smiley is in many ways a Hamlet in reverse: his low-key,
unglamorous pessimism does not tempt self-destruction. As le
Carré said of Smiley, 'He's also very understanding of human
fallibility; he knows that most of life is led below the water's
surface, and that people are very secretive creatures – secret even
from themselves.'

'Secret even from themselves' is a key phrase to describe Alec.
There were other, more personal, similarities between David

Cornwell and Alec. First of all both shared the insecure family background. Le Carré had passed most of his childhood living like a millionaire pauper. His father was a swindler, a cheat, a gambler and a fraud. 'We all knew,' Cornwell said, 'there was absolutely no money – the bills hadn't been paid, the staff hadn't been paid – we knew there was a lot to hide: women, the past, the present.' Le Carré, like Alec, had been turned into what he called 'fake gentry', arriving in educated middle-class society but feeling almost like a spy. He grew up ashamed of himself: similar to Alec's confused state over his illegitimacy. He turned to storytelling as Alec turned to living other people: to organize narrative (in Alec's case, identity and character) out of chaos, to 'make an art' as he put it, 'through jungles of confusion'. Both also had a very staid, conventional side to their personalities. Le Carré joined the Foreign Office, Alec the navy as an officer, then the theatrical establishment.

So, Cornwell and Alec shared the lonely outsider's sense of looking in. Both had from their fathers an imaginary, confused and yet somewhere deeply real sense of power. In their childhoods, passed in private-boarding-school privilege, both felt at an early age what it was like to lead a double life. It was hardly surprising that both, later on when they were famous, felt alarmed at any intrusion into their privacy and grew fiercely reluctant to discuss – except in their own time and on their own terms – anything of a personal or family nature. As C. P. Snow the novelist remarked, closely aligning le Carré with the actor, he was 'putting on another of his disguises . . . Le Carré is a good deal of a chameleon.' On hearing that someone planned to write a biography of him, Cornwell took legal action to forestall him. Alec did all he could to discourage books being written about him.

But there was also a difference between the insecurity of Alec and that of Cornwell. Cromwell's father had always been there, involved with his son who was unsure whether to love him or hate him; they had got on together but later le Carré had found out his father led a double life and committed fraud on a grand scale. Was it surprising, then, that le Carré should have created the 'Circus', which someone once called 'a chorus of male hates' but which le Carré himself felt, while doing 'terrible things for a good cause', contained an element of nostalgia and redressed a sense of balance?

Alec's aggression towards others, especially men, had always been carefully sublimated, expressed in deliberate courtesy and politesse and a disarming kindness. But the anger was always there, deep down. His father had refused to acknowledge him as his son. I was told by male friends that they never really knew if Alec liked them or not: he made them wary, watchful, on their guard. They loved him, but they feared his disapproval, a withdrawal of his favour, a silence in response to a letter instead of the usual alacritous reply, the absence of the usual Christmas card.

Le Carré experienced great delight in the casting of Alec as Smiley in *Tinker, Tailor, Soldier, Spy*. As with all Alec's best performances, most of which had come out of an intensely personal search, Smiley was a product of Cornwell's own family past, his background, and his own unique imagination. 'I naturally warm to this abstraction of myself ... He's flawed enough, obsessed with the enemy.' He confessed that he had great trepidation in adjusting to the idea that Smiley was to be acted by someone, for while a novelist's characters lived in him as his intimates, and he had 'shared his cell' with them, so to speak, they remained '*undefined* for all that, because, for the novelist, to write about them at all is to hunt them, to pursue an abstraction which, in order to lure him, must remain always a little bit beyond his reach'.

Le Carré says he wrote to Alec to ask him to play Smiley and never seriously considered anyone else. After meeting him it was Alec or nobody. At first, working in rehearsals, Alec seemed to find the part formless, which was not very encouraging. 'So hard to be a sort of geriatric ear,' he commented to the author. He seemed, according to le Carré, worried that everyone he spoke to had a different conception of Smiley. Le Carré found it strange to feel Alec hunting for Smiley as once he had hunted for him, and to realize that 'the journey was as intense for him in *his* medium as it was for me in mine'.

This journey took him on an outing to meet Maurice Oldfield, the former head of MI6. Le Carré had 'wondered', said Alec mysteriously, 'whether I wanted to meet *someone* [i.e. Oldfield].

The three of them had lunch together at the Athenaeum Club. None of the trio reported their conversation.

Alec noted Oldfield's cufflinks, his tiepin and his flamboyantly cut suit. 'Perhaps that was his cover.' He seized on his shoes. Naturally he would deny that he based his interpretation of Smiley on what he called 'that man', not mentioning him by name. Nor did the body of the rest of le Carré's work help much: the illustrated editions which showed a pudgy Smiley with hands in pockets; the heavy spectacles, the many comparisons to other animals, in particular to the mole, of course (but also to owls, toads and frogs). The mole was something of a dead end when it came to acting a character – a character must always be visible, while the distinct quality of the mole was his invisibility.

Konrad Lorenz, the naturalist, discovered when he tried to keep a mole in captivity that, apart from its astounding tunnelling ability and its skill in locating earthworms exactly, it proved most disappointing. It never grew any tamer and never remained above earth longer than it took to devour its prey. Lorenz grew tired of procuring the huge amount of worms it required and when he let it free it sank into the earth as a submarine sinks into the water. Perhaps this again underlines the true nature of Alec's so-called 'invisibility' – it was always visible. The mole is not. Alec was not plump in build, and that worried le Carré too.

It was the remarkable toing and froing nature of Alec's mind that le Carré found awesomely similar to his own idea of Smiley. He could think and read and worry and assimilate all at the same time: 'He has a power of response that is like an open wound, and to protect himself he is capable of a sort of social duck-dive which is an almost physical act of self-obliteration.' (Here, perhaps, was a more dramatic resemblance to Lorenz's mole.)

> When he wishes it can be exactly the way I once described
> Smiley; one of London's meek who do not inherit the earth.
> He can affiliate like nobody I have met; a moment later he
> can be luckless, inconsolable and utterly alone.

So le Carré found that in the absolute and final reckoning it was the intelligence that counted: Alec's authority, his powers of deduction, were never in doubt. 'We had a Poirot; we had a

Father Brown; but we also had a man searching for his own lost innocence among the sins of his companions ... Seeing to the heart of his adversary Smiley–Guinness *becomes* the heart; his interrogations ennoble as well as reveal.'

After the transmission of *Tinker, Tailor* Alec received a note from Oldfield which said, 'I still can't recognise myself.' He knew what the game was, but Alec had not tried to mimic him or impersonate him: 'It's just that you nearly always pick up some little thing when meeting a person like that if you are going to play something in the same area.' Most people thought there *were* remarkable resemblances physically and in manner between Guinness and Oldfield, but only 'maybe'. Alec had ended by wearing glasses which were exactly like Oldfield's and his wig was an exact copy of Oldfield's hair.

Something of Smiley rubbed off, too, on Alec, or so he heightened it for the *Sun* newspaper. He said he thought people followed him all the time and when he went to a restaurant he would choose a table, 'where I could sit with my back to the wall'. He noted entrances and exits for a quick getaway. He would be thinking, 'How do I get out of here?' This was what Alec said in the interview, as if playing up to what he felt was required of him, at the same time disguising that this was how he invariably felt.

Overall, though, with the part of Smiley, Alec played along his habit of refusing to fall into a rut; he avoided the permanent, comfortable role. Smiley has to 'be a blank and stay a blank' and never give away to the person he is interrogating what he wants to know. In this role of the interrogator turned martyr inscrutability was all-important. Now and then, as these two serials unfolded, someone or other asked Smiley a question. The answer might clarify. But Smiley said nothing. As le Carré put it:

I don't know what Guinness does then. Perhaps nothing, perhaps a lot. His arts are quite as arcane as Smiley's. But the effect of his silence is to make you feel, not that Smiley is dodging an answer, but that such questions of him are in rank bad taste. I was reminded, the first time it happened, of myself as a small child asking my father whether God had a beard. He simply affected not to hear. It never crossed my mind that he did not know the answer.   *Guardian*

Thus unexpectedly, le Carré reveals how Alec did, at the peak of his professional prowess, remind him of his father. But this revelation only serves further to emphasize the closeness to each other not that they exactly shared but which they reflected in each other.

The skill of Alec was that he could maintain that ability to be real to himself and think along the right lines, yet much of the acting as Smiley was submerged, so all one sees is a periscope gliding swiftly through dark water. Smiley's greatest gift, said le Carré, was 'the gift of quiet . . . to be silent and to make others talk'.

Some, such as Hugh Carleton Greene, the brother of the novelist and a one-time director-general of the BBC, could only see the dull dark water and thought it was tedious and boring. But this was a submarine mole with a periscope, and the periscope signified danger. Clive James found the series 'turgid' and said that it was 'fun' trying to distinguish Sir Alec's performance from previous film performances. This prompted Alec to write to a friend that the series had a 'really first class press with the exception of that jokey shit Clive James – is that his name? – in the *Observer* whose snyde [*sic*] notice could prove to be thoroughly dishonest'.

Smiley took up many hours of film, but it was never a feature film in the Hollywood definition and therefore did not qualify for nomination for an Oscar. In 1979, the year *Tinker, Tailor* was shown on television, Alec was awarded an honorary Oscar for 'advancing the art of screen acting through a host of memorable and distinguished performances'. This now joined the memorable list of awards Alec had already received, including an Oxford Honorary D. Litt. in 1978 (and he was to receive the coveted Hamburg Shakespeare prize, awarded to a British citizen for outstanding success in the arts, in 1985, and be made a Companion of Honour in 1994).

'We are among false biographers, born for the shifty life, the triple personality, sellers of false information and fantasies, sketching their way along, living by the gamble,' V. S. Pritchett had written in his review of *Tinker, Tailor*. It was Smiley's ambiguous motivation, his introspection, his obsession with the great game of not being yourself that would seem to make him so close, as a fictional creation, to Alec in real life. With this mimetic desire of Alec satisfied, fully realized, the autobiographical search was ready to move on.

25. *Either a Man, the Supernatural or an Illusion*

The Church was always there to provide a safety net, ready to save Alec from the 'degrading servitude' of being a child of his own time. He strongly supported Malcolm Muggeridge when he converted to Roman Catholicism in August 1979. Muggeridge, like Alec, approved of Pope John Paul's firm stand on abortion and contraception ('like Orwell Muggeridge had a lifelong distaste for contraception which had nothing to do with religion,' writes his biographer Richard Ingrams). Mother Teresa wrote to Muggeridge, 'Jesus – God is the one in love with you . . . Christ has created you because he wanted you.' Alec wrote to Muggeridge how his reconciliation with Rome had made his day – and how much he rejoiced in it, while Graham Greene told Muggeridge, 'I hope you make a better Catholic than I have done.'

Other destinies still beckoned. Alec feared the sequels *The Empire Strikes Back* (1980) and *Return of the Jedi* (1983) but out of personal loyalty to Lucas made token appearances in Obi-Wan's visitations to guide the destiny of Luke Skywalker. It was fitting his ghost presences should round off the story. 'There won't be a third series,' he said, of Smiley. 'Or if there is, I won't be in it.' He played briefly in an all-star disaster, *Raise the Titanic!*, 'a frail but determined survivor'. After this the next film in which he appeared was *Lovesick* (1983), a light-hearted film with Dudley Moore, in which Alec acted the part of Sigmund Freud. He was back to the safe bet, the portrayal of a genius.

He posed for a photograph in one of Freud's most famous poses and the impersonation was astonishing. Perhaps what was even more remarkable was the difference. The real Freud had a more aggressive tilt of the head. The man was clearly more of a monomaniac than ever Alec could be. Freud's eyes were more certain, almost messianic, his brow unfurrowed. Here was the dogmatist of sex that Carl Jung found so disturbing. Alec's eyes as the great psychoanalyst were shifty, cautious, his pose more passive, his forehead worried, with deep frowning. By nature he probably inclined more to Jung than to Freud, yet he had made up like Freud for his last appearance as the unidentified Guest (the psychiatrist) in *The Cocktail Party*. Both impersonations bore a strong resemblance to Andrew Geddes, photographed at the same advanced age that Alec played these roles. Any doubts remaining that Alec had about Geddes being his father should have by now disappeared. Did Alec himself own the Geddes photograph? An unanswerable mystery for the unauthorized biographer.

A Passage to India (1985) saw David Lean's return to filming after fourteen years. When he had made *Ryan's Daughter* the American film critics, led by Pauline Kael, had so savaged this romantic story (in which Alec had turned down the part of the Priest, which was played by Trevor Howard) that Lean, hurt, had withdrawn from film-making: 'One's awfully easily shaken', he said later. After his recovery Lean spent years of preparation on *A Passage to India*, which became in some ways his own Kwai Bridge, the ultimate gesture of his uncertain obsession and tunnel vision. In it his desire to control every aspect of the film's creation turned into a parody of itself. Although Lean's location manager was looking for something that 'couldn't be built, only by God', Lean had a whole Indian city built in India.

Perhaps the real shortcoming of *A Passage to India* was to stem first from its having no romantic hero and was itself, as were Forster's other novels, a work of flawed vision. The real hero of Lean's *A Passage to India* – the film-maker himself – was manifestly outside the film, which is why a *South Bank Show* about the making of the film emerged as possibly more gripping than the film. 'I'm fascinated by these nuts,' Lean had said of Lawrence of Arabia and Colonel Nicholson; but sweet and kindly Aziz, the Muslim doctor, could never quite equal this pair; while the distorted rape vision of Miss Quested had hardly the right possible qualities for visual inflation on the Lean scale.

'I'm not sure that actors like me very much,' had said Lean. 'I've got to make them measure up to the imagination' – and by imagination he meant the script, which in his Quaker-like sensibility came to wield, when fixed upon, a kind of literal inflexible authority like the Bible. Some actors accepted such authority without complaint. Charles Laughton, who played in Lean's *Hobson's Choice*, never balked at his control. Lean preferred 'no-nonsense' people.

Lean always wanted the same faces; he needed the same sparring partners. How would he fit Alec into *A Passage to India*? Here we go back to shades of Alec's earlier skill of impersonation, to his grotesque Fagin, no less. The answer was the most unlikely role of Professor Godbole, the Indian sage and teacher who befriends Mrs Moore and becomes some kind of mystical chorus, commenting obliquely and enigmatically on the dislocation of soul and body in British India.

Again, as in *Kwai*, although with a less successful result, the actor and the director had an uneasy time together. Alec, as viewed in the *South Bank Show* of the making of the film, grew visibly up in arms when being moved around by Lean as a pawn. (With typical understatement he reported at one moment, 'It's not a problem, but I've just got to make up my mind.') The difficulty was over filming Godbole's startling appearance at the railway station when, just before the trial of Aziz, Mrs Moore departs on the train. Alec had to be placed exactly, and them move 'two foot to his left'. His rebellious spirit rose. 'I hate being fixed like a specimen.' He conceded, perhaps in not altogether good, or convincing, faith, that Lean's genius lay not in what he said to you but 'When he is stuck – visually stuck, and he will say "Come and look through the camera" – you see his vision'.

Godbole was scheduled to end the film with a bizarre Hindu song and dance, part of the muddled eclectic baggage that Forster carried with him all his life. As Peggy Ashcroft described it:

> There was an evening when he danced on an enormous stone circle (of perilous narrowness) clashing cymbals of over four feet circumference. The dance was partly rehearsed, partly extemporised, it lasted well over any expected limit, when finally 'Cut' brought it to an end, the Indian 'crowd' of some hundreds, who had watched breathlessly, burst into applause.

But when he had seen Alec's rendering of this dance, Lean cut it. 'Only some of the mystery of Godbole was revealed in the final version,' commented Ashcroft sadly. Alec complained that it had been taken out, at the same time thanking Lean for taking it out: 'Probably good judgement on his part, even if it left me presenting Professor Godbole as a comic-cuts character without the oriental mystery.' How could this be good judgement?

A Passage to India, or in other words Lean scenery without the hero-colonels Lawrence or Nicholson, was a muddle. Lean, as a man and a film-maker, needed certainties and down-to-earth realities: formed as an editor in the early documentary Balcon regime at Ealing, he had felt initial panic at the ambiguities, hints and half-defined characters. He could not cope with the central incident of the novel, the incident in the Marabar Caves. 'The rape is *either* a man, or the supernatural, or an illusion. And even if I know! My writing mind therefore is a blur here,' Forster wrote to his friend, the scholar Lowes Dickinson.

This was not the stuff of a David Lean picture. Nor was the muddle of Forster's later and sounder assessment: 'I tried to show that India is an unexplainable muddle by introducing an unexplained muddle – Miss Quested's experience in the cave. When asked what happened there, *I don't know.*'

Apart from the incompatible Lean and Forster, Alec tried sensibly, with sound dramatic instinct, to inject some humour – which was one of Forster's saving qualities – into the film's ponderous, elephantine progress. If his performance did sometimes border on a Peter Sellers caricature, so much the better for that. ('There must be people across the world willing to swear on oath that . . . Godbole is played not by Sir Alec Guinness but by Peter Sellers,' wrote Sellers's biographer.) At least someone was viewing the proceedings with a measure of subversive wit. The ironic attitude of prayer adopted by Godbole on Mrs Moore's departure is one of the film's most memorable moments.

'David is a man of genius cocooned with outrageous charm.' Alec's summing-up of Lean has the ring of Antony's words in *Julius Caesar* just after the murder of Caesar: 'For Brutus is an honourable man.' Yet it was to this man, Alec admitted, that he owed his film career. Such were the hostile yet paradoxical feelings towards the authority, or father-figure, that Lean represented. With sound judgement Alec disliked the film.

He rang up Peggy Ashcroft, who was in New York, in the

middle of the night: 'It's a disaster and I'm a failure,' he declared; but American critics and public loved it as a slow-moving feast to the eye and for the way it echoed the hollow anti-British-colonialism sentiments of *Gandhi*; it also focused on rape and upon racial issues in a simple-minded and even muddled way that somehow and unintentionally seemed to mirror American attitudes. Yet the end was an unforgivable travesty of the novel.

One of the last social contacts Alec had with Lean was when they were invited by Margaret Thatcher to 10 Downing Street with a 'great flurry of showbiz and media folk' to a pre-dinner drink. Lean had been next to him when they were propelled towards their hostess whose effect on Alec was mesmeric. Lean, he said, 'kept plucking at my sleeve in a state of high excitement, hissing between clenched teeth, "She is all woman, all woman, all woman."' Alec added, 'And heavens, with his experience he would have known.'

Lean's memorial service, at St Paul's, brought him mixed feelings. He cringed at the star-studded attendance and the military band playing the *River Kwai* 'Colonel Bogey'. Melvyn Bragg in his 'beautifully spoken' address made 'a snide remark of David's about me which caused a few discreet titters'. (Presumably about Alec being the 'most knotted-up man' he knew.)

Alec turned his disdain on the titterers. On balance he felt mistrustful towards Lean because of his unpleasantness in latter years. He depended too much on sycophants, while Alec needed someone 'with whom I could laugh'. Alec, it could be said, had his fair share of sycophants with whom he could laugh. He had the strong temptation to become more and more of a terrible snob. We have already noted his disdainful treatment of Merula and Matthew on occasions, in spite of profuse expressions of love towards them. In an article he wrote for the *Spectator* now he was seventy, Alec quoted Disraeli: 'Something unpleasant is coming when men are anxious to speak the truth.' I think he was trying to check his own tongue as much as other people's.

*

At seventy, Alec played his last major Shakespearean role on the stage, one he had said earlier he hated for its maudlin associations. 'Shylock wasn't my idea. I've never been ambitious to play the role. There are very few roles that I have been ambitious to play in recent years,' he said in 1984, when almost in the same week he reported saying to his wife, 'I wish I'd played Shylock.' When Eileen Atkins had suggested it to Patrick Garland for the Chichester Festival of 1984 with herself as Portia, as described earlier, he had tuned in well to the bush telegraph. Guinness had to face the reality that he was getting on. 'There is a foolhardiness in the old which makes the tactlessness of the young look very circumspect,' he wrote in the same article. Even so he refused to disguise himself as he had as Fagin. He made up for the role with only a beard, some eyeliner and the spirit gum that flattened and sleekened his ears against his skull.

When, in the summer of 1981, he and Merula visited Israel he had remarked upon the strange characters in Jerusalem with black and silver embroidered robes and red, fox-fur hats. This became his mental image for Shylock. He worried over the racial implications of the part but then thought, 'What the hell, Shakespeare is bigger than any temporary racist issues!' In terms of its length Shylock is a small part. Compared to other great roles in Shakespeare he is an enlarged character part, for he appears in only five scenes, one of which is little more than a fragment.

As Shakespeare's best-known character part, Shylock is in many ways like Fagin: he has acquired a life of his own in the popular imagination. Both sprang fully formed, one speculates, from the nightmares of their progenitors' family shame and financial loss. Shylock emerged from the unquelled fears that were once the centre of reality for the son of the prosperous Stratford burgher and town mayor fallen on hard times.

But, as with his earlier attempts at Shakespeare's more passionate roles, Alec went for one aspect of the character that he could control intellectually. He contrived to round out a 'humour', as in the form of a comedy character devised by Ben Jonson, rather than to opt for the whole, many-sided disruptive creation. He was true to form even now, at the age of seventy, and in bringing what Simon Callow calls his 'huge mental force' to bear on Shylock when he was thinking himself into the character 'he eschewed orchestration of all the emotions'.

The Hebrew was what Alec singled out for close attention. His Shylock's experience of the race's suffering had become a deep and wide scar. He incorporated the chip, the enormous resentment Alec once had on his own shoulder and set it bemoaning the Jewish moneylender's lot. Again he brought to the role something very personal and autobiographical.

Shylock's identity *is* his moneylending, just as the black girl out of the ghetto becomes a blues singer, and this becomes her identity. The same could be said of Alec: his deprivation, his sense of shame over it, his secret withholding of it and the other secrets had *made* him into an actor. Deprivation casts its own inescapable mould.

When Alec sat cross-legged on the carpet on the set, when he took the weighing machine, he had assumed the essence of the Jewish moneylender. It was an 'extraordinary revelation of extreme despair', one critic called it, filled in with telling details such as the way he would shape curious little pursings or pouts with his mouth when he wanted to make a point in argument.

'The central element in Guinness's performance,' wrote Irving Wardle, was 'its sense of exclusion.' This was right on target. Wardle noted how, externally, Alec showed the Jew's social affability and modesty while only at danger points did his face turn stony and his eyes burn into the enemy. As with Hamlet's revenge, the rage was muted: the 'huge powers' invoked were somewhere else. He allowed himself one fearsome gesture: placing his ear next to Antonio's heart before plunging his knife into it. But all agreed that the 'crack' when it had come after the departure of Jessica, was tremendously effective. He hugged himself, wailing.

In Jerusalem Alec had been moved by the scenes at the Wailing Wall. For Simon Callow, he himself became 'a weeping wall'. A wall is static: it moves the feelings by what it suggests and symbolizes. The thoughts, memories, have to be intellectually already there in the mind of the beholder. After the breakdown Alec returned to his mask. And even in the expression of the extreme despair he showed an indirectness, a subtlety, which disguised it: as Polonius tells Reynaldo, 'By indirections find directions out.' This was another performance of indirections.

Alec made points of contact with that first production of *The Merchant* in which he had appeared as Lorenzo nearly fifty years before. Directed by Gielgud and designed by the Motleys it had looked wonderful, 'because every sort of kitchen rag was dyed and used', Alec said later. Although he had temporarily stopped smoking three weeks before rehearsals began, he now started again. Garland observed, 'His cigarette was balanced, as always, on a slightly Pisan course and several centimetres of ash tenaciously held their ground.' He worked with his usual concentration: how else does an actor of such name and stature contrive, as he did in this production, to enter unnoticed in the most important scene of the play and discover himself to the audience by the sound of whetting his knife?

After performances, reported Leslee Udwin, who played Jessica, there was always a young man waiting to go out to supper with him. They may not have had an all-male cast, as Alec had first hoped, but Udwin found 'the bisexual thing was present, part of the atmosphere – but suggested, not revealed, not shown'. She found his performance brilliant, but it never varied, 'all set, like a master-craftsman. He learnt his lines early on. He brought the audiences to his talent, to his role.' They had a clash over him making a cut in a Jessica and Shylock scene, and when she stood up to him the director overruled her. She found Alec cold and aloof for the most part, but surprisingly complimentary and encouraging in the first night postcard he sent her. Princess Margaret came to the premiere: 'Patrick Garland made us curtsey and rehearse our bows.' One night during the run Alec invited Udwin together with other leading players to dinner at Kettlebrook Meadows. She noticed his Bafta award on a shelf in the guest toilet. During dinner Merula interrupted a story he was telling. 'He imperiously stopped her. I was incredibly shocked by this. Instinctively my heart went out to her. She was quite gentle and meek.'

Alec did make another late attempt at Shakespeare tragedy, not a fully exposed stage attempt but on radio. John Tydeman, head of radio drama at the BBC, had wanted to do a Welsh Lear with Richard Burton and surround him with Welsh characters: perhaps on the principle of what Elizabeth Taylor once said to Burton – 'Trouble with the Welsh is that they think everybody's Welsh, even Death.' Burton might have made a wonderful Lear. But this did not work out.

Instead, Tydeman managed to persuade Alec to give his Lear. Alec demurred, saying he had not got the weight. Tydeman then convinced Alec he did not need the power to rant and rave and in the end Alec reluctantly agreed.

Gloucester was played by Cyril Cusack. He and Alec had first acted together forty-five years before on the eve of war at the Globe Theatre in the Michel Saint-Denis production of *The Cherry Orchard*. It had never opened. Alec turned up for the first rehearsal with a 'frightfully smart Gucci bag', according to Tydeman. He waddled over to the piano, put down the bag, opened it and took out his pair of extremely chic Gucci slippers, removed his shoes, put on the slippers, all this done meticulously. From the corner of the room Cusack watched.

Next morning Cusack arrived at rehearsals carrying a Marks & Spencer's bag. He arrived before Alec and came into the rehearsal room. At this juncture Alec arrived, stopped, watching Cusack. Cyril crossed to the piano, put down his carrier bag, reached inside for a crumpled and dilapidated old pair of bedroom slippers, then, having removed his shoes, proceeded to put them on.

'Ah-h-ah-h!' responded Alec in the slightly perplexed tone of exhalation, as this peculiar mimetic-envy exercise by two non-upstagers in not upstaging each other came to an end. In fact both actors had the same weight and warmly admired each other. They were natural brothers and later were to play the brothers in *Little Dorrit*. Cusack once said he recognized in Alec his 'familiar', in the metaphysical sense.

The radio Lear never worked for Alec. Tydeman tried to encourage him to 'let go' in the storm scenes, but he held back in a controlled way, 'playing it from within a safe perimeter'. He created a hedge around him, especially in the expression of Lear's sexual disgust which came across as unfeeling and strangely vocalized. One found it hard to believe that Lear ever expressed his feelings like Alec. He loved working with Tydeman, he said, but afterwards he listened only to the last fifteen minutes: 'It slightly shocked me. I'm always a bit shocked at hearing myself. It just doesn't sound what one quite intended.'

At another time Jack Gold, who had directed Alec in the film of *Little Lord Fauntleroy* as the crisply unsentimental Earl of Dorincourt, the boy's guardian, had asked Alec to play Lear on television, but Alec had withdrawn. Alec had been disappointed in

Little Lord Fauntleroy, which had not, he felt, been the fault of Gold – or only occasionally so – but the effect of the ridiculously tight schedule of shooting. 'I haven't seen one frame of it,' was his public comment; but in fact he had seen it all, and now and then was 'a bit embarrassed', or so he informed an intimate.

The Lear idea went back to 1982. Alec heard that Graham Crowden was performing the role at the Bristol Old Vic, and he travelled to Bristol to see it. Peter Copley was playing Gloucester. After the performance Alec took some of the cast including Copley out to supper: they had a table at Renato's and here, shortly after they arrived, the review artiste Danny La Rue, also playing that week at Bristol, came into the restaurant with his entourage and sat down at an adjoining table.

'Suddenly,' said Copley, 'the atmosphere was electric. Like two old queens at proximate tables, ruffling their feathers and competing.'

'I'd love to play in *Lear*,' pouted La Rue, 'I'd like to play *all* the daughters.'

In the end Alec decided not to play Lear: he felt he could not match what was required. Afterwards he went into what Copley termed 'a strange withdrawal'.

26. Friendships Both Jealous and Altruistic

> The doorbell rang and she let in two surprise visitors, Stephen and Natasha Spender. They came on like Burton and Taylor, a couple of copper-bottomed literary primadonnas, quickly sizing up the company and deciding Ken [Tynan] was the star.
>
> **Peter Nichols**

Given the depth and breadth of Alec's involvement over the years with literary figures, it was perhaps inevitable he should now become a celebrity in this field. He wrote the bulk of *Blessings in Disguise* before or just after his seventieth birthday. John Mortimer, when he reviewed *Blessings in Disguise* for the *Sunday Times* in the year following Shylock, while admiring Alec's style and ease, believed 'he and his book are clearly happier when describing other people ... rich and strange enough to allow the central character to slip out of the limelight'. For Mortimer one passage was worth the price of the book:

> Coming off the stage as Yakov the butler in *The Seagull* [in 1936] Guinness had won a laugh and a round of applause. In the wings he met Edith Evans and looked at her proudly. The next night there was no laugh and no hand on his exit and he asked Miss Evans, who was again waiting in the wings, for her explanation. 'You're trying too hard', she told him. 'You didn't know how you got it in the first place. But it's natural to you, one day you will find it again. Take it lightly. But when it comes back make a note of what you were feeling *inside*.'

For most readers *Blessings in Disguise* confirmed Alec's skill by showing that autobiography could now be his ultimate disguise as well as tease. The master magician or self-transformer could perform just as well in print as on stage or film. But certain of the critics, perhaps masters or seasoned observers of the same game of constructive deceit themselves, found this method irritating and perhaps also, not being Christians, blamed his Roman conversion. 'No wonder, perhaps, that the inner serenity which his faith and his marriage have given him,' wrote J. W. Lambert in his review in *The Times*, 'should, at least to this outsider, have seemed to produce in his acting a sense of a man with a built-in halo, a look, whether in an Alan Bennett play or in a John le Carré creepie on television, of an Ineffable, not to say patronising, Something.'

Blessings in Disguise deservedly became a bestseller and was reissued together with Alec's two later books after his death. True, it did descend at times into an orgy of self-effacement, yet the lasting impression it created of its protagonist – the imitative skills apart – was that he was a model of attractive self-doubt. He wanted to make friends, dispel hostility, be accepted; and, after all, was not making friends a perfectly reasonable and normal aspiration? As one reviewer wrote, this book would make him many more. But there was in Alec still, as Hamlet says, 'that which passes show'.

As a schoolboy Alec had read *Great Expectations*, *Oliver Twist* and *David Copperfield*, and in the navy *Bleak House*, but his enthusiasm for reading Dickens had died down in later years. In late middle age he became more an Anthony Trollope man and an admirer of Edith Wharton. When he had turned seventy, Christine Edzard approached him to play William Dorrit in her film of *Little Dorrit*. He liked the script but found it very difficult to read the book; it took him three or four attempts to get into it, although the idea of the debtors' prison appealed to him as an apposite image for our own age. As he joked, 'We all might be sitting in the next Marshalsea.'

Dorrit is the most complex of all Dickens's central figures. Comic and tragic at one and the same time, he is shifty, distraught and above all without shame, continuously reminding us of his own peculiar brand of self-delusion. Because of this, Dorrit has been judged closest to being based on Dickens's own father who, when Dickens was twelve, was imprisoned in the Marshalsea for debt. As the whole novel revolves round this central scarring experience, as reflected through Dorrit's daughter Amy, one might be looking for bitterness and anger, qualities that Alec had never shown himself powerful at portraying, yet had continually within himself. Dickens, with affecting compassion, presented the character of Dorrit as a helpless victim rather than as agent of the awful circumstances which had been inflicted upon his family. Dickens's aggression had been redirected into dealing a satirical onslaught on the powerful social influences that affect the lives of his characters: religion and the law, using the popularly distorted idea of Providence – 'Nobody's Fault' – as a particular target.

In playing Dorrit, therefore, it was the mobilization of the passive sides of Alec's gift that were called for, above all his ability to show the set of weaknesses revolving round a particular form of deception. Christine Edzard said, 'William Dorrit is all about self-delusion.' Alec commented:

> William Dorrit is a very complicated man. To start with . . .
> I couldn't make head nor tail of him – he was so up and
> down: he could have been an actor, he could have been all
> sorts of things. What appealed to me was the variety of it –
> some of it amused me very much.   *Guardian*

Like himself, he might have said, 'a very complicated man'. Edzard gave him confidence in the grasp she showed of the character, and pointed out he should remember that Dickens was a reporter and had been a journalist: that what he wrote was what he saw and what he heard. This became a good lead, for although Alec realized how Dickens exaggerated and 'tipped things up', to understand that there was a reality behind Dorrit brought him the key to the character:

> Of course it's supposed to be one side of Dickens' father, in
> the way that Micawber is supposed to be another side, but I
> imagine William Dorrit is the closer picture, because it's a
> more varied character, and not so comic. He's a very mon-
> strous man in some ways.

To show the different viewpoints of Amy Dorrit and Arthur Clennam, Edzard said to me in 1989 that she conceived the film in two parts and she intended to shoot some of the scenes twice with two different versions of the script. For instance, to Clennam the Marshalsea Prison would be no more than a slum and Dorrit

an old faded failure giving himself airs. But for Amy, in her view
of her father, the beauty and pain were first and foremost apparent,
so she would see the family room in the prison as much bigger:
the geraniums would be in flower, the curtains much brighter and
more elaborate.

This approach at first puzzled Alec: as he pointed out, 'Saying
the same lines with some missing, or words slightly altered, is very
difficult to hold in the head.' When they rehearsed it carefully,
and always shot the differences in sequence, then Alec fell 'into it
in the most natural way'. The important thing was that Alec had
built up and retained trust in his director. Christine Edzard made
him feel secure in those areas where other directors, perhaps
especially David Lean, could upset him. He called her, with her
tactful, easy way, 'a joy to work with'. Later he was to tell Alan
Bennett she was the best film director he had worked with. She
used little camera movement, so the camera gave him a unique
scope for showing how important small things could be. Alec
knew, Edzard told me, 'exactly where his little finger would be in
relation to the edge of the frame. He knows exactly where he is
and how much you see.' He was content to leave this to the
director, although sometimes he might wander over and ask,
'Where are my knees?' Edzard also noticed that she knew no actor
who could switch off so quickly and conclusively as Alec did at
the end of shooting a scene when she called 'Cut'.

Not only did the director and her collaborators inspire his
confidence (and like most actors he refused to watch the nightly
'rushes' of the day's filming), but he found himself loving the
atmosphere of this unusual enterprise, most of which was filmed
in tiny studios in Rotherhithe in south-east London. Everything
here was originated by the director, her producer-husband Richard
Goodwin, his partner John Brabourne and their staff – 'the crew
they have around them', Alec called it, 'and the whole ramshack
oddity of it: the fact that it's on the Thames, down from Tower
Bridge, with the river flowing, the tide coming in and out – that
gives it all a curious life – I think that has something to do with
it. I've never enjoyed anything so much.'

He also respected the authenticity of what was created, something he said he had never felt so powerfully before in a film. This

impressed him in the detail applied to everything, so that the costumes, to take one example, were hand-sewn.

'Walking into the Marshalsea Yard, for a moment I had an uncomfortable feeling that I had walked back 150 years, into something which was actually there and like that.'

Three and a half months was a long time and so it became something of a way of life. It had its exacting side, as Alec expressed it: 'In the part of William Dorrit I probably explored unpleasant things in myself – faced up to my own fecklessness and weakness and shelving important decisions, which is part of the character.'

Here, as at other times, he owned up to small faults as a kind of propitiatory ceremony performed so that, as always, the inner core of privacy could remain untouched. The instinctive covering up of himself from himself went on. This was how he had learned to deal with himself.

'It's very easy to caricature Dickens's characters into a kind of papier mâché figures, and great fun to do. But to find the reality in them, and the reality he observed,' Edzard told me, 'is quite salutary – and once something is real you've got to find it in yourself.'

Edzard gently, and with perceptive objectivity, encouraged him. She found the dialogue lent itself well to his needs and to his 'discreet type of diction – his slightly precious way of putting things in a tiny space'. He asked her for images and suggestions – 'What [Alec's] Dorrit made me think of,' she pointed out to me, was Charlie Chaplin eating his boots in *The Gold Rush*. 'He was by nature the essence of forever seeking inside himself to find the truth of his character. I've seen few actors do it as honestly. He had to be autobiographical – uncomfortably close to himself – and he did it with real respect for truth and sometimes with anguish.'

This probably did not go down well with Alec who was not a Chaplin admirer. Yet the grandiose vision of the self-deluded man, his bafflement at reality, both were perfectly handled by Alec – from within. Was not self-delusion by now a part of him, as it could be part of everyone, perhaps increasing as he grew older? Possibly so, as he sometimes unguardedly revealed in some self-reassuring pieces he published later in the *Spectator*. But if he clothed and hid himself in words, he could still explore the insight and empathy he had with the victim. Dorrit is yet another of those helpless people who are life's casualties, this time writ large and flamboyantly. Dorrit is also the dupe of himself. He is Abel Drugger from *The Alchemist* multiplied by a hundred.

The truth Alec reveals in this performance was uncomfortably close to what had been inflicted on him when he was young by Agnes de Cuffe: it radiated an unconscious femininity. It was even absurdly camp in places, as if at heart Dorrit was an old queen. He may not have wanted to know this himself, but he wanted to draw on and did reveal what his mother had done to him. He did this without any inhibition or restraining factor imposed by his intellect, or by shyness or self-awareness. His sensibility nourished the role, feeding it with everything from the past he could muster:

> It's been very swift on the floor – we haven't had to hang around for much lighting changes – that's what's been marvellous. I just sit and daydream and wonder if I know my lines for the next scene. The most I've ever done is look at scenes ahead and revise lines. I always learn the whole thing before I start. That's what I've done on my journeys here in the car, learning lines. Nothing else, I can't read – I can read newspapers briefly, but I can't concentrate on anything else. At least in a film that's as long in the making as this you become familiar with certain people who are constantly here, and you fall into each other's way of working easily if there's plenty of time.   **BBC Radio**

If his imagination and his sense of shame and his mother's self-delusion and all these personal qualities were so carefully focused on revealing Dorrit through his own experience as broadly as possible – and in a kind of muted narcissism, a pantomime-damish sexual self-sufficiency which Dorrit often seems to exude – the actor's intellect was also working during the filming at full stretch on the practical, technical aspects of the character.

Edzard told me how she found Alec very controlled in everything he did. He timed everything with precision so that he would know, for instance, when eating, when to put down his fork, when to swallow a mouthful. Everything was remembered, nothing left to chance. Of course something might occasionally throw him off balance, such as a sudden noise off or on the set. Edzard discovered he used everything. Curiously enough, too, he never blinked in front of the camera. 'Very few people can do that. He knows everything is switched on, and his concentration is total. It's like playing a finely tuned instrument.'

Towards the other actors, Edzard observed, he behaved with considerable courtesy, yet he seemed not 'someone who gets a lot out of other actors'. He would not pick up a spontaneous movement or gesture and do something unexpected with it. With him every little effect had been worked out, then created with the know-how and skill to appear spontaneous. 'Never is he doing things that he doesn't know about or doesn't want to happen. And if he did, he wouldn't have it.'

She found him quite remote, and that he could put people off, but although it might seem to be so, it was not selfishness on his part or lack of generosity to others, it came from the intensity of his concentration. He didn't give the others advice. Of Sarah Pickering who played Amy, he said, 'She was determined to help me.'

It was Alec who suggested that Cyril Cusack play Frederick Dorrit, William's brother. Alec perceived 'a kind of similarity in the shape of our faces'. He was now seventy-one years old while Cusack, whose performance in this film was outstanding, was seventy-five. Each of them appeared to be, or acted, men in or barely past their prime.

William Dorrit has a brief but moving death scene. As Alec commented in 1986, 'I can't think how many times I've died ... Never very well. This time, earlier in the year, I was *at* a deathbed – the first time ever, [it had been his mother's, who died on 17 February 1986] and, it's awful to say this now, but I couldn't help absorbing it for future use ... I'm never going to be caught out again ...'

Agnes had something about her of William Dorrit's 'forlorn gentility': in company with Frederick Dorrit he was 'so courtly, condescending, and benevolently conscious of a position'. He was also always afraid on the Continent and in London, when he had left prison, that the secret of his past would emerge.

Actors have their own vanity. Derek Jacobi, playing Clennam, betrayed on occasions to their affectionate director (or so she told me) a need to please visually, to seduce, to be loved. He worried about his hair, or whether or not his trousers were too tight. Alec's over-riding vanity was intellectual: his mortification was manifest on losing a line, something which never bothered the Cambridge-educated Jacobi. Alec became obsessed with how he would manage the long and final speech of Dorrit towards the end of the second part when, in the midst of his wealth at the Merdles' dinner table, his over-burdened mind reverts to his former life in the Marshalsea:

> Welcome to the Marshalsea: The space is-ha-limited; but you will find it apparently grow larger after a time, ladies and gentlemen – and the air is, hmmm, all things considered, very good. Blows over the Surrey hills, over the Surrey hills ... Those who are habituated to the-ha-Marshalsea are pleased to call me its Father.

He does this movingly, in spite of every older actor's fear of 'stumbling around for words. Pray God they'll shoot me before I get to that stage.'

Dickens had 'never dared tell anyone, not even his wife and children,' wrote the critic John Carey, 'about his father's incarceration in the Marshalsea, or his own childhood degradation as a "little labouring hind" in a boot-blacking factory'. When William Dorrit lets out the shameful secret of his past at the grand banquet he succumbs to a nightmare that pursued Dickens for years. Similarly a nightmare had pursued Alec, so its purging through Dorrit must have been an important stage of his autobiographical quest.

'One finds things in oneself,' Alec had said many times when asked if he thought of the character he was playing as someone apart. The shame and secrets of his early life, however well guarded for the energy they could supply, were past their prime. Had he the self-knowledge, or had he been given the grace, to own and forgive the homosexual side of his nature? If so, he was not going to tell us. He spent fourteen happy weeks of 1985 filming *Little Dorrit*; it formed a natural background against which to camouflage himself during, that same year, the publication of *Blessings in Disguise*.

*

On Monday 20 June 1988 fell the golden wedding anniversary of Alec and Merula. Many of their joint friends went back to even before their wedding. They had met Peggy Ashcroft fifty-three years before in Gielgud's production of *Romeo and Juliet*; Margaret Harris, the designer of Motleys, a year or two earlier; Gielgud himself. The strength of Merula's family background had been a great support to Alec, his much-loved father-in-law in particular, whom Alec would often quote on growing old and not being 'past it'. He might reflect now on the past, such as how, when a young actor, he had often thought of old actors, 'Oh God, I wish some of them would die off. Now I'm an old actor I don't feel quite the same about it.'

For many years, they had, as Merula said, 'been opposite in all things . . . he was a shopping addict whilst I hated shopping' and so on. They were Mr and Mrs Jack Sprat. 'Grounds for divorce' was a household joke; but now they were more Darby and Joan, soon to be helping each other along on sticks.

Merula had rarely been photographed but she had been described as 'an intensely shy woman' who had been for many years 'behind the Guinness boom'. It may again be noted that their marriage to outside eyes had always been a close one whatever its hidden realities. Alec's public affectionate and grateful references to his wife with the years had increased. *Blessings in Disguise* was dedicated to her. So were *My Name Escapes Me* and *A Positively Final Appearance*. She had been content to remain in the background, painting and tending to pleasures quieter than her husband's public life, while it was her more gentle virtues that had always shone through him, and which he had celebrated.

'I think reclusive is a bit strong,' she said of herself (*Daily Mail*, 30 October 1992). 'I am simply a quiet person who prefers to stay in the country. I've been like that since I was a little girl. We only like to see a few people at a time.' Her painting studio had become her private territory; Alec did not intrude. But did he encourage her painting? 'He usually comes round to it. But I think he'd prefer me to be cooking.' (Pause) 'Well, I don't particularly like cooking.' More guilty laughter.

In 1992 under the name Merula Salaman, she published *The Kingdom of Heaven is Like*, a book of twenty-four of her oil paintings illustrating Christ's parables, an enchanting collection revealing a sweetness of vision and a child's innocent eye for landscape. She painted them when Alec was in India making *A Passage to India*. John le Carré said, 'Her paintings are full of magic, comedy and love.' Alan Bennett wrote the introduction.

Alec never had reservations about the judgement she made of his own work: 'She doesn't have to be critical. She is very, very tactful and knows when comments might be injurious. But I know what she is thinking, and when she finally tells me I half listen, half resent it. But maybe she only drops one word about the whole performance and she is usually right.'

Over their long married life until their deaths in 2000 one is left perhaps with a picture of them having grown in some ways similar to their mentors Tyrone and Judy Guthrie, radiating on visitors an easy and gracious eccentricity. Attentive to the needs of others they would depart for Mass on Sunday morning and tell their weekend guests, 'Back in an hour.' The guests might notice the Bafta award in the toilet, an Oscar casually tucked away on the mantelpiece, so 'one' saw it if 'one' wanted to see it. Later they might be asked if they would like to take the goat for a walk. The mild gentle evenings would be loved most of all. Merula and Alec were a devoted and loyal couple, and she had possessed the breadth of spirit and quality of resolution to embrace the complex and not always easy nature of her husband. 'One of the few really good people I know,' says Eileen Atkins of her, 'who is also huge fun.'

Can we reach into Guinness in the solitude of his last years? We can try. His garden, his modest acreage of Kettlebrook Meadows, its remote, buried quality off the beaten track and yet its very cosy, familiar and still English quality, can tell us something. Later in his life there had been an increasing roar of traffic from the new A3 dual carriageway cutting through the hill only a few hundred yards from the garden. 'The river is within us,' wrote Eliot in *The Dry Salvages*. 'Drift, wait and obey': Kipling's words about when your 'Daeman' is in charge, apply, Alec thought, to Merula who often did so. She surprised him by planting a kiss on Jim Callaghan's cheek when she had never met him before, saying she loved him. 'That boy can't play tennis,' she observed crossly of Tim Henman after seeing him serve a double fault, yet in finding out it was Henman added, 'I like him.' Alec's gentleness towards her came out in his writing (to redress the balance perhaps of the rough treatment he could mete out). In one sensitive passage he compared their long marriage to the courtship of ravens. The male slid about and fell all over the place, until she got the idea and joined in. Then they stayed together for the rest of their lives.

The year before, in late 1988, Alec had agreed to appear in *A Walk in the Woods* by Lee Blessing, an American two-hander based quite closely on certain aspects of the arms-control treaty signed between Russia and America. The play had been successful on Broadway earlier in the year, receiving two Tony Award nominations and an Outer Circle Critics award. It was a warm-hearted, almost sentimental germ of a play about that most elusive of subjects, reconciliation between enemies: it took, or rather presupposed, its dramatic power from the context, the threat of nuclear annihilation, just as certain classical Greek plays assumed for their malignant and dramatic impetus the mindless destructive force of some god's passion.

Alec's imperiousness declared itself – briefly – over casting the director. He left a message on Simon Callow's answer machine, saying he would like him to direct *A Walk in the Woods*. When Callow called back two days later Alec told him, 'Sorry, I've already got someone.' This was Ronald Eyre.

How do you anthropomorphize the threat of a nuclear holocaust? Greek plays showed gods on the stage, and while Peter Sloterdijk might write, as he did in his *Critique of Cynical Reason*, that the atomic bomb was the 'real Buddha of the West, a perfect sovereign apparatus without bonds. It rests unmoving in its silos, purest reality and purest possibility,' it was difficult to turn this into a dramatic presence.

By late 1988 the fear of nuclear death had lost some of its urgency, and while the programme for *A Walk in the Woods* had its quota of apocalyptic citations expressing the hype of the day – 'There is no doubt that art . . . is in radically altered circumstances if the future is placed in doubt . . . Masterpieces cannot be timeless if time itself stops . . . Without confidence that we will be followed by future generations . . . our life is impoverished' – there was a certain if not post-coital, then déjà vu, mood about the whole evening.

The events on which *A Walk in the Woods* was based had

happened six years before. Paul Nitze, the American diplomat who was two years Alec's junior, had entered into a covert and unauthorized negotiation-within-the-negotiations with Yuli Kvitinsky, his Soviet counterpart in the Intermediate-range nuclear forces (INF) talks. They strolled together in the wooded Jura mountains outside Geneva, 'sat on a log and sheltering their papers from the rain', according to Strobe Talbott, US Deputy Secretary of State, put the finishing touches to what they called a joint exploratory package. Tentative compromise had been reached primarily by breaking through at a human level to make contact with one another.

Later, when the compromise foundered in a series of complex, fractious and prolonged 'deliberations' on both sides, they met again, this time in a Geneva park, to try and resurrect the original 'walk in the woods' formula. This new deal also failed to go through, although as one State Department official complained, Nitze was 'still off there in the goddam woods with Kvitinsky, cooking up deals to kill the Pershing II'. Still, it was an unusual, even inspired, move on the part of the playwright Blessing to write up what *Time* much later called 'one of the most extraordinary episodes of creative insubordination in the annals of diplomacy'.

Blessing reversed the roles, making his Russian, Andrey Botvinnik, the elder of the two men, and his American, John Honeyman, about forty-five and a rising star (as Yuli Kvitinsky actually was). This showed, as one might expect, a certain pandering to popular taste (America youthful and temperamental, Russia old, tired and traditional). But the Russian realist and the American idealist (again reversal of the truth) were persuasively underplayed by Alec and by Edward Herrmann, whose earlier triumph as T. S. Eliot at the Royal Court in London in Michael Hastings's *Tom and Viv* gave the pair plenty to talk about offstage. Their performances were, in a meditative way, thought-provoking.

Recently I read the text for the first time. I found I had forgotten Alec was playing a Russian and not a reserved Englishman and that the location had been Geneva. Little of the touchy, explosive nature of Botvinnik, his temperamental flights, had been shown in Alec's performance: instead he had continued his autobiographical journey, travelling this time with a calm, evasive, cunning and suavely witty elder negotiator. His timing, as ever, had been perfect. In a discussion, for instance, about boredom (always tricky, this, on stage), the way he said the somewhat banal line, 'There is a difference between frivolity and boredom,' had the audience hanging on every half-syllable. So it was amazing how Alec, as a veteran performer, could inspire worship and affection simply by the accomplished way he paced the whole play, and displayed the good man at the interior of what would have seemed, without examination of the text, this passive, stage stooge. Yet while it was exquisite and memorable – in the manner, for example, in which Alec received the gift of a pen from the American with a little nod of his head and the gesture of the hand on his heart over the pen now in his pocket – there was much more that could have been done to stir the passions. He had abandoned disguise in favour of a calm, meditative centre. He was still a giant. But perhaps he was now a giant with nothing much more to hide. Or to fear. At the end of the run he told Ed Herrmann, 'That's the last performance I shall give on any stage,' to which Herrmann replied 'Balls!' or something like that. He regretted, he said later, that the play hadn't been something of greater distinction.

Even so, after *A Walk in the Woods* Alec agreed to perform in one more stage play, *Bookends*, written by Keith Waterhouse, based on Craig Brown's *The Marsh – Marlowe Letters*, a spoof of the Lyttelton – Hart-Davis correspondence. They had sent it to Alec and he had been very excited. Manager Michael Redington and director Ned Sherrin had lunched at L'Epicure and Alec had, as far as he was able to allow himself, rhapsodized over the play, especially the drunk scene at the end of act one: 'I can see myself going a little far,' he said with a chuckle.

After three weeks he wrote to Redington that he could not do it, because he was finding it too difficult to learn the lines. 'Do you think Dr Alzheimer is knocking at my door?' (Later it was performed by Michael Hordern who received, on the first night in Brighton on the pre-London tour according to Sherrin, thirty-five prompts.) Was it fear not only of memory loss, or the loss of a sense of certainty through having concrete business to perform on stage – and as a consequence to feel rooted in simple behaviour? To have the right props becomes important to older actors.

It would also seem he had grown unhappy at appearing again

on the West End stage; Peter Copley came round to visit him
after a performance of *A Walk in the Woods* and recalled that Alec
had a terrible cold. He greeted him in his dressing-room and he
was now 'like a barrel, but still chain-smoking. "We're going out
to supper," Alec told him. "It's very plain. You may not like it.
It's by the river." ' When they arrived at the restaurant Copley was
struck by the number of elegant Italian ladies with fur coats over
their arms. Alec suggested (i.e. implied he must) take a dish with
six different kinds of pasta and six different sauces. When they
were leaving Alec tipped everyone and Copley noticed he gave
the manager as well some enormous sum. 'Do you have to tip
so much?' Copley asked. Alec replied, to his amazement: 'I'm so
terrified of them all – I have to buy my way through.'

*

As might be expected, Alec had mixed feelings, or cold feet, about
the tribute of essays collected by Ronald Harwood for his seventy-
fifth birthday in April 1989. When Ion Trewin, the book's publisher, first wrote to Alec suggesting a book, he replied testily.
They had lunch at the Garrick Club. Alec did not want it done at
all, but he wrote to Trewin that he would 'try to tag along'.

Graham Greene could not contribute, replying from Antibes
that he was very fond of Alec and would have liked to have written
something. The essay had never been an easy form for him and
now he was approaching eighty-four it was a nightmare to promise
anything. Peter Glenville replied that he was Alec's godfather and
directorial architect of some of his best performances; he agreed
to write but nothing arrived; he then disappeared to Mexico
promising he would send something from there. No more was
heard. John le Carré agreed, planning to do a 3,000-word essay
on 'making a spy of Alec', but was chary of abandoning work on
a new novel. Among those who said no straightaway were John
Mills, who needed what he called his 'brilliant writing time' for
himself, and Anthony Quayle who would find, he said, Alec, as a
dear and close friend, extremely difficult to write about. Snowdon
made his truthful and revealing photographs available, saying he
had more admiration for Sir Alec's work, both on stage and in the
cinema, than anyone he could think of.

Cyril Cusack, perhaps better than anyone else, summed up in

his contribution how the real actor was aware of the elements at war in our humanity and how Alec had trodden 'this dangerous pilgrim path'. Eileen Atkins, under the title of 'A Different Pin-Up' confessed that under her desk-lid at school she had stuck a photograph of Alec as Herbert Pocket. Alec rounded off the contributions by asking the editor to call the whole thing off, and wait till his 'unlikely' eightieth. He would be gaga by then and 'no one who knew me in my twenties likely to be alive. So you needn't do it at all.'

The reviews were consistently affectionate (and echoed those of his own book). About half of them said that the volume gave a number of insights into what he was and who he was; the best picked out the constant reminders in the book to his qualities of stillness and quietness: a value compared to the 'stabiliser of a great ship'.

The most repeated story was the self-told tale (perhaps always a little suspect) in Harwood's introduction of the cloakroom ticket. Invited to a grand luncheon at a West End hotel Alec hands his hat and coat to the attendant, and asks for a ticket. Oh no, smiles the attendant, reassuringly, this will not be necessary at all. Alec is secretly pleased at this gesture of recognition and departs. After lunch he collects his hat and coat and on his way out reaches into the pocket where he finds a piece of paper. On this is written the words, 'Bald with Glasses'. But the reality was that in the last decade of his life Alec was recognized everywhere. The great game of anonymity had worn thin, come to seem a bit of a pose, again like that of T. E. Lawrence in *Forty Years On*.

Telling jokes against oneself ('*My Name Escapes Me*') is by now also time-honoured if sometimes tiresome. The famous compete with each other. And of course it is the standard practice of the stand-up comedian. Alec and Merula are one night dining with Ralph Richardson and his wife Mu when, unaccountably but characteristically, Richardson gets up from the table and says, 'I'm going for a walk,' then leaves. Later they find him sitting all alone on a bench. He has found an old tramp and sat down next to him. The tramp says nothing. After a while looking at Richardson he says, 'I know you, you're John Gielgud.' 'Fuck off!' says Richardson. I like more Alec's later dream of Richardson entering a grand hotel in Zurich with Alec on his arm, saying to the maître d'hôtel, 'Two tables, please.' Again, a soupçon of the dominant male figure – with Dame Alec on his arm?

The most repeated snatch of gossip (appearing in the reviews) is Coral Browne's account of how she was served breakfast in bed by 'Sir Alec' at Kettlebrook Meadows, who then left her bedside. Browne turned her attention to the three books on the bedside table, which she called an unmistakable touch, selected and inviting, they spoke for him:

> 'I thought you might like these!' Indeed, the only problem was which to tackle first. Alec reads a great deal and his choices, while off-beat and unusual, always have been right and have never failed to divert me. It would be heaven to have him always – not only this day – as my own, special librarian, infallible and challenging.

The other half of the reviews, less favourable, on the question of the personal or biographical insights the book provided about Alec, said it gave none. Some reviewers said, at £12.95, it was expensive. Three reviewers commented on Alec's postcard to Harwood, printed as the epilogue: 'Wouldn't it be good to call the whole thing off? etc. . . .' using this quotation against the book. 'You finish this slender volume,' wrote Sheridan Morley, 'knowing even less about his private persona than you did at the outset.' Alec had been victorious once more. Another critic dragged up the ghost of Tynan, quoting from the early monograph: 'He exists in a histrionic air-pocket, isolated and circumscribed by his own eccentricity.'

Douglas Dunn in the *Glasgow Herald* expresses this accurate reaction: 'Impersonality is an ambivalent or contradictory objective in a form of art as physical and humanly present as acting in the theatre or film. Yet it is tempting to think of it as a goal that Guinness has made into an incontestable virtue.' Dunn compares him to T. S. Eliot: as Eliot delineates how the calm remains at the centre of being, so Guinness finds 'an actorly equivalent of a poet's grace and its imaginative withdrawal of the ego from the centre of the creative impulse.' It also suggests how similar Alec was to Macavity the Mystery Cat – never seen but mischievously evident and defiant of discovery.

Someone else captures the contradictoriness, calling Guinness 'the sultan of self-effacement' – with its hint of smugness and self-satisfaction. There were those who said that when Alec lost his sexual adventurousness as a man, he lost his danger and ability to surprise as an actor. I think the jury will be out for eternity before reaching a verdict.

*

Snowdon had been given permission to photograph Alec in the garden at Kettlebrook. When Alec appeared in his garden with Melvyn Bragg on *The South Bank Show* in 1985, as carefully guarded as he had ever shown himself, he made Bragg feel 'unaccountably nervous', the reason being, surmised Bragg, 'because I wasn't being allowed to find a rock to which I could anchor myself'.

Bragg, noting Alec had 'never been a tall poppy, never been slashed down', commented on his studied personality and on how difficult it was to get near him: 'Is that the way he is – or the way he wants to be?' He inclined to the former view and ventured to suggest, in conversation with me, that it may have been due to him being at cross purposes with himself, part of which was due to feeling the 'inclination of intellectuals', while 'he doesn't move among intellectuals'. Having agreed to do the interview, Alec, Bragg found, gave him no help at all and he felt they were playing 'a silly superficial game', while under his breath Alec was saying, 'You're not going anywhere near me.' He would have responded better, Bragg told me, to Alan Bennett's breeziness: 'If I saw him again I think I would be much more jolly and buffeting.' There was only one 'thoroughly unbuttoned moment' in the programme, Bragg felt. When Alec was playing with his and Merula's puppies near their outbuildings he voiced yet again his sentiments over acting as something you can't explain, 'like an empathy with animals'.

Alec told Bragg, 'I'm a very simple person really, but I don't want people to know everything about me.' Contrast this with Merula quoting Peter Glenville – ' "He's the most complicated person I've ever met" and if Peter says that goodness he ought to know because of the very complicated people he has known' (and do not overlook the fact that Merula must surely have known Glenville was homosexual). Alec then went on to Bragg, 'I've got nothing to hide.' The understatement of all time? 'It's just that I'm an actor and as an actor although I enjoy having my name stuck up on billboards I also want not to be there. I like to be private, I like my life to be private, but on the other hand there's been that urge to make new friends, thousands of friends, possibly, maybe enemies, and to be different people to all those friends out there.'

Some of Alec's other statements and jottings at this time have a disconcerting as well as evasive air about them. 'Flamboyance doesn't suit me. I enjoy being elusive' is one. He contributed several diary pieces to the *Spectator* in 1992–3 which later he was to work into the memoirs. On 17 July 1993, for example, he writes about how he sat on this lovely summer morning lolling in a newly acquired steamer-chair set up on his patio at Kettlebrook, pretending 'it is the sundeck of the beautiful *Mauretania*', his favourite of the old Cunard liners. He tricked himself into believing we 'are in mid-Atlantic and in the mid-1950s in time. But there is no charming steward to bring beef-tea or chicken-broth.'

He went on to deflate this little dream – with the bottled iced lemonade which tasted of the smell of gasworks. This was well away from the image of the ordinary little man which he spent much time in the 1950s conveying to the public. The fantasy of the beautiful *Mauretania* brought a stern rebuke from one *Spectator* reader who had been a Cunard crew member at the time and had no such nostalgia about the ship. Sir Alec, he said, had not shared a crew cabin with seven others, smelt the 'farts, the smelly socks' or seen the 'uplifting sight of underpants hanging up to dry on a line slung across the cabin . . . I'm afraid I missed the charming steward.'

Five years later, in 1998, Alec had stored up enough resentment over this letter to emerge in a two-page-long reply in *A Positively Final Appearance* (four years later, Alec mistakenly wrote). 'I find the ignorance, chilliness and smugness shown in the letter still irritates, even if it doesn't exactly rankle.'

Alec claimed, in his indignation, that he could not have afforded the first class fare out of his own pocket (the theatre company was paying). He asked if the 'curmudgeonly letter-writer' suffered his experiences at Chatham during the war; 'Perhaps he was too young to know about such things' (e.g. puddles of urine and lumps of vomit). 'When I looked at his letter I heard his voice, the whine of that perennial, unpleasant plant, "the barrack-room lawyer".'

'If he took against you he could be rather chilling' voiced Ian Richardson in a television documentary about Alec shown in 2001; Peter Copley noted how to his wife Shosh, who used to be a stage manager, Alec represented something grand but very alien: whenever he phoned he would ask brusquely, without courtesy or greeting, 'Is Peter there?' Unbuttoned with Peter he could be both depressing and depressed about events, such as a holiday in the Camargue, which he represented to others, or in print, in a rosy tone. Frith Banbury, as old if not older than Alec, could not stand the 'pussyfooting' when Alec gave lunch for him at Kettlebrook, the long discussions over whether they should have lunch 'in here or out there' irritated him. Banbury's sentiment was, 'I don't give a fuck, all I wanted was to talk.' Merula, to Banbury a kind of saint, would again be on the receiving end of Alec's sharp tongue.

Nostalgia for the vanished space of the past extended also to the Sistine Chapel, now a 'horrific experience'. It had not been the same in 1939 when he found only one visitor, an elderly lady in tweeds. We are, he wrote elsewhere, 'throwing ourselves like lemmings into some overcrowded, over-publicised cultural sea'. True this may be, but it did not occur to him that not only were there considerably more people on the planet, but that most of them enjoyed a life culturally enriched and materially beyond the dreams of their parents.

So, between the cherished privacy and the public urge to exhibit, continued to fall the shadow. Sometimes the dichotomy became too great for him to contain discreetly. In October 1992 he had an 'outburst' about the West End theatre, reported on the front pages of newspapers. The 'outburst' was well timed, before the screening of his new role as Heinrich Mann in Christopher Hampton's *Tales from Hollywood*. Over-publicized?

The statement that reporters claimed he made was that he would never act again in the West End because he 'hated' the 'blank faces' of the uncomprehending tourists. 'It's so hard to

respond when the audience doesn't respond because they don't
understand.' He was seventy-eight, and his last stage performance
had been in *A Walk in the Woods* three years before.

'I'd rather go to the provinces where they still speak English
and not Japanese.' He conceded that tourism helped put 'bums on
seats' and thus keep the London theatre alive, but the expense
involved now made him seldom tempted to see plays in the West
End. 'I do go occasionally, but only if my pockets are sufficiently
full,' he cavilled (still on £12,500 a week from *Star Wars*). He
recalled that for his 1938 *Hamlet* twelve gallery seats were provided
free by the *Sunday Pictorial* for those who could not otherwise
afford tickets.

Then, irritated at what he himself had said, or what he had
been reported as saying, Alec spoke through the *Spectator*: 'Thirty
years or so ago, the West End theatre was self-sufficient; the
audiences were almost entirely home-grown (as they still are in the
provinces) . . .' Oh dear, he was getting beside himself. In the
1960s when he played in *Ross* foreign visitors flooded London.
Often plays were presented, during the summer in particular,
purely for their tourist appeal. Alec had benefited. *Wise Child* had
attracted a great many American tourists who flocked to see it
because of his film reputation. Many provincial theatres today are
packed with foreigners, especially foreign students who know
much more about the English theatre than local residents.

Alec back-pedalled: 'Recently, in answer to a sudden question
about all this while being interviewed about something else, I
replied tactlessly (not for the first time in my life), and this was
treated as if it was some *ex cathedra* pronouncement from the
Vatican. The flippant tone in which I spoke was entirely misjudged.' He claimed praise for the 'truth' of his remarks and by
'tactless' he meant 'from the heart'; at the same time he was not
being entirely accurate about the kind of reports he received. The
Daily Telegraph did not treat his statement as if it had been made
by the Pope.

Alec went on to say that the point he laboured was 'that it is
hell for actors to play light comedy to an audience if there exists
an acute language barrier. It is nothing new.' But were West End
comedies full of blank, uncomprehending faces, and was there

less laughter than in the 1950s? Alec told a story which had no relevance, as far as I could see, to the point he was making: a comedian playing to an unresponsive audience comes forward to the front of the stage:

'Anyone here speak English?' he asks. 'Yes, I do,' comes a voice. 'Well, f— you for a start.'

The point of Alec's story proves to be that the whole audience is English and that the comedian could not make contact with them. The joke is about the deadness of *English* audiences, especially in former days when they were exclusively English. As Timothy West observed to me, 'I don't think Alec liked audiences very much.' Perhaps an attitude similar to his view of audiences was taking place in Alec's last screen performances which had become more minimal and honed down, like line drawings.

In the first of these, in a role offered to Paul Scofield and turned down by him, Alec played Heinrich Mann, a victim part, in *Tales from Hollywood*, a play about the German literati in exile. Mann, who wrote the original story of the *Blue Angel*, is humiliated by Nelly, his wife.

Mann's passive and exploited state is established over and over again by Alec, whose performance seemed both timid and wafer-thin. It was unconvincing to me that Mann had ever been full-blooded enough to have been attracted by Nelly (played as an attractive tart by Sinead Cusack: Nelly had been the original of the Blue Angel and so the cause of Marlene Dietrich's fame). Yet, according to Benedict Nightingale in *The Times*, 'The weariness, the sick misery, the increasingly debilitating attempts [of Mann] to sustain his self-respect and disguise his inner disintegration: they were all there, understated yet overwhelming.'

Dominic Lawson in the *Spectator*, in a diary piece, pointed out how Alec observed of John Major, during his first term of office, that he always followed Neil Kinnock's physical mannerisms.

'If Mr Kinnock asked a question with a sunny beam, Mr Major would reply with a similar expression on his face. If Mr Kinnock led with a scowl, Mr Major's face would darken in turn.' This meant to Alec that Kinnock was more decisive. Major should look at Kinnock's expression and do the opposite, Alec prescribed, to make Kinnock appear either pompous or flippant by turn, and at the same time impose his own different character. Good advice, but unheeded.

Opinion was mixed about Alec's second-to-last television film, *A Foreign Field*, made by Roy Clarke in 1993 about a group of, mainly, ex-servicemen who return to the landing beaches of Normandy to recapture that moment of greatness – or feeling of something anyway – in which they had participated. It was trounced by the *Daily Mail* critic as similar to war in that it consisted of 'interminable periods of brain-numbing boredom interrupted by brief moments of excitement'.

A Foreign Field was a quiet and still piece, with a tenuous storyline, and huge, empty-headed gaps to be filled with viewers' awe and the memory of the celebrated players. These included Lauren Bacall, Jeanne Moreau and Leo McKern, who had not long before played with Alec in the television adaptation of *Monsignor Quixote*, by Graham Greene. McKern plays the gruff but benevolent minder of Amos, the Guinness part, who is, but for five words, silent. His brain had been irreparably damaged by mortar fire on D-Day plus whatever – when Brigsy, the comrade he asks about, died.

Amos enables Alec to give a touching display of that early Pierrot-like charm in this sketch of 'second childishness' and 'mere oblivion'. He explores hotel-room appliances with the gentle skills of Jacques Tati and reminds one of Chaplin in his sense of loneliness and rejection (even of Jean-Louis Barrault as Baptiste, the clown of clowns in *Les Enfants du paradis*).

Brain damage is a bit of a misnomer here, holy innocent would have been more appropriate. One more television appearance, as James, the father of the tutor at Queens' College Cambridge, in *Eskimo Day* by Jack Rosenthal followed during Easter 1996. In this Alec, in his two main scenes with James Fleet, has quite a long speech: on the way to visit the old people's home to which he is referred – 'Who wrote this balderdash – cantankerous old sod,' he comments on the report. He then explodes:

Ask me why tribalism produces globalism? Ask me why life-supporting technology makes life so complicated? Ask me why the more we learn, the less we know. Ask me why the highest seats of learning produce cabinet ministers with the nous of an earthworm? Ask me why children turn their parents into children?

But is he a father? It seems he can only play the father at last when the father has become the child of the son – which points to the aptness of the questions he asks.

He was a bit unhappy during the filming, says Ken McReddie, his agent for his last five years. McReddie took over representing Alec from Alistair Blackie, who, a much-admired young agent, had from the time of Van Thal's retirement handled Alec's affairs before dying from Aids. 'He frustrated himself over it – whether it was the character or the man I'm not sure.' Telling me Alec did little in these last years – an exception was the voice for an Inland Revenue advert for self-assessment – he was frequently asked to promulgate religion and religious products. He said no. 'He was not fulsomely pious. He did not want to posture in that way. A genuinely modest man – he had a healthy sense of his own worth.' McReddie had never been to Italy, and Alec, hearing of this, wrote him a three-page letter from a cross-Channel ferry of places to visit, hotels to stay in. 'The descriptions got tighter and tighter and smaller and smaller till they tailed off to a point in the bottom right-hand corner – something to do with the deep and dark personality which had been pushed away. I respected him hugely. He had lived with and overcome his demons.'

*

Alan Bennett has been called 'Curmudgeon Laureate', but also National Teddy Bear, and he is another very complicated person with, one friend has said, 'a weight of emotions, blackness, hurt, that one senses and walks around'. When I asked him for an interview, he sent me a curious postcard, a photograph of a small boy in a one-piece bathing costume on a seaside rock advertising Lindsay Anderson's 1994 film *Is That All There Is?* He wrote on the back a comment about not wanting to talk to an unauthorized biographer: 'I've just about had my fill of the genre.' It seemed like a cloned reply of Alec's.

The apparent fascination of these two men for one another has continued to intrigue me. Both successful self-deprecators in a charming fashion; both safe, cute, unchallenging while apparently rebellious and yet acceptably so: an editor could compile a dictionary of the collected self-deprecations of Guinness and Bennett. Was or is the oblique, self-recorded humility genuine, or in the end but a game and only skin-deep, to defuse envy and maintain a self-satisfied *hauteur*? Is it manipulative, perhaps, because it disguises a need or desire for power (or for constant attention, which is a form of power)?

The meeting and partnership of Alec with Bennett over *Habeas Corpus* began an intimate friendship which was to last until Alec's death. It was as if he had found and could adopt someone who was so like himself in many ways that he saw him as an extension of himself, as a member of his family, as a son almost who looked up to him as a father and mentor. Did their relationship go deeper in terms of shared confidences? 'There is a lover of Alec's who is alive – but I don't want to say who,' reports a close colleague. 'Alan Bennett would know.'

In *My Name Escapes Me* Alec mentions Bennett more than anyone else except for Merula, whose ill-health dominates the references, and his dogs, which numerically top both. Anthony Daniels had noticed how, during the filming of *Star Wars*, Alec, suffering from his hurt back, had not lost his temper and how it 'made me realize how angry he was'. This underlying anger struck Simon Callow as more important than Alec's fear or anxiety (although they may well have been the same thing and come from the same source). I wonder if the same could not be said of Bennett, whose sexual complexity, as well as aridity, has received twilit exposure in the biography he mentioned, called *Backing into the Limelight* (I first heard this phrase used of Alec, but it has quite comfortably been transposed to Bennett). When Alec first met Bennett he must have experienced instant recognition; he might well have thought: 'That's me, twenty years younger, gone to Oxford, yes, first-class degree, but with the switching of a few major elements, essentially me.'

Of course he would have been unlikely to express this because self-knowledge – beyond a certain point – was not a quality in Alec. The recognition would have had to have been instinctive, half-hidden, and impulsively shut down. Who knows what might have gone on, what confidences exchanged over the next twenty-five years or so, what mutual irritations suffered or expressed (or more likely hidden)? No doubt, while decrying the whole process of biography – ('This is persecution.' 'No it's not. It's biography' – from Bennett's *Kafka's Dick*) – Bennett will at some point change his mind. I cannot venture beyond reporting my own observations based on what I have found.

In *A Positively Last Appearance* Merula regains her rightful place as main mention (Alec was acutely conscious of the hierarchy he imposed on those close to him), while Bennett takes more of a back seat. Bennett's final appearance occurs, appropriately, as a non-appearance on page 231, when he is reported as feeling unwell and at the last moment calls off a dinner with Alec. He makes one or two prior fleeting visitations.

It is reasonable to assume that Alec, who pursued, or related to, a series of mirror-images, as well as pursuing romantic embodiments of the unattainable male (such as Richard Burton, Robert Shaw and later in his serial infatuations, or wining and dining such figures as Anthony Daniels, Alex Jennings, Piers Paul Read, Piers Haggard and so on and so on), became more enamoured of Bennett than Bennett of him. He courted him and found him consoling, while Bennett, normally a great chatterer and spiller of confidences in private, deferred. For example, on 15 May 1996, among these many mentions in the earlier book, Alec mentions a trip to Italy which, it seemed, might have to be cancelled because Merula suffered spells of vertigo. He turned to Bennett, noting 'As often, when feeling anxious and low-spirited, I got in touch with Alan B and asked him to spend the evening with me. He is always sympathetic and reassuring and never thinks it is comforting to pour out his own troubles, which many people do.' They strolled off together to eat at the Berkeley.

How loyal or true Alec was to his friends behind their backs may be seen if against his instructions the contents of his private diaries are published. Alec declared that he had kept diaries for thirty years or more, thereby indicating that he began in the early 1960s. If our assumptions are correct, there will be found little or no reference to his sexuality. Alec called these private diaries his 'small, strictly private, almost illegible series of daily jottings'. More significantly he added, especially as this wish has not been carried out, 'I have left instructions for them to be destroyed at my death.' Their only use, Alec added, had been to settle arguments between himself and Merula when they disagreed about some past detail.

To have made sexual confidences in these diaries would seem to be out of character: like Samuel Butler, Alec would not allow to himself certain thoughts about himself. Yet he could always spring surprises. But what of shocking revelations or his thoughts about those who adhered so firmly and loyally to him? These are more likely. Judging by Kenneth Williams's back-stabbing in his classic diaries and letters both published and unpublished, Alec, in certain ways a personality similar to Williams, although more robust and secure because of his faith, might often have had a sharp word or two to say about friends.

The best of Alec's publicly airable memories from his diaries are included in the two final books. Many are delightful, if not profound or revealing. Alec wrote that these two last books were 'unavoidably self-revealing', which is just what they are not. His skill and conviction are such that you believe you are being treated to confidences. For these books he must have drawn on what he could find in his diaries, and this process continues in his *Commonplace Book*, published in 2001, which illustrates Montaigne's observation, 'I get others to say what I can't say myself.'

Bennett, after Alec's death in August 2000 seemed to show almost indecent haste to distance himself. In a card to an actor friend of Alec's, saying he would miss him, he pointed out he could be 'infuriating' – but that he had been immensely kind to him. In the diary extract published in early 2001 and previously referred to he accused Alec of being patronizing to Merula, going into some detail. Report of Alec's belittling of Merula was nothing new. But it caused attention in the newspapers: 'Playwright Alan Bennett has jeopardised his benevolent uncle image with an unprovoked attack on the late actor Sir Alec Guinness's deficiencies as a husband,' began one article (in the *Daily Express*).

How far did the mirror-imaging go? When Peter Cook died in January 1995, not perhaps an occasion for snide comment, more for genuine sorrow, Alec remarked to Bennett that his obituaries seemed to take up more press coverage than would the assassination of the entire royal family. (So incidentally did Alec's own obituaries and subsequent serials and features.) Alec asked Bennett if he could account for it. 'He was a journalist,' Bennett told him. (Bennett has a public attitude of despising journalists.) This kind of comment, both from Bennett – and from Alec in repeating it – was indicative of a rather unpleasant side to the characters of both, especially Bennett, whose rise to stardom and celebrity had been closely involved with Cook. Not a journalist by any means, Cook was a magazine proprietor.

Another example: the endearing old actor friend John Warner sent Alec a letter from his mother, dating from just before the Normandy landings of 1944. Warner was the minute, almost elf-like gifted character actor who played Osric in Alec's 1951 Hamlet. He was discreetly homosexual, and he had been a naval officer like Alec: his long-term lover had been a BBC producer. He commanded a wartime minesweeper named HMS *Rattlesnake*. Photographs of him in naval uniform bear a strong resemblance to Alec similarly kitted out. On the eve of the invasion in 1944 Warner's mother exhorted her son and his fellow officers to dose themselves up with Epsom salts (which she sent along with the letter). Use them, she admonished, if you seem unusually merry or bad tempered. 'It is almost certainly due to faulty elimination of bowels . . .' She went on in this vein at length.

Alec forwarded the letter to Bennett with the po-faced reply to Warner that it was a remarkable document which could have been written by Queen Victoria. He enclosed a stamped addressed envelope to Bennett for its return to Warner, and the former sent it back saying it was almost too good to be true. 'Alec said it had him in stitches and me too.'

Well, everyone's sense of humour is different, but my reaction is that while Warner might have intended to show Alec the letter to share it or provoke a quiet chuckle in an old friend, it was quite bizarre to send such a private document to Bennett. Didn't it breach a sense of privacy? Perhaps Alec should have asked Warner's permission. Perhaps I am exaggerating.

Maybe it touched a nerve. Agnes de Cuffe probably never wrote such solicitous and caring letters to her son. Humour is cruel – but also self-protective. Sometimes the humour can be both cruel to oneself *and* self-protective (cocooning of a self-inflicted wound). One day Ian McKellen allegedly wrote to Bennett asking him if he was gay and suggesting that he should 'out' himself, i.e. come out of the closet.

'Dear Sir Ian,' Bennett is alleged to have written back, 'asking me if I'm homosexual is like asking a man who is crossing a vast and lonely desert by himself and when he is faint and dying of thirst, with no rescue in sight, if he would like to choose between Perrier and Evian.' (Or Malvern water – or even Thames water in other versions!)

Self-protective, too, and notably different from Alec, whose bisexuality Bennett must have studied and thought about carefully before revealing his own homosexuality. What ironies and game-playing can be found in the way Bennett produced his bombshell in the *New Yorker* magazine in September 1993 that he was gay: 'I'd always been in love with guys, you know, but always unhappily. They were always straight and it was always totally unfulfilled.'

This Bennett confession is wrapped up and cushioned in a disclosure – that he has had a long-standing heterosexual affair with a woman, Anne Davies, who helped him about the house. As Alexander Games writes, 'To some extent the revelation about Anne was a Trojan Horse. In all the media onslaught, the issue of his sexuality was more or less ignored. Bennett had managed to reveal that he was gay, but only as a by-product of revealing his relationship with Anne.'

Subsequently there was no reaction in November 2000 when a *Daily Telegraph* article named a thirty-four-year-old man (thirty-two years younger than Bennett) as Bennett's lover. This announcement was *after* Alec's death, and perhaps connected. Did Bennett want to observe the rules of discretion while his friend was still alive, for fear of showing him up? If Bennett had come out of the closet sooner, why, of course – could have been the implicit suggestion – should not Alec?

One can speculate endlessly and he cannot be pinned down (e.g. the significance of Bennett's boyfriend, Rupert Thomas, being editor of *World of Interiors* magazine, suggesting rooms versus views, gloom versus light – the Forsterian theme of self-deception). Maybe it's ultimately silly. The important factor in the Guinness–Bennett intimacy, however far it went, is that both men shared and practised a strong mimetic desire towards one another, were almost outdoing one another in the bravura of not being who they were. And their controlling artistry in concealing themselves frequently revealed their mutual similarities.

To take one example, Bennett makes himself out to be hunched and crab-like when, with his eminent confidence and effortless ability to excel at everything he does, he uses this persona to disguise himself. Similarly did Alec use the persona of the anonymous, faceless man. Perhaps, in all the range of possibilities and similarities one might list (and Alec's power of imitating in real life others often seemed without boundaries, while his mimetic envy and power to devour others was quite voracious), it had been Bennett's witty perception of Lawrence of Arabia which most identified the pair as similar.

> Shaw, or Ross as Lawrence then called himself, returned from the East in 1919. Shyness had always been a disease with him, and it was shyness and a longing for anonymity that made him disguise himself. Clad in the magnificent white silk robes of an Arab prince, with in his belt the short curved, gold sword of the Ashraf descendants of the Prophet he hoped to pass unnoticed through London. Alas, he was mistaken. 'Who am I?' he would cry despairingly. 'You are Lawrence of Arabia,' passers-by would stop and say, 'And I claim my five pounds.'

Bennett continues, in the Headmaster's speech in *Forty Years On*, that Lawrence feared his body. It was a wild beast to be tamed and cowed into submission, and there was something feminine about his make-up, 'but his was always so discreet'. At the back of his mind 'there was that ready snigger'. Prophetic stuff. Self-portraiture? Even Bennett's desert response over his sexuality provides an echo of Lawrence. While in *The Lady in the Van*, Bennett's much later play, which opened in London some eight months before Alec's death, the slipshod piece of humanity that parked her van in Bennett's garden in NW1 carries traits linking her, in the mind of this writer at least, to Alec's mother Agnes, who suffered from the same 'delusion of reference' – imagining bombs had been planted by Irish revolutionaries in pillar boxes to blow her up. Alec himself had similar premonitions and neuroses. Alec and Bennett might have written, along with Donne, his lines:

> 'Tis much that glass should be
> As all confessing, and through-shine as I . . .
> But all such rules, love's magic can undo
> There you see me and I am you.

Would Alec be tempted onto the stage again after *A Walk in the Woods* and *Bookends*? Patrick Garland, who directed him as Shylock, and Alan Strachan believed he might. Garland tried with the part of Lob in *Dear Brutus*, while Strachan wanted him to play Father Keegan in *John Bull's Other Island*. He said no to both. There were other offers.

In June 1996 Peter Glenville died in New York, causing in Alec's life after a 'close' friendship of over fifty years, 'a considerable full stop'. Alec telephoned Father Caraman in Somerset, to ask him to say a Requiem Mass at the London Oratory. Glenville's death shocked him and left him numbly blank, but there were 'dozens of happy or absurdly funny memories'. He promised to write something about Peter, but never did. Fearful that few would turn up for the Requiem Alec phoned around for attendance. Frith Banbury was one of those who turned him down. 'Why should I go,' he told me brusquely, 'I'm a non-believer – and for someone I didn't know at all.'

In 1996 Alec recalled in his diary Ron Eyre, another important figure in his life, who had died in April 1992. Alec had taken out Christopher Good who had worked with him and Eyre in *Habeas Corpus*. Eyre had been one of Alec's favourite directors and he expressed surprised that as a stage director Eyre left over £700,000 in his will. Eyre had been Good's mentor and Good had looked after him during his final illness. 'This was Alec's way of saying thank you,' Good told me. 'In emotional moments he always knew exactly what to say.'

Good had gone down to stay with Alec and Merula in Hampshire for three weeks – as well as being an actor Good was a gardener. He found Merula, 'Such a beautiful person . . . wonderful eyes, beautiful skin, surprisingly modest, the centre of Alec's existence because utterly different from him, she seemed to epitomize everything that he wasn't. She went off at night to perform charitable acts, she would go out and feed tramps.' But there came a moment, and here Good compared Alec to Benjamin Britten who used people then threw them away – 'Difficult for the person on the receiving end of his affection.' Good felt he had 'got through that carapace with Alec and then he could suddenly cut you . . . I then found it was hard to revive and he withdrew. The formality might have been a defence.' Good had been happy to leave their friendship at that.

27. Move Heaven and Earth to Avoid a Memorial Service

> Today, characteristically, mourners like to personalize funerals, using the service as an occasion to eulogize their loved ones, and expunging, as far as they are able, mention of death itself. And so they are robbed of a most significant moment to self-existence into a realistic context. We are given life as a gift; we leave the earth with an added value known only to God.
>
> **Rev Dennis Duncan, from Guinness's notebook**

Aristotle never answered the question of why impersonation should be pleasurable. Acting owes its uncanny and ambivalent prestige to the mimetic *translations* that it effects. As a role becomes really our own, as soon as we are officially and culturally empowered to play it, so it loses its prestige. The roles of others always seem more fascinating than our own. Like Helena and her friends in *A Midsummer Night's Dream*, Bottom and his friends want to be *translated* into prestigious models. Their desire for mimesis has the same ontological goal as the mimetic desire of the lovers.

Alec had a lifelong, ever unsatisfied appetite for mimesis, to peruse people and translate himself into them. He enjoyed this not only because he enjoyed the attention it brought him, made him millions of friends and admirers, but also because he was not happy with or fully reconciled to himself. He remained full of shame. Conversion, for both Alec and Merula, must have emphasized the distance between any psychoanalysis or therapy, and religious belief. For a Catholic to look for complete fulfilment in idealized, intimate relationships is not an aim; the belief is that this can do more harm than good; because the nature of man renders human relationships necessarily imperfect.

All that hatred that Simon Callow correctly identifies in him,

he learnt to channel and fashion into someone else, and above all
to show how the feelings were contained – as was so much about
himself – except when they emerged on rare occasions, when he
bitched and quarrelled with his wife, or fled from his proper,
upright self into what he thought of as guilt-ridden, illicit sex
(whether it was or not is unimportant). If he had not felt shame
and guilt over what he saw as his defects, then we would not have
had his great performances. 'Best men are moulded out of faults,'
says Mariana in *Measure for Measure*. Claudio, in the same play,
on the nature of lust, declares

> Our natures do pursue
>   Like rats that raven down their proper bane,
>   A thirsty evil; and when we drink, we die.

Alec kept going into a *noche oscura* – out of which, each time
he emerged into a new, pristine role – then disappeared again –
each a link in a chain of search for self. Did the chain form by the
end a whole? Yes, but there remained weak links. The more
mimetic we are, the less we perceive the mimetic law that governs
our behaviour as well as our language. The lovers in *A Midsummer
Night's Dream* keep teaching each other a language that none of
them ever understands. Shakespeare lets us see what they never
see:

> *Hermia:* The more I hate, the more he follows me.
> *Helena:* The more I love, the more he hates me.

Mimetic desire effectively programmes its victims for maximum
frustration. As the Stanford philosopher René Girard writes, 'The
four lovers keep desiring because, each time, they magnify purely
positional differences into a false absolute. A revolving illusion of
transcendence propels the entire system.'

In his first book Alec managed, because of the stored up power
and energy (it was quite some time since he had worked flat out)
to give the characters he wrote about and escaped into – the
Sitwells, Martita Hunt, Ernest Milton – a vivid life of their own.
At the same time Alec was there inside it, disguising himself as all
the characters he wrote about just as he disguised himself in his
acting roles. In the later two books, however, this doesn't quite

happen, because Alec, the *bon viveur*, the nature lover, the raconteur – the censored, but real person – is half here, keeping a diary. The danger when you are commissioned to keep a diary, as Alec was by Charles Moore, editor of the *Daily Telegraph*, is that you provide a heavy ration of self-justifying content and name-dropping. This does not happen on the whole with Alec, but sometimes, we do get a grumpy old snob and worse, a Catholic one who is making a positively last appearance. True, he has many saving virtues, like putting out food on the bird table, but sometimes, aside from the authority he carries from whom he is, there seems little substance. But the levitation of wit, the appreciation of life's ironies, the fastidious taste for accessible prose, these prevail.

He has come to terms with his acting, which he had now given up, but the observations of craft are not original or revealing because he never knew or understood what exactly he was doing as an actor. He did not need to. To repeat, the more mimetic we are the less we perceive the mimetic law which governs our behaviour.

He has sensible good advice and he was quite a good critic of others. Not all that good, it may be said, because he is solipsistic, he tends only to admire within the range of what he himself has done and the kind of actor he was. Gielgud apart, to whom he pays his debt, he skirts round or avoids the great. His generosity extends more to the weak, the casualties, the curiosities, whom he dominates: his giving comes from a kind of dependence.

He constantly meets people in his old age travels, such as Profumo, the disgraced war minister, and his ex-actress wife Valerie Hobson, an old acting colleague. The endless friends – it's not that he does not find something interesting to say about each, because he will always pick up something clever – but it is cleverness, it is safe, it is unthreatening, it is sometimes too tame – and it is not the real Alec, who could be bitchy with gleeful malice behind their backs about his friends, or who sat silently with a cold baleful stare in the corner of a room. The headmaster of Shaftesbury Avenue offers a few encouraging words to those following along, and gives recommendatory reports or mentions at the end-of-term assembly.

The thread of Melvyn Bragg, as he crops up in the first

memoir, is an intriguing one to pursue: he is one of the score of talented courtiers taken out to lunch or dinner with or without wives on their arm. Bragg, possibly because of his elevation to the peerage, gets singled out. 'Today I was supposed to have lunch with Melvyn Bragg at the Ivy,' writes Alec on 23 October 1995 (he has given a favourable mention to the latest novel of another novelist, Piers Paul Read). The lunch, where is it? The humble (prurient? inquisitive? voyeuristic?) reader is tempted. 'Lunch?' 'Ivy?' 'Melvyn Bragg?' Wow!

What happens? Answer, not the lunch, but the literary equivalent of a small sherry and a packet of posh crisps. But wait! The promised lunch like the promised land arrives. Two months later. Ivy. Bragg gives him lunch. 'I was impressed to be at what was obviously one of the No 1 tables.' Melvyn (nice young chap, good manners) – dowager Alec speaks – 'Took the deference shown him with modesty and charm.' End of lunch. No report of their conversation.

Later, at David Lean's memorial service, amid some bitching and recrimination (paying off old scores) over Lean's dependence on sycophants, Bragg 'gave an admirable address, beautifully spoken'. (But again includes, as Alec notes as already reported, the snide remark of Lean's about Alec.) Next spring sees Alec at lunch at the Ivy with Barry Humphries – (in Melvyn's corner, he says). Bragg crops up finally in Alec's *Commonplace Book*: Alec is miffed that Bragg on Radio 4 implied his comment on West End theatre was snobbish. 'If asked about him, I'd say, "one of our better second-class novelists".' *Et tu Brute*, but gently, like the tapping of the egg in *A Voyage round my Father*.

Here the mimesis, as practised in his acting and with considerable success in *Blessings in Disguise*, has descended to the mimetic envy of journalistic tittle-tattle, to Tynan without the tiger in Tynan's tank, to being surrounded by a chorus of self-sustaining names (with no offence intended to those I mention). Alec more often than not sees himself as the celebrity conferring favour (thanks, gratitude, buying love, conferring attention) on those he likes. There's nothing essentially wrong or immoral in this, of course, but we are examining these works in relation to Alec's personality and character, and what they tell us about him.

The other side of old age is the health aspect: this is popular

and fashionable – failing eyesight, old dears getting to and back
from hospital. We are in John Bayley and Iris Murdoch land.
Compassion as a new and remunerative cultural commodity:
'selling cheap what is most dear', in Shakespeare's words. Putting
a brave face on the ageing process endeared Alec to millions of
readers and listeners (he read both books on the radio). Given
who he is, however, the admissions of defeat and shortcomings,
although comforting to middle England ('Oh, look, how ordinary
I am,' Sir Alec is confessing to this and that and the other – a bad
cold, failing eyesight – showing his wounds) again here is condescension. But here too Alec performs admirably. I should have
liked to have seen more professional remorse: 'The guilty goddess
of my harmful deeds / That did not better for my life provide /
Than public means which public manners breed.' There is again
little of the real and whole Alec revealed.

Yet he does express this England well – the ordinary common
sense of the Englishman; the absurdity; the strutting, antic postur-
ing of its politicians, civil servants, artistic panjandrums; the
corruption and power of money, the decline of culture. Alec's
troubled illegitimate background and his desire for men created
for him a lifelong mimetic double bind. The only escape or radical
solution would have been either to renounce the possessive desires
once and for all – making the real choice between tragic conflict
and total renunciation (the Kingdom of God, the rule of the
Gospels) – or to give in to chaos and complete self-gratification.
This second alternative could be so frightening that Shakespearean
heroes and heroines try to elude it, and therefore are condemned
to the distortion and perversion of ever-renewed mimetic duplica-
tions. Alec escaped into his parts, but had to end up himself. 'The
search for compromise, satisfactorily achieved . . .' possibly, but
the very public and continued public utterance of his love for
Merula was a bit suspicious, in this so-called very private man. It
would always be difficult. Did she read his books?

> The search for a compromise produces an unhealthy combi-
> nation of things that are not supposed to be combined –
> renunciation becomes parody of itself, tinged with the slipper-
> iness of sexual perversion. Values and meanings that should
> remain separate contaminate each other, friendship and Eros,

possessiveness and generosity, peace and war, love and hatred all jostle together uneasily . . . [Summed up by] the offer to the would-be rapist in *Two Gentlemen of Verona* –
All that was mine in Silvia I give thee.

René Girard, A Theatre of Envy

Reluctant to jump on the bandwagon, 'particularly when the bandwagon is a hearse,' remarked Bennett. At the end of his life Alec would seem to have eliminated the first of Samuel Butler's 'Three Most Important Things', namely the private parts, as an over-riding or even active concern: or at any rate he wryly observes twice in the later books, 'the first two diminish with age', adding that the third becomes 'rigid'. But he remained a frequenter of plays and now had a kind of guru-like authority in the theatre, for he could not, when attending these examples of other's work, refrain from a high degree of visibility in his invisibility. If man is, as Catholic theologians especially Pope John Paul II have suggested, the 'visibility of the invisible' (in other words, God), then Alec did have, as Angela Fox suggested, a godlike quality, for he was somewhere there, a being, a larger than life presence to his contemporaries. He had found safe lodging in the Kingdom of Heaven – even if this sometimes seemed a perch on the edge of a precipice.

On a more practical level he would go round backstage and offer heartening praise or comments, or write to those he had just seen, gentle, humorous, warm, appraising letters. The aura was powerful, but with his imposing manner, and while he might say only very simple things he managed to make everything sound oracular – up to and including his own very studied modesty and evasiveness. He often had sound, or civilized and sophisticated, judgement. Autobiographical search had always, from the very start, been central to the practice of Alec's art. From the age of eighty to his death at eighty-six, he appeared in only two small parts, on television, so he may be said to have retired from acting. In the last twelve years of his life he had not acted on stage. In fact, the complex and complicated paths of his acting had simplified and converged into that of writing his memoirs, much in the same way as he had acted this out in many, if not most, of the parts he had played.

The essential fact about Alec's art was that he transmuted, or had transmuted, his inner drama – that of his own life – into acting, although not in any directly autobiographical sense. Simon Callow describes this as being achieved by his 'becoming a sort of ontological magician. He was able to release himself into character, or rather, he was able to allow himself to be seduced by, to be taken over by, another self.'

All these other selves, as far as I have been able, I have explored. Always there, the need to control and release the emotions of rage, the feelings of impotence and other primary experiences of his childhood (and these continuing all through his life), which produced, says Callow, 'the powerful mental instrument that is central to Guinness's work'.

That powerful mental instrument remained intact in his retirement, taking different forms and occupations. He had pondered deeply his experiences of his early life and the gay scene in particular and had opted for his strong liking and desire (as a companion) for a woman. He had stuck with her, committing his will to married 'normal' life. The other side always tugged at him: as Callow told me, he loved the company of gays in his late years, to drink and gossip, he liked the whole lifestyle, and while expressing admiration for those who were open about and unashamed of their homosexuality, he regretted he could not identify himself with it and come into the open. The crucial thing is that love for a man never came to occupy a central place in his life: the priorities of his love were his wife and family. His physical fastidiousness also played a part, his instinctive dislike of any kind of squalor or incontinence. The impact of Aids, especially as its significance struck home in the mid 1980s possibly played a part, confirming his detachment from 'that sort of thing'. As Spencer wrote in his *History of Homosexuality*, 'AIDS made bisexuals question where their sexual orientation really lay, and provided a powerful motive for examining the strength of their commitment to their sexual preference.' Sexuality had, also, become politicized, while sexual politics as well as its practice had assumed identity as a growth industry with large commercial possibilities. Alec shied away from this.

Anyway, by this time, Alec was quite old, which may or may not have deterred him from exercising a sexual preference either in his marriage or outside of it. Further evidence one way or other is unlikely to be found. As old age gathered force, however, it was natural he should fall back more on himself and that his mimetic assumption of others, even now they were only other writers (such as, for example, Bennett, his favourite novelists like Updike, Butler, the mystics and so on – not to forget the Bible) should continue to the end. Alec, as an autodidact, continued to be a great reader.

But the shadowy, troubled spirit of the earlier memoir, *Blessings in Disguise*, which dug up some notable glimpses of his strange childhood and confronted the loony outlines of other great eccentrics with comparable majesty, had gone. For the most part, *My Name Escapes Me* and *A Positively Last Appearance* are – the pleasure apart of hearing that authoritative voice and being mesmerized by the presence and aura – gentler and in lower key. They lack that essential quality that earlier in his life made him such a great actor, namely his anonymity. They are the work of a charming letter-writer engaging his surface personality but little more. He gives himself away too often – humility? – 'There are only a few handfuls of CHs, which is what makes it such a desirable honour.' He confesses that he dislikes it when those outside his circle fail to show him due deference as a knight; he lists the price of chairs bought (£1,000 at the Conran Shop), or a hat (£97 at Lock's). The name-dropping, with clichéd descriptions, does tend to pall; anecdotes, having built up expectation, irritatingly tail off with the witticisms of the 'witty' and promised, teasing indiscretions omitted. As one reviewer, Paul Bailey in the *Daily Telegraph* commented, this was 'unkind to the reader. Can a riveting diary ever be commissioned? The great diarists are there to answer in the negative.'

On the other hand, there are sharp glimpses of the vanished geography of earlier years, of the backstages of long demolished theatres, while the light is thrown vividly on a forgotten great actor or actress, a curious disappearance, an old, long-dead piece of gossip. The meandering details of the feathered visitors to Alec's bird bath, his love for his dogs and his meticulous record of his and Merula's ailments, comforting though they are to elegiac time-travellers, hardly sustain more than temporary interest. The intensity of non-stop remembrance would be refreshing, but an annoying habit is Alec's tendency to pass comment on the week's events in the news. This was fine for the *Spectator* articles. But it all helps to create the idea that Alec in old age was decent, dignified, wise, selfless, an exemplary Jedi Knight, a caring father and grandfather, a devoted if sometimes waspish friend.

Someone must have told Alec as a grandfather to mention his grandchildren in *A Positively Final Appearance* because in neither of the previous books is there a single mention. His first grand-daughter, Sally, from Matthew's first marriage (name of wife not mentioned, divorce not spoken of), was born in 1972. Sally partnered or married a Barbadian named Walker (otherwise anonymous) and gave birth to Otis Marlon Simeon in 1995: his surname is Guinness-Walker, and great-grandfather says he 'looks like a very appetizing chocolate éclair'. Matthew's second wife, Joanne, gave birth to Bethany, who is ten months old at first mention, and nearly two when Alec and Merula celebrate their sixtieth wedding anniversary. There was, notes Alec brusquely, a gap of twenty-four years between Bethany and half-sister Sally, and he wonders how it will work out for them (he hopes lovingly).

The old demons or trolls still lurked in Alec's spirit to the end. Simon Gray met him in the street once or twice long after his play was over and he noticed what a lot of people, myself included, felt: the face had become strange, full, as Gray described it, of 'unlived vices'. But beautifully covered by the liquid, courteous voice. Perhaps it was that, reading his words on the radio, that really made the last two books so seductive, the liquidity, the endless malleability of his voice, its modulated cadences and his mischievous laugh. Sheridan Morley remarked on his unsteady, more than occasional drunken appearances at the Garrick Club. He met him late one night: 'Derek Nimmo had just got killed falling down some steps and Alec was very very unhappy, seriously drunk. Was it homosexuality unfulfilled?' asked Morley. These incidents of an increasingly darkened complexion I report were not isolated. The figure of a portly roué had long supplanted the eager active young man of Herbert Pocket vintage. But he fought hard to keep the mental characteristics at bay.

When he puts down the telephone one day after ordering flowers and books Alec can't help speculating that almost all exchanges of words have become meaningless, friendly rubbish.

No one uses surnames. Who the hell are these Christian names, what do they mean? He hates the self-righteous petulance of women, mostly, who are vindictive on television towards the royal family – in former times, he points out, they would have suffered the chop for high treason.

*

Alec continued to the end to be a generous host. His letters to his former Osric of 1951, John Warner, show a touching solicitude, repeated over and over again to other friends. He insisted, as always, when he went out to lunch he would pay. That magnificat, mainly of his generosity to others, edited by Christopher Sinclair-Stevenson, had been published for his eightieth birthday in 1994. 'I sometimes suspect,' he told Piers Paul Read in 1988, 'I am only generous for effect.' Sinclair-Stevenson recounts how he took Alec to Paris for the launch of the French *Blessings in Disguise*. Eating at a restaurant, Alec was asked to write a comment in the *livre-d'or*: 'What shall I write?' he asked Sinclair-Stevenson. 'I suggested that he should look at the most recent insertion. Alec turned to it. 'You won't believe this. It's David Lean. And he says, I am lost for words. The first time *that's* ever happened!"

Please bear in mind that we lead a simple life, he wrote, inviting Warner to lunch in Steep. (This example of hospitality should be multiplied by fifty or a hundred.) His modest house, he says, is really 'a dog basket. I suggest oldest shabbiest clothes you can lay your hands on.'

Warner was playing at Chichester in *Henry IV* in the summer of 1998 when he visited Alec, who asked, 'Is it Shallow, or is it Silence?' He and Merula saw the performance but they would not, he told Warner, be stage-door Johnnies as they had to get back and let the dogs out. He thanked Warner for the bottle of wine he brought: they elaborately 'broached' it with lamb cutlets and Lyonnaise potatoes. Alec usually looked on this practice with disfavour, often sending guests back with their offerings and condemning the practice as 'American'. At another time he regrets that an old actor, Robert Harris, who once spoke so beautifully, did not like Denville Hall, saying that if the retired actors' home wasn't so inaccessible and in such a dreary part of London he would be 'happy to shuffle in there'.

He refers, in one of many spates of nostalgia, from a seaside location, to intrepid young men in noisy speed boats who are 'very much an élite. Nostalgic names – Vir, Bra, Hvar and Korula – brought back memories of my naval insufficiencies.' Warner must have known. Surely there was some discreet double meaning between old gay friends intended here. Warner had suffered with him the humiliation of Hamlet. Alec brought up the subject of this production several times: it had stuck in his gullet as life-long resentment: 'I had picked a first-class starry cast for the grim Hamlet (with about two exceptions – well three) and I live for the day when I can twist Harold Hobson's crutches round his neck.'

Discovering he was going blind in one eye in his mid-eighties he opted for some optical engineering. 'It took me a long time to notice that I couldn't see as well as other people,' he told Roger Lewis on the telephone, and he claimed to have started mixing up Merula with the milkman. When the surgeon wanted to explain what was about to happen and how his left eyeball was going to be scooped out and fiddled with, he stuck his fingers in his ears. 'To this day,' he said in spring 1999 when he had full vision for the first time for twenty-five years, 'I don't know what they got up to. [But it was] like being in a tropical forest with brilliant butterflies fluttering around, all the colours of the spectrum but greatly intensified.'

He voiced unhappiness about the new *Star Wars* film, *The Phantom Menace*, in which his former self was to be played by Ewan McGregor. 'Mention *Star Wars* and the old Jedi Knight grows cranky.' The dialogue, 'It's all frightful rubbish!' said Alec. 'And you do all your acting against a blue screen. You are a caged animal for the special effects from the word go.' But while he might denounce the false mythology of *Star Wars*, it was his performance as Luke Skywalker's mentor that gave the saga its extra dimension and reverberations. When he came round from the operation for his cataracts he found doctors and nurses crowded round his bed wanting him to write, 'May the Force be with you,' on scraps of paper.

Hard on the surgical engineering that restored brightness to his vision came the deterioration of a prostate cancer which he told few about, but which had plagued him for two years. In the final few months of life he filled exercise books with thoughts and jottings, either from the Bible, Cardinal Newman or John Donne. Earlier he had written down Woody Allen's quip, 'I'm not afraid to die, I just don't want to be around when it happens,' and penned rude ditties and reminiscences from a party on the set of *Little Dorrit*.

According to a new but apparently close friend he had acquired eight years before, aged seventy-eight, his death, like his life, was quicksilver and unpredictable. In February 2000 he had been told, so he wrote to Keith Baxter, actor and former lover of Binkie Beaumont, prolific correspondent of Kenneth Williams, that the prostate cancer would not spread and he had reasonable expectation of years to live. On Thursday 4 August they informed him, when immobilized by a thrombosis – and while Merula was away in hospital having caught pneumonia – that he had cancer of the liver and only forty-eight hours to live.

Baxter saw him two days before his final departure to hospital. He had found him downstairs, in the dining room, to where his bed had been moved, resting. He was lonely and in low spirits and offered Baxter wine or martini. It was only noon, protested Baxter. 'I lose track of time lying here,' he replied. When he struggled out of bed, saying, 'I've got to have a pee,' Baxter remarked that he was wearing a bright lilac nightshirt, and complimented him on it. 'There was a flash of a smile,' reported Baxter, 'and he batted an eyelid coyly. "Well, you never know who might come to call!"'

On Saturday night, 5 August, Monsignor Murtagh of Petersfield heard Alec's last confession and said prayers with him. The final undated entry in his exercise book is from the Book of Wisdom: 'But the multiplied brood of the wicked shall not thrive, nor take deep rooting from bastard slips, nor lay any fast foundation.' Quite a dark thought to record on the threshold of eternity. And so he died during the night, his family were with him and he was calm, reposed, and at peace. He thought 'Paradise was awaiting him after death,' said Piers Paul Read.

He had left Merula a note in an envelope in the safe with an instruction written on it, 'not to be opened until after my death'. This was dated 29 December 1999, so he predicted his death would be soon. Addressing his wife as 'My Darling', he tells her that this is a 'tiresome' letter to put her in the picture of his affairs 'when I drop off the twig'. Then, going into details, he lists, under separate headings, his solicitor, accountant, bank, retirement annuity, money in the bank, adding, perhaps as a final exercise in self-diminution, that he imagines from time to time 'some bits of money will come from *Star Wars* or direct from my books.' And that these would go mostly to Matthew.

The final point (7) is 'I don't much care where I am buried. Move Heaven and earth to avoid a memorial service. I imagine there will be a requiem for me at St Lawrence. That is sufficient.'

And then he adds to this the most moving valedictory: 'I hate to think of all the distress I may have caused you. I love you dearly. Forgive me. I cannot imagine what life would have been without you. All my love. Alec. Take great care – particularly with electrical appliances and cigarette ends.' Here is the final proof, not that it is needed, of Alec's unswerving love and loyalty for wife, family and Church.

> We are in a world in which 'elite' has become an insult, 'discrimination' a swear word, 'quality' a joke and 'excellence' an incomprehensible concept . . . in literature it encourages lust at the expense of spirit.   **Bernard Levin**

Alec quotes this, surely his own view, in his *Commonplace Book*, published posthumously in 2001. 'You get to know Alec so much more through this than anything else,' Eileen Atkins told me. 'When I read it I realized how much I missed him.' The one-liners are particularly sharp. 'The steady direct looks of the congenital liar, thief and dipsomaniac' (Alec condensed a comment earlier made to Alan Brien); 'Norman Lamont's mouth like the neck of a party balloon.' Alec also, he told me over lunch, incidentally did not have a high regard for Prince Charles, whom he had sat next to once at dinner and found a bit dull and dim although the Prince had told him, 'I enjoyed seeing you play my ancestor Charles I.' Alec would seem to have endorsed A. N. Wilson's view, for he quoted it in his *Commonplace Book*: 'A tactless, cranky, ill-tempered figure . . . he would be fitted for about any form of employment better than he would be fitted to be King of England.' As *A Commonplace Book* was published after Alec's death I wondered if he had had the final say in what should be included, whether he would have left this out. There is also recapitulation of the mildly shocking motif, as when he records the remark of the young Irish transvesite Jaye Davidson, who was up for an Oscar at the Los Angeles ceremonies, and was asked what he'd really like. His reply: 'Richard Gere. Right now. Here. Lying at my feet. Naked.'

Much of the comment and quotations circle warily round the truth versus concealment preoccupation: 'No one is at liberty to speak ill of another without justifiable reason, even though he knows he is speaking the truth, and the public knows it,' or '. . . a just indignation would be felt against a writer wantonly exposing the weaknesses of a great man, though the whole world knew they existed'. (Cardinal Newman, *Apologia Pro Vita Sua*) Most thoughts would seem to prefer concealment, with Montaigne's the exception, 'Pliny says each man is an excellent instruction unto himself provided he has the capacity to spy on himself from close quarter.'

The most consistent of Alec's aspirations reveals itself in Simone Weil's 'Imaginary evil is romantic and varied; real evil is gloomy, monotonous, barren, boring. Imaginary good is boring; real good is always new, marvellous, intoxicating. "Imaginative literature", therefore, is either boring or immoral or a mixture of both.' It doesn't sound so good, but maybe this does sum up the paradox, the very human paradox that was Guinness (and also points to a universal predicament). It demonstrates too, through Alec's continuous need and attempt to find a balance between the two or more sides of his nature, how sometimes he walked on a broad plain, sometimes on a tightrope. He could not have been the great entertainer he was if he had not delved into – and sometimes walked on – the dark side, yet the quality of the new, the marvellous, the intoxication, came from his goodness, from that other spring that Herbert Pocket so beautifully exemplifies. He would not have been the magician he was if he had come clean about himself.

*

Merula, not surprisingly, so closely had their lives become inter-twined, their needs and practices so mutually dependent, survived Alec by almost two months.

Alec Guinness had made a final will on 15 March 2000, only

five months before he died, in which he reiterated his desire to be buried in Petersfield according to Roman Catholic rites, and forbade any memorial Mass or celebration ceremony. The nine-page document, in character, is complicated and even, in the epithet of Angela Fox, ducal. With son and wife, and with actor friends Mark Kingston and Richard Leech as executors, he disposes of personal mementoes and art treasures among relatives and friends. To Matthew goes the gold pocket watch bought when he felt he had 'arrived' and inscribed 'The readiness is all', together with Edward Lear's watercolour of Elephants in Bengal and a Vogel bronze head of Merula. Eileen Atkins receives the Suther-land oil of a stork wading in a Venetian boathouse, Alan Bennett – in an appropriate touch – the Lytton Strachey drawing by Max Beerbohm. Tom Courtenay's gift was six first-edition volumes of D'Israeli's [sic] *Curiosities of Literature*. Some sixteen beneficiaries include Piers Paul Read (letter of St François de Sales) and Matthew's wife Joanne (Russian icon of Virgin and child).

In the rest of the will and apart from the bequests to Merula, Alec set up a trust for the disposal of the rest of his estate, entailing a division of proceeds into 398 (!) equal parts which were then to be split among twenty-five beneficiaries. These consist of relatives, neighbours, friends, servants, charitable funds and so on – graded, so to speak, by virtue of the number of gifted parts. Wife and blood relatives are to receive 328; at the bottom of the scale many get one or two.

Alec gives his full and unrestricted power to invest the money or buy property or to delegate power to advisers. This will, with its complicated strands of generosity, its Byzantine breadth and meticulous attention to detail – will anyone ever be able to administer it? – bears Alec's distinctive signature. There is even a grandson double, or an up to now unmentioned one – named in the will as Samuel Pierre Guinness. Is this Otis Marlon Simeon Guinness-Walker whose name is left out? The mysteries and omissions march on. The value of the estate given to the press in 2002 was £2.5 million while the films still earned large sums.

Alan Bennett occupied the literary high ground of Alec's funeral, his diarist's eye surveying the 'oddly primitive Catholic rites', and publishing his account five months later in the *London Review of Books*. 'The note of "Alec wouldn't like this" keeps recurring and is perhaps the most vivid way in which he is recalled.' Alec might have expected Alan Bennett at his funeral, but asked him to leave his pen behind. On Alec's coffin when it was borne in there sat a cushion with decorations, including his CH. 'The service is simple and being Catholic to me is utterly mysterious, as I never understood how they get the mass over with quite so quickly.' The Bennett of crabby posture is playing his game, not owning his privileged overview. '. . . It's quite hard,' he continues, 'to see how someone as fastidious as A.G. managed it all these years; Merula would have been one of his neighbours so perhaps he always sat on the aisle.' After the funeral they went back to Kettlebrook: 'Now it is within 200 yards of the A3, the roar of which was never absent in this last decade of their lives.'

The last time Bennett had seen Alec had also been two days before he died, like Baxter. Could he have been so lonely, as Boswell One and Two (One for the *Daily Telegraph*; Two for the *London Review of Books*) made out? Their accounts would not have been quite so lively if Baxter had written, 'As I left I could see Alan Bennett, who had walked from the railway station, puffing up the drive,' or if Bennett had said, 'Alec asked me to clear away Baxter's martini glass before I sat down to chat.' In his bed in the dining room, with a handkerchief over his head against the sun, Bennett had felt Alec was effectively turning his face to the wall. (But perhaps he was grumbling to himself, 'God, I wonder who's going to turn up next?') Almost the last thing Alec said to Bennett was to ask him when leaving, where he was getting the train.

'Petersfield.'

'Liss is better. It takes ten minutes off the journey.'

'This bending you to his will, gently though he did it, was entirely characteristic of the way he had always been, particularly on the hundreds of occasions he took me out to supper.'

On 27 August Merula, recovered from pneumonia, was in bed, having broken her shoulder in two places wiping her bottom. 'One can't be too careful,' she told John Warner. Matthew was being a rock, but he had broken his Achilles tendon and hopped around on crutches. She felt she ought to volunteer to go back to hospital but could not face it. 'I want to opt out. I hope it won't be too long,' she ended.

Doubt (and, I'm reluctant to say, snobbery) had been an

endearing element of Alec's spiritual make-up. When Graham
Greene died in June 1991 Monsignor Rod Strange gave a homily
at the memorial requiem Mass, in which he pointed out that
Thomas was the name Greene took at his confirmation ceremony
after his conversion to Roman Catholicism. Thomas was a 'kind
of patron saint for those who wrestle with faith and doubt'.
Strange suggested that God's presence could be detected in people's lives in different ways, and that in Greene's case 'the angels'
he was sensitive to were to be found in the dreams he experienced
and wrote down.

Greene's most powerful and rare grace, Strange continued,
which showed his instinct for the heart of the Gospel, was his
sympathy with the virtue within failure. 'If we can learn from him
also to see and value the virtue in our defeats, and to recognise
that all is not lost when we fail, then we will have still greater
cause to give thanks for his life.' Alec, who with Merula had been
at the Mass, came up afterwards to Strange and they talked. He
had been moved by the homily, and deeply, Strange felt, here was
someone who had struggled long and hard with temptation. A
little later Alec wrote to Strange that his homily was the finest he
had ever heard (Alec must have heard many) and that he was sure
Graham must have rejoiced in it. 'It was,' wrote Alec, 'one of
those happy statements which, when one's faith has been a bit
wobbly, set one firmly on one's feet again.' After Alec had died,
Merula wrote to Strange, who had written her a letter of condo-
lence, that she remembered his wonderful talk about Greene. She
was at the bottom of the barrel, she said, ill and

> on top of it sciatica. I just want Alec to come and fetch me,
> but –
>
> > 'He cometh not' she said.
> > She said, 'I am aweary, aweary
> > I would that I were dead'
>
> My loving dutiful son, and granddaughter are being angels
> and I am still at home with lovely view from my window,
> and dear dogs lolling on my bed. So you see it's me to be
> prayed for, I'm sure Alec's just fine. Sorry about big moan.
> > Yours sincerely,
> > Merula Guinness.

Only a few days before she died, she had written a poem praying that she and Alec would be reunited. As in her letter to Rod Strange, she scarcely had the strength to lift a pen and the writing had become very wobbly. The poem was read out at her funeral. Her last book of text and illustrations, published in 1992, had been *The Kingdom of Heaven is Like*.

Dead, Alec will continue to haunt us. Will his degree of invisibility be seen, ultimately, as a measure of his saintliness? Will his elusive nature continue to make sure that however well we know him, we will desire and seek to know him better? Greene wrote ten days before his death, 'Perhaps in paradise we are given the power to help the living. Sometimes I pray not for dead friends but to dead friends asking for their help. I picture paradise as a place of activity.' If this is so, we can be sure Alec will be very busy.

Perhaps he will even be glimpsed from time to time, assuming other guises. He recalled towards the end of his life when attending a performance at the Olivier auditorium of the Royal National Theatre, being mistaken for the dead Olivier. 'Fancy seeing you here, Mr Olivier, and in your very own theatre.' It is unlikely that others will be mistaken for him, extraordinary force that he was.

Epilogue – Was Guinness a Great Actor?

We have attempted to document Alec's quest to find himself through the many parts he played. Every actor has dreams, but only a handful realize their dreams. The successful ones have instinctively and successfully fished and chosen well, in the maelstrom of their souls. So did he. He became an enduring British institution, closely identified with key roles in some of the most famous, mid- to late-twentieth century films and television series.

It is hard to consider Alec anything like a great man of the theatre, as he rightly called Tyrone Guthrie in his address at Guthrie's funeral in 1971. The clue to Guthrie's greatness, said Alec, was that he was never 'all things to all men. He never cut his cloth, or trimmed his sails, to suit other personalities, but gave wholly himself . . . He had great personal humility – and rather hoped for it in others.'

On the stage Alec avoided characters who were caught in the search for the truth about themselves. Crisis in a role frightened him, which is why more often than not he fell back on character instead of great roles. The nearest he came to trying was when he played Hamlet, and this nearly destroyed him. He was prepared to observe, but not to confront. In creative terms he became stuck at Hamlet, and he failed here because his self-instruction stopped short of self-knowledge. He was too imitative, too mimetic to perceive and understand the mimetic law which governed his behaviour. Every part he played was, however, at heart, informed with the wisdom of the sad clown.

This was why, as much as anything else, he couldn't play the other great tragic figures with success. His Macbeth was a qualified disaster, his Lear never happened, his Othello – or Iago – well, the first was beyond his reach physically, the second demands self-knowledge, a knowingness, which was alien to him. On several occasions he said that he had never dared enough, but added, 'I never dared at all,' which went too far, betraying that trace of self-hatred and desire to belittle himself which was not altogether genuine humility, but often a fishing for reassurance or compliments. But he dared much more than he gave himself credit for.

So, like Charles Laughton's, Guinness's career and its impact remained predominantly in films: wherever he appeared he tried to convey the inner life of the character by tapping into some inward experience of his own. He never really was wholly a comic impersonator – the disguises went always so much deeper. Any actor, we have quoted him as once saying, needs 'a slight mystical appearance . . . you can't force a character on yourself'.

Alec often asserted that he was not at all a nervous man, but there had always been something measured about his need to assert how cool he was which suggested inner anxiety and tension. Interviewing him in 1958, Alan Brien summed up the Guinness manner: 'the voice cool, smooth and soft as a Polar bear's fur, the style as measured and impersonal as a bulletin from Buckingham Palace'. When Brien asked him if it was true he never looked anyone in the eye except when hiding himself inside one of his favourite eccentric roles, Alec replied (untypically) in the first person, while, as Brien wrote, 'his eyes kept sweeping restlessly across me like the beams of a lighthouse': '. . . I find that I only look somebody straight in the eye when I am about to tell him a lie. All the biggest frauds I have ever met have been men with that steady, unwinking gaze.'

Guinness was never an actor who relaxed *at heart* and could therefore allow an unpredictable inspiration to take over and change a performance. Pre-planning and calculation: they were supremely in control. As Melvyn Bragg said of him, he wished to have control not only of himself but of everything about him. Every effect was meticulously staged or prepared. Perhaps Tynan's notion that a great actor needs complete physical relaxation did not apply in his case. What you watched and anticipated in Alec's performances were a great magician's transformations which were breathtakingly complete because they happened from the inside.

As an actor it was Alec's commanding intelligence which made him a giant. He had as well what Komisarjevsky considered the first essential of the good actor: imagination. He had the ability to communicate the workings of the human heart. He had never fitted the conventional idea of the great stage actor. He had never had a larger-than-life stature, he never wanted to be stretched, pushed to the limit. Balance, to him, given his background and the lessons of a very difficult early life, became much more critical: 'The most important thing in life is a sense of balance: Oh, I don't mean spending one's whole existence on an even keel, daring nothing. But to be conscious that a human personality is many-sided and to be sufficiently balanced to know which side to bring out in a given situation.' (And, typically, when he said this he smiled sadly and shrugged his shoulders: 'Not that I have it myself but I know several people who have and how I envy them.' *Evening Standard*, 2 October 1957)

This ceaseless striving for courtesy and humility was always at the centre of that quality of intimacy Guinness communicated and which, to many people, had wrongly seemed innate. Sensitive actresses who were also sensitive women picked up this attractive element. Eileen Atkins as a schoolgirl kept a photograph of him as Herbert Pocket under the lid of her desk. Jeanne Moreau reacted to this special quality when she first met him in 1992: 'Though I had never met him before it's as if I knew him from all his films.'

Observation, too, was an outstanding quality in Alec, hardly needing more examples; so was personality, that instinct and practice of self-projection with which an audience does or does not identify. The following passage from Tyrone Guthrie's *Good Acting* can be seen to refer specifically to the stage acting of Guinness:

> It is only theoretically impossible to separate the actor's skill from his personality. Theoretically, then, the most skilful actor is the most protean, the actor with the widest range. It so happens, however, that the actors with the widest range do not usually go very deep. I have known many protean actors who could achieve startling changes in their appearance, voice and mannerisms, but their performances were apt to be superficial ... Some of the greatest actors have no protean quality at all. In every part, though the make-up and costume may vary, the performance is almost exactly the same. John

Gielgud is a case in point; matchless in declamation, with extraordinary intelligence, insight and humour, he commands almost no skill as a character actor. Like many other eminent players, he is 'always himself'.

Alec achieved depth with the range, and this was what made him unique. While no one would dispute his ability to be protean in his disguises, what was truly extraordinary was how he could match the characters he was playing with degrees of profundity and insight to every level, even the deepest, although they had to have qualities like his own.

But the admission of weakness is not the same as self-knowledge, which again is not quite the same as a sense of one's limitations. While richly capable of the first and third, his knowledge of himself fell short. 'I'm a very simple person really,' I have already quoted him saying, 'but I don't want people to know everything about me. I've got nothing to hide.'

Michael Meyer, biographer of Ibsen, was outspoken about this evasiveness of Alec towards truth. 'Since he got converted,' Meyer told me before he died, 'he's only ever acted the Pope.' From the early days of promise, he 'shrank from tragedy . . . never found the emotional freedom to confront things. You have to look deep into yourself.' Meyer recalled there was some talk (in 1973) of him performing in Strindberg's *Creditors* with Mai Zetterling; but Alec didn't want her: 'He didn't want sexy ladies, he wanted Eileen Atkins,' Meyer said (he might have added, if he had known, that he didn't even want Atkins as Portia, preferring an all-male cast). As far as I can ascertain Alec never, in sixty years of acting, played an Ibsen character. He must have been offered *one*. Ibsen directly confronted and explored his own problems and family. 'His credo: to live is to war with trolls in the vaults of the heart and brain. To write: that is to sit in judgement over one's self.' Alec's preferred method had been towards the creation of existences rather than characters, taking much trouble to realize – then hide carefully more than reveal – what the personage he played was feeling.

The Ibsen problem was more: Ibsen required passion. 'His men and women are passionate men and women. In Ibsen you have to act relationships,' Meyer told me. Alec could not act relationships beyond a certain limited span. He could act genius, the outcasts, the eccentrics – those who had attributes that set them apart. 'Can you remember Alec acting a father?' Meyer asked me. Yes, a few, but the tyrant, the weak father, the father who has become the child of his offspring.

Finally, there had always been the life apart. 'Otherwise,' as he said, 'I love dappled sunlight and being out of doors and meeting one or two chums'. It didn't worry him in the last years if no one offered him anything more to act. He was not going to do something for the cash, or for the sake of working. He had had a tough life to begin with, had had to work hard to become the communicator he did, and had tried to give virtue her form. Le Carré was right when he wrote in the eightieth-birthday book in 1994, 'The deprivals and humiliations of three-quarters of a century ago are unresolved. It is as though he were still striving to appease the adult world about him; to winkle love from it, to beg its smile, to deflect or harness its monstrosity.' But perhaps it was the darkness in the first place which made him learn to forgive the betrayal. If he could not always practise it he would have agreed with Antony's forgiveness of Enobarbus for deserting him; or with Prospero's 'The rarer action is / In virtue than in vengeance.'

Peter Bull wrote what it was like being an actor:

> They try to fashion us according to their whim. They cannot believe that hard work, discipline, and above all, immense talent are essential to the artist if he is to make a lasting effect on the industry or indeed posterity . . . They would rather have it that an actor's life is a bed of roses, grossly overpaid, oversexed and possibly overdrugged. They quite fail to realize that the stars who stay the course have disciplined themselves probably more completely than leaders in other professions. The path to lasting fame and success is so tricky and treacherous that many potential stars fall by the wayside.
>
> *I Know the Face But . . .*

Guiness, 'best-known and loved English actor of the 20th century' according to his *Guardian* obituarist, had that discipline. He remained spiritually awake and watchful; ever loyal to Hamlet's precept, 'The readiness is all'.

The Career of Alec Guinness

All theatres are in London unless otherwise indicated.   d = director

PART ONE

1933

Walk-on role in *Evensong*, d. Victor Saville.

1934

2 April   Non-speaking Junior Counsel in *Libel* by Edward Wooll, d. Leon M. Lion, Playhouse Theatre.

August   Chinese coolie, French pirate, English sailor in *Queer Cargo* by Noël Langley, d. Reginald Bach, Piccadilly Theatre.

November   Osric and Third Player in *Hamlet*, d. John Gielgud, New Theatre.

1935

July   Wolf in *Noah* by André Obey, d. Michel Saint-Denis, New Theatre.

October   Sampson and Apothecary in *Romeo and Juliet*, d. John Gielgud, New Theatre.

1936

May   The Workman (and later Yakov) in *The Seagull* by Anton Chekhov, d. Theodore Komisarjevsky, New Theatre.

September 1936–April 1937   Season with the Old Vic Company:

Boyet in *Love's Labour's Lost*, d. Tyrone Guthrie.

Le Beau and William in *As You Like It*, d. Tyrone Guthrie.

Old Thorney in *The Witch of Edmonton* by William Rowley, Thomas Dekker and John Ford, d. Michel Saint-Denis.

Reynaldo and Osric in *Hamlet*, d. Tyrone Guthrie.

Sir Andrew Aguecheek in *Twelfth Night*, d. Tyrone Guthrie.

Exeter in *Henry V*, d. Tyrone Guthrie.

1937

June   Osric, Player Queen and Reynaldo in *Hamlet*, d. Tyrone Guthrie, Old Vic Company at Elsinore.

September 1937 to May 1938   Season with John Gielgud's Company at the Queen's Theatre:

Aumerle and the Groom in *Richard II*, d. John Gielgud.

Snake in *The School for Scandal* by R. B. Sheridan, d. Tyrone Guthrie.

Fedotik in *The Three Sisters* by Anton Chekhov, d. Michel Saint-Denis.

Lorenzo in *The Merchant of Venice*, d. John Gielgud.

1938

June   Louis Dubedat in *The Doctor's Dilemma* by George Bernard Shaw, d. Bernard Miles, Richmond Theatre.

September to December   Season with the Old Vic Company:

Arthur Gower in *Trelawny of the 'Wells'* by A. W. Pinero, d. Tyrone Guthrie.

Hamlet in *Hamlet*, d. Tyrone Guthrie.

Bob Acres in *The Rivals* by R. B. Sheridan, d. Esme Church.

1939

January to April   Tour of Europe and Egypt with the Old Vic Company:

Hamlet in *Hamlet*, d. Tyrone Guthrie.

Chorus in *Henry V*, d. Tyrone Guthrie.

Bob Acres in *The Rivals*, d. Esme Church

Emile Flordan in *Libel*, d. Leon M. Lion

May   Macbeth in *Macbeth*, d. Geoffrey Ost, Playhouse, Sheffield.

June   Michael Ransom in *The Ascent of F6* by W. H. Auden and Christopher Isherwood, d. Rupert Doone, Old Vic Theatre.

July   Romeo in *Romeo and Juliet*, d. Willard Stoker, Perth Scottish Theatre Festival.
Herbert Pocket in *Great Expectations*, adapted by Guinness from Charles Dickens, d. George Devine, Rudolf Steiner Hall.

1940

Richard Meilhac in *Cousin Muriel* by Clemence Dane, d. Norman Marshall, Globe Theatre.
The Dauphin in *Saint Joan* by George Bernard Shaw, d. Norman Marshall, charity matinee, Palace Theatre.

May   Ferdinand in *The Tempest*, ds. George Devine and Marius Goring, Old Vic Theatre.

September to December   Charleston in *Thunder Rock* by Robert Ardrey, d. Herbert Marshall, English tour.

1942

December   Flight Lieutenant Graham in *Flare Path* by Terence Rattigan, d. Margaret Webster, Henry Miller Theater, New York.

1945

Nelson in *Hearts of Oak* pageant by Edward Neil, d. Albert Locke, Royal Albert Hall.
Herbert Pocket in *Great Expectations*, d. David Lean.

1946

June   Mitya in *The Brothers Karamazov*, adapted by Guinness from Fyodor Dostoevsky, d. Peter Brook, Lyric Theatre, Hammersmith.

July   Garcin in *Vicious Circle* (*Huis Clos*) by Jean-Paul Sartre, d. Peter Brook, Arts Theatre.

September 1946 to May 1947   Season with the Old Vic Company at the New Theatre:
The Fool in *King Lear*, d. Laurence Olivier.

Eric Birling in *An Inspector Calls* by J. B. Priestley, d. Basil Dean.

De Guiche in *Cyrano de Bergerac* by Edmond Rostand, d. Tyrone Guthrie.

Abel Drugger in *The Alchemist* by Ben Johnson, d. John Burrell.

King Richard in *Richard II*, d. Ralph Richardson.

September 1947 to May 1948   Season with the Old Vic Company at the New Theatre:

Richard II in *Richard II*, d. Ralph Richardson.

The Dauphin in *Saint Joan* by George Bernard Shaw, d. John Burrell.

Khlestakov in *The Government Inspector* by Nikolai Gogol, d. John Burrell.

Menenius Agrippa in *Coriolanus*, d. E. Martin Browne.

Fagin in *Oliver Twist*, d. David Lean.

1948

September   Directed *Twelfth Night* for Old Vic Company at the New Theatre.

1949

D'Ascoyne family in *Kind Hearts and Coronets*, d. Robert Hamer.

Whimple in *A Run For Your Money*, d. Charles Frend.

February   Dr James Simpson in *The Human Touch* by J. Lee Thompson and Dudley Leslie, d. Peter Ashmore, Savoy Theatre.

August   An Unidentified Guest (Sir Henry Harcourt-Reilly) in *The Cocktail Party* by T. S. Eliot, d. E. Martin Browne, Lyceum Theatre, Edinburgh.

1950

George Bird in *Last Holiday*, d. Henry Cass.

Disraeli in *The Mudlark*, d. Jean Negulesco.

January   An Unidentified Guest in *The Cocktail Party*, d. E. Martin Browne, Henry Miller Theater, New York.

1951

Henry Holland in *The Lavender Hill Mob*, d. Charles Crichton.
Sidney Stratton in *The Man in the White Suit*, d. Alexander
  Mackendrick.

May Hamlet in *Hamlet*, ds. Guinness and Frank Hauser, New Theatre.
Denry Machin in *The Card*, d. Ronald Neame.

1952

The Ant Scientist in *Under the Sycamore Tree* by Sam and Bella Spewack,
  d. Peter Glenville, Aldwych Theatre.

1953

1st Lt. Peter Ross in *Malta Story*, d. Brian Desmond Hurst.
Henry St James in *The Captain's Paradise*, d. Anthony Kimmins.

July to September Season at the Shakespeare Playhouse, Stratford-on-
  Avon, Ontario:
King of France in *All's Well That Ends Well*, d. Tyrone Guthrie.
Richard III in *Richard III*, d. Tyrone Guthrie.

Father Brown in *Father Brown*, d. Robert Hamer.

1954

Colonel Fraser in *To Paris with Love*, d. Robert Hamer.
The Cardinal in *The Prisoner*, d. Peter Glenville.

March The Cardinal in *The Prisoner* by Bridget Boland, d. Peter
  Glenville, Globe Theatre.

May Boniface in *Hotel Paradiso* by Georges Feydeau and Maurice
  Desvallières, d. and translator Peter Glenville, Winter Garden
  Theatre.

PART TWO

1955

Professor Marcus in *The Ladykillers*, d. Alexander Mackendrick.

1957

William Horatio Ambrose in *Barnacle Bill*, d. Charles Frend.
Colonel Nicholson in *The Bridge on the River Kwai*, d. David Lean.
Prince Albert in *The Swan*, d. Charles Vidor.

1958

Gulley Jimson in *The Horse's Mouth*, d. Ronald Neame.

1959

John Barrett, Jacques de Gue in *The Wicked Scheme of Jebal Deeks*, d.
    Franklin Shaffer, for US television.
Jim Wormold in *Our Man in Havana*, d. Carol Reed.

1960

May   Aircraftman Ross in *Ross* by Terence Rattigan, d. Glen Byam
    Shaw, Theatre Royal, Haymarket.
Lieutenant-Colonel Jock Sinclair in *Tunes of Glory*, d. Ronald Neame.

1961

Koicho Asano in *Majority of One*, d. Mervyn LeRoy.

1962

Captain Crawford in *HMS Defiant*, d. Lewis Gilbert.
Prince Feisal in *Lawrence of Arabia*, d. David Lean.

1963

August   Berenger the First in *Exit the King* by Eugène Ionesco, d.
    George Devine, Royal Lyceum Theatre, Edinburgh.

September   Berenger the First in *Exit the King*, Royal Court Theatre.

1964

January   Dylan Thomas in *Dylan* by Sidney Michaels, d. Peter
    Glenville, Plymouth Theater, New York.

Marcus Aurelius in *The Fall of the Roman Empire*, d. Anthony Mann.

1965

Herr Frick in *Situation Hopeless but Not Serious*, d. Gottfried Reinhardt.
General Yevgraf Zhivago in *Doctor Zhivago*, d. David Lean.

1966

January   Von Berg in *Incident at Vichy* by Arthur Miller, d. Peter Wood, Phoenix Theatre.

October   Macbeth in *Macbeth*, d. William Gaskill, Royal Court.

Boniface in *Hotel Paradiso*, d. Peter Glenville.
Pol in *The Quiller Memorandum*, d. Michael Anderson.

1967

Major Jones in *The Comedians*, d. Peter Glenville.

October   Mrs Artminster in *Wise Child* by Simon Gray, d. John Dexter, Wyndham's Theatre.

1968

An Unidentified Guest in *The Cocktail Party* by T. S. Eliot, d. Guinness, Chichester Festival Theatre; Wyndham's Theatre; Haymarket Theatre.

1969

Executioner in *Conversation at Night*, d. Rudolf Cartier, for television.

1970

Charles I in *Cromwell*, d. Ken Hughes.

July   John in *Time out of Mind* by Bridget Boland, d. Stephen Barry, Yvonne Arnaud Theatre, Guildford.

Marley's Ghost in *Scrooge*, d. Ronald Neame.

Sir Andrew Aguecheek in *Twelfth Night*, d. John Dexter, for television.

1971

August   The Father in *A Voyage round my Father* by John Mortimer, d. Ronald Eyre, Haymarket Theatre.

1972

Narrator in *Solo* – e.e. cummings's book, d. David Cellan Jones, for television.

Adolf Hitler in *Hitler – The Last Ten Days*, d. Ennio De Concini.

1973

May   Dr Wickstead in *Habeas Corpus* by Alan Bennett, d. Ronald Eyre, Lyric Theatre.

The Pope in *Brother Sun, Sister Moon*, d. Franco Zeffirelli.

1974

Jocelyn Brome in *The Gift of Friendship*, d. Mike Newell.

1975

Julius Caesar in *Caesar and Cleopatra*, d. James Cellan Jones for television.

April   Dudley in *A Family and a Fortune* adapted by Julian Mitchell from Ivy Compton-Burnett, d. Alan Strachan, Apollo Theatre.

1976

Bensonmum in *Murder by Death*, d. Robert Moore.

October   Dean Swift in *Yahoo* adapted by Guinness and Alan Strachan from the works of Jonathan Swift, d. Alan Strachan, Queen's Theatre.

1977

Obi-Wan Kenobi in *Star Wars*, d. George Lucas.

September   Hilary in *The Old Country* by Alan Bennett, d. Clifford Williams, Queen's Theatre.

1979

George Smiley in *Tinker, Tailor, Soldier, Spy*, d. John Irving for television.

1980

Obi-Wan Kenobi in *The Empire Strikes Back*, d. Irvin Kershner.
Bigalow in *Raise the Titanic!*, d. Jerry Jameson.
The Earl of Dorincourt in *Little Lord Fauntleroy*, d. Jack Gold.

1981

George Smiley in *Smiley's People*, d. Simon Langton, for television.

1982

Sigmund Freud in *Lovesick*, d. Marshall Brickman.

1983

Obi-Wan Kenobi in *Return of the Jedi*, d. Richard Marquand.

1984

Professor Godbole in *A Passage to India*, d. David Lean.

June   Shylock in *The Merchant of Venice*, d. Patrick Garland, Chichester Festival Theatre.

1985

Publication: *Blessings in Disguise*.
Father Quixote in *Monsignor Quixote*, d. Rodney Bennett for television.
Edwin in *Edwin*, d. Rodney Bennett for television.
William Dorrit in *Little Dorrit*, d. Christine Edzard.

1987

Mr Todd in *A Handful of Dust*, d. Charles Sturridge.

1988

October Andrey Botvinnik in *A Walk in the Woods*, d. Ronald Eyre, Comedy Theatre.

1992

Heinrich Mann in *Tales from Hollywood*, d. Howard Davies, for television.

1993

Amos in *A Foreign Field*, d. Charles Sturridge, for television.

1996

Publication: *My Name Escapes Me* (Hamish Hamilton).
James Fleet in *Eskimo Day*, d. Piers Haggard, for television.

1999

Publication: *A Positively Final Appearance* (Hamish Hamilton).

2001

Publication: *A Commonplace Book* (Hamish Hamilton).

Sources

(i) By Alec Guinness

'I took my landing craft to the Sicily Beaches', *Daily Telegraph*, 20
    August 1943.
'Money for Jam', *Penguin New Writing*, No. 26, 1945.
'My Idea of Hamlet', *Spectator*, 6 July 1951.
'A Helping Hand from Gielgud', *Sunday Times*, 22 April 1956.
'The "Horse" and I', *Observer*, 1 February 1959.
'Cakes and Ale No More', *Spectator*, 22 October 1983.
Essay on Gielgud, *The Ages of Gielgud* (ed. Ronald Harwood), Hodder
    and Stoughton, 1984.
Blessings in Disguise, Hamish Hamilton, 1985.
'Don't Leave Your Fan on the Seat', *Spectator*, 5 September 1987.
'Jottings from My Notebook', *Spectator*, 19/26 December 1992.
Diary, *Spectator*, 17 July 1993.
My Name Escapes Me, Hamish Hamilton, 1996
A Positively Final Appearance, Hamish Hamilton, 1999
A Commonplace Book, Hamish Hamilton, 2001

(ii) By others (for the most part these are interviews with Guinness; the list is by no means comprehensive):

Daily Mail, 16 February 1939
Leader, 15 September 1945
Picture Post, 10 May 1947
Observer, 9 March 1952
Life magazine, 24 November 1952
Daily Telegraph, 12 April 1953
Punch, 25 May 1955
Daily Telegraph, 30 October 1955

Daily Mail, 5 February 1956
Sunday Times, 19 February 1956
News Chronicle, 31 March 1956
Sunday Times, 22 April 1956
Evening Standard, 2 October 1957
Evening News, 1 January 1958
The Times, 10 February 1958
Daily Mail, 7 March 1958

Everybody's, 23 March 1958
The Times, 28 March 1958
Time, 21 April 1958
Guardian, 10 January 1959
Daily Mail, 3 February 1959
Daily Telegraph, 8 May 1959
Sunday Express, 7 May 1964
New York Times, 5 February 1965
New York Times, 2 August 1965
Sunday Express, 19 December 1965
Daily Express, 22 October 1966
The Times, 4 December 1967
Daily Mail, 5 May 1968
Punch, 19 June 1968
Daily Mail, 26 June 1970
Daily Telegraph, 19 October 1970
Daily Telegraph, 1 August 1971
The Times, 7 August 1971
Daily Mail, 7 August 1971
Sunday Times, 25 August 1971
Evening Standard, 1 September 1972
Daily Mail, 17 December 1972
Daily Telegraph Magazine, 4 May 1973
Guardian, 19 May 1973
Daily Telegraph, 9 December 1974
Evening Standard, 2 February 1975
Daily Mail, 20 May 1975
Daily Telegraph Magazine, 9 September 1975
Evening Standard, 10 September 1976
The Times, 4 October 1976
Sunday Express, 19 February 1977
Evening Standard, 5 August 1977
Sunday Times Magazine, 2 October 1977
The Times, 8 December 1977

Sunday Express, 17 February 1978
Vogue, September 1979
Guardian, 8 September 1979
Daily Mail, 10 April 1980
Sunday Times, 8 February 1981
The Times, 30 November 1981
Guardian, 5 October 1982
Mail on Sunday, 4 December 1983
Mail on Sunday, 2 April 1984
Sunday Times, 29 April 1984
Mail on Sunday, 29 July 1984
Observer, 9 December 1984
Express Sunday Magazine, 3 July 1985
The Times, 30 September 1985
Sunday Express, 16 March 1986
Guardian, 7 October 1985
Sun, 10 March 1987
Today, 11 May 1987
Daily Telegraph, 13 May 1987
Daily Telegraph, 16 May 1987
Daily Mail, 7 December 1987
Sunday Telegraph, 13 December 1987
Observer, 10 January 1988
Independent Magazine, 1 October 1988
The Times, 10 October 1988
Daily Telegraph, 21 October 1989
Daily Telegraph, 29 October 1992
Spectator, 17 July, 7 August 1993
Telegraph Magazine, 31 July 1993
Independent on Sunday, 20 March 1994
Daily Mail, 16 May 1995
Daily Mail, 18 May 1995
Sunday Express, 15 December 1996
The Times, 20 May 1997
Mail on Sunday, 25 April 1999

Daily Express, 25 April 2000
The Times, 23 May 2000
Sunday Times, 28 May 2000
Guardian, 7 August 2000
Daily Telegraph, 8 August 2000
The Times, 8 August 2000
New Statesman, 1 October 2000

Sunday Times, 12 November 2000
London Review of Books, 25 January 2001
Daily Express, 5 February 2001
Sunday Times, 29 July 2001
Mail on Sunday, 10 February 2002

(iii) Radio and television broadcasts

28 February 1942 (*The Rape of the Locks*, BBC).
4 October 1946 (*Huis Clos*, BBC).
4 October 1960 (*Desert Island Discs*, BBC, int. Roy Plomley).
7 October 1971 (BBC, *Tribute to Michel Saint-Denis*).
18 March 1974 (BBC, reading and introducing T. S. Eliot's poems).
29 January 1975 (BBC, int. Derek Parker).
17 December 1977 (BBC, *The Parkinson Show*).
6 May 1981 (BBC monologue, Peter Barnes's *People*).
30 September 1982 (BBC, on John le Carré).
10 September 1984 (BBC, on Graham Greene at eighty).
30 August 1985 (BBC, int. Alan Strachan).
17 February 1985 (LWT, *David Lean: A Life in Film*, int. Melvyn Bragg).
6 October 1985 (LWT, *The South Bank Show*, int. Melvyn Bragg).
1987 (Mavis on Channel 4, *Sir Alec Guinness*).
11 July 1989 (BBC, Funeral of Lord Olivier).
July 2001 (Carlton TV, Profile of Guinness).

There are hardly any contemporary autobiographies or memoirs – or books on the British theatre since the mid-1930s or on film since the late 1940s – that do not contain some reference or other to Guinness. The following list includes only those works on which I have drawn most frequently. (The place of publication is London unless otherwise indicated.)

Agate, James, *Ego* (9 vols., 1935–48: vol. 1, Hamish Hamilton, 1935; vol. 2 Gollancz, 1936; vols. 3–9, Harrap, 1938–48);
— *Brief Chronicles* (Cape, 1943);
— *Red Letter Nights* (Cape, 1944).

Alec: A Birthday Present for Alec Guinness (Sinclair-Stevenson, 1994).

Atkinson, Brooks, *Broadway, New York* (Macmillan, New York, 1970).

Bagnold, Enid, *Enid Bagnold's Autobiography* (Heinemann, 1969).

Bair, Deirdre, *Samuel Beckett* (Cape, 1978).

Balcon, Michael, *Michael Balcon Presents . . . A Lifetime of Films* (Hutchinson, 1969).

Barker, Felix, *The Oliviers* (Hamish Hamilton, 1953).

Barr, Charles, *Ealing Studios* (Cameron and Tayleur/David and Charles, 1977).

Baxter, Keith, *My Sentiments Exactly* (Oberon, 1999).

Beaton, Cecil, *Self-Portrait with Friends* (Weidenfeld & Nicolson, 1979).

Beauman, Nicola, *Morgan* (Hodder & Stoughton, 1993).

Bennett, Alan, *Forty Years On* (Faber & Faber, 1969).

Billington, Michael, *The Modern Actor* (Hamish Hamilton, 1973);
— *Peggy Ashcroft, 1907–1991* (Mandarin, 1991).

Blakelock, Denys, *Advice to a Player* (Heinemann, 1957);
— *Round the Next Corner* (Gollancz, 1967).

Blunt, Wilfrid, *Cockerell* (Hamish Hamilton, 1964).

Bragg, Melvyn, *Laurence Olivier* (Hutchinson, 1984).

Brandreth, Gyles, *John Gielgud, A Celebration* (Pavilion, 1994).

Brook, Peter, *The Empty Space* (MacGibbon and Kee, 1968).

Brown, Ivor, *The Way of My World* (Collins, 1954);
— (ed.), *Theatre 1955–6* (Reinhardt, 1956).

Buckle, Richard (ed.), *Cecil Beaton, Self-portrait with Friends: Diaries 1926–74* (Weidenfeld & Nicolson, 1979).

Bull, Peter, *To Sea in a Sieve* (Peter Davies, 1956);
— *I Know the Face But . . .* (Peter Davies, 1956);
— *Life is a Cucumber* (Peter Davies, 1973);
— *Bulls's Eyes* (Robin Clark, 1985).

Callow, Simon, *On Being an Actor* (Methuen, 1984).

Casson, Lewis, *Lewis and Sybil: A Memoir* (Collins, 1954).

Cavell, Stanley, *Disowning Knowledge* (Cambridge University Press, 1987).

Clarke, T. E. B., *This is Where I Came In* (Michael Joseph, 1974).

Corrigan, Dame Felicitas, *The Nun, the Infidel & the Superman* (John Murray, 1985).

Cottrell, John, *Laurence Olivier* (Wiedenfeld & Nicolson, 1975).

Coward, Noël, *The Noël Coward Diaries* (Macmillan, 1982).

Dale, James, *Pulling Faces for a Living* (Gollancz, 1970).

Danischewsky, Monja, *White Russian – Red Face* (Gollancz, 1966).

Daubeny, Peter, *My World of Theatre* (Cape, 1971).

Davies, Russell (ed.), *The Kenneth Williams Diaries* (HarperCollins, 1993).

Davis, Bette, *The Lonely Life* (Alfred Knopf, New York, 1962).

Dean, Basil, *The Theatre at War* (Harrap, 1956).

Devlin, Diana, *A Speaking Part: Lewis Casson* (Hodder & Stoughton, 1982).

Dexter, John, *The Honourable Beast* (Nick Hern, 1993).

Drake, Fabia, *Blind Fortune* (Kimber, 1978).

du Maurier, Daphne, *Gerald: A Portrait* (Gollancz, 1934).

Duff, Charles, *The Lost Summer* (Nick Hern, 1995).

Durgnat, Raymond, *A Mirror for England: British Movies from Austerity to Affluence* (Faber and Faber, 1970).

Eliot, T. S., *Selected Essays* (Faber and Faber, 1932).

Ellmann, Richard, *Oscar Wilde* (Penguin, 1988).

Fairbanks, Douglas, Jnr., *The Salad Days* (Doubleday, New York, 1985).

Findlater, Richard, *Michael Redgrave: Actor* (Heinemann, 1956);
— *Lilian Baylis: The Lady of the Old Vic* (Allen Lane, 1975);
— *The Player Kings* (Weidenfeld & Nicolson, 1971).

Forbes, Bryan, *Notes for a Life* (Collins, 1974);
— *Ned's Girl* (Elm Tree Books, 1977).

Ford, Boris (ed.), *The Arts in Britain*, Vol. 9 (Cambridge University Press, 1988).

Forsyth, James, *Tyrone Guthrie: The Authorized Biography* (Hamish Hamilton, 1976).

Fox, Angela, *Slightly Foxed* (Collins, 1986);
— *Completely Foxed* (Collins, 1989).

Fox, James, *Comeback* (Hodder Christian Paperback, 1983).

French, John, *Robert Shaw: The Price of Success* (Nick Hern, 1993).

Games, Alexander, *Backing into the Limelight* (Hodder Headline, 2001)

Gielgud, John, *Early Stages* (Macmillan, 1939);
— *Stage Directions* (Heinemann, 1963);
— *Distinguished Company* (Heinemann Educational, 1972);
— *An Actor and His Times* (Sidgwick and Jackson, 1979).

Greene, Graham, *The Pleasure Dome* (Secker and Warburg, 1972).

Guinness, Michele, *The Guinness Legend* (Hodder & Stoughton, 1990).

Guthrie, Tyrone, *A Life in the Theatre* (Hamish Hamilton, 1960);

— *In Various Directions* (Michael Joseph, 1965);

— *Tyrone Guthrie on Acting* (Studio Vista, 1971).

Hall, Peter, *Peter Hall's Diaries* (Hamish Hamilton, 1983).

Hardwicke, Cedric, *A Victorian in Orbit* (Methuen, 1961).

Harrison, Rex, *Rex* (Macmillan, 1974).

Harwood, Ronald, *Sir Donald Wolfit CBE* (Secker and Warburg, 1971);

— (ed.), *The Ages of Gielgud* (Hodder & Stoughton, 1984);

— (ed.), *Dear Alec: Guinness at 75* (Hodder & Stoughton, 1989).

Hawkins, Jack, *Anything for a Quiet Life* (Elm Tree Books, 1973).

Hayman, Ronald, *John Gielgud* (Heinemann, 1971).

Hobson, Harold, *Ralph Richardson* (Barrie and Rockliff, 1958);

— *Unfinished Journey* (Weidenfeld & Nicolson, 1978);

— *Theatre in Britain* (Phaidon, 1984).

Holden, Anthony, *Laurence Olivier: A Biography* (Weidenfeld & Nicolson, 1988).

Huggett, Richard, *Binkie Beaumont* (Hodder & Stoughton, 1989).

Hunter, Allan, *Alec Guinness on Screen* (Edinburgh, 1982).

Jones, Ernest, *Oedipus and Hamlet, Essays in Applied Psychoanalysis* (New York, 1923).

Kemp, Philip, *Lethal Innocence: The Cinema of Alexander Mackendrick* (Methuen, 1991).

Keown, Eric, *Peggy Ashcroft* (Rockliff, 1955).

Korda, Michael, *Charmed Lives* (Random House, New York, 1979).

le Carré, John, *A Perfect Spy* (Hodder & Stoughton, 1986);

— *Tinker, Tailor, Soldier, Spy*, with le Carré's Foreword (Hodder & Stoughton, 1991).

Lejeune, C. A., *Thank You for Having Me* (Hutchinson, 1964).

Lewis, Roger, *The Life and Death of Peter Sellers* (Century, 1994).

Meynell, Viola (ed.), *Further Letters to Sydney Carlyle Cockerell* (Rupert Hart-Davis, 1956).

Mills, John, *Up in the Clouds, Gentlemen, Please* (Weidenfeld & Nicolson, 1980);

— *Still Memories* (Hutchinson, 2000).

Morley, Sheridan, *Review Copies* (Robson, 1974);

— *Tales from the Hollywood Raj* (Weidenfeld & Nicolson, 1980);

— *Robert, My Father* (Weidenfeld & Nicolson, 1993);

— *The Authorised Biography of John Gielgud* (Hodder & Stoughton, 2001);

— (ed.), *The Theatre Addict's Archive* (Elm Tree Books, 1977).

Mortimer, John, *In Character* (Allen Lane, 1983).

Nichols, Peter, *Diaries* (Nick Hern, 2000).

Olivier, Laurence, *Confessions of an Actor* (Weidenfeld & Nicolson, 1982);
— *On Acting* (Weidenfeld and Nicolson, 1986).

Payn, Graham, and Sheridan Morley (eds.), *The Noël Coward Diaries* (Weidenfeld & Nicolson, 1982).

Perry, George (ed.), *Forever Ealing* (Pavilion, 1981).

Priestley, J. B. *Particular Pleasures* (Heinemann, 1975).

Quayle, Anthony, *A Time to Speak* (Century, 1990).

Raby, Peter, *Samuel Butler, A Biography* (Hogarth, 1991).

Redgrave, Michael, *In My Mind's Eye* (Weidenfeld & Nicolson, 1983).

Sinclair, Andrew, *Spiegel: The Man behind the Pictures* (Weidenfeld & Nicolson, 1987).

Sinden, Donald, *A Touch of the Memoirs* (Hodder & Stoughton, 1982).

Speaight, Robert, *The Property Basket* (Collins, 1970).

Spencer, Colin, *Homosexuality – A History* (Fourth Estate, 1995).

Storr, Anthony, *The School of Genius* (André Deutsch, 1988).

Taylor, John Russell, *Alec Guinness: A Celebration* (Pavilion, 1985).

Trewin, J. C., *Edith Evans* (Rockliff, 1964);
— *Drama in Britain 1951–64* (Longman, 1965);
— *Five & Eighty Hamlets* (Hutchinson, 1987).

Turner, Daphne, Alan Bennett, *In a Manner of Speaking* (Faber and Faber, 1997).

Kathleen Tynan, *The Life of Kenneth Tynan* (Weidenfeld & Nicolson, 1987);
— (ed.), *The Letters of Kenneth Tynan* (Weidenfeld and Nicolson, 1994).

Tynan, Kenneth, *Alec Guinness* (Rockliff, 1953);
— *Curtains* (Longman, 1961);
— *A View of the English Stage* (Davis-Poynter, 1975);
— *Letters* (Weidenfeld & Nicholson, 1994).

Ustinov, Peter, *Dear Me* (Heinemann, 1977).

Vickers, Hugo, *Vivien Leigh* (Hamish Hamilton, 1988).

Vickers, John, *The Old Vic in Photographs* (Saturn, 1947);
— *Five Seasons* (Saturn, 1950).

Walker, Alexander, *Hollywood, England* (Michael Joseph, 1974).

Wansell, Geoffrey, *Terence Rattigan: A Biography* (Fourth Estate, 1995).

Wardle, Irving, *The Theatres of George Devine* (Cape, 1978).

Warre, Michael, *Designing and Making Stage Scenery* (Studio Vista, 1966).

Webster, Margaret, *The Same Only Different* (Gollancz, 1969).

Wilcox, Herbert, *Twenty-five Thousand Sunsets* (Bodley Head, 1967).

Williamson, Audrey, *Old Vic Drama* (Rockliff, 1951).

Williams, E. G. Harcourt, *Old Vic Saga* (Winchester, 1949).

Williams, Kenneth, *Just Williams: An Autobiography* (HarperCollins, 1993).

Young, B. A., *The Rattigan Version* (Hamish Hamilton, 1986).

Index